AF334974

History's Most Devastating Disasters

MACMILLAN
PROFILES

History's Most Devastating Disasters

Macmillan Reference USA
an imprint of the Gale Group
New York • Detroit • San Francisco • London • Boston • Woodbridge, CT

Contents

Preface

Macmillan Profiles: *History's Most Devastating Disasters* is a unique reference featuring 109 articles describing major natural and technological disasters. Macmillan Reference recognizes the need for accurate and accessible reference materials in history, science, and the arts. The Macmillan Profiles series can help meet that need by providing new collections of articles that were carefully selected to appeal to young readers and to compliment the middle and high school curriculum.

This volume includes articles describing disasters of the following types: hurricanes, tornadoes, floods, earthquakes, volcanic eruptions, fires, shipwrecks, aircraft accidents, and industrial accidents. Particular events were chosen for coverage based on the following criteria: the magnitude of the disaster in casualties and damage; the importance of the disaster to history; and the relevance of the disaster to the science, history, social studies, or current issues curriculum. We further attempted to achieve representation of as broad a geographic and chronological range as possible, although some sections include a heavier representation of recent events that occurred in the United States because these will be of greatest interest to many students and readers. Due to space constraints, most sections include only natural or accidental disasters and exclude history's countless deliberate acts of war and terrorism. However, the sections on shipwrecks and aircraft accidents do include the *Lusitania*, USS *Vincennes*/Iran Air, and PanAm Flight 103 incidents because any listing of history's major shipwrecks and aircraft accidents would have seemed incomplete without them.

FEATURES

To add visual appeal and enhance the usefulness of the volume, the page format was designed to include the following helpful features:

- Definitions and Glossary: Brief definitions of important terms in the main text can be found in the margin. A glossary at the end of the book provides students with an even broader list of definitions.
- Sidebars: Appearing in shaded boxes throughout the volume, these provocative asides relate to and amplify topics.
- Pull Quotes: Found throughout the text in the margin, pull quotes highlight essential facts.

- Additional Resources: An extensive list of books, articles, films, and websites about the disasters covered in the volume will help students who want to do further research.
- Index: A thorough index provides hundreds of additional points of entry into the work.

Macmillan Profiles: *History's Most Devastating Disasters* would not have been possible without the hard-work and creativity of our staff. We offer our sincere thanks to all who helped create this work.

Macmillan Reference USA

Hurricanes

Great Caribbean Islands Hurricane

The Great Hurricane of 1780 occurred in the Lesser Antilles of the Caribbean Islands and is considered to be the deadliest Atlantic Ocean hurricane ever recorded in history. Sweeping through the islands of Barbados, St. Vincent, St. Lucia, Martinique, Puerto Rico, and Bermuda, between October 10 and 18, 1780, this storm ultimately killed 20,000 to 30,000 people.

According to hurricane scholar William C. Redfield, the Great Hurricane of 1780 originated approximately 400 miles southeast of Barbados on October 10. However, other scholars believe this great storm was born off the coast of West Africa's Cape Verde Islands earlier in the month. Either way, the great storm matured rapidly over the warm waters of the Caribbean, casting a brilliant red light over the island of Barbados near sunset on October 9. By dark, rain from the storms outer fringe began lightly covering the island, increasing in duration and intensity throughout the evening. By 10:00 the next morning, the winds had increased to more than 35 miles per hour, creating a tropical storm. Almost 100 ships that were anchored in harbors all across Barbados began breaking their lines and drifting aimlessly toward rocky shores. Many of these were saved by competent sailors. However, one army transport, an ordnance vessel, and two navy ships were driven ashore at the entrance of the Carlisle Bay, causing them to burst open. The lives of some 200 sailors were lost at this point.

Piers and dock-side warehouses were torn to shreds.

torrential a violent or sustained flow of liquid, commonly used in association with heavy rainstorms.

Late in the evening on October 10, the hurricane's winds had intensified to levels greater than 155 m.p.h. In one Barbados harbor, the storm's powerful winds actually carried a 12-pound iron cannon a distance of 420 feet. Inland, a stone prison housing French and Spanish prisoners of war was completely demolished, releasing 800 prisoners. The island's governor, concerned that the prisoners would begin looting the stores of local merchants, immediately ordered that troops be called to duty. However, after his house collapsed he realized that there would not be much left on the island to loot and so he recalled the troops, leaving the prisoners to find shelter wherever they could. A bit after midnight on October 11, the eye of the storm passed north of Barbados, traveling rapidly towards St. Vincent. Unfortunately, because the eye did not pass directly over the island, islanders were unable to experience the reduction in storm intensity that comes from the eye's associated lull. Thus, in one continuous reign of terror, the hurricane tore apart plantations and bungalows alike, spreading **torrential** rains all across the island and drowning hundreds.

Shortly after the storm's eye passed Barbados, the Great Hurricane began affecting the volcanic island of St. Vincent, which is 100 miles west of Barbados. Officials reported that 550 houses were destroyed as flash floods and winds gusting at 172 m.p.h. wracked the small island. In one particularly tragic event, the storm threw ashore two ships resting just off the island's east coast, killing around two hundred French and British sailors.

Throughout the early hours of October 11, the storm continued to move northwest. Traveling at a speed of 7 m.p.h., the storm quickly reached St. Lucia. Needless to say, with winds still at the level of a category five hurricane (the Saffir-Simpson Hurricane scale defines a category five hurricane as having winds greater than 155 m.p.h.), the hurricane caused considerable damage to the island. Piers and dockside warehouses were torn to shreds, as boats were picked up off the water and thrown inland. Meteorological reports indicate that for an entire day the storm lashed this island with this kind of fury. When, around 1:00 in the morning of October 12, the hurricane began to move on, it left 700 islanders dead.

By midmorning the Great Hurricane had covered the fifty miles of ocean water that separate Martinique from St. Lucia. To announce its arrival, the storm, with a surge of water many feet high, demolished 150 buildings situated along one harbor's edge in one large gulp. Inland, at Fort Royal, a cathedral, several churches, the senate house, the governor's house, and a prison were left as little more than rubble. A hospital that housed 1,600 patients was similarly pounded to the ground. In yet another maritime tragedy, the storm sank a 40-ship convoy bringing **provisions** and troops to Martinique from France. Probably 3,000 people died from this event alone.

Moving rapidly northwest, the Great Hurricane next hit the islands of Dominica and St. Kitts and moved into the open waters of the southeastern Caribbean. At this point, the storm surge (the increase in water level that comes with a hurricane) was reported at towering over 22 feet. After traveling over open waters for two days, on October 15, the storm passed through the Mona Passage, which separates Puerto Rico from Hispaniola. High winds and rain were consequently brought to both islands, uprooting trees and destroying much property. Fearing the worst, people scrambled to reach higher ground and take cover. Luckily, the hurricane did not remain stationary and kept traveling towards the Bahamas. On October 16, the storm shifted and began moving northeast towards Bermuda. By October 18, it was located approximately 50 miles off the southern coast of Bermuda. Here, the storm wrecked at least fifty merchant ships and caused a tremendous degree of damage to building structures and the natural environment of Bermuda. Continuing northeast, the hurricane finally **dissipated** over the North Atlantic's cold waters.

In the end, the storm left a terrible legacy in the Caribbean. In Barbados an estimated 4,326 people were killed by the storm's rage. With 9,000 lives lost, Martinique suffered a death toll twice that of Barbados. After adding the countless number of sailors who perished at sea, the number of deaths caused by the Great Hurricane reached upward of 22,000 people. This was and remains a storm not easily forgotten. ◆

provisions material such as food, water, clothing, and other necessities needed during or after a hardship or disaster.

dissipate to break apart or spread out before vanishing.

Galveston Hurricane

AUGUST 1900

Located off the coast of Galveston, Texas, in 1900, Galveston Island was a one-mile wide **sandbar** that rested only nine feet above sea level. Both a bustling port and a popular seaside resort, geographers believed that the sloping ocean

sandbar a ridge of sand built up by the currents of water, especially in coastal waters and rivers.

Galveston residents survey the damage caused by the Galveston hurricane in 1900.

barometric pressure measure of the atmospheric pressure usually expressed by the height of a column of mercury.

floor off the coast of Galveston, Texas, made the low-lying island relatively safe from hurricanes. They could not have been more wrong.

On August 27, 1900, just west of the Cape Verde Islands in the Caribbean, storm winds began to form. Moving northward over Cuba, and across the Florida Keys, what had been a tropical storm became, by September 5, a full-blown hurricane. As the hurricane moved just south of due west along the Gulf Coast on September 7, it became clear that Galveston Island lay directly in the path of this increasingly intense storm and the Weather Bureau in Washington issued a warning to the people of the island. Unfortunately, despite these warnings and rapidly falling **barometric pressure**, overconfident tourists remained on the beach, secure in the belief that they would be safe from the storm.

By the next morning, the weather at Galveston Island had significantly worsened. As of 10:10 A.M., the Weather Bureau in Washington predicted a storm center landfall west of Galveston. This not only put the city in the right semi-circle of the hurricane, but also posed the threat of a deadly storm surge. Within two hours, Washington's predictions were becoming a reality, and winds blowing out of the northeast were steadily increasing to speeds of more than 30 m.p.h. Waves had increased in size by more than four feet, and rising water levels not only filled the streets with five feet of water, but submerged the wagon bridge and train trestles that acted as the only way off the Island.

The situation continued to deteriorate rapidly. As of 2:30 P.M., Isaac Cline, chief of the Galveston weather office wired Washington with the news that half of the city was under water. At some point soon after this message, the bridge to the mainland completely collapsed. By 5:15 P.M. winds blew at 100 m.p.h., and water levels had increased by four feet. At 6:30 P.M., the barometer was at 29 inches and water levels elevated to 15.2 feet above sea level. With at least 10 feet of water in the streets and storm wreckage being catapulted through the air, people were beginning to die by the hundreds, either struck by flying debris, or pinned underwater by the remnants of crumbling buildings.

As the evening progressed, the deaths and damage continued to increase. Winds were now greater than 120 m.p.h. and water levels increased yet another four feet, making the Galveston Hurricane classifiable as a category four. According to the Saffir-Simpson Hurricane Scale, a category four hurricane has winds between 131-155 mph and storm surges 13-18 feet above normal. Extensive damage to residences, trees, and shrubs, along with excessive flooding may occur. Indeed this was the case with Galveston. It is reported that by 7:30, almost nothing remained rooted in place under the power of the storm. Houses, torn from their foundations, floated through the city, knocking into other buildings and crushing the stranded citizens who floated by on bits of wreckage. The corpses of domestic pets and livestock filled the streets, accompanied by uprooted trees and telephone poles.

And yet, amazingly enough, amid all this chaos and destruction, life emerged. After being carried through the streets on the roof of a wrecked cottage and hurled into a floating steamer trunk, a woman named Mrs. William Heideman eventually found herself pulled into the Ursuline Convent to give birth to a healthy baby boy, William Henry Heideman, Jr.

Finally, around midnight the winds began to subside, the rain ceased, and some of the water started to drain out of the streets of Galveston. What the dawn revealed was a gruesome scene. According to the National Hurricane Center, roughly 3,500 homes were destroyed, and more than 8,000 people died. At the time, the Governor of Texas reportedly estimated as many fatalities as 12,000. In a National Hurricane Center

As the evening progressed, the deaths and damage continued to increase.

report comparing all U.S. hurricanes between 1900 and 1996, the Galveston Hurricane ranks not only as the most deadly, but the seventh most intense. Barometric pressure is reported to have reached an all time low of 27.49 inches mercury. The irony of this tragedy is that a shift of about 50 miles in the course of the hurricane could have drastically reduced the number of deaths and the extent of the damage. For that matter, if better precautions and evacuation procedures had been taken on the island the story would be much different.

Luckily, the Galvestonians learned from their lesson and as they began to clean up the wreckage that Hurricane Galveston caused, they implemented a number of changes. Amongst these was the construction of a seawall across the harbor mouth and the elevation of the sandbar city 17 feet above high-tide levels. Some damage appears to have been irreparable; it is believed that the Galveston Hurricane ended Galveston's position as Texas's key city, paving the way for the ascendancy of Houston.

Interestingly, the story does not actually end in Galveston. Although the storm soon lost hurricane status, as a storm it turned north and went on to cause damage in northern cities such as Chicago, Buffalo, and St. John's, Newfoundland. At times a tropical storm can become a mid-latitude cyclone that is pushed by temperature differences. This transformation is what happened on September 11, 1900. Fed by temperature differences in St. Louis, Yankton, and Bismark, the storm traveled 1,000 miles towards the Great Lakes and by the afternoon of September 11, winds gusted at hurricane strength (72 m.p.h.) over Chicago and Buffalo. As a consequence, several vessels sank, many schooners were lost, and around 30 fishermen died. Moving northeast, it eventually crossed the North Atlantic and disappeared over southern Greenland on September 20. ◆

Lake Okeechobee Hurricane

SEPTEMBER 1928

The Lake Okeechobee Hurricane of 1928, also known as the San Felipe Hurricane, is one of the fiercest Cape Verde Storms on record. With a barometric pressure as low as 27.76 inches and winds gusting as high as 150 m.p.h.,

this storm ended up killing between 2,000 and 3,000 people, making it the third deadliest hurricane disaster in United States history.

The San Felipe/Lake Okeechobee Hurricane most likely developed near the Cape Verde islands during the first week of September 1928. By September 10, the storm had become a true hurricane and was moving northeast towards the Leeward islands with winds of 135 m.p.h. The island of Guadeloupe was the first to be struck by the immense strength of the storm. On September 12, the hurricane covered islanders with 11 to 12 inches of rain and blew down houses with wind gusts as intense as 160 and 170 m.p.h. Palm groves were entirely mowed down, hundred of buildings were destroyed, and nearly 500 people were left dead when San Felipe finally decided to move on to Puerto Rico.

After killing another 100 people on the two islands of Montserrat and St. Kitts, on September 13, San Felipe blew ashore the southeast coast of Puerto Rico. First striking the port town of Arroyo, the storm then traveled diagonally across the nation and ended in the northwestern town of Isabela. At the

The September 19, 1928, edition of *The New York Times* headlines the hurricane in Florida.

deluge an overflowing of natural liquids or material on land.

time, the National Weather Service recorded winds of 150 m.p.h. and a barometric pressure of 27.50 inches. Within only 12 hours, more than 30 inches of rain covered the central highlands of the island. The storm produced considerable damage throughout Puerto Rico, inundating low-lying areas, destroying coffee, banana, and citrus crops, and obstructing roads. In the town of Cayey, dozens of townspeople were decapitated by airborne sheets of tin roofing. In another town, 14 parishoners who were gathered around an altar to pray were crushed when the church's dome collapsed. The mountainside towns of Caguas and Adjuntas were virtually erased from existence when landslides covered them in a **deluge** of mud and rock. In total, $50 million in damage (in 1928 dollars) came from the hurricane's devastating trip over the island. At least 1,400 Puerto Ricans died.

From Puerto Rico, San Felipe moved on toward Hispaniola and the southern Bahamas. For two days the hurricane terrorized islanders with 119 m.p.h. winds and torrential rains. Meanwhile, Floridians were scrambling to predict where the storm was likely to hit the United States. If the hurricane continued to travel northwest, it was believed it would touch down in West Palm Beach. However, it seemed just as likely that the storm would fall under the influence of a high pressure air mass that would push it out to the North Atlantic.

Early on September 16, the storm began its destruction in the United States, lashing a 90-mile strip of coast between Jupiter and Miami, Florida. At 10:30 A.M., as waves 15 feet high smashed against the shore at Pompano Beach, the Weather Bureau began sending out hurricane warnings over the radio. Frantically, citizens retreated towards safer ground. As the day progressed, heavy winds gusting at speeds of 160 m.p.h. caused communication to go down, so facts regarding when and where the hurricane first touched down are hazy. However, it is believed that the storm center hit between West Palm Beach and Miami sometime in the evening of September 16. At the estimated point of impact, barometric pressure was approximately 27.43 inches. The damage was immense. Parked cars were lifted up and slammed into walls. Dozens of oceanfront homes were completely demolished. An 11-foot storm surge (the increase in water level that accompanies a hurricane) wiped out the main highway that linked Palm Beach with the nearby city of Delray. In total, $11 million (in 1928 dollars) in damage was reported throughout southern Florida.

Little known to West Palm Beach citizens, in between 5:00 P.M. and 10:00 P.M., the storm made one powerful hit at Lake Okeechobee, which is located in the southern portion of Florida on the north edge of the Everglades. It was here around 6 P.M., that wind gusts as high as 160 m.p.h. caused lake waters to overflow their shores, burst through the earthen **dike** on the south end of the lake, and spill out into low-lying fields. In the nearby towns of Belle Glade, Pahokee, Port Mayaca, and Moore Haven, the consequences of such flooding were tremendous. Houses and livestock were swept away and hundreds of unprepared citizens drowned. In fact, as water rushed over the countryside, only one building, the Glades Hotel, was left standing. Some people who did not drown climbed into trees only to be bitten and killed by poisonous snakes who had similarly tried to escape from the floods.

dike an artificial course for water; a bank of usually natural material to confine or control water.

However, the disaster at Lake Okeechobee remained unknown, and the next day, newspaper headlines only reported that hundreds were injured between Palm Beach and Miami. Red Cross volunteers focused their attention on gaining relief aid for Puerto Rico and Palm Beach, taking a full-page advertisement out in *The New York Times*. As for the storm, in the days following its devastating touch down in Florida, it moved northeast. Warnings went into effect for South Carolina and the Atlantic Coast. Three people were killed in New Jersey before the storm dissipated over the North Atlantic. Two days later, a frantic telegraph requesting relief aid was sent to officials in the town nearest to Lake Okeechobee.

As relief efforts spread to Lake Okeechobee, it became apparent that the storm was much more of a tragedy than was previously thought. As survivors from the storm walked through six miles of flood waters to ambulances, rescue workers were forced to string dead bodies together and tow them behind their boats. In fact, a precise death toll cannot be given because until the flood waters receded, alligators were eating some of the floating corpses. Today, it is estimated that 1,836 people were killed and 1,879 individuals were injured at Lake Okeechobee.

Luckily, the tragedy of the San Felipe/Lake Okeechobee Hurricane was taken as a lesson by the U.S. government, which helped begin a $5 million flood-control program for the lake. Part of this program was the construction of a 85-mile-long **levee**, named after the president at the time Herbert Hoover. Towering 34-38 feet high, this levee covers nearly the entire southern shore of Lake Okeechobee. In August 1949, when

levee a river landing place or embankment for flood prevention.

another hurricane, with sustained winds of 110 m.p.h., and gusting to 153 m.p.h., swept through the region, the levee held Lake Okeechobee in and only two people died. ◆

Hurricane Audrey

A trench holds a row of coffins containing unknown victims of Hurricane Audrey.

Hurricane Audrey hit Louisiana in June of 1957. Responsible for the deaths of 390 people, Audrey is ranked by the National Hurricane Center as the sixth deadliest hurricane to hit the United States between the years of 1900 and 1996. In terms of intensity, the National Hurricane Center ranks her as the eighteenth most intense hurricane ever. Ultimately, though, the story of Hurricane Audrey is a tale of how the unexpected should be expected.

Late in the day on June 25, 1957, reports came in to the National Weather Service that a tropical storm depression had formed in the Bay of Campeche, which is located in the southwest portion of the Gulf of Mexico between the Yucatan Peninsula and Mexico City. According to the National Hurricane Center, a tropical depression is characterized by wind speeds that exceed 25 m.p.h. This depression can grow into a hurricane only if it crosses an area of very warm water. This movement across an expanse of warm, moist space is what Audrey performed. Consequently, after chartering a Navy Hurricane Hunter to fly through the area in search of the storm, instead of finding a tropical depression, the Weather Bureau discovered a hurricane. This storm had winds of 75 m.p.h. and was moving in a northern fashion. According to the 1950s practice of naming hurricanes after women, they named it Hurricane Audrey.

Audrey intensified rapidly, and as of June 26, the storm was registered to have winds of 104 m.p.h. and a barometric pressure as low as 28.73. Traveling 17 m.p.h. north-northeast, Audrey appeared to be headed directly towards Galveston, Texas. Consequently, the warnings of the Weather Bureau were primarily directed at Southern Texans. Later that day Audrey performed its first act of aggression, upsetting a 70-ton workboat and drowning nine men. Despite its evident power, the people of Louisiana felt moderately safe from Audrey, underestimating both its power and direction.

Early in the morning of June 27, barometric pressure dropped even lower to a pressure of 27.91 inches. At this point, **gale** wind warnings were put into effect from Grand Isle, Louisiana, to Corpus Christi, Texas, and tides were predicted to be around five to eight feet by late afternoon June 27. A little past midnight on June 27, Audrey's eye was located 50 miles southeast of Galveston, and it became very clear that the region to be most affected by its ferocity would be Louisiana, not Galveston, Texas. Weather officials scrambled to evacuate the residents of southwestern Louisiana. Unfortunately, radio stations given the task of broadcasting storm warnings, took it upon themselves to paraphrase or shorten the warnings in a way that left out crucial information regarding the storm. In one instance, citizens were told the time of landfall for only the eye of the storm. They did not realize that the storm would be half over at this time, and thus incorrectly estimated the time at which they would need to evacuate their homes and seek higher ground. When Audrey hit the coast of Louisiana near Texas on June 27, many people were unprepared.

At Audrey's early morning landing its winds were blowing at speeds as great as 155 m.p.h., and its waves were cresting at approximately 24 feet. Storm surges, bulges of water that hurricanes carry around with them, exceeded 20 feet. In Texas, this cresting surge was so powerful that it sheered 60 feet of shoreline off the northeast tip of Bolivar Island. As for Cameron, Louisiana, at landfall, Audrey's great storm surge poured gulf waters and debris almost 25 miles inland. In the process, hundreds of wooden cottages were swept away, many with people still in them. Victims struggled to climb atop bits of wreckage that bobbed in the chaotic waters that **inundated** streets. Unfortunately, hundreds of poisonous snakes also swam

gale a wind measuring from 32-63 miles per hour.

inundate to cover or overflow.

through the water-filled streets, biting and killing at least five people. One boy was apparently bitten seven times.

From Louisiana, Audrey curved northeast, and moved up through Ohio, Illinois, Indiana, New York, and Ontario Canada. Wreaking havoc everywhere it went, during this day-long trek across the United States, Audrey eventually managed to kill 30 people and cause several million dollars in damage. It finally dissipated on June 29, over Northern Canada.

The bloated corpses of Louisiana citizens continued to be found throughout the entire month of July. According to federal relief agents dispatched by President Dwight D. Eisenhower, as of July 3, the death toll stood at 296. By July 22, number of deaths grew to 518 people. Half a dozen casualties were also reported in Texas. As for property damage, in Cameron Parish, Louisiana federal relief agents reported the loss of at least 1,900 buildings. Another 19,000 buildings were listed as being in very poor shape. Additionally, at least 50,000 head of cattle drowned in the storm. In total, damage is estimated to have cost the United States $150,000,000.

Besides leaving behind several hundred deaths and millions of dollars in damage, Hurricane Audrey also set off a civil rights crisis throughout Louisiana. When citizens learned that 90 percent of Audrey's victims were African American, local and state civil defense authorities faced an onslaught of criticism. For months after Hurricane Audrey's brief reign of terror, nearly every organization that played some role in warning the public about the hurricane was faced with charges of bigotry and willful disregard of public safety. Today it cannot be said if or how much racial prejudices directed the series of events that occurred in relation to Hurricane Audrey. However, because the storm caused such devastation to Louisiana and set off such an intense period of civil rights strife, the name "Audrey" has been retired from the cyclical list of possible hurricane names. ◆

Hurricane Flora

Septic	ember–October, 1963

Hurricane Flora is yet another of the deadly storms to have caused considerable damage throughout the Caribbean. Between the days of September 30 and

October 8, 1963, Flora moved through Trinidad, Tobago, Grenada, Jamaica, Hispaniola, and Cuba, destroying homes and lives. Officials estimate that Flora's path of destruction eventually claimed 8,000 lives, left millions homeless, and caused several million dollars in property damage.

Late in September 1963, a rare storm, born below a latitude of ten degrees north, quietly began forming over the warm waters just south of Trinidad and Tobago. Weather officials called this storm Flora. On September 30, Flora struck its first victim, Tobago. With winds blowing at speeds of 110 m.p.h., in Tobago, Flora uprooted trees and shrubs, broke windows, and snapped telephone poles in half. Bits of rock, trees, and garbage flew through the sky, striking citizens as they ran to find shelter. Releasing a downpour of six inches of rain over Trinidad, Tobago, and Grenada, Hurricane Flora also set off mudslides that swept away many houses and killed 36 people. Approximately 500 more individuals were left moderately injured from Flora's intense winds and waters.

Moving northeast, Flora next threatened Haiti. Over the days of October 3 and 4, it hit the southwestern tip of Haiti with sustained winds of 140 m.p.h. and gusts as great as 170 m.p.h. According to the Saffir-Simpson Hurricane Scale, a hurricane with winds of 140 m.p.h. is classified as a category 4 hurricane. Storms of this caliber are generally characterized by storm surges (the increase in water level) 13-18 feet above normal. Trees, signs, and telephone poles are all blown down. Land lower than 10 feet above sea level is often flooded and evacuation of these areas is usually necessary. Indeed, in Haiti, much of the damage caused by Flora was due to flash floods and landslides. Unfortunately, because of poor communication, evacuation of residents in low-lying areas largely went undone. Consequently, when Flora, which was accompanied by 18-foot seas, swept away entire fishing villages, it also swept away many fishermen and their families. Villagers not immediately washed away by Flora's initial onslaught rushed to escape into trees as Flora's terrific winds and waves chased them through the land. A storm surge of 11 feet washed inland, entirely destroying Haiti's coffee crops, killing 4,000 individuals, and leaving at least 100,000 people homeless. As for the nearby Dominican Republic, Flora's fierce winds tore up trees and telephone poles, pushing splinters of these objects into windows and doors. Government officials in the Dominican

Villagers not immediately washed away by Flora's initial onslaught rushed to escape into trees.

How to Prepare for a Hurricane

What can you do if a hurricane warning has already been issued, and it's too late to head to higher ground? A little pre-hurricane planning can seriously reduce your risk of injury and property damage.

Before the storm hits, make sure that all furniture or other loose items outdoors are brought inside, or at least securely anchored, so that they will not be picked up and tossed by the high winds. If there is time, clear deadwood from trees near your home, so that it doesn't come crashing through the roof later on. If you have a boat, make sure it is safely moored. Secure your window shutters, or tape your window glass to keep it from breaking inward. Wide masking tape works best, placed in long strips that run diagonally from corner to corner, like a giant "X." People who live in trailers are at particular risk; they should secure their homes with "over-the-top" strapping to reduce the possibility of the trailer being blown away.

Remember that you are likely to lose electricity during the storm. Find candles, or better still a flashlight, and make sure you have matches on hand. You will also want a portable radio, so you can stay informed of the storm's progress—and make certain you have batteries for this and any other small electric appliances you are planning to use. A hand-operated can-opener is another useful item to have when the power goes out, as is a supply of canned foods.

Hurricane flooding causes damage not only to property but also to the water supply. If you are stuck at home, move yourself and your supplies above the ground floor if possible, and create a supply of clean water by filling all your sinks and bathtubs, as well as large jugs, cooking pots, or even clean garbage cans with water. The Federal Emergency Management Agency (FEMA) hosts a web site with further tips on making it through the storm: visit it at www.fema.gov.

Republic report that Flora, in its short stay, was responsible for $60 million in property damage and the deaths of another four hundred people.

After this nine-hour encounter with Haiti and the Dominican Republic, Flora curved northwest and approached Cuba. Luckily, as it traveled, its winds slowed to 107 m.p.h., and the barometric pressure in Cuba rose from 27.64 inches to 28.64 inches. It was in this reduced state that Flora roared into the southern port city of Santiago de Cuba. In this bustling seaport town, Flora bulldozed buildings with torrential rains and winds. The nearby towns in the provinces of Oriente and Camaguey were washed out by flashfloods. Surrounding highways and railways were rendered useless and local sugarcane fields were devastated by seawater. Flora did not stop here though; moving inland into central Cuba, Flora brought terrified islanders lightning strikes, gale-force winds, and much rain. Unfortunately, in a stroke of bad luck for Cuba, Hurricane Flora's passage north-northwest away from Cuba was checked by a warm front. Consequently, it spent the next three and a half days trapped directly over the island's mountainous interior. At the time, records from the United States Weather Bureau did not demonstrate any other instances of a storm lingering over one area for such a prolonged period of time. During this four-day reign of terror, the storm released between 15 and 20 inches of rain over the cities of Las Tunas and Santa Clara. Floods and bloated rivers poured through the countryside, destroying 90 percent of the year's sugar and coffee stocks. In particular, the Cauto and Contramestre rivers swelled to record heights, causing many thousands of citizens to flee their homes. When, on October 8, the warm front blocking Hurricane Flora gave way and allowed it to drift away from Cuba, it left more than 1,000 Cubans dead and 175,000 were homeless.

Leaving Cuba behind, Flora next spun towards the Bahamas. Luckily, resting over Cuba for so long, zapped some of Flora's strength, and so, when it hit the Southeastern edge of the Bahamas, it caused minimal damage. One day later Hurricane Flora dissipated, leaving nothing more than death, property damage, and a string of economic and political problems in its wake. For example, because of the damage done to Cuban sugar crops, for weeks after the storm, world sugar prices rose daily. Eventually, Great Britain was forced to freeze retail sugar prices so that the problem would not get out of hand. Unfortunately, because of a political and ideological disagreement, the United States did little to aid this Cuban economic crisis. Arguing that they could not condone Cuba's "aggressive course," United States government officials refused to lift the economic **blockade** it had imposed on Cuba before Hurricane Flora. Consequently, Fidel Castro, angered by U.S. resolve, reportedly accused the United States of rejoicing in Cuba's plight. This claim was without basis though, because the American Red Cross did offer extensive aid to Cuba and was rejected. Finally, Cuba accepted some U.S. aid, but only help that came from non-governmental sources. For the most part, the country relied upon aid from several Latin American and Communist nations. Despite this extensive international aid, Hurricane Flora ultimately set back Cuba's **agrarian** economy by four years. The economies of Haiti and Tobago were similarly disabled, making Flora a hurricane of some significance. ◆

blockade economic and/or social isolation of an enemy nation by another nation in response to particular policies or actions by means of obstructing movements of ships, supplies, etc.

agrarian rural; farm-based.

Hurricane Camille

Hurricane Camille struck the United States Gulf Coast in August 1969 as a category five hurricane. According to the Saffir-Simpson Hurricane Scale, a category five hurricane is characterized by winds greater than 155 m.p.h. and a storm surge greater than 18 feet above normal. The complete destruction of buildings and roofs is common. Major damage is often done to the lower floors of buildings located less than 15 feet above sea level and within 500 yards of the shoreline. Massive evacuation is typically required, although flooding can often inhibit this process. In the case of Camille, at landfall, winds were gusting at speeds of 200 m.p.h., storm surges reached 22 feet high, and central barometric pressure lowered to 26.84 inches. The consequences of this intense storm were the deaths of 400 people and property damage exceeding $5.2 billion. The second of only two category five hurricanes to touch down in the United States, Hurricane Camille is also the United States' fifth costliest disaster.

The history of Camille began in early August 1969 somewhere over the Caribbean Sea south of Hispaniola. Starting out as an unnumbered, low pressure tropical disturbance, for the first two weeks of August meteorologists and storm watchers largely ignored this would-be storm. On August 14, centered approximately 320 miles off the southern coast of Cuba, what had seemed to be a minor tropical disturbance took meteorologists by surprise as it intensified rapidly to a storm with winds of 65 m.p.h. The next day, as barometric pressure dropped to 28.67 inches and winds rose to 82 m.p.h., the storm was given hurricane status and named Camille. Camille continued to intensify swiftly, and by evening on August 15, winds at speeds of 115 m.p.h. were blowing across the extreme western portion of Cuba. On this first night of terror, several people were killed and considerable property damage occurred.

Early in the morning on October 16, Hurricane Camille stalled over the southern Gulf of Mexico, where it continued to intensify speedily. Despite this intensification, Camille retained a small cloud pattern. Meteorologists at the time believed that hurricane intensity was directly related to cloud pattern and so, after seeing this small cloud pattern, they dras-

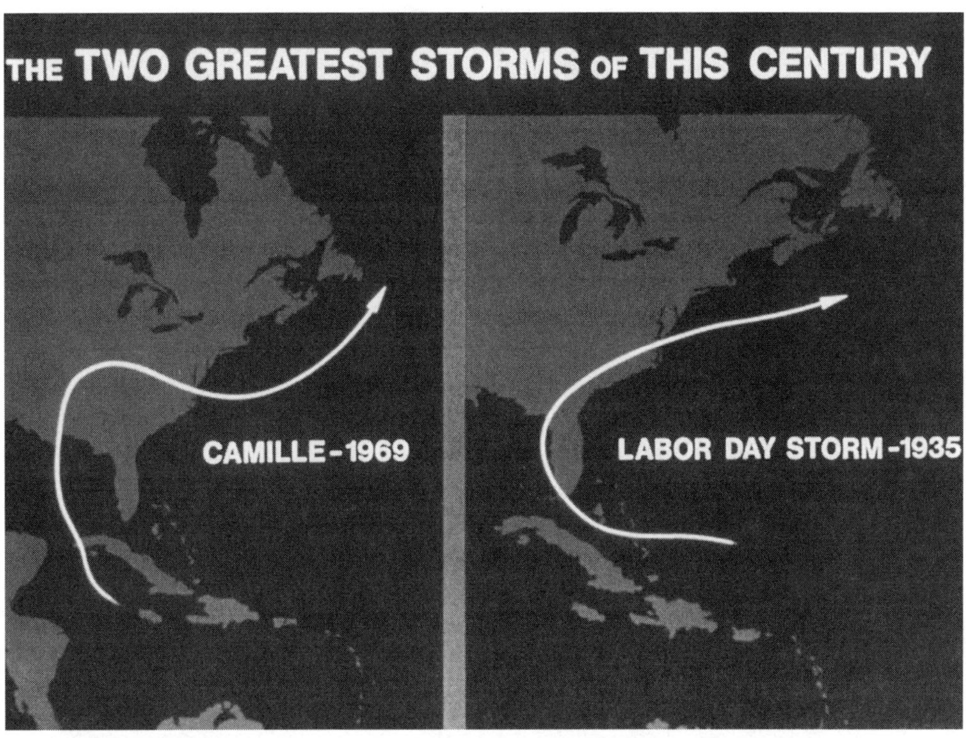

tically underestimated the power of Camille. They also drastically misinterpreted Camille's pattern of movement. As late as August 16, meteorologists believed that Camille was headed straight for the Florida Panhandle. Consequently, storm warnings were focused at Florida, not Louisiana, Mississippi, or Alabama.

The map on the left shows the path of Hurricane Camille.

After hundreds of Floridians evacuated their oceanfront homes, Camille **capriciously** shifted its course and headed straight toward Mississippi. On August 17, 1969, the eye of Hurricane Camille made landfall just west of Pass Christian, Mississippi. With a barometric pressure of 26.84 inches, sustained wind speeds of 170 m.p.h., and wind gusts as great as 200 m.p.h., at landfall, Camille proved to be a formidable force. Storm surges in the Pass Christian, Long Beach area towered over 24 feet high. Winds were so fierce that one house was blown off of its foundation and onto a set of railroad tracks nearby. In Pass Christian, 11 **parishioners** took refuge in a stone church, only to be crushed alive after Camille's 210 m.p.h. gusts smashed the place to pieces. Mile-long sections of the coastal highway were left as crumbled messes when seawalls gave way

capricious characterized by unpredicatable or rapidly changing behavior or patterns.

parishioners members of a church.

The Naming of Hurricanes

Hurricanes and tropical storms were once identified only by numbers assigned by the scientists tracking them. This gave rise to great confusion, however, particularly when several storms were being tracked by more than one group of scientists. Even in those days, however, many hurricane trackers would informally name a big storm they were watching, usually choosing the name of a wife or girlfriend.

In 1950, the National Weather Bureau and the U.S. Air Force, which tracked hurricanes throughout the world, decided to rationalize the way they named the big storms at sea. The first naming system they adopted used a phonetic alphabet (Able, Baker, Charlie) employed by radio operators and the military, and worked sequentially down through the list.

Clearly, this approach had its limits. There were only 26 possible names, so after they were all assigned the scientists had to cycle back to the beginning of the list. A new, more flexible naming system was begun in 1953, still based on the alphabet, but with each letter used to select a unique personal name.

The earliest names were all female and drawn from the English language. A set of six lists was drawn up, each list beginning with an "A" name and working through the alphabet. The first storm of a season was always given an "A" name, after which the names on the lists were assigned sequentially until all had been used. Names were repeated frequently, but the name used for a storm that received a lot of publicity, such as Hurricane Camille, would be retired, never to be used again.

This basic system is still in use, but with some modifications. In the 1970s, women's groups objected to the exclusive use of female names, claiming that equating hurricane destruction with women was sexist. In 1979, therefore, male names were added to the lists. In the Atlantic, French and Spanish names are now also used, so that all the nationalities in that hurricane zone are represented. Similarly, regionally familiar names drawn from Asian cultures are given to storms tracked in the Pacific hurricane regions.

under the wind's fury. In total, Camille's wrath forced at least 200,000 individuals to flee from their homes. Unfortunately, many individuals did not seem to take the ferocity of Camille seriously. One motel on the Gulf shore advertised a "hurricane party" for those more adventurous vacationers who desired to see the development of a storm. Needless to say the party turned out to be less than fun when 20-foot waves completely destroyed the motel, sweeping at least a dozen of the "partygoers" out to sea. Similar tragedies appear to have occurred all along the Gulf Coast, as people who believed they did not lie in Camille's path invited friends over to watch the storm only to discover that it was heading right for them.

After damaging Mississippi so badly that the governor was forced declare **martial law**, Camille moved on to Louisiana,

martial law law applied by military forces invoked by a government in an emergency situation to restore order when civilian law enforcement is unable to maintain safety.

where it struck New Orleans with winds gusting up to 92 m.p.h. At Lakeshore Drive, these winds caused the waters of Lake Pontchartrain to flow over the town's sea wall, flooding the streets and homes of locals. Elsewhere in Louisiana, Camille practically flattened the town of Buras. Camille also ran at least 24 ships aground near the New Orleans-Mobile area. Camille then moved northward into the Mississippi Delta, striking Hattiesburg, Mississippi, on the way. Weakening to a tropical storm with winds reduced to 50 m.p.h., over the next couple of days, Camille shifted east and crossed the Blue Ridge Mountains in Virginia.

A strange meteorological phenomena occurred at this point. As moist air moving inland from the Atlantic Ocean met Camille's winds, the tropical storm was funneled through the two narrow Virginian valleys of the Rockfish and Tye Rivers. Moving through these valleys, Camille met an advancing cold front that was producing thunderstorms. The consequence of this meeting was the production of a moist low-pressure bit of air that rose up the cold front, causing both extreme quantities of rain and intense winds. Due to this rare meeting of cold front and low-pressure tropical storm, in a mere eight hours, Camille covered Virginia with 27 inches of rain. Traveling with sustained winds of 100 m.p.h. and gusts of 175 m.p.h., Camille's rain caused such extensive flash floods that 109 people died and 41 remained unaccounted for. In particular, it caused the James River to flood. Finally, around August 22, Camille dissipated over the Atlantic Ocean north near Newfoundland.

As government officials looked over the wreckage that Camille left in its wake, it became clear that a relief effort of millions of dollars needed to be implemented. President Richard M. Nixon declared parts of Louisiana and Mississippi to be disaster areas and allocated $1 million in disaster funds. Food, medical supplies and fresh water were shipped from all over the country to these U.S. Gulf Coast states. Meanwhile, the American Red Cross scrambled to **inoculate** refugees against **typhoid** and **tetanus** and the National Guardsmen worked overtime in an effort to bar looters and sightseers. Leaking gas mains endangered dozens of coastal areas. In Breton Sound, which is located off the Louisiana coast, storm damage to oil storage tanks caused two large oil slicks to form, threatening populations of local wildlife. It would be an understatement to say that Camille was one of the most terrible storms the U.S. had ever witnessed. Luckily, with the help of sympathetic communities

inoculate to introduce an active material such as an antibiotic or other medicine into the bloodstream to prevent disease.

typhoid a disease of domestic animals resembling human typhus or typhoid; typhus is marked by high fever, intense headache, and delirium.

tetanus an infectious disease characterized by spasm of voluntary muscles caused by the toxin bacillus.

all across the United States, within the next year, the lives of citizens of the U.S. Gulf Coast and Virginia, though changed with the memory of Camille, returned back to normal. ◆

Pakistan Cyclone/Bangladesh Cyclone

NOVEMBER 1970

In November 1970, a great oceanic storm struck East Pakistan. This storm is often referred to as the Great Cyclone of 1970. With winds of 131 m.p.h., a barometric pressure of 27.88 inches, and a colossal storm surge that towered 34 feet high, the Great Cyclone of 1970 ultimately claimed 350,000 lives, left nearly a million people homeless, and set off the bloody civil war that produced Bangladesh.

The story of the Great Bangladesh Cyclone begins November 10, 1970, in the Bay of Benegal, which is off the eastern coast of India. At 9:00 A.M., meteorologists sighted the development of a low-pressure area moving northwest. Low-pressure areas that develop over warm water are typically monitored very carefully by meteorologists who know that the combination of a warm, low-pressure area above the sea with an area of high atmospheric pressure is likely to create a cyclone. Indeed this was the case in the Bay of Benegal; by mid-afternoon air was rapidly being drawn into the low-pressure area, creating a cyclonic storm with winds near 55 m.p.h. This pattern continued into November 11, causing wind intensity to jump to 85 m.p.h.

Still 650 miles southeast of Chittagong, East Pakistan, over the next two days the storm traveled quickly north. Government officials in Pakistan, warned of the storm by the National Hurricane Center, made some, but little effort to alert the public of this **imminent** disaster. Luckily, radio stations in Calcutta, India, and Dhaka began independently broadcasting warnings to citizens. Unfortunately, for the most part, the inhabitants of the islands who were scattered throughout the Bay of Benegal did not have electricity and therefore did not hear these radio warnings.

imminent fast-approaching.

A steamer ship rests in a field in East Pakistan after being run aground during the 1970 cyclone.

By midnight of November 13, the cyclone reached the mouth of the Ganges River. With a barometric pressure of 27.88 inches, winds of 100 m.p.h. and a storm surge (the increase in water level above what is normal) 15 feet high, the cyclone was of **cataclysmic** proportions. To make matters worse, when it struck, the Bay of Bengal was in the midst of its lunar tide, which is when water levels are naturally at their highest. When the typhoon's storm surges, fed by the high lunar tide, hit the land, whole areas were simply swept away. The islands of Bhola, Dubla, Jabbar, and Hatia were entirely submerged beneath 20 feet of saltwater. In almost an instant 8,000 lives were lost. One man, seconds before being thrown out to sea, attempted to save the lives of his grandchildren by locking them into a large wooden trunk. Amazingly enough, days later this trunk was found with the children still alive and healthy. Others who managed to survive did so only by climbing the sturdiest and tallest of trees. Even up in the trees though, these individuals were forced to fight off poisonous snakes and other wildlife smart enough to seek refuge high above the seething mass of

cataclysmic description of a violent and momentous event marked by extreme devastation and damage.

ambivalent indecisive or uncaring.

cholera any number of several diseases in humans and domesticated animals usually characterized by severe gastrointestinal problems.

water that engulfed the countryside. Within hours, nearly one-fourth of East Pakistan's total landmass was entirely underwater.

Luckily, only a day after this initial furious onslaught, the storm seemed to dissipate over the uplands of Bhutan and Tibet. Unfortunately, what the storm left behind was little more than the complete and utter destruction of much of East Pakistan. In total, over 1.1 million acres of rice paddies and 800,000 tons of grain vanished under the force of the storm. Hundreds of boats and ships were destroyed or found beached inland. The bloated corpses of both humans and animals were strewn about the landscape. Officials arriving from the World Bank, United States, and Great Britain soon realized the seriousness of the tragedy.

To make matters worse, the Central Pakistani government seemed **ambivalent** to the losses incurred by the eastern half of the nation. Responding slowly and with minimal assistance, the central government and its inaction increased the tragedy two-fold. For at least a week after the storm, the government remained immobile while storm-devastated citizens succumbed to disease and starvation. In particular, dirty drinking water made the threat of typhoid and **cholera** especially intense. Luckily, political differences were largely set aside as the international community pulled together to aid the disaster-struck citizens of Pakistan. In a particularly compassionate act, India, putting aside years of territorial disputes with Pakistan, granted permission for Pakistani helicopters to enter Indian airspace. Needless to say, Red Cross groups across the world organized and sent bundles of vaccines, food, and clothing to the victims of the cyclone.

Despite this international aid, the situation in Pakistan deteriorated. East Pakistanis, angry and frustrated, accused the central Pakistani government of being unconcerned with their plight. This resentment towards the central government only intensified when, on November 23, a relief helicopter injured several survivors. When the remaining storm refugees fled to Calcutta, tension and resentment were simmering just below the surface. In 1971, with the devastation of the storm still on their minds, East Pakistan rebelled and declared independence from the central government. Bangladesh is the consequence of the short, bloody civil war that followed.

After its installation, the new Bangladeshi government took many efforts directed at protecting itself from the tragedy of November 1970. One of these protective devices was the construction of cyclone shelters. These concrete shelters are two to three stories high and stand on high concrete stilts. When there is no threat of storm, the buildings are used for municipal purposes. The government also funded a project to plant mangrove trees along the coast. These forests can somewhat absorb the shock of the storm surge and since 1970, the government has planted more than 60,000 acres of these trees. At some locations, embankments that delay flood water have been built behind the trees. ◆

Hurricane Fifi

Hurricane Fifi hit Belize and Honduras on September 18 and 19, 1974, and is most often remembered by the massive destruction of banana crops and the high death toll that it caused. With winds of 109 m.p.h. and torrential rains, Fifi is believed to have caused $900 million in damage and 5,000 deaths.

On September 14, 1974, a tropical depression began to form over the southeastern Caribbean Sea. Moving northwest at a speed of 16 m.p.h., by September 16, 1974, this tropical depression shaped itself into the season's sixth tropical storm, Fifi. Located just 32 miles south of Kingston, Jamaica, throughout September 16, Fifi covered Jamaica in rain, leaving streets with two feet of water and causing hundreds of thousands of dollars in property damage. On September 17, poised some 400 miles east of Trujillo, Honduras, Fifi intensified her winds to 74 m.p.h., and thus became a full-blown hurricane. The next day, after first skirting the Swan Islands, it made its first landfall on the north

Hurricane Fifi caused massive flooding, covering this row of houses in Honduras.

National Hurricane Center

In 1970, the National Oceanographic and Atmospheric Administration (NOAA) was formed by the United States Congress by merging several previously independent but related agencies, including the National Weather Service, the Environmental Data Service, and the National Satellite Center. From this wide range of scientific resources, the NOAA created several subagencies, each devoted to specialized areas of environmental concern.

The National Hurricane Center (NHC), partnered with the Tropical Prediction Center (TPC), is one of these special research units, headquartered at the Florida International University in Miami. These paired agencies share a twofold mission: to advance scientific understanding of ocean-based storms, with particular interest in learning how to predict their occurrence; and to improve public awareness of these storms in order to reduce the destruction and loss of life that they can cause.

From May 15 to November 30 every year, the NHC and the TPC monitor storm formation over the Atlantic and Pacific Oceans, the Caribbean Sea, and the Gulf of Mexico. To do this they use satellite imaging as well as data supplied by the fabled Hurricane Hunters—an Air Force Reserve battalion that flies specially outfitted planes directly into storms in order to gather data. Researchers back in Miami use this data to prepare hurricane watches and warnings to alert the public to danger, and they provide marine and military advisories as well.

During the off-season, from December 1 to May 14, the NHC remains busy. They provide training in emergency management for U.S. and foreign officials and conduct workshops to increase public awareness of the need for hurricane planning and preparation.

coast of Honduras. Lashing the island with winds of 132 m.p.h. and a barometric pressure of 28.67 inches, Fifi set off a series of flash floods that battered more than 182 towns. Banana trees were torn from the ground, leaving their fruit as little more that smashed yellow mush. The Red Cross estimates that within this first 12-hour time slot after landfall, Fifi killed between 800 and 1,500 people.

The next day, September 19, Hurricane Fifi headed straight into southern Belize near the port town of Monkey River. With winds reduced to 109 m.p.h., Fifi acted as any hurricane would, uprooting trees, damaging buildings, carrying bits of debris through the air, and covering the island in rain. By mid-afternoon, it had moved into Guatemala with winds of such a degraded intensity that it could only be classified as a tropical storm. In spite of this reduction in power, Fifi's rains triggered numerous mudslides throughout the country, destroying dozens of roads and bridges. Some 200 people are estimated to have drowned in Guatemala on this day, making Fifi the deadliest storm to strike the country for almost two decades. Meanwhile, Fifi's rains continued to pound down upon Honduras, triggering cataclysmic landslides and mudslides all across the island.

In fact it was ultimately the flooding and landslides that really caused the most damage to Honduras and its neighboring countries. According to National Emergency official Col. Eduardo Andino, the northern lowlands of Honduras was the region where most of Fifi's flooding was concentrated. Unfortunately, these northern lowlands were also the location of most of the country's agricultural crops. It is estimated by Honduran government officials that roughly 80 percent of Honduras' banana crops were destroyed by the mudslides caused by the storm. Additionally, a great deal of the country's cattle were killed in these floods. Some estimate that as many as two-fifths of the country's cattle population was swept away in Fifi's deluge. In terms of people, in one Nicaraguan village, at least 50 people were killed when a landslide of rock and mud swept through their town. The number of fatalities in Honduras, though debated, is even larger. In the time after the storm, the Honduran government estimated between 7,500 and 8,000 deaths. In comparison, the U.S. Army put the death toll at 1,000 individuals. *The New York Times* reported that some foreign diplomats believed that the Honduran government was intentionally inflating the number of dead so that they could ensure international aid. Today, a figure between 5,000 and 6,000 dead is probably most accurate.

The area hardest hit by Fifi was Choloma, Honduras. It was here, on September 20, that Hurricane Fifi performed one last major act of destruction, triggering an avalanche of trees, water, and rock that ultimately killed nearly 3,000 villagers. Originally this avalanche dammed the river that ran through the town, but later this dike burst, engulfing the entire city in water. Government officials report that approximately one square mile of Choloma was covered with mud and debris. It is estimated that almost half of the town's residents died. The survivors, for the most part, had lost their homes and all their belongings. Consequently, in the days following the initial avalanche, the surviving Choloma residents camped out at the railroad station and the town square. In the meantime, officials scrambled to cremate the bodies of dead villagers that threatened to pollute drinking water with cholera and other epidemics. By September 23, the Honduran Army reported that 2,700 bodies were burned

It is estimated that almost half of the town's residents died.

or buried at Choloma. Another 1,000 bodies were burned at La Ceiba, another town that was hit hard by Fifi.

As thousands remained homeless and the total amount of property damage rose in Honduras, the international community pulled together to offer aid. These relief efforts consisted of monetary aid, cattle, water, gas, clothing, and medicine. In particular, Cuba played a major role in the relief effort. American owned fruit companies United Fruit Company and Standard Fruit Company also offered helicopters to carry food to survivors. Despite the promptness with which other nations and corporations responded to Honduras' plight, help seemed slow in reaching residents. As of September 23, at least 8,000 people were still stranded on roofs, treetops, and high ground. Many hurricane victims, threatened with starvation, were reduced to looting nearby stores. The government reported as many as 40,000 people without food and water.

There are two reasons for the slowness of the relief effort: hurricane devastated transportation routes and corrupt government officials. First of all, floodwaters washed out bridges, roads, rail lines, and air strips to such a large degree that it was virtually impossible for relief supplies such as food, gas, and medicine to reach the places most devastated by the storm. Additionally, poor organization and a lack of fuel made it difficult to distribute materials over what roads were not destroyed. Unfortunately, many flood relief supplies appear to not have reached their intended destination because they were confiscated by Honduran officials. On October 17, Honduran Foreign Minister Cesar A. Batres resigned under allegations of mishandling relief efforts.

As for Fifi, on September 21, after obliterating the city of Choloma, Honduras, in a rare meteorological shift, Fifi rejuvenated and became a tropical storm named Orlene. After making one last landfall in Mexico, Orlene/Fifi dissipated in the early morning hours of September 22. ◆

Bangladesh Cyclone

1985

Bangladesh, which is located in the northeast portion of India and borders the Bay of Benegal, has historically been plagued by hurricanes. In fact, the Bangladesh Cyclone of 1970 was one of the causes for the separation of

Bangladesh, then East Pakistan, from the rest of Pakistan. That stated, in many aspects, the Bangladesh Cyclone of 1985 is not much different from the other cyclones that have plagued the Bay of Benegal. What makes this storm unique is the contrast between its low intensity and the extent of damage it caused. With winds of only 80 m.p.h., this cyclone managed to affect six districts and change the lives of roughly 1.3 million people over an area of 5,000 square miles. Consequently, some officials have stated that this 1985 cyclone comes in second to the 1970 storm in terms of fatalities and overall destruction.

The scene begins early in the week of May 19, 1985 when a low-pressure area began forming in the Bay of Benegal. Midweek, Indian meteorologists warned Bangladesh that their radar indicated that a storm was headed for the Grange Delta. They estimated two days before this storm would hit. Six hours later, as the storm shifted its course, Indian meteorologists were forced to retract their warning, realizing that actually the storm would arrive a day earlier than expected. Acting on this advice, Thursday, May 23, the government of Bangladesh began sending out hurricane warnings over Radio Bangladesh every half an hour. Red Cross volunteers are also said to have warned islanders and citizens of the coastal district. However, the warnings, which urged villagers and islanders to take refuge at higher elevations largely fell on deaf ears, if they fell at all. Many villagers felt that the warnings were a false alarm. Others, without access to a radio, claim they never heard a warning. Still others felt they did not want to leave their land and animals unprotected.

This reaction, tragically enough, proved fatal, when late in the evening of Friday, May 24, 1985, a cyclone struck Southern Bangladesh. According to the Dhaka Meteorological Center, this storm was characterized by winds between 80-100 m.p.h., and waves 15 feet high. This cyclone was not very strong, and yet somehow, over the period of a day and a half, it managed to kill 10,000 people, leaving at least 80,000 homeless. The Bangladeshi Red Cross estimates an even larger death toll, figuring fatalities to be closer to 40,000. Part of the reason the number of deaths is so high is because of the large tsunami that engulfed seven islands off the coast of Bangladesh. A **tsunami** is literally a great wave, and in this case, it demolished an embankment constructed to hold back such tragedies, before flooding islands located off Bangladesh's coast. Indeed, the Bangladesh government estimated that approximately 90

Many villagers felt that the warnings were a false alarm.

tsumani large sea waves capable of moving thousands of kilometers and caused by the sudden and violent displacement of water; generally generated by earthquakes, volcanic eruptions, and underwater landslides.

percent of the cyclone's victims were on just one of these islands, Urichar. Urichar is a recently formed **silt** island that stretches four miles wide in the delta of the Meghna River. It is located 220 miles south of Dhaka and at the time was believed to be populated by approximately 7,000 people. Tragically, 4,093 individuals who had lived on Urichar were reported missing after the storm.

On June 1, 1985, bodies of the cyclone's victims continued to wash ashore. News reports at the time estimated that 500 fishing boats were at sea when the storm hit, causing the loss of at least 2,000 crew members. Unfortunately, the bodies of these fisherman, as with the bodies of many of the residents of Urichar and Sandiwap were swept out to sea, destroying the possibility for citizens to properly bury their dead. This factor also hindered the ability of officials to estimate an accurate death toll.

The aftermath of the storm continued to take victims, as hundreds of people succumbed to disease and diarrhea. As of June 2, 1985, medical teams who were working around the clock to aid the disaster areas, reported the deaths of at least 100 people from diarrhea. Cholera and other water-born diseases were beginning to appear with increasing frequency as thousands of people were without clean drinking water. In order to correct this problem, President Hossain Mohammad Ershad ordered the immediate digging of wells. However, because transportation routes were so devastated and communication was wiped out, his orders could not be carried out as quickly as they needed to be. Fuel, food, and medicine were also scarcities. At the time, President Ershad estimated that only 15 percent of the country's needs were being met.

Besides the loss of human life, government officials estimated property and crop damage at a sum of $200 million. Included within this figure are crop losses worth $100 million and the price of reconstructing 100 miles of protective embankments and 500 miles of roads. Additionally, the Bangladesh government estimated a loss of 15,000 cattle head.

Luckily, the international community pulled together and came to Bangladesh's aid. A total of $12 million in aid was pledged by 13 different countries such as Canada, the United States, the Soviet Union, Saudi Arabia, and Japan. Saudi Arabia, in particular contributed a large portion of this figure. Divisions of the Red Cross from many different nations also contributed medical supplies, food, and clothing. In the city of Dhaka, Bangladesh, which was not directly affected by the storm, collec-

What is the Difference Between a Cyclone, a Hurricane, and a Typhoon?

Cyclones, hurricanes, and typhoons, along with their inland relatives, tornadoes, are all major storms that are characterized by powerful winds swirling around a central, calm region, called an "eye." The terms are easily confused with one another, but they differ in important ways.

The term "cyclone" is generic, and refers to any atmospheric low-pressure zone that gives rise to circularly flowing winds. These weather systems can grow to vast dimensions, but as they increase in power they tend to pull into themselves, becoming more compact. If they occur over land, cyclones are called tornadoes, and can range from 300 to 8,000 feet (90 to 2,400 meters) across.

If this same weather pattern occurs over the ocean, it is called a tropical cyclone, in part because they are found only in the tropics and subtropics. Tropical cyclones begin as a set of easterly winds which, as they pick up speed, form a weather system known as a tropical depression. When the speeds increase even further, they are called tropical storms or tropical cyclones–the names are used interchangeably. When wind speeds exceed 73 miles per hour (117.5 kph), however, the name is changed once again.

In the eastern and northern Pacific, and in the Atlantic, these supercharged cyclones are called hurricanes. In the Western Pacific, however, they are called typhoons, a word drawn from Greek and Arabic, meaning "great wind." Thus the distinction between a hurricane and a typhoon is purely linguistic. To add to the confusion, when these extremely high-wind weather systems occur in the Indian Ocean, they receive no special designation; there they are called cyclones no matter how powerful they become.

tion boxes were established within the city in the hopes that citizens might donate money to aid their fellow countrymen.

One week after the storm struck, planes and ships continued to drop off much needed medical supplies and food. In comparison to the negligence of the Pakistani government during the storm of 1970, the Bangladeshi government implemented a massive relief effort that included the distribution of preventative medicines to check the spread of disease, and the distribution of free seeds, fertilizers, and cattle to farmers whose crops were devastated. According to government officials, a total of 100 medical teams and 20,000 members of armed forces participated in this rehabilitation program.

Finally, the Bangladesh cyclone of 1985 appears to have had one very positive impact. Acting as a reminder of the extent to which the Bay of Benegal and the southeast Asian area in general are **susceptible** to cyclones, this storm somewhat prompted the United Nations Economic and Social Commission for Asia and the Pacific to begin to monitor the frequency of cyclones in Bangladesh. ◆

susceptible unresistant and open to a particular agency, stimulus, of influence.

Hurricane Gilbert

Hurricane Gilbert was one of the most intense hurricanes ever to be recorded in the Western Hemisphere. Extending over some 500 miles, with an eye of only eight miles, at one point Gilbert's barometric pressure reached a low of 26.22 inches. Over the course of eight days in September, 1988, the hurricane wreaked chaos in nine nations, ultimately causing millions of dollars in damage and hundreds of deaths.

Hurricane Gilbert was born out of a group of clouds moving west from the coast of West Africa. By September 9, these clouds had shaped themselves into a tropical storm near Guadeloupe. Only a day later, this tropical storm, now named Gilbert, had increased to hurricane intensity and was causing a great deal of flooding as it thrashed the coast of Puerto Rico with waves 12 feet high. By 2 A.M. Sunday, September 11, the National Hurricane Center in Miami located Gilbert at a latitude of 16.1 north, longitude 67.5 west, making the hurricane 140 miles south of Puerto Rico. Traveling northwest with sustained winds of 75 m.p.h. and **gusts** as strong as 92 m.p.h., Gilbert next swept past Haiti and the Dominican Republic, causing torrential flooding and much crop damage.

Linked with five deaths in the Dominican Republic and 10 in Haiti, on Monday, September 12, this "monster-storm" pushed towards Jamaica. Jamaicans, who had not witnessed a hurricane since 1951, did their best to prepare by moving inland, boarding up houses, and stocking up on food and water. However, as waves 20 feet high pounded the shores of the popular resort Ocho Rios, and sustained winds at a speed of 115 m.p.h. ravished Jamaica's southwest coast, it soon became clear that Jamaica would not emerge from the storm without heavy damage. Trees and telephone poles were uprooted and sent flying through the air as tourists and locals huddled in schools, hospitals, and government buildings for protection. Roughly four out of five houses had their roofs torn from their foundations, leaving a fourth of the island's population, half a million people, homeless. Safe drinking water and power sources were devastated, leaving Kingston, a major city on Jamaica's southwest coast, and other places without these basics.

gust a sudden, brief rush of wind.

With a Jamaican death toll of at least 30, Gilbert continued to move northwest at a speed of 15 m.p.h. towards the Cayman Islands and Yucatan Peninsula. Meanwhile, people everywhere prepared for the worse. The National Civil Defense System ordered an evacuation of all individuals living less than 15 feet above sea level and within 2,000 feet of the Caribbean coast. The Cayman Islands Airlines began running flights to Miami every two hours in hopes of evacuating as many people as possible. In the Bay of Campeche, the Mexican state oil company Pemex began evacuating its 5,000 employees at all 146 oil drilling locations. Early morning September 13, Gilbert, with winds now as strong as 140 m.p.h., passed about 20 miles south of Grand Cayman Islands, causing extensive damage to crops and property. Later in the day these winds increased to over 150 m.p.h. and the atmospheric pressure in the eye of the storm was one of the lowest ever recorded for an Atlantic hurricane. Five Cuban fishing boats with a total crew of about 80 people sank under Gilbert's power.

On September 14, over the warm waters of the Yucatan Channel between Cuba and Mexico, Gilbert was at its

A ship forced ashore at Cancun, Mexico by the enormous waves caused by Hurricane Gilbert in 1988.

strongest. As early as dawn Wednesday morning, waves 23 feet high thrashed the beaches of the Mexican states Quintana Roo and Yucatan. By 8 A.M., winds were tracked at speeds of 160 m.p.h., making Gilbert classifiable as the highest category of hurricane, a category five. According to the Saffir-Simpson Hurricane Scale, a hurricane is classified as a category five if it has winds greater than 155 m.p.h. At this level, roof failure, extensive window and door damage, and the complete destruction of mobile homes, shrubs, trees, and signs is common. In general, structures located less than 15 feet above sea level and within 500 yards of shoreline experience high levels of damage. Gilbert seemed to greatly exceed this level of intensity. By mid-morning, the Mexican National Weather Service reported winds to be gusting at 218 m.p.h. and sustained winds to be blowing at 179 m.p.h.. Gilbert had truly become an embodiment of the Caribbean Indians' god of wind whom they call Huracan.

After pouring more than 10 inches of water over Central America and killing 15 people in Honduras, Gilbert struck the tourist hub and 110-hotel Mexican resort island of Cancun. Ironically, the location of this resort was chosen after a 1970s computer-generated study demonstrated that its chances of being hit by a hurricane were slim. The devastation was terrible. At one point, 450 refugees in a banquet room were forced to hold up a wall as it collapsed under Gilbert's strength. Water and electricity were completely wiped out, eliminating running water and properly functioning toilets. Still moving northwest, Gilbert next blew through the resorts of Cozumel and Isla Mujeres, where it uprooted laurel plants and palms, snapped telephone poles, and demolished huts and houses alike. Gilbert's strength was so powerful that after the storm a 118-foot Cuban fishing boat was found washed up next to a hotel. Additionally, the Nichupte Lagoon that separates Cancun from mainland Yucatan overflowed. In total, at least $300 million in damage, 24 deaths, and the complete destruction of many fruit crops were the gifts that Gilbert left behind as it moved towards the Gulf of Mexico.

On September 15, Gilbert, still a category five storm, moved toward Texas. The Weather Bureau issued warnings for all residents of the coastline between New Orleans and the Mexican border. Residents, remembering the wrath of Hurricane Camille (the only other category five hurricane to hit the United States in the 1900s) expected the worst. However, on

September 16, Gilbert began to lose energy and winds decreased to 125 mph, downgrading it to a category three storm. It was perhaps because of this decrease in energy that Gilbert swerved inland to Mexico, just 100 miles south of Brownsville, Texas. Here, in the state of Tamaulipas, Gilbert pushed ocean waters roughly three feet deep inland, killing several coastal villagers. In the meantime, Haiti had declared a state of emergency and relief funds from Canada and the U.S. were pouring into Jamaica and Cancun.

After flattening the fishing village of La Presca, Gilbert continued inland, approaching the 2.8 million person town of Monterrey, Mexico. With winds now reduced to 75 m.p.h., Gilbert, in one final and ferocious act smacked into the 14,000 foot-high mountains that surround Monterrey. The rain released by Gilbert over this mountain caused such flooding and mudslides that four buses, packed with a total of 190 passengers, were washed away as they traveled across the dry riverbed of the Santa Catarina River. Only 12 people escaped alive from this disaster. On September 18, Gilbert entered the United States near the Mexican town of Nuevo Laredo and dissipated into several tornados that caused yet more damage throughout Texas.

When all was said and done, Gilbert had caused approximately $300 million in damage to the tourist industry in Mexico, and as much as $1 billion in damage to Jamaica. It caused approximately 300 deaths and left an inestimable number of people homeless. ◆

Hurricane Mitch

OCTOBER 1998

Of all the Atlantic Ocean storms ever measured, Hurricane Mitch was the second most intense. The bulk of Mitch's damage came not from wind damage, but from the post-storm flooding and mudslides that the hurricane set off. Ultimately killing 11,000 people, leaving 2 million homeless, and causing between $6 and 10 billion in damage, for two weeks in October 1998.

The story of Mitch begins in Africa, where, during the first two weeks of October, a series of atmospheric disturbances and thunderstorms were charted traveling out over the Atlantic

A satellite photograph shows Hurricane Mitch covering part of the Carribean.

Ocean. On October 19, 1998, this tropical wave extended out through the Caribbean, near Lesser Antilles. Feeding on the moisture and heat that come from waters with a surface temperature of at least 80 degrees, by October 21, the tropical wave became a tropical depression named Mitch. At this point, the storm was 360 miles south of Jamaica and moving north.

From this point on, Mitch continued to develop rapidly. Early in the morning on October 22, Mitch's winds increased to 45 m.p.h., and it was given tropical storm status. Two days later and 200 miles south-southwest of Jamaica, these winds had doubled to 90 m.p.h., officially classifying Mitch as a hurricane. Almost as a **portent** of the devastation to come, torrential rains from Mitch flooded the streets of Costa Rica, killing several individuals.

It was around this time when Cubans and Jamaicans alike began preparing for the worst, buying up canned goods and filling sandbags. However, on Sunday, October 25, Mitch shifted west and began traveling more in the direction of Belize and Mexico. The next day, Mitch, still traveling west, developed

portent a foreshadowing or omen of an event yet to occur.

winds of 180 m.p.h., making it a category five hurricane. According to the Saffir-Simpson Hurricane Scale, a category five hurricane has winds greater than 155 m.p.h. and storm surges (an increase in water level) at levels 18 feet above normal. Roof and building failures are common and evacuation of low-lying towns is usually necessary. Thus, as Mitch swirled near the Honduran Swann Island, army members evacuated Belize and coastal towns in Mexico. Similarly, Honduran President Carlos Flores Facusse declared a state of alarm, urging coastal residents to take refuge inland.

By chance, a high-pressure system north of the hurricane deflected Mitch more west than northwest, causing the storm to meander aimlessly off the coast of Honduras. As a consequence of this shift, Mitch's wrath was focused on several Honduran Islands. In particular, the island of Guanaja took a beating; after a three-day period of intense winds and fierce waves, the island was denuded of both buildings and trees. Luckily, despite this property damage, only six people died on Guanaja.

By Wednesday, October 28, Mitch hovered 30 miles north of Honduras. However, at this point, its winds had decreased to 115 m.p.h. and the Weather Bureau degraded Mitch to a category three hurricane. Despite this reduction in storm intensity, Mitch's rains were causing severe flooding throughout many Caribbean countries. Government officials estimated that nearly 1 million people were affected by this flooding. In Nicaragua, 20 towns were placed on alert, 10,000 individuals were forced to flee inland, and thousands of **hectares** of rice, beans, and corn were completely destroyed. Storm drain systems were stressed to such a degree that they were nearing collapse. The Red Cross in Nicaragua reported as many as 19 dead. The situation in Costa Rica was less severe, but still grim; by Wednesday, Mitch had left 5,000 Costa Ricans injured, causing the government to declare a state of emergency. Late Wednesday evening, Honduran President Flores also declared a state of emergency and publicly requested international aid.

hectare a metric measurement of an area equalling 2.47 acres.

On October 29, Mitch hit the north coast of Honduras, near Trujillo. Winds slowed to 85 m.p.h., significantly downgrading Mitch's hurricane status, but rains, deluging Honduras with more than 25 inches of water, continued to do significant damage. Rivers and creeks swelled across the countryside, flooding towns and forcing the evacuation of 70,000 Hondurans. Coffee and banana crops were washed away, as local families struggled to remain dry high up in the trees or on rooftops. This

Hurricane Hunters

Long before Hurricane Mitch made landfall, a unique crew of Air Force Reserve pilots were already in the air, tracking the storm and sending meteorological data back, as they have done since 1945. These are the Hurricane Hunters, who combine aerial weather reconnaissance with relief assistance throughout the Atlantic Basin during hurricane season.

In September of 1945, Lt. Col. Joe Duckworth became the first Hurricane Hunter by accepting a dare to fly his plane into the eye of a storm. Duckworth was a member of the 53rd Weather Reconnaissance Squadron, which was formed in 1944 to collect data for the U.S. Weather Bureau on weather patterns throughout the world. Among the squadron's planes were four B-25s that were specifically charged with tracking hurricanes. This unit came to be known as "Hurricane Hunters," and the nickname has stuck ever since.

In 1947, the mission of the 53rd squadron was formally merged with the U.S. Weather Bureau's program for issuing hurricane warnings during the storm season. In this pre-satellite era, data collected by the Hurricane Hunters were crucial for accurate forecasting.

Congressional cuts in the military budget at the end of the 1940s led to a temporary disbanding of the 53rd squadron, but it was restored to active status in 1951. In 1953 the squadron took on a new and very special annual mission that continues to this day: they accepted letters from Western Europe and the United States, all addressed for delivery to Santa Claus. Over the years the 53rd has been based in Bermuda, England, and Puerto Rico. When Hurricane Camille hit U.S. shores in 1969, however, Congress decided to establish a permanent base closer to the local action. Thus in 1973 the Hurricane Hunters came home to Keesler Air Force Base, near Biloxi, Mississippi. In the mid-1970s, this "regular" Air Force squadron faced a rival when the 815th Weather Reconnaissance Squadron of the Air Force Reserve also began tracking storms. The two units cooperated for a decade and a half, until budget cuts finally sidelined the 53rd in 1991. The Air Force Reserve squadron carried on alone, for a time, but in 1993 the Reserve unit was split in two, with the 815th devoted solely to running cargo flights. The newly created second unit, charged with storm tracking, honored its predecessor by taking its name and traditional nickname, becoming the newest incarnation of the Hurricane Hunters.

trend continued into Friday, at which point, Mitch, 55 miles south of Limon and with winds under 55 m.p.h. could only be called a tropical storm. Despite its reduced status, rain from Mitch continued to plague Caribbean states. By afternoon, 25 villages along the Aguan River were completely under water. The Choluteca River, swollen beyond belief, similarly put much of Tegucigalpa, the capital of Honduras, under water. Livestock, trees, telephone poles, and furniture floated through the deserted streets of cities and towns.

For the entire weekend, Mitch's presence continued to be felt in the shape of devastating landslides and mudslides. The most tragic of these landslides, made possible only by deforested landscapes, occurred at Casita Volcano, in northwestern Nicaragua, where the collapse of a rain-filled crater's wall buried 14 villages in mud and killed at least 1,500 people. One family told reporters that they woke up to a rumbling sound only to discover that 15 of their neighbor's houses had been swept down the mountainside. By Sunday Mitch had moved west across Honduras and into Guatemala and El Salvador, significantly slowing, but also forcing 17,000 people to evacuate and killing several people. It finally lost power near Tapulcha.

On November 2, 1998, as the sky resumed a sunny **countenance**, Caribbean governments looked over the devastation of their countries with sorrow and disbelief. Ninety-three of the country's bridges were out of commission; 45 of these were completely destroyed. Lines of communication were also completely knocked out, forcing cities to cope on their own and hindering relief efforts. Storm waters destroyed roughly 70 percent of the year's grain harvest and covered most of Honduras' coffee and banana crops in mud. More than 600,000 people left homeless crammed into schools, government buildings, and other temporary shelters.

As the week wore on and bloated corpses were hauled out from under the water and mud, it became clear that Mitch's wrath was responsible for the deaths of at least 10,000 people. It also became clear that the relief effort in Honduras needed to be stepped up. Food was quickly disappearing off grocery shelves, and gas was increasingly rare. Traveling between cities over rocky roads and crumbling bridges was dangerous. Fears mounted regarding sanitation and the availability of drinking water. Luckily, international aid came in full to Honduras, which sustained the most damage from Mitch. Japan offered to repair two bridges, and the U.S. pledged $70 million to help rebuild and sent 30 tons of food. Ultimately, a total of $1.5 billion was given in aid to the Caribbean nations struck by Mitch.

One year after Hurricane Mitch, many Caribbean nations were still trying to put the pieces of their countries back together. For example, as of October 1999, storm drainage systems were still backed up, silt left from Mitch was causing increased water levels, some roads were still damaged, and at least 21 bridges were in terrible shape. On a positive note, within that time period the Honduran National Emergency organization COPECO was overhauled and equipped with a larger staff and better operating strategies. ◆

Storm waters destroyed roughly 70 percent of the year's grain harvest.

countenance mood or expression.

Tornadoes

Natchez Tornado

The Natchez Tornado was one of the most devastating tornadoes in United States history. According to the National Oceanic and Atmospheric Administration (NOAA), it was the second deadliest tornado in U.S. history. When the tornado broke out, most people in the area of Natchez, Mississippi, were enjoying a pleasant spring day, unaware that a deadly tornado was about to strike. Suddenly the sky turned black and a massive tornado swept through Natchez demolishing the town in a matter of minutes.

Natchez was the first city formed on the Mississippi River, two years before history-rich New Orleans, Louisiana. It was named for a group of native Americans who were among the first to develop the area, the Natchez Indians. Natchez was a highly developed town at the time of the tornado; wealthy **prospectors** flocked to it from around the nation to take advantage of the area's rich land and natural resources. Natchez also served as the original capital city of the state of Mississippi.

prospectors individuals who explore area for mining deposits in particular.

The massive tornado developed on May 17, 1840, approximately 20 miles southwest of Natchez and moved northeast through Natchez up the Mississippi River. The tornado began at around 1:00 P.M. and caused the majority of its death and destruction in 30 minutes. Historical reports of the tornado indicate that at some points the "funnel" of the tornado, which was a mile wide, ripped out trees and tore down homes on both sides of the river as it moved up the Mississippi. It was on the banks of the Mississippi River that most of the 317 lives were lost. Many of the people lost in the storm were aboard flat boats along the river. When the tornado hit, these people were thrown from the boats and swept beneath the raging water. The steamboat *Hinds* was pulled completely beneath the river, killing its entire crew and all passengers.

Although the "official" death toll has been marked by the National Oceanic Association of America at 317, it is likely that many more people were killed. The tornado occurred before the Civil War (1861-1865) when slavery was still in practice. It was then common to exclude the deaths of slaves from official death tolls because they were not given equal consideration as citizens, but treated as property. According to newspaper reports at the time it was believed that hundreds of slaves were killed on plantations during the storm. An estimated 109 people were injured by the tornado and the total amount of damage caused was estimated to be $1.2 million. One of the most tragic events of the tornado destruction occurred when a young woman was rescued at the Steam Boat Hotel. The badly injured woman was rescued while holding the lifeless bodies of two children in her arms. ◆

St. Louis Tornado

MAY 27, 1896

On May 27, 1896, a massive tornado swept through eastern Missouri and southern Illinois causing massive property damage and loss of life. An estimated 255 people were killed and 1,000 injured in the tornado outbreak which ended as the worst natural disaster in St. Louis's history, and one of the deadliest tornadoes in U.S. history. The tornado's path was more than one mile wide at times. Historians suspect that the death toll was actually much higher because the deaths of African Americans were not recorded at the time.

On the morning of May 27, 1896, the skies were cloudy and the people of St. Louis, Missouri, were expecting a springtime thunderstorm but nothing out of the ordinary. However, a mass of cool air over St. Louis was mixing with warm air from the southwest and developing into a massive tornado.

At approximately 4:30 P.M. on May 27, 1896, the clouds began to darken and the temperature began cooling down in St. Louis. The tornado outbreak of 1896, which has been called the

"Great Cyclone of 1896," touched down at around 5:00 P.M., approximately six miles west of Eads Bridge, near the St. Louis State Hospital. A large portion of Eads Bridge was destroyed and the hospital was badly damaged. The tornado then moved up Jefferson Avenue on its way toward Lafayette Park. The tornado demolished homes, hospitals, schools, and businesses causing an estimated $10 million worth of property damage. The areas struck in St. Louis were heavily populated industrial areas. A hospital was hit by the tornado, killing several patients and staff members, and injuring several more. When the tornado swept through Lafayette Park it all but transformed the tree-filled park into a pile of sticks and debris.

Residents of St. Louis stand near the ruins of a building following the 1896 tornado that swept through the city.

The tornado then moved east across the Mississippi River into Illinois where it destroyed homes along the water. Some accounts claim that when the tornado passed over the Mississippi River it was possible to see straight down to the bottom of the river. An estimated 16 boats were destroyed along the Mississippi before the tornado picked up additional momentum and moved into East St. Louis, Illinois, where it caused heavy damage. The majority of deaths caused by the tornado occurred in St. Louis, where 137 people were killed, and East St. Louis, Illinois, where 118 people were killed.

After the tornado laid waste to East St. Louis it began to break up. In approximately 15 minutes the tornado had completely dissipated. The tornado destroyed entire blocks in both St. Louis and East St. Louis. Many people were crushed inside collapsed buildings. An estimated 8,000 buildings were damaged or destroyed.

The scene after the tornado disaster was one of grief and despair. There were mounds of debris from wrecked homes and buildings, people were desperately trying to find loved ones, and the dead bodies of horses and mules were scattered about. Rescue workers were searching vigorously for survivors. The day after the tornado hundreds of people went down to the city's overcrowded **morgue** looking for friends and relatives. The

morgue a place where bodies of persons found dead are kept until claimed or identified by relatives.

crowd grew so large that the police were called in to maintain order.

According to newspaper accounts of the time, the force of the tornado was so strong that it lifted freight train cars from the track and threw them several feet. A row of homes next to the Eads Bridge was completely swept away.

One street in particular was left in a complete state of ruin by the tornado. South Seventh street in St. Louis was hit directly by the tornado. A saloon on South Seventh street that had been full of 15 to 20 men was demolished and everyone inside was killed. Newspaper reports of the time explained how telegraph polls had been snapped in half by the force of the tornado. According to a St. Louis newspaper, a three story brick boarding house "went up like a dry puff ball burying dozens."

According to the National Weather Service the storm that devastated the St. Louis area in 1896 would probably not be as destructive today. Weather tracking and warning systems would have provided people sufficient warning to move out of harm's way. It is very unlikely that a tornado would take a city completely off guard today the way it surprised people in Missouri and Illinois in 1896.

In 1999 a $2.5 million, state-of-the-art tornado detection system was installed in St. Louis. The system that was replaced had been installed in the 1950s and, at the time, only 35 out of 127 sirens were functioning. Prior to the installation of the new system, residents of St. Louis had to rely on television and radio broadcasts as well as fire truck warnings. Officials agreed that the time had come for the state that had experienced the nation's two deadliest tornadoes (in 1896 and 1925) to develop a sophisticated warning system in the event of another outbreak. ◆

Tri-State Tornado

MARCH 18, 1925

In the early morning of March 18, 1925, the sky was sunny and the temperature was a comfortable 70 degrees in eastern Missouri. Residents of Missouri, Illinois, and Indiana had no idea that a cold front from Canada had just met with a

stream of warm air from the Gulf of Mexico to form the deadliest tornado in U.S. history. The tornado began at approximately 1:00 P.M. on March 18, 1925, approximately three miles northeast of Ellington, Missouri.

At 2:00, the storm moved eastward to Leadanna and Annapolis where it destroyed a village, killing four people and causing $500,000 in damage. The tornado gathered momentum as it crossed the Mississippi River and moved into Illinois, where it caused the majority of deaths and damage (540 people killed and 1,423 injured). The tornado laid waste to the town of Gorham, Illinois, killing 34 people and injuring nearly half of the town's population of 500. At 2:30 the storm sped toward Murphysboro, Illinois, where it caused the most death and destruction to a single city in U.S. history. The tornado killed 234 Murphysboro residents, 25 of whom were school children, destroyed several buildings, and caused $10 million in damage.

At 2:34 the tornado moved into DeSoto, Illinois, where it killed another 69 people, 33 of whom were school children. Tragedy then struck the town of West Frankfort, Illinois, at approximately 2:38. In this small mining town, 800 men were 500

Residents of Griffin, Indiana, survey the damage caused by the 1925 tornado outbreak.

feet below the earth mining in the afternoon of March 18, 1925. They remained helplessly trapped in the mine. When the miners finally emerged they discovered that the tornado had killed 127 people, injured 450, and caused over $800,000 in property damage. At approximately 4:00 the tornado then crossed over the Wabash River and moved into Indiana, where it caused the death of 71 people in the towns of Griffin and Princeton. The tornado caused approximately $1.8 million worth of damage in Princeton. The storm broke up around 4:30, after moving through Princeton.

Most of the towns took at least a year to rebuild after the storm. Directly after the storm there were food and housing shortages and well as a shortage of medical supplies. Many of the towns experienced sanitation problems and people were forced to live in tents until their homes could be rebuilt. Aid workers came from across the country to help with the recovery effort. Construction companies traveled from as far as California to help rebuild homes. Fund raising drives were also organized to help the many families who had lost everything. The New York Police Department Orchestra put on a concert in St. Louis to raise money for families in Murphysboro.

The Tri-State Tornado of 1925 was one of the deadliest tornadoes ever to hit in the United States. No series of tornadoes caused more deaths and destruction. The Tri-State Tornado moved at an average speed of 62 miles per hour, an average width of three-fourths of a mile, killed 695 people, injured another 2,027, and caused approximately $16.5 million in damage.

One of the primary reasons that this tornado was so deadly was that people did not see it coming. Farmers were usually cautious about tornadoes in the Midwest because they occurred fairly regularly compared to other regions of the country. However, this particular tornado came in disguise. When the tornado touched down in Missouri it had picked up so much dust and debris and the sky had darkened so much that the funnel could not be seen. Residents of the tri-state area were given no advance warning of the tornado because there was no **radar** system to detect the storm system.

The massive tornado that devastated the tri-state area of Missouri, Illinois, and Indiana brought national attention to the need for a national tornado warning system. The U.S. military lead the effort in developing a national tornado warning system. By 1948 the Tinker Air Force Base in Oklahoma issued the first tornado forecast. A radar system was not put in place until the late 1950s, however. A network of weather-warning radio stations was established in an effort to prevent killer tornadoes such as the Tri-State Tornado of 1925 from catching people off guard. Today, people receive warnings through several different sources an average of 12 minutes before a tornado strikes.

One individual who was particularly moved by the event took it upon himself to increase awareness of the storm and the danger of tornadoes. Peter Felknor compiled newspaper articles and eyewitness accounts of the tornado in a book called *The Tri-State Tornado*. The intent of the book is to increase public awareness of the danger of tornadoes and provides tips on the safest place to be if you are caught in a tornado. Felknor suggests that if caught in a tornado one should get inside a building, preferably in the basement, avoid trying to outrun it if inside a car, and stay away from buildings with free-standing roofs. ◆

Tupelo Tornado

APRIL 5, 1936

The Tupelo Tornado of April 5, 1936, was the fourth deadliest tornado in U.S. history. This tornado was part of a larger storm system that broke out in Georgia in the spring of 1936. An estimated 466 people were killed by the storm system and over 3,000 people were injured. Among the casualties, approximately 216 occurred in Tupelo. The tragedy that occurred in Tupelo, Mississippi, is not only known for the number of lives that were lost; it is also known for sparing the life of one-year-old Elvis Presley.

When the tornado broke out people had been expecting a storm, but certainly not one of the magnitude that hit. The tornado appeared as a large dark cloud releasing massive amounts of lightening. At the time the tornado struck, many residents were filing out of church, and were taken completely by surprise.

The tornado that caused massive damage to Tupelo began its destructive path near Coffeeville, Mississippi, in Yalobusha County. It then entered Lee County and moved northeast through northern Tupelo. In western Tupelo many of the homes

Protecting Yourself During a Tornado

Dorothy from the *Wizard of Oz* knew the most important technique for surviving a tornado: finding a safe place. Tornado winds can reach incredibly violent speeds, and because they occur over land they can pick up and carry large, dangerous debris in their black funnels.

Getting indoors is your first priority, because in addition to the tornado itself, some of that flying debris can easily strike you. In addition, outside you risk being caught under falling power lines or even being trapped in a flash flood.

If you are caught outdoors and you see the telltale funnel shape of a tornado bearing down on you, your best bet is to run for the nearest building and hurry to the lowest accessible floor. If there are no buildings nearby, find cover where you can, and anchor yourself as best you can. Crouch down low and protect your head and face with your hands or arms. If the tornado is accompanied by rain, avoid culverts or ditches, because flash flooding is common during these storms.

If you are in your car, it is never wise to try to outrun the tornado. The storm moves very quickly, and tornadoes have been known to "jump," so that the storm that appears behind you now can suddenly seem to materialize directly ahead. The tornado's high winds can easily pick up vehicles and carry them great distances before dropping them violently back to earth, so you are far safer getting out of your car and into shelter.

The safest rooms are specifically designed to withstand a tornado. This is why, in tornado country, storm cellars are often dug into the ground and securely closed off by a well-anchored door. An interior room in the basement is another good choice for shelter. It is best to avoid rooms with windows and doors that access the outside. Wherever you are, remember that tornadoes generally come from the south, southwest, or west, so it is wise to get as much protection as you can between yourself and the outside in those directions.

were poorly built. The tornado crushed many of these homes, killing entire families who sought shelter in them. It took very little time for the tornado to leave the town of Tupelo, Mississippi, in a state of devastation.

The official death toll from the tornado has been listed as 216, however, many experts estimated that the death toll was closer to 230. The number of people injured by the tornado has been estimated to be 700. The path of the tornado's destruction covered nearly 50 blocks leaving ten churches, over 200 homes, and several businesses in ruin. Among the most tragic of the tornado's losses was the death of Jim Burroughs and his family of 13 who were killed just west of Tupelo.

A series of rainstorms after the tornado actually helped prevent further damage to Tupelo. A series of fires broke out and the rainfall extinguished the flames before they could cause excessive injury or damage. Several schools were destroyed during the tornado and as a result students had to attend classes in churches and the Tupelo Military Academy.

During the recovery period over 100 train cars were brought to Tupelo to provide shelter for people who had lost their homes to the tornado. Because of overcrowding in Tupelo's hospitals, health officials converted a movie theater into a makeshift hospital. People came from all parts of Georgia as well as surrounding states to assist in the recovery. Doctors, nurses, ambulance crews, and construction workers flocked to Tupelo to help the survivors recover from the devastation. Several organizations including the Red Cross, National Guard, and American Legion helped with the relief effort. In addition, several local newspapers helped coordinate fundraising events.

In 1938 the residents of Tupelo decided to construct an elementary school that was better prepared to protect children against future tornadoes. The tornado of 1936 destroyed the Tupelo Primary School. Had school been in session at the time the tornado struck, hundreds of children would have perished. The Church Street School, constructed two years later, was engineered to be tornado resistant. The building's walls are eight inches thick and reinforced with steel. ◆

Gainesville Tornado

APRIL 6, 1936

In 1936 the United States experienced extreme weather patterns. Temperatures were abnormally high and low in several parts of the country throughout the year. During the winter months several states experienced below freezing temperatures for extended periods of time. In the summer months, record high temperatures were set in 11 states. According to weather experts, the abnormal weather patterns during the winter and summer months of 1936 set the right conditions for stormy weather during the spring of 1936. When cold air flows into warm air, tornadoes can begin to form.

On April 6, 1936, two tornadoes devastated the city of Gainesville, Georgia, killing 203 people and injuring more than 1,600. Approximately 750 homes were destroyed and 254 were severely damaged. The tornado caused $12.5 million in property damage. The Gainesville Tornado set a record for killing the most people in a single building when it tore through the Cooper Pants Factory killing between 70 and 100 people. When the tornado hit the factory, the building collapsed and caught fire. Several children were killed in Newman's department store, which collapsed when it was struck by the tornado.

On the morning of April 6, at approximately 8:15 A.M., a tornado broke out in Hall County, Georgia, moving northeast. After tearing down several homes it began moving toward the city of Gainesville. At the same time a second tornado also approached Gainesville from the west. The two tornadoes merged at approximately 8:27 when they reached Gainesville, causing massive destruction.

When the two tornadoes met, they were approaching a Catholic church, but shifted direction momentarily, completely avoiding the church. After the tornado swept around the church it resumed its course, heading directly toward downtown Gainesville. Approximately 200 people were working at the Cooper Pants factory at the time. When the storm hit the workers had nowhere to go to protect themselves from the tornado. The double tornado hit the factory and caused a fire to break out. Between the fire and the tornado destruction, between 70 and 100 people were killed at the Cooper Pants factory. Historians suspect that the tornado probably caused more deaths than the official count of 203 people that has been documented. At the time, the deaths of African Americans were not recorded after natural disasters.

In the aftermath of the tornado, the recovery and rebuilding process moved swiftly. This was led, in part, by President Franklin Roosevelt, who took a tour of the area three days after the storm. Forest Rangers from the Georgia National Forest also contributed to the relief effort bringing in supplies, helping clean up the area, and providing radios that allowed residents of Gainesville to speak to friends and family outside of the community. Within two years, the city had been almost entirely rebuilt.

During the period between 1950 and 1995 Georgia has experienced several tornadoes. Although Georgia does not experience as many tornadoes as other states, those that did break out were dangerous because they were unexpected. Researchers have also found that the number of tornadoes that occur in Georgia has been steadily increasing. In 1974, 16 people were killed and 74 were injured by a tornado outbreak in Georgia

and, in 1994, another rash of tornadoes killed 18 people and injured 206.

In April and May 1998, tornadoes hit the southeast United States causing an estimated $4 million in damage and killing 16 people in Georgia. In light of these unexpected disasters, the Federal Emergency Management Agency (FEMA) conducted a poll among southern states and found that 56 percent of the people did not know how to protect themselves if a tornado broke out. In response to these findings FEMA initiated Project Impact to educate residents of the southeast United Sates, including Georgia, some of the more common ways to prepare for a violent storm.

Scientists conducted research in order to help people in Georgia protect themselves against violent tornadoes. According to the National Weather Service Storm Prediction Center, tornadoes hit in the months of March, April, and May between the hours of noon and 7:00 P.M. April was found to be the most common month for tornado outbreaks in Georgia. Scientists also discovered specific regions of Georgia in which tornadoes

The buildings in this lumberyard in Gainesville, Georgia, were damaged during the 1936 tornado.

seemed more likely to break out. Although tornadoes will always happen unexpectedly, the research conducted has helped Georgia citizens be better prepared for violent storms. ◆

Palm Sunday Tornado Outbreak

APRIL 1965

In the late afternoon of April 11, 1965, there was little indication that a destructive batch of tornadoes was about to be unleashed in the Midwestern part of the United States. The sun was shining and it was a little breezy. Temperatures throughout the Midwest were in the 70s. However, as people celebrated the Christian holy day of Palm Sunday, a massive storm formed in the sky above them.

The tornadoes that broke out affected six states: Illinois, Indiana, Iowa, Ohio, Michigan, and Wisconsin. Indiana, Michigan, and Ohio were hit hardest by the tornadoes. During the tornado outbreak, an estimated 50 tornadoes emerged, 21 of which were deadly. The tornadoes killed 256 people and injured over 3,000 others. The total amount of property damage caused by the outbreak was estimated to be $230 million.

The first tornado broke out in Iowa around 2:00 P.M. Tornadoes then broke out in Wisconsin and Illinois at approximately 4:00 P.M. Shortly afterward several tornadoes formed in Michigan and Indiana. Near 3:00 P.M., a tornado warning was issued for Indiana and at around 6:00 P.M., the Chicago Weather Bureau issued warnings for all areas in northern Indiana and southern Michigan.

In the early evening of April 11, a swarm of tornadoes swept through Indiana. The Palm Sunday tornado outbreak of 1965 was the most destructive tornado disaster in Indiana's history. In Indiana 137 people were killed by the tornadoes and an estimated 1,700 others were injured. The storm hit Marshall County at approximately 5:50 P.M. where it killed four people. Five destructive tornadoes ripped through Elkhart County killing 52 people. One of the tornadoes that devastated Elkhart laid waste to Dunlap, Indiana. At approximately 6:00 P.M. the South Bend Weather Bureau spotted the tornado. The tornado then moved northeast and continued its path of destruction in LaGrange County at 6:30 P.M.

At approximately 6:15 P.M. a tornado swept through the north and western part of Elkhart and another tornado came through causing further destruction an hour later, which caused massive death and property damage at the Midway Trailer Park in Dunlap. An estimated 100 trailer homes were destroyed. Between the storm that broke out at 6:15 and the one that hit at 7:15 people had already begun searching for survivors of the first tornado. Experts believe that the twin tornadoes that touched down in Elkhart, Indiana, was one of two tornadoes that stuck during the outbreak. A massive tornado then struck Russiaville, Indiana, destroying approximately 90 percent of the buildings there.

The storm system then moved into central and southern Michigan where tornadoes caused significant property damage and loss of life. The areas hardest hit were Branch County, where 18 people were killed; Hillsdale County, where six people were killed; Lenawee County, where nine people were killed; and Monroe County, where 13 people were killed. In Michigan the Palm Sunday tornadoes killed 53 people, injured approximately 800 people, and caused an estimated $50 million in property damage.

Later in the evening a devastating tornado hit Strongsville, Ohio. This was the second of two tornadoes that broke out during the storm. In Michigan a bus was hurled through the air, killing seven passengers. The storm system then broke up and reappeared later in the evening in central Indiana and Ohio before dissolving.

One of the reasons many lives were lost during the tornado outbreak was that the tornadoes struck in the evening while most people were settling in for the night and had already cut themselves off from television and radio communication. The tornadoes also struck heavily populated areas.

The Palm Sunday tornado outbreak of 1965 caused greater demand for better warning systems. The National Weather Bureau reviewed the warning systems of the states that were affected by the 1965 outbreak and found that several improvements were needed. Among their findings was that some states were unable to issue warnings during the storm, which could have decreased the number of deaths. This resulted in the creation of the NADWARN or Natural Disaster Warning System. In the 1990s the National Weather Service created

Most people were settling in for the night and had already cut themselves off from television and radio communication.

the NEXRAD (or Next Generation Radar). The NEXRAD Doppler radar system has significantly improved the ability of forecasters to provide warnings when tornadoes break out.

The survey conducted following the Palm Sunday tornado outbreak of 1965 also resulted in the creation of the Skywarn system. The Skywarn system is a network of professional and amateur "weather spotters" who release a chain of communications when severe weather breaks out. SKYWARN serves as a back up to the Doppler Radar system. Through SKYWARN eyewitness accounts of tornado outbreaks are communicated to areas that are about to be hit by a tornado. Amateur radio stations and the Red Cross also participate in the program. ◆

Tornado Outbreak

APRIL 1974

The Tornado Outbreak of 1974 was one of the worst series of tornado storms in history. According to all major categories, such as the number of tornadoes recorded, the length in which the tornadoes traveled, and the amount of damage, this was the worst tornado outbreak to occur in the United States.

On April 1, 1974, a series of 20 relatively mild tornadoes broke out in the southeastern and central United States killing three and causing significant damage. These storms turned out to be a mere warning of what was to come. To a certain extent, the storms that occurred on April 1 were a blessing in disguise in that people began to prepare for worst. In addition, when formal tornado watches and warnings were issued two days later, people were much more likely to take the warnings seriously. According to the National Weather Service a tornado "watch" means that conditions are right for tornadoes to develop within the next few hours and a tornado "warning" means that a tornado has actually been spotted. On April 2, the day before the tornado outbreak, forecasters were beginning to see a far more severe storm system developing than what occurred on April 1.

Although forecasters at the NSSFC could see the storms developing on April 2, they had no way of knowing when or where the storms would break out. Severe storms were expected to occur in the general area of the Mississippi Valley. As a result, radio stations in Kansas, Nebraska, Missouri, Michigan, Iowa, Minnesota, Kentucky, Oklahoma, Texas, Arkansas, and Indiana began to alert communities of the coming storm system. On the morning of April 3 it was still not clear to forecasters where the storms would break out. Warnings were issued in the lower Mississippi Valley. Between the morning of April 3 and the afternoon of April 4, the NSSFC issued 28 severe weather watches and National Weather Service issued 150 tornado warnings.

During the 16-hour swarm of tornado outbreaks, 330 people died and 5,484 people were injured and the total length of tornado paths was 2,500 miles. At one point during the outbreak, 15 tornadoes were on the ground at once. One of the deadliest tornadoes was on the ground for more than two hours.

The majority of the tornadoes occurred on April 3 between 2:00 P.M. and 10:00 P.M. Thirteen states experienced tornadoes during the Super Tornado Outbreak (Alabama, Georgia, Illinois, Indiana, Kentucky, Michigan, Mississippi, North Carolina, Ohio, South Carolina, Tennessee, Virginia, and West Virginia). Among the hardest hit states were Alabama, Georgia, Tennessee, Kentucky, Indiana, and Ohio. At 2:00 P.M. tornadoes hit Bradley County, Tennessee, and within minutes more tornadoes touched down in Gilmer County, Georgia. At 2:20 severe tornadoes broke out in Perry and Lawrence counties in Indiana and at 3:30 tornadoes broke out in Ohio. Ten minutes later tornadoes hit Brandenburg, Kentucky, and at 4:30 Birmingham, Alabama, was struck by severe tornadoes.

Alabama suffered the greatest amount of property damage and loss of life. Alabama was hit by eight tornadoes which killed 86 people, injured 949, and caused over $50 million in property damage. Counties in the northern part of the state suffered the most damage. On April 3, at approximately 4:30 P.M. the first tornado broke out west of Birmingham. An hour later a second storm hit Jacksonville, Alabama, causing some power outages but no injuries or property damage. However, at 6:30 P.M., a major tornado broke out and remained on the ground for 85 miles tearing up Limestone and Madison counties in northern Alabama. At 7:35 P.M., a second major tornado broke out and nearly followed the exact same path. Several towns and counties were hit twice by these two tornadoes that killed 55 people, injured 408 people, and heavily damaged more than 1,100 buildings and 200 mobile homes.

> **During the 16-hour swarm of tornado outbreaks, 330 people died and 5,484 people were injured.**

Doppler Radar

All weather radar systems bounce a burst of radio waves against clouds or rain, then listen for the return of the signal in order to determine how far away these targets are located. Modern meteorologists, however, now use a refinement of this radar technology, known as Doppler radar, which one that provides even more detailed data than conventional radar ever could.

A nineteenth-century Viennese mathematician, Christian Doppler, was intrigued by the way sound travels. He noted, for example, that the sound of a train whistle changes as the train moves toward, then passes, an observer standing on the railway platform. Doppler discovered that the pitch of the train whistle varied according to the speed and direction of the train was traveling and its distance from the observer.

Doppler radar uses these principles of sound change. A continuous series of short bursts of radio waves are beamed outward from radar dishes. Between the bursts, sensitive equipment records the frequency of the returning waves, which have been bounced back off of particles of dust or precipitation in the air. From this data, scientists can determine the location and intensity of weather systems, just as conventional radar has always done. In addition, however, an analysis of frequency changes in the returning waves tells scientists if the systems are moving toward or away from the radar installation, and how fast they are going.

The increased detail and accuracy provided by Doppler radar over older technology has made storm tracking much more efficient. As a result, the National Weather Service has switched entirely over to Doppler radar technology, retiring its last non-Doppler installations in 1996.

While these tornadoes were destroying communities in northern Alabama, another tornado broke out in the southern part of the state at 7:00 P.M. This tornado began in Pickens County and stayed on the ground for nearly an hour before reaching Walker County. At 8:50 another tornado broke out killing 23 and injuring 250 in Marion County. Alabama's final tornado hit at round 11:00 P.M. in Jackson County where 28 people were killed, 332 injured, and 850 buildings were severely damaged or completely destroyed.

Several other states were struck by the outbreak while Alabama was being ravaged. The northern part of Georgia was hit by seven tornadoes which killed 17 people, injured 104, and caused $15 million in damage. Indiana experienced its largest tornado outbreak in that state's history. A total of 20 tornadoes broke out in the state killing 49 people, injuring 768 and causing property damage to nearly 6,000 homes. Kentucky also experienced its worst tornado outbreak on April 3, 1974. Kentucky was hit by 26 tornadoes which killed 77 people, injured 1,377, and caused approximately $110 million in property damage. The first storm that hit Kentucky was the worst. It was an F-5 tornado which broke out at 3:40 P.M. in Breckinridge County. The tornado, which was 500 yards wide, killed 31 people, including several children who were playing outside after school. Tornadoes struck Ohio between 3:30 and 5:30, killing 41 people, injuring 2000 and damaging 7000 homes.

Despite the massive amount of property damage and lives lost, the Super Tornado Outbreak of 1974 presented a learning opportunity for researchers and scientists. Prior to the outbreak, it was generally believed that tornadoes would not touch down on rivers and that tornadoes were unable to travel up or down steep hills. The 148 tornadoes that ravaged through 11 states on April 3 and 4, 1974, put an end to these misconceptions. Some of the tornadoes were reported to travel up and down 3,000-feet mountains. In addition, the Super Tornado Outbreak inspired engineering studies designed to determine the safest areas to remain indoors while weathering a tornado storm. The studies concluded that hallways are the safest places inside schools and that larger buildings such as gyms and classrooms whose walls are exposed to the elements are least safe. ◆

East Florida Tornado Outbreak

FEBRUARY 1998

On the evening of February 22 and the morning of February 23, 1998, the state of Florida experienced the worst series of tornado storms in its history. The storms claimed 42 lives and injured more than 260 people. They left more than 135,000 people without power during the storms, however, the major theme parks in Florida including Walt Disney World, Universal Studios, and Sea World were not affected by the tornadoes.

On Friday, February 22, 1998, the National Weather Service saw storm systems developing and the potential for tornadoes to break out. The National Weather Service had been on full alert at the time because of the damage El Niño had been causing. El Niño is the gradual warming of the Pacific Ocean which causes a stream of warm air in the upper atmosphere to move slightly further south than normal. El Niño had been blamed for an outbreak of tornadoes in South Florida on February 2, 1998. Perhaps the primary reason that these particular tornadoes were so destructive was the fact that they came with no advanced warning. One of the reasons that scientists blamed El Niño for Florida's tornado disaster was the unusual strength of the twisters. Scientists noted that the force of the tornadoes that hit Florida were the type that usually only break out in the Midwest.

When the National Weather Service spotted the potential for dangerous storms to break out in central and eastern Florida, they did not hesitate to issue a warning. A tornado watch was issued for central Florida at approximately 2:00 P.M. on Sunday, February 22, 1998. Seven hours later, three violent tornado storms began developing around Tampa, Florida. The National Weather Service began issuing tornado warnings approximately 15 to 20 minutes before the first tornado touched down in Daytona, Florida. (According to the National Weather Service a tornado "watch" means that conditions are right for tornadoes to develop within the next few hours and a tornado "warning" means that a tornado has actually been spotted.)

In the late evening of February 22, 1998, twelve tornadoes broke out between Tampa Bay on the Gulf Coast to Daytonal Beach on the Atlantic Coast. Osceola and Seminole counties were hit the hardest during the storm. In Osceola County 25 people were killed and in Seminole County 12 people were killed. In Orange County three people were killed and 74 were injured and two people were killed in Volusia County. The force of the tornado was so strong that some bodies were found a mile away from their homes. In Seminole County an 86,000 square foot shopping center was completely obliterated. The only thing that remained after the tornadoes swept through was a slab of concrete and some metal remains from the former structure.

The tornado warnings were broadcast on televisions and radios throughout Florida. Unfortunately, the tornadoes came at a time when many people had already gone to bed and were not listening to their radios or watching television. In addition, because Florida does not experience many tornadoes, they did not have a siren system in place.

The National Weather Service in Melbourne provided the warnings for the residents of central and eastern Florida with the help of the **Doppler Radar** system. However, they were greatly assisted by a group of amateur weather watchers who communicated with them while the storms were developing. A group of amateur weather watchers have formed an organization called Skywarn whose purpose is to provide eyewitness accounts of developing storm systems. Their participation in the East Florida Tornado Outbreak showed that word of mouth can be just as useful during a tornado outbreak as advanced technology.

President Bill Clinton visited east Florida after the tornadoes and declared 34 counties disaster areas, making them immediately eligible for federal funding. The relief effort was led by the Federal Emergency Management Agency (FEMA). Volunteers from Florida Christian College also pitched in to help in the rescue effort. One hundred and eighty students helped bring blankets and food to the residents of the Ponderosa Trailer Park community that was hit hard by a tornado.

The 1998 tornado outbreak in East Florida overturned this motorhome in Kissimmee.

Doppler Radar a radar system using the Doppler effect for measuring the velocity of a storm.

Fujita Tornado Intensity Scale

Tornadoes are officially classified not by the size of their funnels or the speed of their winds, but by the degree of damage they leave behind. The classification system is based on the Fujita Tornado Intensity Scale, the brain-child of Tetsuya Theodore Fujita and Allen Pearson, two University of Chicago meteorologists who specialized in studying severe weather patterns.

Tornado classification is done according to the Fujita scale's 6-point system, as follows:

F0: These tornadoes have wind speeds of 40 to 72 miles per hour. Chimneys may be knocked over, branches are torn from trees, and other relatively minor damage occurs.

F1: Tornadoes at this phase are described as moderate, with winds of 73 to 110 miles per hour. A moderate tornado can peel up the surface of roads, push mobile homes over, and force cars off the road.

F2: This designation is given to what are known as significant tornadoes, with wind speeds 113 to 157 miles per hour. F2 tornadoes can rip roofs off of buildings, snap trees, and demolish mobile homes.

F3: At the F3, or severe phase, wind speeds reach 158 to 206 miles per hour and are powerful enough to overturn train cars or uproot trees.

F4: This refers to devastating tornadoes in which wind speeds can range from 207 to 260 miles per hour. Houses may be flattened, and cars and other large objects are picked up and thrown by the winds.

F5: An F5 storm is, fittingly, called an incredible tornado. Wind speeds can range from 261 to 318 miles per hour. These storms can pick up houses and carry them through the air, and even concrete structures are badly damaged.

F6: This final category is purely theoretical, and refers to storms in which winds range from 319 to 379 miles per hour. No tornado has yet received an F6 classification.

Tornadoes rarely receive a classification of F4 or higher. The 1998 tornado outbreak in Florida consisted of several F2 and F3 funnels.

Thirteen people had been killed in the trailer park and several mobile homes were torn to shreds. There was also an enormous amount of support for the tornado victims immediately after the storm. According to the American Red Cross $2.3 million was raised in an outpouring of generosity to cover the rebuilding costs in Osceola, Orange, and Seminole counties.

The tornadoes were particularly horrifying for central Florida residents Manuel and Judy Rincon. It took them a decade to save enough money to buy a home, but moments for a tornado to destroy it. They were fortunate, however, that their home was the only thing they lost. The tornado nearly snatched up their five-year-old daughter, Elissa. The tornado blew open their kitchen door and started pulling Elissa into its vortex (center of the tornado). Elissa's mother held on to her daughter by the ankles with all of her might. Fortunately, she held on long enough for the tornado to pass. The thought of losing their daughter helped Manuel and Judy Rincon put losing their home in its proper perspective. A resident of a trailer park in central Florida was not as fortunate, however. When a tornado swept through the trailer park community near Kissimmee, Florida, his 18-month-old boy was pulled from his arms and killed. One man who survived the storm was pulled from his car and thrown about 150 feet by a tornado. ◆

Oklahoma Tornado Outbreak

MAY 1999

On May 3, 1999, a series of 76 tornadoes tore through Oklahoma and parts of Kansas. The tornadoes claimed 45 lives and injured 748 people. Forty of the 45 deaths were in Oklahoma. The tornadoes destroyed or seriously damaged approximately 2,000 homes in Oklahoma City alone. The tornado outbreak was the worst to hit Oklahoma since 1947 when 119 people were killed in Woodward, Oklahoma.

The storms began at approximately 4:51 P.M. and lasted past midnight on March 3, 1999. During the outbreak 76 tornadoes were documented. Forty-five of the tornadoes broke out in Oklahoma, causing 40 deaths; 14 tornadoes broke out in Kansas, causing five deaths; twelve tornadoes broke out in Nebraska; three tornadoes broke out in Texas; and two tornadoes broke out in South Dakota. According to the National Oceanic and Atmospheric Administration (NOAA) the estimated amount of damage to the area was $1.2 billion. The storm system lasted for approximately 20 hours.

One tornado was particularly destructive. According to the National Weather Service, the tornado stayed on the ground in Chickasha, Oklahoma for approximately four hours and maintained a width of one-half mile. The National Severe Storms Laboratory indicated that the tornado may have been as wide as one mile at times.

This home in Dell City was one of around 2,000 homes completely destroyed or severely damaged by the Oklahoma tornado outbreak of 1999.

The first violent tornado broke out in Stecker, in southwest Oklahoma. A massive tornado then broke out in Chickasha at approximately 6:00 P.M. and moved into Bridge Creek and Newcastle, Oklahoma, approximately one hour later. Between 7:00 and 9:00 P.M. the tornado struck Moore, Oklahoma City, Midwest City, and Choctaw, Oklahoma. At approximately 10:00 P.M. a tornado hit Logan County and Lincoln County before breaking up in Tulsa at around midnight.

The force of the tornadoes was so severe that cars were launched across highways and homes were torn to splinters. In regions of Texas and Oklahoma pieces of hail fell that were reported to have been over four inches wide. The most destructive tornado broke out near the heavily populated Oklahoma City.

During the storm a woman from Moore, Oklahoma, tried to hide from the storm beneath her mattress. The padding of the mattress shielded her from some of the debris but she suffered head and arm injuries. Another woman sat out the storm in her bathtub, one of the safer places to be during a violent storm. She indicated that she heard the popping noise of the approaching

National Weather Service

The National Weather Service (NWS) got its start in 1849, when researchers at the Smithsonian Institute decided to conduct a nationwide study of weather patterns. The Institute sent specialized scientific instruments to every telegraph operator in the country, along with a request that the operators take weather readings every day and report their findings to the scientists in Washington, D.C.

In 1870, President Ulysses S. Grant signed a bill to transfer this research effort to the federal government. Authority over the project, now officially named the National Weather Service, was granted to the Secretary of War, largely because the data collected was thought to be of particular importance to military planning.

In 1890, the agency was made a part of the Department of Agriculture, which began offering forecasts to the nation's Farm Bureaus. At that time, however, forecasting was of limited accuracy, because only data from within the U.S. borders was available for study, whereas weather systems are global by nature. This shortcoming was partially remedied in 1900, when undersea cable made it possible to exchange data with European meteorologists. In 1914, the ground-based readings were further supplemented when Air Force planes were pressed into service for data collection, and from then onward the Service has always incorporated technological innovations, such as radar and, later, satellites and Doppler radar to improve the accuracy of their forecasts.

The NWS is today a member agency of the larger National Oceanographic and Atmospheric Administration, which is dedicated to the study of a wide range of environmental sciences. The NWS still fulfills its longstanding mission of analyzing weather-related data, in addition to issuing long-term forecasts to farm bureaus, the military, and the general public.

tornado and immediately knew what it was. One eyewitness said the scene in Oklahoma after the tornado looked like the Murrah Building, the federal building which had been the target of a massive bombing attack in 1995.

On May 4, 1999, President Bill Clinton declared 11 Oklahoma counties (Caddo, Cleveland, Creek, Grady, McClain, Oklahoma, Kingfisher, Lincoln, Logan, Pottawatomie, and Tulsa) and Sedgwick County in Kansas to be "disaster areas" which made them eligible for federal financial assistance. Rescuers came into the area almost immediately. They helped search through the scattered cars, and mobile homes, and destroyed homes and buildings looking for survivors. One woman was found who had been trapped inside a trailer.

Given the severity of the storm system the death toll could have been much worse. Thanks to widespread warnings, people were given time to prepare for the tornadoes. Two hours before the tornadoes struck Oklahoma City, there local news outlets broadcast warnings of the approaching tornadoes. The television warnings gave those people who heard the broadcasts sufficient time to find refuge from the storm underground.

The technological advances in weather forecasting undoubtedly saved lives during Oklahoma's 1999 tornado outbreak. New systems such as NEXRAD and Doppler radar helped to spot the storm system developing and allow members of the media to communicate to residents of Oklahoma and surrounding states that tornadoes were approaching. NEXRAD is the newest generation of a national weather radar grid, established by the National Weather Service and the U.S. military. In addition the National Weather Service developed a system for radio broadcasters to communicate to one another called the Emergency Alert System (EAS). The Emergency Alert System is a network of 14,000 radio and television stations that uses special equipment to allow emergency broadcasts to break into regular programming when something dangerous threatens a community. Radar technology can spot the vortex, or center, of a large tornado forming in time to warn people that a tornado or other violent storm is developing.

According to the National Weather Service, tornado watches were issued for central Oklahoma 30-90 minutes before the tornadoes began to break out and torando warnings were issued between eight and 30 minutes before the first tornado touched down in Oklahoma. A tornado "watch" means that conditions are right for tornadoes to develop within the next few hours and a tornado "warning" means that a tornado has actually been spotted. Although 45 lives were lost during the Oklahoma Tornado Outbreak of 1999, the death toll could have been much worse had it not been for existing radar technology and a network of television and radio warning systems. ◆

Floods

Yellow River Flood

SUMMER 1887

The Huang Ho (also spelled Hwang Ho or Huang He), commonly referred to in English as the Yellow River, has been the source of the majority of deadly and destructive floods that have occurred throughout China's history. The 1887 flood was particularly devastating, causing an estimated 900,000 to one million deaths.

The Yellow River is the second longest river in China next to the Yangtze River. It extends approximately 2,900 miles. The river runs east through China starting near Tibet and ending at the Yellow Sea. Yellow River floods have caused more deaths than any other river in the world and it has therefore been called the "Unmanageable river." Western scholars often refer to the Yellow River as "China's Sorrow." The quality that makes the Yellow River prone to flooding is that it carries an enormous amount of silt, or thick muddy residue. An estimated 1.6 billion tons of silt runs through the river each year. The silt causes the river to shift courses unpredictably, causing frequent flooding.

Since around 3,000 B.C. the Yellow River has flooded over 1,500 times. Between the years 1194 and 1887 there were approximately 50 major floods along the Yellow River. In 1939 a major flood was intentionally created causing the deaths of an estimated 900,000 people. Chang Kai-shek, China's leader at the time, ordered the destruction of dams along the Yellow River in an effort to halt invading Japanese soldiers. Destroying the dams caused massive flooding to several communities along the Yellow River.

Entrance of the Yellow
River in Eastern China

province an administrative district or division of
a country.

During the summer of 1887 China experienced an unusually high amount of rainfall. The continuous rainfall caused the
banks along the Yellow River to overflow into hundreds of
nearby towns in September and October of 1887. The area that
was most severely affected by the flooding was the **province** of
Henan in eastern China. The flood claimed between 900,000
and one million lives. In addition to drowning, many people
died by starvation due to the massive amount of crop damage
caused by the flooding.

As destructive as the Yellow River has been, it also serves
an important economic function for China. Through the years
China has learned to harness the power of the river to use it for
agricultural production and electricity. The Yellow River also
provides drinking water for many areas of China. However, due
to economic development the amount of pollution in the river
has steadily increased and, at times, caused shortages of drinking water.

Over the years Chinese officials have made several different
attempts to control the flow of water along the Yellow River. In
the third century B.C., an engineer attempted to improve the
flow of water by removing some of the silt from the river. The

project was only mildly successful. Later attempts to control the Yellow River involved building dams, levees, and digging channels to redirect the flow of water. The most successful measure the Chinese have taken to control flooding is building large dams along the river to prevent water from building up and overflowing into heavily populated areas. In the 1950s Chinese officials put a major plan in motion to prevent flooding along the Yellow River.

The plan was inspired by a massive flood that occurred along the Yangtze that killed thousands of people. The plan involved constructing 40 dams. One of the dams created through this project was the San-men Gorge Dam which was completed in 1974 and is 295 feet high. The dam collects a large portion of the silt that is built up in the river and has successfully protected northern China from major flooding. However, experts believe that the dam will reach its full capacity by the year 2050, which may causes problems in the future.

A second dam also helps to protect China from major flood disasters occurring along the Yellow River. The Liu-Chia Gorge Dam prevents water from overflowing near the Yellow River's middle basin. The Liu-Chia Gorge Dam also serves as hydroelectric power generated, providing power to thousands of homes and businesses in China. It is China's largest hydroelectric power station. The efforts the Chinese have put into bringing the "unmanageable river" under control have been largely successful. The Yellow River has not experienced a major flood since the 1970s. However, in the summer of 1999, Chinese officials were forced to relocate over 150,000 people because of heavy rains and expected flooding along the Yellow River. ◆

Johnstown Flood

1889

The Johnstown Flood of 1889 was one of the worst peacetime disasters in U.S. history. In terms of lives lost, it was the second worst disaster in United States history, next to the Galveston hurricane of 1890, which killed 6,000 people. Johnstown is a small city located about 70 miles southeast of Pittsburgh in a river basin of Pennsylvania's Appalachian Plateau. In 1889, the city had a population of about 10,000,

The Johnstown flood of 1889 killed over 2,200 people and left homes like this in its wake.

many of whom were laborers in the steel industry. Some 20,000 more people lived in the surrounding area. On May 31, 1889, the citizens of Johnstown, Pennsylvania, were busy tending to their daily lives when disaster struck without warning. At 3:10 P.M. a large earthen high dam, which was built to contain Lake Conemaugh, collapsed and sent a wall of water into Johnstown, located 70 miles east of Pittsburgh. The flood and a fire caused by the flood claimed a total of 2,209 lives.

South Fork Dam, located about 14 miles north of Johnstown, had been built between 1838 and 1853 by the Commonwealth of Pennsylvania as part of the state's canal system. The 72-foot high and 900-foot wide dam held back the waters of the Conemaugh River, forming a lake that was over two miles long, a mile wide, and about 60 feet deep where the water met the dam. Conemaugh Lake was used for recreation by the South Fork Fishing Club, whose members included the wealthy industrialists Henry Clay Frick, Andrew Carnegie, Andrew Mellon, and many affluent Pittsburgh area residents.

The dam had been weakening before it broke. It was suffering from a lack of maintenance and had taken on 10 inches of rain the day it collapsed. When the South Fork Dam broke it released 20 million tons of water in a 40-foot high wave. Moments after the dam broke, water flooded down the Little Conemaugh River Valley washing away everything in its path including homes, barns, carriages, trains, animals, and people. An estimated 20 to 30 homes were destroyed in the small town of South Fork moments after the dam collapsed. The rushing water was temporarily blocked by a railroad **viaduct**, but the flood pushed its way through. With renewed power the water then rushed into the town of Mill Point where every home was completely washed away and 16 people were killed. The flood then tore through the towns of East Conemaugh and Woodvale, killing 364 people. Within one hour from the time the South Fork Dam broke, the flood roared into Johnstown, where it caused the most death and destruction the state of Pennsylvania had ever known.

The only warning the residents of Johnstown received came from the engineer of a train that was traveling nearby on an elevated track. John Hess, the train's operator, let out a howling whistle from Pennsylvania Railroad Engine 1124 in an attempt to warn the people below. In an act of heroism, Hess saw that the dam had broken and decided to tie his whistle down and jump from the moving train while it motored along the tracks above Johnstown. Survivors of the flood claim that nearly everyone who heard the whistle understood what it meant.

After the dam broke it took approximately one hour for the water to reach the small town of Johnstown. Johnstown had been experiencing heavy rainfall and some areas were flooded up to two feet. Residents who saw the flow of water coming were in awe of the approaching disaster. They described the dark cloud of air that rolled toward them smashing trees like toothpicks as "the death mist." Among the 2,209 victims claimed by the flood, an estimated 663 bodies were never found. One victim from the flood was found 15 years later. Some of the bodies were found 100 miles away, in Ohio. In addition to the lives lost, 1,600 homes and 280 businesses were destroyed.

An eyewitness claimed to have seen an entire house floating down the river. The witness said that he could see people praying inside the house. Moments later the house turned over and everyone inside drowned. According to David G. McCullough, author of *The Johnstown Flood* (1968), residents of Johnstown who witnessed the tragedy said that the rush of water "crushed houses down like eggshells" and "snapped trees like pipestems." Several people who were thrown into the rushing

One victim from the flood was found 15 years later.

viaduct a bridge resting on a series of narrow reinforced concrete usually carrying a road or railroad tracks over a particular obstruction.

water managed to find temporary relief atop a heap of debris that accumulated near the stone railroad bridge. Tragically, the pile of debris caught fire killing 80 people.

The rescue effort moved quickly after the disaster. Within days people came with supplies of tents, lumber, food, clothing, and construction equipment. Approximately $3.5 million was donated to help the victims. Among the people who helped with the rescue efforts was Clara Barton, the founder of the American Red Cross. Barton set up a small recovery shelter in an abandoned boxcar. The Red Cross helped nurse the wounded and set up kitchens for the devastated families.

Johnstown experienced two other destructive floods after the flood of 1889. On March 17, 1936, a flood caused by melted snow claimed 25 lives and caused an estimated $41 million in damage. On July 22, 1977, another flood caused by 11 inches of steady rainfall resulted in 80 deaths and approximately $350 million in damage. In 1989 the Johnstown Flood Museum was created in memory of the victims. In the same year Johnstown also commemorated the one hundredth anniversary of the Johnstown flood under the slogan "A Triumph of the American Spirit." The event which included ethnic art concerts, a banquet for flood survivors, and survivor story telling was a celebration of the town's ability to overcome tremendous hardship. In addition, the National Park Service maintains the Johnstown Flood National Memorial, located about 10 miles northeast of Johnstown. The memorial comprises about 165 acres and preserves the remains of the South Fork Dam. ◆

Heppner Flood

JUNE 1903

In June 1903, the state of Oregon experienced one of the worst natural disasters in its history; a thunderstorm broke out in the town of Heppner causing a flash flood that claimed approximately 250 lives.

The climate in Oregon is rainy throughout much of the year. The rainy season in Oregon runs from October to May and heavy rainfall can also occur during the summer months. When rain falls during the summer months in Oregon, it is usually very hard and concentrated in particular areas; this is what occurred in 1903. The heavy rainfall that Oregon regularly experiences has caused several floods throughout history. None, however, have been as deadly as the Heppner flood of 1903.

On June 14, 1903, the town of Heppner, Oregon, experienced a flash flood. Flash floods are usually caused by heavy rainfall during a short period of time. However, they can also be caused by dams breaking or some other unexpected event that causes a large, unexpected, release of water. The thunderstorm that hit near Heppner came swiftly and was accompanied by outbreaks of hail storms. The storm occurred in a very small, concentrated area, approximately 50 square miles. When it first began raining, the people of Heppner were not concerned about flooding. The majority of the people in Heppner were pleased that it was raining because it was good for the crops.

The flood caused Willow Creek to overflow with water. Willow Creek is usually a small, calm creek that runs through Heppner. However, the massive amount of rain that collected in the creek in addition to flowing water that ran into the creek from higher ground, caused an enormous amount of water to rush into Heppner. Within 15 minutes from the time the thunder storm began, the town of Heppner was almost completely flooded. According to newspaper reports at the time of the disaster, the town was struck by a 40-foot-high wave of water. The flood damaged or destroyed the majority of the town's homes and buildings. The flood unleashed an estimated 59 million cubic feet of water through the town of Heppner.

When the flood hit the town, the residents of Heppner were caught completely off guard. No one heard the water rushing in over the sound of the rain and thunder. Townspeople began running for higher ground to escape the rushing water. In downtown Heppner, the flood was so powerful that homes and buildings were carried away from their foundations. One man decided to remain in his house when the flood hit and began carrying his home away. The floodwater eventually destroyed his home and he was caught in the rushing water trying to cling to floating debris. After being drawn underwater several times he finally managed to swim to safety.

The town of Ione, Oregon, also suffered severe property damage as a result of the flooding. However, very few people in Ione were injured because they were notified by residents of Heppner before the flood struck the town. Ione is located approximately 20 miles down from Heppner and was in the direct path of the floodwater. After being notified that a massive flood

The flood unleashed an estimated 59 million cubic feet of water through the town of Heppner.

was on its way to Ione, local officials immediately communicated the news to the residents of Ione. Fortunately, the residents there had enough time to evacuate their homes before the water rushed in.

In the aftermath of the flood the town of Heppner received several donations including from Portland, Oregon. People from all parts of Oregon came to Heppner to help the city recover from the disaster. It took several months to reconstruct the city.

The state of Oregon has also sustained major damage and destruction due to other floods in its history. In May 1948, a massive flood struck the town of Vanport, Oregon, after a dike collapsed killing 15 people. In 1964 a rainstorm hit central Oregon which lasted for five days. Hundreds of homes and buildings were destroyed by the flood and 17 people were killed. In February 1996, Oregon experienced four days of steady rainfall which melted snow causing 10 inches of water to be released near Portland. Five people were killed in the 1996 flooding.

In 1972 a plan was proposed by the United States Congress to construct a dam on Willow Creek Lake that was designed to protect the people of Heppner from future floods. The project was abandoned, however, in 1976 because federal and local officials could not agree on the specific design and implementation of the project. ◆

Ohio Flood

MARCH 13, 1913

On March 13, 1913, Ohio experienced one of the worst floods in the state's history. The flood claimed approximately 400 lives and caused approximately $100 million in property damage.

Floods are a way of life in Ohio; nearly the entire state is exposed to the threat of flooding. At some point every year a flood occurs in Ohio, however, the degree of damage and the location of the flooding varies. Some of the more destructive floods in Ohio's history have occurred in 1913, 1937, 1945, 1948, 1959, 1963, 1964, 1969, 1990, 1992, 1996, and 1997.

In the spring of 1913 Ohio had an unusually high amount of rainfall. Four straight days of rain occurred before the flash flood of 1913. Flash floods are usually caused by heavy rainfall

The front page of *The New York Times* describes the flooding in Ohio.

during a short period of time, however, they can also be caused by dams breaking or some other unexpected event that causes a large, unexpected, release of water. The area most severely affected was Dayton, Ohio. The majority of the damage caused by the flood occurred in approximately two hours. As a result, the 1913 disaster has often been referred to as the "Great Dayton Flood."

The floodwater came rushing down the Ohio River causing tributaries such as the Miami River to overflow. The 1913 flood affected the cities of Dayton, Columbus, Cincinnati, Hamilton, and Middletown. Initial estimates were that thousands of people were killed; however, the actual number of deaths caused by the flood was an estimated 400. The flood caused over 40,000 people to lose their homes. In addition to the loss of life the flood also damaged several hundreds acres of land and killed enormous amounts of valuable livestock. When the floodwaters washed away there were reports of hundreds of dead horses lying throughout Dayton.

The floodwaters covered approximately 3,000 square feet of land. In some areas of Dayton the water level rose nearly 30 feet high. The flood current was powerful enough to carry away homes and cars. Hundreds of homes were completed washed away by the flood in Portsmouth, Ohio.

Residents of Dayton were forced to stand in line to obtain **rations** of fresh drinking water after the flood. The city was covered with silt from the river. One family was lucky to escape with their lives. The Ludwig family decided to climb to the second story of their home when they got word that the town was flooding. Shortly after reaching the second story of their home they could see several feet of water accumulating on the streets below. As the flood waters increased in the first story of their home they could hear their piano banging against the ceiling. Fortunately the family was saved by a rescue worker the following day. The flood waters were so high by the time they were rescued that they climbed out of a second story window into the boat.

Shortly after the disaster of 1913 the residents of Ohio raised funds that were specifically designed to come up with a way of preventing disastrous floods from occurring in Ohio in the future. An estimated $2 million was raised which went toward the creation of America's first flood control project. The project was called the Miami Conservancy District and is still in existence today. By 1918 the Miami Conservancy District began creating dams and expanding channels to prevent future floods in Ohio.

Several local, state, and federal agencies have worked to minimize the amount of damage caused by flooding in Ohio since the 1913 flood. Some of the measures taken by officials in Ohio include constructing dams, levees, and floodwalls; expanding the channels through which water flows through Ohio waterways; improving warning systems; and discouraging the construction of homes and businesses near flood-prone areas.

After the Great Dayton Flood of 1913 another deadly and destructive flood hit Ohio in January, 1937. Western Ohio and southern Indiana experienced unusually warm weather. On January 9, 1937, however, temperatures cooled dramatically causing a large amount of precipitation the following day. In addition to the flood, residents of Cincinnati also had to contend with massive fires that were set off when gasoline tanks erupted in fire. The 1937 flood caused nearly 400 deaths and over $500 million in property damage through states in which the Ohio River runs.

In 1996 Congress allocated $2.8 million for flood control projects in Ohio. The funds were designed to help pay for the completion of a massive floodwall to protect the city of Columbus, Ohio. The floodwall is over five miles long. Funds were also designated to help complete the construction of a 4,300-foot flood channel near Dayton. ◆

Netherlands Flood

JANUARY–FEBRUARY 1953

The Netherlands, also know as Holland, lies approximately 38 percent below sea level. When land rests below sea level the possibility of flooding inevitably exists. The Netherlands as well as other countries surrounding the North Sea have therefore spent tremendous amounts of time and energy preparing for a possible flood. At the time of the flooding, in the middle part of the twentieth century, the Netherlands had dikes and walls set up along its southwest coast to protect itself against the North Sea. However, when hurricane force winds stirred up the North Sea in January 1953, all of the defenses they put together to contain rising water levels could not protect them.

Much of the farmlands of northern Europe are exposed to the potential flooding by the North Sea. These regions lie beneath sea level and have only a few dikes shielding them from the waters of the North Sea. (A dike is an embankment or wall built to control the flow of water. They are often used to redirect water away from communities in an effort to prevent flooding.) A series of floods in the eighteenth century inspired officials to establish a water management ministry in 1798. In 1953 water levels in the North Sea were expected to rise to abnormal heights.

On the evening of January 31, 1953, high winds and heavy rain developed in the North Sea, northwest of the Netherlands. The next morning, hurricane force winds, along with already unusually high water levels in the North Sea, caused massive amounts of water to crash into the coasts of England, Belgium, and Denmark. The majority of the flood damage occurred at the southeast of the North Sea where the water level rose 18 feet higher than normal. By 4:00 A.M., many of the dikes that protect areas surrounding the North Sea began to break as high waves came crashing against them. The waves were so powerful

A Dutch woman watches helplessly as flood waters cover her farmland.

that the water rushed approximately 40 miles inland killing hundreds of people in their homes. In some areas along the coast of The Netherlands the water levels rose as high as 33 feet. The hardest hit areas of Holland were the province of Zeeland and an area near Rotterdam.

The flood killed 1,853 people and caused massive amounts of property damage. The flood also had a major impact on the farming industry in Holland. The salt water that came rushing inland coated acres of farmland. Even though some farming areas were not beneath water, the salt from the sea water ruined the land and crops. It takes approximately two years for agricultural land to recover when it is damaged by salt water.

After the massive flood of 1953 government officials worked out a plan to protect the country from future disasters. The government of Netherlands passed The Delta Act in 1958 with this goal in mind. They had to decide whether to construct dikes to steer water away from land or put up storm surge barriers around the land. The engineers had to consider how to best maintain the safety of the residents who lived near the water as well as environmental issues such as how a barrier might affect the sea life in estuaries, which are sensitive to the ebb and flow of tides. They decided that barriers would be the safest option, even though it was more costly and meant the destruction of some historic buildings. The Delta Project was considered the best way to satisfy both safety and environmental concerns.

The project consisted of building ten dams and water surge barriers around the southwest coast of Holland. The Delta Project was officially completed on October 4, 1986. However, it was not until 1997 that the final barrier to the North Sea was constructed at the Nieuwe Waterway. The project was a triumph in modern engineering technology. One of the walls, called the Eastern Scheldt Barrier, was designed with swinging doors to control the water flow and allow ships to pass through during calm periods. ◆

Buffalo Creek Flood

February 1972

Several years before the Buffalo Creek Flood of 1972, residents of the community firmly believed that one day a nearby dam would break and cause great damage. In the early morning of February 26, 1972, their suspicions were confirmed. Sixteen communities in West Virginia were affected by the flooding which occurred on that day, and 125 lives were lost.

On the morning of February 26, 1972, there was little to suggest that something dreadful was about to happen. Buffalo Creek had been experiencing heavy rainfall, but this was not out of the ordinary for February. Eventually, the heavy rainfall had filled a pond owned by the Pittston Coal Company with water beyond its capacity. It only took four inches of rainfall over a 24-hour period for the unfit dam to break. When the "dam" which contained the mud and coal-filled water finally gave way, millions of gallons of water was unleashed on the town of Buffalo Creek. The dam that contained the water was

Sixteen West Virginia communities were affected by the Buffalo Creek flood in 1972.

actually an impoundment of dust, shale, clay and coal, that had been dumped there by the Pittston Coal Company.

The flood caught the town off guard and caused devastating amounts of death and destruction to the town below. The force of the flow of water, which was claimed to be 30 feet high, up-rooted homes, knocked down telephone polls, and ripped out railroad tracks as it made its way through the town. Some people were fortunate enough to have the chance to run for higher ground, others climbed atop homes that were floating on top of the water, and others had no time to react to the onslaught of water.

It took approximately 20 minutes for the flood to cause the majority of its destruction. According to the West Virginia Library Commission, the flood killed 125 people and injured another 1,100. Among the 125 people killed, seven bodies were never found. The property damage caused by the flood mounted to $50 million from over 500 destroyed homes, 44 destroyed mobile homes, and 1,000 ruined automobiles. In addition, approximately 4,000 people were left homeless because of the floodwaters which pumped out an estimated 135 million gallons of water.

One survivor lost his wife and two of his children. During the flood he was holding to one of his children but the force of the raging water tore her from his arms. After the flooding he was unable to move back to Buffalo Creek. In the aftermath of the flooding local officials converted a high school into a recovery ward. The Department of Housing and Urban Development also helped out by providing shelter for those who had lost their homes. It took several months and millions of dollars for the town to return to normal. In Kistler, West Virginia, a monument was created in honor of those who died in the flood. Each year on February 26, residents of Buffalo Creek gather at the monument to pay their respects to those who lost their lives in the tragic accident.

One survivor recalled searching for bodies after the flood and finding them all over the place, covered with black dirt from the coal-muddied water. Another survivor explained that railroad tracks had been twisted around trees like pretzels. One woman who lost 11 family members during the flood explained, "I just think they should've made everyone evacuate. The company should have warned people."

Some experts believe that the flood did not have to happen. The dam that kept water away from the town was not constructed by engineers. It was formed by years of waste, stone, and debris being dumped across the hollow along Buffalo Creek. For several years the Buffalo Mining Company disposed of its coal mining **byproduct** and debris in the Buffalo Creek until it eventually dammed up the flow of water. The Pittston Mining Company, which at the time had been one of the nations top coal producers, had developed a poor reputation for safety. In 1971 the company had several safety violations issued against it by state officials and in 1972 they experienced the second most fatal and non-fatal accidents among coal mining companies in the nation. In 1971 the federal government warned state officials in West Virginia that several of the dams in the state, including the ones at Buffalo Creek, were unsafe.

After the flood some residents of the 16 communities that were devastated by the flooding took the Pittston mining company to court. The Buffalo Mining Company was owned by

byproduct something produced in an industrial setting in addition to the principle product.

Pittston Coal Company. They sued for $64 million. In 1974 Pittston settled with the residents out of court for $13.5 million. In addition the state of West Virginia sued Pittston for $100 million to help pay for the some of the reconstruction costs. However, Pittston was only forced to pay $1 million to the state.

Through all of the pain and suffering caused by the flood there was a positive development. The disaster inspired new laws designed to prevent such disasters in the future. One such law forced coal mining companies to more carefully dispose of their waste, stone, and debris which had built up the faulty dam and released the floodwaters in the 1972. ◆

Rapid City Flood

JUNE 1972

The morning of June 9, 1972, showed little sign that a massive thunderstorm was gathering above the skies of Rapid City, South Dakota, a city located on the eastern side of the Black Hills of South Dakota. There were patches of fog, but temperatures in the spring air were between 70 and 80 degrees. However, in the afternoon, clouds began to gather and the National Weather Service forecast thunderstorms for the region later that day. In the afternoon, at approximately 3:40 P.M., rain began falling and would continue for six hours bringing 10 to 15 inches of rain in parts of the Black Hills.

The first reports of dangerously high water levels came between 6:00 and 6:40 P.M. in Boulder Canyon, South Dakota. By 7:15 the Black Hills region received its first flood warning and a warning was issued to Rapid City a half hour later. Between 9:30 and 10:00 P.M. flood waters began to filter into Rapid City. Residents along Rapid Creek began to evacuate the area and at 10:30 the mayor of Rapid City, Don Barnett, appeared on television and radio telling residents of the lower areas to leave the area immediately. At 12:15 A.M. on June 10, floodwater began rushing into downtown Rapid City. At the time of the flood, many of the 43,000 residents of Rapid City were sleeping, unaware that their town was about to be almost completely submerged in water.

The majority of the rainfall came down in an area between Pactola and Rapid City. The unusually heavy rainfall transformed the normally calm, 15 feet wide and three feet deep, Rapid Creek into a raging river in six hours. Rapid Creek, which had a normal water flow of 200 to 300 cubic feet per second, had water flowing through it at an astounding 50,000 cubic feet per second as a result of the rain. The flooding in Rapid City was worsened by the damming up of water beneath bridges. Debris and automobiles began to pile up beneath bridges causing the floodwater to spread out to a wider area. At 10:45 P.M. a dam gave way at Canyon Lake releasing a wave of more water into Rapid City.

Although several communities were affected by the flooding, the majority of the damage occurred in Rapid City. The flood eventually killed 236 people and injured approximately 3,057, 118 of whom were hospitalized. The flood destroyed approximately 1,335 homes, 565 mobile homes, and 5,000 automobiles. The total cost of the damage caused totalled $160 million; $35 million worth of the damage occurred in Rapid City alone.

During the flood a police officer was driving down a street in Rapid City when his car was completely surrounded by water. He radioed in and said that he was forced to abandon his car because he was about to be hit by a house. The officer nearly drowned as a part of the house broke off and began pulling him under as it sunk. The officer was then rescued by a group of firefighters. Ironically, the man did not want to leave the water because he could hear screams from people trapped in the flood. Scenes like this were the most horrifying for the survivors. Many residents of Rapid City who survived the flood recall seeing people trapped on top of cars or houses and eventually being launched into the rushing water. Survivors said that they could hear screams that would fade away as people were being engulfed by the raging floodwater.

As the sun came up the following day the water levels began lowering. A massive search and rescue team made up of National Guard units, law enforcement officers, and firemen immediately began searching the area for survivors and aiding flood victims. A local radio station announced names of survivors and victims in the days that followed the flood. The federal government also

The flood destroyed approximately 1,335 homes, 565 mobile homes, and 5,000 automobiles.

contributed to the rebuilding effort, offering $48 million in aid through the federal urban renewal program.

Rapid City has put in place several precautions designed to prevent or limit the potential of future floods. City engineers created a "Green Way" along the banks of the Rapid Creek to filter any excess water away from homes and businesses. In addition, laws were passed prohibiting new businesses and homes from being built in the "Green Way." A system of keeping debris from clogging up Canyon Lake Dam was put in place. City engineers also restructured the town's bridges to keep water from building up beneath them. There has also been an elaborate satellite system put in place which monitors the water levels of streams in the Black Hills of South Dakota around the clock. In 1997 developers tried to build a supermarket along the Green Way. Several members of the community, led by those who survived the Rapid City Flood of 1972, protested the construction. ◆

Big Thompson River Flood

1976

The Big Thompson River flood was one of the worst natural disasters ever to occur in the state of Colorado. On July 31, 1976, an unusual thunderstorm hit the Big Thompson River in Colorado along the Rocky Mountains. The storm began at approximately 6:30 P.M. and, unlike normal thunderstorms which eventually pass through an area, it brought heavy rainfall over the Big Thompson River for four and a half hours straight. By 7:00 the water level in the Big Thompson River began to noticeably rise.

The thunderstorm produced 10 to 12 inches of rain. When the rainfall hit, the water began to come down the Rocky Mountains in thousands of small passageways called **rivulets**. These rivulets flowed into the streams that led into the Big Thompson River. The rainfall was accompanied by periods of hail storms. As the rainfall continued the river ballooned from its normal depth of 18 inches to 19 feet. Eventually the water level rose too high for the mouth and the water came gushing out flooding the canyon where approximately 3,000 people lived. Water came pouring out at an astounding rate of 31,200

rivulets a small stream or brook.

cubic feet per second (the river ordinarily flowed at a rate of 165 feet per second).

The flood caused hundreds of tons of mud and debris to come crashing down on homes, cars, motels, and restaurants in the Big Thompson Canyon causing massive destruction. The flow of water was so powerful that it destroyed portions of U.S. Highway 34 which runs from Loveland to Estes Park. The flood killed 145 people, injured 88 people, destroyed 52 businesses, wrecked approximately 400 homes, and caused over $39 million in property damage. The storm came on a Saturday during the peak tourism season. Therefore there were far more people camping in the Big Thompson Canyon than usual. Among the people who were killed by the flooding, only 41 actually lived in the Big Thompson Canyon. The remaining 104 were vacationing in the area. Among the 145 people killed in the storm, six of the bodies were never found. According to public officials there were several warnings issued from police and neighbors regarding the approaching flood. However, very few people took the warnings seriously.

An aerial view of a highway washed away by the Big Thompson River floodwaters.

The flood water was so strong that, according to one eyewitness, it lifted and overturned a station wagon with two passengers, and carried it down river. Ten years after the flooding a former law enforcement officer said it was still too painful to drive through the canyon. Whenever he had to drive past the Big Thompson Canyon, he took an alternative route. Another officer who was approaching retirement was killed in the storm. While he was trapped in the storm he issued a dispatch warning to people below that the flooding was far worse than they thought. One of the survivors saw that the road ahead was getting too drenched with rain to travel. He decided to leave his car and start climbing a hillside. This decision saved his life as he could later see cars with their headlights on being carried down river, engulfed in water. Another survivor indicated that

Federal Emergency Management Agency

Whenever a major natural disaster occurs in the United States, the Federal Emergency Management Agency (FEMA) is first on the scene to organize relief efforts and assess the damage. FEMA combines both a full-time professional staff and an army of reservists, and was created in 1979 under President Jimmy Carter. Its roots can be traced back to the early twentieth century.

In 1903, Congress passed a law to provide assistance to a New Hampshire town that had been devastated by fire. This was the first time that federal intervention was provided to a community struck by a major disaster. Over the next 30 years, individual congressional acts were passed to address disaster relief needs throughout the nation for calamities as diverse as earthquakes, flooding, fires, nuclear power-plant accidents, and tornadoes.

Help originally came primarily from loans, granted through an agency called the Reconstruction Finance Corporation. In 1934, however, the Bureau of Public Roads was called in to assist in rebuilding damaged bridges and highways, and the U.S. Army Corps of Engineers joined the effort by taking charge of flood control.

This piecemeal approach continued until, in the 1960s and 1970s, its limitations were exposed in the aftermath of Hurricanes Camille (1969) and Agnes (1972), as well as earthquakes in Alaska and California. The government responded by creating the Federal Disaster Assistance Administration, under the authority of the department of Housing and Urban Development. The new agency, however, was largely administrative–it continued to rely on a patchwork of individuals and organizations to get the job done.

To address this issue, President Carter merged all disaster relief agencies into a single unit, FEMA, and charged the organization providing relief and disaster insurance. The agency also works with the public in disaster preparedness programs. FEMA was reformed and streamlined during the Clinton Administration, through Vice President Al Gore's "Reinventing Government" efforts, and during these years the first professional emergency manager was made head of the agency.

the flood had so thoroughly wiped away two hotels that there was no sign that they existed.

The clean-up effort after the storm took months. Several volunteers, search and rescue teams, and the Colorado State Police helped search for survivors and clean up the wreckage. It took approximately two years and $16 million in funding for the repairs on Interstate 34 to be completed. Although homes that were only 50 percent damaged were allowed to be rebuilt, any new home construction was prohibited by zoning regulators. Twenty-three bridges had to be rebuilt.

In response to the Big Thompson River flood public officials in Colorado took steps to decrease the amount of death and destruction of future floods. Signs have been placed all over Colorado canyons telling people to climb to higher ground in the event of a flash flood. They have also established more sophisticated warning systems and built more dams. The warning systems consist of rain gauges which indicate when rainfall is dangerously heavy. The construction of dams help to minimize the potential for flooding because they allow greater control over the flow of water as river levels rise. However, some question the effectiveness of dams because the dam in the Thompson Canyon did little to prevent the massive flooding that occurred. In addition, the growth of home building as well as environment concerns have slowed down the construction of dams in Colorado. Although tremendous effort has been put into warning systems and preventing floods in Colorado, some experts believe that the biggest danger is how to evacuate people after the floods occur.

Despite the nightmare of the Big Thompson Flood people continue to live along dangerous canyons in Colorado such as Boulder, Golden, and Colorado Springs. Boulder is particularly prone to flooding. Very few steps have been taken since the Big Thompson River Flood to decrease the potential for death and destruction in the event of another flood. According to some estimates, depending on the time of day a flood hits, thousands of people could be trapped in a flood and hundreds of millions of dollars could be lost. An advanced warning system has been put in place in many of the canyons in Colorado. However, there is some question as to just how effective the warning system would be because people are unlikely to heed flood warnings and floods are very unpredictable. It is also unknown how people might react during a flash flood warning. During the Big Thompson River people seemed unwilling to leave the safety of their homes and head for higher ground, which is what experts recommend.

The canyon in Boulder, Colorado, faces a terrifying possibility. If the Boulder Canyon were hit by a powerful flood there is a possibility that the bridges that separate the north side of town from the south could be torn down. The danger is that all of the town's hospitals are on the north side of town. ◆

Bangladesh Flood

SUMMER 1988

Bangladesh, a country to the northeast of India on the Bay of Bengal, is one of the most flood-prone countries in the world. Bangladesh (which was known as East Pakistan until 1971) has a tropical monsoon climate. A monsoon is a wind system, common in Asia, characterized by heavy rainfall and shifting and wind patterns that change with the seasons.

Because of the climate, over half of the country is affected by floods each year in Bangladesh. In 1988 Bangladesh suffered a particularly devastating flood which affected nearly 85 percent of the nation's population, put approximately 75 percent of the nation under water, and nearly destroyed its economy. The president of Bangladesh, Hoosain Mohammed Ershad, described the flood as the worst in Bangladesh's history.

On June 3, 1988, a flash flood along the Kushiara River washed over an entire community killing over 200 people. This marked the beginning of the devastation. After a brief period of relief in July when the water levels in the Ganges, Brahmaputra, and Meghna Rivers actually declined, the flooding then continued in August. On August 27, 1988, the water levels reached record highs. On September 2, Dhaka International Airport was shut down because of the flooding, which not only cut the nation off from international relief, it also prevented people from leaving the country.

Part of the cause of the flood was the filtering of water down the Himalayan Mountains from India, China, and Nepal. The flow of water from melted snow from the Himalayas usually runs through the Ganges and Brahmaputra Rivers in Bangladesh and out into the Bay of Bengal. However, because so many trees and plants had been removed from the base of the Himalayas, there was nothing to buffer the rivers from the massive amounts of incoming water. As a result, the seasonal rainfall caused these passageways of water to overflow, destroying the surrounding areas. The overflowing rivers caused 54 of the nation's 64 districts to be covered with water. By early September the death toll was estimated to be around 1,300.

Flooding began in the middle of July when monsoon passageways began overflowing with rain water. The flooding caused 85 percent of the capital city of Dhaka to be covered with water. Flooding in the city ranged from several inches to over four feet. During the flood millions of people were stranded on rooftops and stranded in areas with no access to medicine, clean water, or cooked food. By September 1988, an estimated 21 million people were homeless because of the flooding. Economically, the flood could not have come at a worse time for Bangladesh. At the time of the flooding, one half of the country's 16.5 million tons of rice, which feeds as well as employs much of the country, was planted. The country lost an estimated 2 million tons of rice due to the flooding. This was disastrous for Bangladesh, which is one of the poorest and most densely populated countries.

According to estimates by the United Nations, approximately 1,500 people lost their lives as a result of the flooding, approximately 4 million homes were destroyed, and 28 million people were homeless when the flooding stopped. The flooding also caused a major problem with drinking water. Contaminated drinking water caused hundreds of thousands of people in Bangladesh to contract various forms of **dysentery**, a bacterial disease which, if untreated with proper **antibiotics**, can lead to death. The flooding caused impure water to filter into the wells.

Many communities rely upon well water for their drinking water and had no choice but to drink the water during and after the flooding. In addition to facing drowning, landslides, starvation, disease, and a lack of clean drinking water people who were stranded in the water also had to deal with the possibility of being bitten by poisonous snakes. In September 1988, an estimated 30 people had been killed by snakebites.

Starvation is usually not a problem for Bangladesh during the monsoon season. Because Bangladesh is prone to flooding, the government makes a point to prepare for food shortages. However, the flooding was so severe that several of the buildings that store the food supplies were covered with water up to their roofs. In many areas people were forced to eat uncooked food just stay alive.

Recovery came slowly for Bangladesh after the 1988 flood. In September, the government of Bangladesh made an appeal to the international community to help with food and supplies. The government asked for millions of tons of grain, helicopters, and boats, among other supplies. Relief efforts were hampered by the closing of Bangladesh's airport. The flooding began in June and substantial relief did not reach Bangladesh until September, in part because of the continued flooding.

Several countries contributed food and money to help the devastated country. Japan was one of the most generous supporters, pledging $13 million in aid. Japan also sent a medical team to help the victims. Canada pledged $4 million. The United States contributed $3.6 million in cash as well as thousands of tons of food, corn, and wheat seed to the relief effort. Great Britain donated $927,000, Australia pledged $241,000, Denmark donated $275,000, and Pakistan gave $568,000 food supplies and cash. In addition, the United Nations sent funds as

dysentery a disease characterized by severe diarrhea and the passage of mucus and blood caused by infection.

antibiotics a substance produced to dilute, inhibit, or kill a microrganism.

well as hundreds of staff members to help the people of Bangladesh.

In 1991 and 1998 Bangladesh was also hit by severe floods. A flood in summer of 1991 killed hundreds of people and flooded 30 out of Bangladesh's 64 districts. The 1991 floods affected approximately 600,000 people. In July of 1998 monsoon flooding killed hundreds people and left ten million people stranded. The 1998 floods ruined approximately 350,000 tons of rice crops, the value of which amounted to $150 million. Tens of thousands of people were also infected with diarrhea caused by contaminated drinking water. By August of 1998 diarrhea had killed an estimated 50 people. Although the Bangladesh floods after 1988 were destructive, they were mild compared to the disastrous flooding of 1988. ◆

Yangtze River Flood

Summer 1998

In the summer of 1998 China's longest river, the Yangtze, swelled to levels seldom experienced in the nation's history; not since 1954 had the Yangtze taken on so much water. Experts believe that the primary reason that flooding was so severe along the Yangtze in 1998 was the result of El Niño, a large patch of warm water in the Pacific Ocean. The warm water causes abnormal changes in weather conditions, one of which is higher than normal amounts of rainfall. A second major factor that played a role in the 1998 flood was the continued removal of trees along the Yangtze River.

The Yangtze River is the longest river in Asia and the third longest river in the world. The health of the Yangtze is vital to China's agricultural production. The majority of the land used for agricultural production in China is located in the eastern part of the country which also happens to be subject to heavy rainfall, known as monsoons. The eastern farmlands of China are flooded nearly every year. Three floods in China's history have been exceptionally damaging: the flood of 1931, the flood of 1954 and the flood of 1998. The damage caused by these floods caused thousands of deaths, destroyed millions of acres of farmland, and affected millions of people.

The flooding of 1998 occurred between the months of June and September. During this period China experienced nearly

The Wuhan Bridge over the Yangtze River

twice the average amount of rainfall along the Yangtze and the rain fell progressively harder. According to public officials in China, the vast majority of people who were killed by the flooding between June and August were killed by flowing mud and landslides. During the flooding the Chinese government assisted approximately 14 million people relocate to safer areas.

Throughout the months of June and July, continued rainfall caused the Yangtze River to swell. The rising water level put pressure on dams and levees along the river. On July 23 and 24 a flash flood occurred in Wuhan, in the province of Hubei, the hardest hit province during the flood. By August 1998, the flood was reaching record levels in central China. At this point an estimated 2,000 people had been killed during the floods.

There were also outbreaks of diseases such as dysentery. The water levels of the Yangtze reached dangerously high levels in cities such as Wuhan and Jiujiang. In regions of Wuhan and Jiujiang the flooding had already caused serious damage and loss of life, however, by August a population of half a million people were relying on the dikes to protect them from the rising water levels. (A dike is an embankment or wall around bodies of water to control the flow of water. They are often used to redirect water away from communities in an effort to prevent flooding.) On August 9, Chinese government officials decided to start destroying dikes in order to shift the path of the running water away from heavily populated areas such as Wuhan, home to 7 million people. The decision to deliberately blast dikes was difficult because it meant flooding smaller towns and communities in order to protect larger cities along the Yangtze. The Chinese government had to evacuate over 300,000 people from these smaller towns, which were sacrificed in the interest of damage control.

On August 19, the water levels of Dongting Lake and the Yangtze River rose to record highs. According to the headquarters of China's Flood Control and Drought Relief department, the water levels were reported to be 35.68 meters at 2 P.M. In an effort to control the flood the Chinese government sent approximately 10,000 troops to monitor Yangtze River dikes. Over 1.5 million members of the military as well as civilians were put on alert along the banks of the Yangtze to monitor the flooding.

In the aftermath of the flood, thousands of Chinese were forced to live in tents on higher ground along the Yangtze River. They were helpless as the water raced through their former communities destroying their homes. In the rescue effort thousands of Chinese soldiers risked their lives to save millions of people who lived along the banks of the Yangtze River. In addition to risking their lives the Chinese Army also provided tents, food, and life preservers to flood-drenched communities. On September 10, 1998, the people of Wuhan held a small ceremony honoring soldiers for their bravery during the flood.

After the Yangtze Flood of 1998, officials in China embarked on a new approach to prevent future floods from occurring and minimize the amount of death and destruction if they do occur. Addressing the issue of flooding along the Yangtze River was not only a matter of public health and safety for officials in China, it was a serious economic issue. According to government officials, China had suffered 166.6 billion yuan (China's currency) in damage, equivalent to $20 billion in economic losses in 1998 due to flooding. The damage caused by Yangtze floods in 1998 affected 223 million people (nearly one-fifth of the country's population) and brought agricultural production to a halt on approximately 51 million acres of cropland.

China's Water Resources Ministry confessed that the majority of flood control facilities in China's major cities need improvement. The United States donated tents, blankets, water containers, in addition to $250,000 in recovery assistance.

According to government officials, part of the cause for the 1998 floods is the logging that occurs along the Yangtze River. Trees and other plant life are one of the best natural defenses against flooding because they absorb so much of the rainfall. The president of China was so concerned about how to address the flooding issue in August 1998 that he canceled visits to Russia and Japan in order to focus on the problem.

In 1999 the Chinese government began helping 2 million people move from dangerous low level territories along the Yangtze to safer, higher ground. In addition, the government moved 150,000 people who lived along the Yellow River to higher ground. The relocation project was heavily influenced by the destructive Yangtze River floods of 1998. China has also taken steps to prevent future flooding along the Yangtze. In 1998 the began constructing tree dams along the Yangtze and began putting a forest shelter system in place. Researchers in China have discovered that after floods occur along the Yangtze River, they tend to occur along the Yellow River, and as a result, China has taken several measures to prevent flooding along that particular water. In 1999 the Chinese government spent over $200 million on strengthening the banks of the Yellow River. A set of flood response teams have been put in place in designated areas along the Yangtze and Yellow rivers and residents have been educated on how to react to best react to a severe flood, if and when disaster strikes again in the future. ◆

Venezuela Floods

DECEMBER 15, 1999

An onslaught of heavy rains beginning on December 15, 1999, brought flooding and mud slides to Venezuela, killing an estimated 20,000 to 30,000 people and destroying massive amounts of property. The Red Cross estimated that as many as 50,000 people may have died as a result of the flooding. In northern Venezuela 36,000 people lost their homes due to the avalanche of water. Several of Venezuela's states, as well as the nation's capital city of Caracas, were declared disaster areas. Private economists estimated the damage caused by the flood to be $20 billion. It was the worst natural disaster in Venezuela since an earthquake killed 300 people in 1967, and undoubtedly the worst in the country's history.

The heavy rainfall began on December 15, 1999, the day before Venezuelan citizens were scheduled to vote on a **referendum** for a new constitution. The rain fell on a mountain range which is an extension of the Andes, and separates Caracas from the Caribbean Sea. The water loosened rocks, mud, and debris which eventually made its way into the communities below. The heavy rainfall continued through the end of December.

The region hit hardest by the flooding was a 60-mile coastline in the province of Vargas. Vargas was completely devastated by the floods. In some areas entire towns had been covered over in water and mud. Homes were submerged in water up to their rooftops, large rocks had fallen from the mountains and covered many roads. Some areas of the state were covered with mud up to two to three feet and creeks swelled into rivers. An estimated 15,000 people were killed in Vargas alone.

Venezuela's capital city of Caracas was also hit hard by the flooding. On December 16, 1999, one day after the heavy rainfall, rivers were overflowing which forced several schools, banks, and government office buildings to shut down. Although the city of Caracas has an altitude of 3,020 feet the city was covered with mud, water, and trees that had been dragged down from the mountains along side the city. The subway system, which normally carried a million passengers per day was shut down and the international airport in Caracas was also closed. Approximately 2,000 people were left homeless and hundreds of homes were damaged beyond repair. Several people were trapped inside their homes. People were seen carrying bodies on top of doors that had been ripped away by the flood waters, and carrying furniture to other parts of the city to help homeless flood victims.

As the heavy rain continued to fall and rocks and debris continued to slide down the Andes the death and destruction mounted. By December 20, 1999, approximately 150,000 people had lost their homes, an estimated 5,000 had been killed, and another 6,000 people were missing. On December 22, the Red Cross estimated that the death toll could be as much as 30,000 and by December 25, Venezuelan officials estimated that anywhere between 10,000 and 20,000 people had been killed by the floods.

In the aftermath of the tragedy members of the Venezuelan Army were investigated for beating looters to death during the floods. Human rights organizations including PROVEA (Venezuelan Program for Action on Human Rights) claimed that 60 people were killed during the floods. There were eyewitness reports from Vargas who claimed that the looters were killed with blunt instruments in an attempt to make it seem like they were among the flood victims.

Among the dozens of countries that offered assistance to Venezuela during the floods were the United States, Cuba, Colombia, Japan, Mexico, Peru, France, and Aruba. Several countries, including the United States, helped purify water. One of the biggest threats to survival after the flooding. Water had become contaminated by debris and decaying bodies which could cause further loss of life through the spread of disease. The United States sent 18 purification machines capable of purifying 500,000 gallons of water per day. The United States also sent city engineers, food, and helicopters to help transport victims. Other countries such as Israel, Uruguay, and Spain also sent water purification machines to Vargas. The European Union donated $5.6 million to the relief effort including a fundraising drive in February 2000, specifically put together to help the flood victims.

Unfortunately, all of the donations sent across the globe to help Venezuela recover from the flooding merely put a dent in the $20 billion worth of damage. Six months after the flooding residents from the state of Vargas, which suffered the most damage during the floods, held a protest rally in an effort to secure more funding for the central government. The roadways, school systems, and drinking water systems in Vargas had still not been repaired from the flooding.

Initially, Venezuelan President Hugo Chavez refused to receive any aid from the United States. In terms of foreign policy it was in the interest of the United States to attempt to forge good relations with Venezuela because they were such an important supplier of oil. However, President Chavez was suspicious of the United States and had made efforts to strengthen relations with Cuba, a nation which has had historically poor relations with the United States. But the magnitude of death and destruction forced Chavez to put political concerns aside. In the end Chavez accepted much of U.S. humanitarian aid and expressed gratitude. ◆

> **The United States also sent city engineers, food, and helicopters to help transport victims.**

Mozambique Floods

FEBRUARY–MARCH 2000

Mozambique is a country on the southeast coast of the continent of Africa. It is located to the northeast of South Africa. The climate of the country is primarily hot and humid. Mozambique is one of the poorest nations in the world; a majority of people earn a living through agriculture. Because many of the people depend on the climate for their livelihood, floods occurring during the rainy season are particularly harmful to the national economy. In February and March 2000, heavy rains caused massive flooding in Mozambique. According to reports from the government of Mozambique, over 700 people were believed to have died in the flood. The exact number of people killed is unknown.

The government also estimated that one million people were directly or indirectly affected by the floods. It was the worst flooding Mozambique's history. The flooding in Mozambique was particularly tragic because just months before the disaster, according to the Economist Intelligence Unit's World Outlook, the nation had been listed among the fastest growing economies in the world, with 10 percent Gross Domestic Product growth since 1995. (Gross Domestic Product is a measure of the goods and services produced by a nation's economy.)

The provinces of Gaza and Sofala were hit hardest by the floods. The Mozambique government estimated that 80 percent of the fertile land had been damaged by the floods, which resulted in 124,000 families losing their crops and farming equipment. Thousands of acres of sugarcane fields, the nation's main crop, were ruined by mud and floodwater. An estimated 250,000 people were forced to relocate because of the floods, according to the government.

The town of Chockwe, which is part of the province of Gaza and lies 120 miles north of Mozambique's capital city of Maputo, was devastated by the floods. The February flooding caused the Limpopos River to swell, putting enormous pressure on the dam. On February 26, 2000, town officials decided to open the gates of the dam to prevent it from breaking. Shortly after opening the gates, Chockwe was covered in six feet of water and mud. The flood forced the town's population of approximately 70,000 people to flee the city and relocate into accommodation centers run by the state.

The government of Mozambique estimated that 60 people drowned in Chockwe between February 26 and 27, 2000. Farmlands were ruined and a rice factory, a logging company, and a brick company were submerged in water. Chockwe's railways, roads, buildings, and homes were destroyed. The town's hospital, covered in water, was invaded by snakes. The cost of rebuilding the town of Chockwe was estimated to be $756,000. People in Gaza and Sofala were scrambling to flee from the water that came rushing into their community. Hundreds of people had to climb trees to get relief from the onslaught of water. At one point, a pregnant woman was forced to give birth while stranded in a tree. A Coca-Cola plant near the nation's capital of Maputo was destroyed beyond repair by the floodwater.

Experts believe that a combination of global warming and weather patterns related to global warming known as El Niño and El Niña, were probably the cause of the Mozambique flood disaster. Meteorologists contend that the large amount of pollutants that is sent into the air through industrial production is causing the earth to gradually warm. This warming, scientists contend, causes drastic climate changes and among the consequences is heavier rainfall than usual.

In the aftermath of the flooding the government set up relief areas for families that had lost their homes. The government set up 121 camps to provide food, shelter, and medical attention. Bodies were still being discovered in April 2000, and the smell of decomposing bodies lingered in the air. However, the Mozambique government possessed limited resources to combat the flooding and aid flood victims. The government only had two helicopters with which to rescue stranded victims at the time, and only one of the two was functional. The threat of disease was also a major problem after the flooding. A lack of clean drinking water caused outbreaks of cholera and **malaria**. There was also a rash of looting that broke out which the police were unable to control.

malaria a human disease caused by the bite of anopheline mosquitoes causing periodic episodes of chills and fever.

Although donations to Mozambique during and after the flood were generous, some believe that the international community was slow to react to Mozambique's needs. In addition, because of the political climate in Africa, very few African countries contributed to the relief effort. The Organization for African Unity was criticized for only donating $20,000. The

The Red Cross and Red Crescent

The International Red Cross and Red Crescent, headquartered in Geneva, Switzerland, had its origins in 1859, with the humanitarian efforts of a young Swiss man named Henry Dunant. Traveling through a battle zone in Solferino, Italy, Dunant viewed the appalling sight of some 40,000 dead or wounded soldiers of the contesting armies of Austria, France, and Sardinia. He galvanized the local citizens into action, providing medical care, food, and comfort to the injured, regardless of nationality.

After this experience, Dunant called for the establishment of national relief organizations, and four years later his call was answered. With four other Swiss nationals, Dunant founded the International Committee for Relief to the Wounded. In 1876 it was renamed the International Committee of the Red Cross, after its emblem. The committee met to develop rules according to which soldiers wounded in battle could be cared for, later also addressing rules and customs regulating the conduct of war. These came to be known as the Geneva Conventions. Almost immediately, many of Europe's major powers had accepted the conventions and established Red Cross Societies in their countries.

In 1919, after the devastation of World War I, the European powers recognized the need for a more international scope for Red Cross activities, and the International League of Red Cross Societies was formed in Paris. The five original members were France, Britain, Italy, Japan, and the United States. Since then the organization has grown to include 176 member countries, and the name was changed in 1986 to the International Red Cross and Red Crescent to reflect participation by Muslim nations. The organization remains committed to the principles that first inspired Henry Dunant in 1859: humanity, impartiality, neutrality, independence, voluntary service, unity, and universality.

The Red Cross and Red Crescent does not limit its assistance to wartime. It is the principal provider of disaster relief throughout the globe, wherever natural disasters bring widespread suffering to humanity.

South African Development Community was also criticized for not responding faster and contributing more of the relief effort. South Africa was one of the few African countries that helped in the recovery effort, sending seven helicopters that helped save thousands of stranded Mozambique citizens. European nations contributed between $70 and $80 million to relief efforts but it was still not enough. In April 2000, it was estimated that Mozambique would require $500 million to rover from the floods. Some of the items that required rebuilding after the flooding were railway lines, bridges, roads, dams, schools, hospitals, and homes.

In May 2000, the international community held a conference on the disaster in Rome, Italy. The attending nations decided to donate $450 million to the reconstruction effort. In addition, several nations decided to forgive large amounts of debt owed to them by Mozambique. France alone forgave $485 million in debt. According to the World Food Organization approximately one half million people were in need of food supplies after the flooding. The WFO promptly made plans to deliver 53,000 tons of food to Mozambique to aid the victims. ◆

Earthquakes

Egypt Earthquake

1201

In 1201 a massive earthquake struck northern Egypt and western Syria. Many historians believed the earthquake of 1201 was the deadliest earthquake in history, as an estimated 1.1 million people died in the disaster.

Egypt is located in northeast Africa. Over 95 percent of the land in Egypt is desert and an estimated 2 percent of the land is **arable**, or able to be cultivated for crops. Egypt has a long history of destructive and deadly earthquakes because it is located in a seismically active region. (Seismology is the study of energy produced by activity beneath the earth's surface.) Two major plates meet beneath Egypt: the Arabian Plate and the African Plate. Tension between these two plates causes excess energy to be created which is released in the form of earthquakes. Earthquakes are believed to have occurred in Egypt as far back as 5,000 years ago.

One of the earliest known earthquakes to cause massive death and destruction in Egypt occurred in 365 A.D.. An estimated 50,000 people were killed in the earthquake, which occurred near Alexandria, Egypt. In more recent years destructive earthquakes have occurred in Egypt in 1955, 1969, 1981, 1992, and 1995. In the September 1995 earthquake, an estimated 300 buildings were destroyed.

The year 1201 was a difficult year for Egyptians to begin with. In addition to the massive earthquake, the water in the Nile River began to dry up, causing a devastating famine. According to some historians, food was so difficult to obtain that many people were reduced to cannibalism.

The earthquake also coincided with a period of intense political and religious conflict in Europe, north Africa, and western Asia. The earthquake occurred during the Christian Crusades. The Crusades were military efforts launched by Christians to attempt to capture the holy land of Jerusalem from Muslims. The Muslim center of power at the time was in Egypt, which was ruled by the Byzantine Empire, that had emerged after the fall of the Roman Empire.

In July 1201, an earthquake struck near the eastern Mediterranean Sea. Many historians believe that the earthquake was the deadliest natural disaster on record in history. The earthquake killed an estimated 1.1 million people, most of whom lived in Egypt and Syria. In addition to the destruction on land, the earthquake is believed to have caused massive tsunamis along the shores of the eastern Mediterranean Sea. A tsunami refers to a larger than normal wave of water that hits land after there has been a disturbance in a large body of water.

On October 12, 1992, Egypt suffered another destructive earthquake. The earthquake occurred approximately 20 miles southeast of the capital city of Cairo and measured 5.9 on the Richter scale. The Richter scale, developed by Charles Richter in 1927, is a measure of the amount of energy released by an earthquake. An earthquake that measures 7.0 on the Richter scale is considered by experts to be a "major" earthquake, capable of serious damage and loss of life. Although the earthquake did not qualify as a major earthquake in terms of its intensity, a large amount of damage was caused to Cairo, in large part because of the way buildings were constructed. The quake, which lasted approximately 20 seconds, was powerful enough to be felt 250 miles away in Jerusalem.

Over 1,000 people were killed and an additional 10,000 people were injured in the 1992 earthquake. The cities that were the most severely affected by the earthquake were Cairo and Giza. Egyptian officials estimated that the damage of the earthquake amounted to $200 million and over 500 buildings were destroyed. A majority of people killed in the 1992 earthquake were crushed to death when older buildings as well as poorly constructed newer buildings collapsed.

The government of Egypt does not enforce strict building codes and, as a result, a greater amount of damage is caused by milder earthquakes in the area. Buildings have been known to collapse in the complete absence of an earthquake. Just days before the 1992 earthquake a four-story building collapsed killing six people in Cairo. Prior to the earthquake of 1992, inspectors estimated that 60 percent of the buildings in Egypt were unsafe. Egypt suffered another major earthquake on September 22, 1995 which measured 7.2 on the Richter scale. The earthquake was felt in many Middle Eastern states from Sudan to Lebanon. ◆

Sicily Earthquake

JANUARY 11, 1693

On January 11, 1693, the island of Sicily experienced a deadly and destructive earthquake. The earthquake was one of the deadliest to occur in Sicily's history. An estimated 100,000 people were killed in the tragedy.

Sicily is an island located on the southern tip of Italy. Sicily has its own parliamentary system which meets in the city of Palermo, but it is a region of Italy. Sicily has a history of destructive earthquakes and volcanoes. It is considered by experts to be one of the more seismically active regions in the world. Sicily is located where two major plates meet. The Eurasian plate extends to the north of Sicily and the Arabian plate runs to the south. The tension produced by the meeting of these two plates can cause massive amounts of energy to be released in the form of earthquakes and volcanoes.

The majority of land in Sicily is mountainous. Sicily is home to one of the most active volcanoes in the world, Mount Etna, which has erupted several times throughout history. Perhaps the most famous eruption occurred in 1669, claiming the lives of nearly 20,000 people. Sicily is also home to another extremely active volcano called Stromboli, also referred to as the "Lighthouse of the Mediterranean." On December 28, 1908, Sicily was struck by a massive earthquake that devastated the city of Messina. The earthquake killed more than 120,000 people.

On January 9, 1693, at approximately 3:45 A.M., Sicily was near the first in a series of earthquakes that would leave the majority of civilization on the island in ruin. The first earthquake caused little damage. However, about one hour after the first earthquake, a second earthquake shook the island. Historians consider the second earthquake to have been a "foreshock" which killed thousands of people. A "foreshock" is

Mt. Etna

an earthquake that precedes a major earthquake. On January 11, 1693, at approximately 9:00 P.M., a catastrophic earthquake struck southern Sicily claiming an estimated 100,000 lives.

The earthquake completely destroyed several towns and villages throughout southern Sicily. Among the regions affected by the earthquake included: Modica, Ragusa, Vittoria, Ispica, Giarratana, Monterosso, Siracusa, and Catania. Shortly after the earthquake a massive tsunami crashed into the shores of Sicily. A tsunami refers to a larger than normal wave of water that hits land after there has been a disturbance in a large body of water. In addition to the many homes and buildings that were destroyed by the earthquake, Sicily also lost several historic buildings and churches.

In addition to the massive earthquakes of 1663 and 1908, Sicily has experienced moderate earthquakes in recent years. On December 13, 1990, the eastern coast of Sicily was struck by an earthquake that killed over 20 people and injured 400 others in Carlentini which lies between Syracuse and Catania. The earthquake registered 4.7 on the Richter scale. The earthquake caused an estimated $400 million in property damage. ◆

San Francisco Earthquake

The San Francisco Earthquake of 1906, often referred to as the "Great Earthquake," was the most destructive earthquake to ever occur in the United States. Although the earthquake itself was destructive and deadly, many of the lives lost during the tragedy were a result of the fires that broke out after the earthquake.

San Francisco, California, is sometimes referred to as "Earthquake City." The city sits atop the San Andreas Fault line. The San Andreas Fault line is a 600 mile crack in the earth's crust that runs from northwest California to the Colorado Desert. The movement of land along the San Andreas Fault line causes numerous earthquakes in California. San Francisco has suffered several earthquakes throughout its history, including eight in the nineteenth century alone. However, in terms of lives lost and property damage, none of these earthquakes could compare to the power of the 1906 earthquake.

San Francisco developed quickly as a city after gold was discovered in 1849. But it was not prepared to accommodate the rush of settlers that flocked to the city when gold was discovered. As a result, buildings and homes were constructed hastily and without much concern for safety in the event of a catastrophe in the city, which had a population of over 300,000 at the time of the quake.

As a consequence, on the morning of April 18, 1906, the city was poorly equipped to deal with an earthquake or major fire. Tragically,

San Franciscans watch the fires caused by the 1906 earthquake from the safety of Russian Hill.

the head of the San Francisco fire department, Dennis T. Sullivan, had warned city officials that San Francisco's fire fighting ability was poor and he requested additional funding the fire department prior to the earthquake. Unfortunately, his requests were not satisfied. Sullivan died on April 22 from injuries caused by fighting the "Great Fire." At 5:13 A.M. on the 18th the city was struck by a massive earthquake. The entire earthquake lasted approximately two minutes. The city shook for approximately 40 seconds. After a period of around 20 seconds of relief from the quaking, it was struck by another earthquake which lasted approximately 90 seconds.

The earthquake was so powerful that its shock waves were felt as far away as Oregon. The destruction zone of the earthquake extended approximately 400 miles long and 25 to 30 miles wide. Perhaps equally destructive to the "Great Earthquake" were the fires that broke out after the earthquake and burned for approximately four days.

Several large fires broke out almost immediately after the earthquake. The entire city was in a state of chaos. Some people fled for their lives, others stayed and tried to help rescue people, while a few took advantage of the tragedy by looting homes and buildings. The fire soon began to grow out of control. As a result the federal government sent in 15,000 troops to help rescue victims and control the fire. At approximately 3:00 P.M. on April 18, 1906, the mayor of San Francisco gave troops the order to shoot any looters or other criminals "on sight."

According to reports at the time of the earthquake, officials initially suspected that about 650 people were killed in the earthquake and fires that followed. However, further research after the event, according to some historians, places the death toll between 2,000 and 3,000. Researchers estimate that the earthquake measured 8.2 on the Richter scale. (The Richter scale, developed by Charles Richter in 1927, is a measure of the amount of energy released by an earthquake.) The total amount of property damage caused by the earthquake and ensuing fires was an estimated $500 million.

One of the primary reasons that city officials had such a difficult time putting out the fires was that many of the water lines were destroyed by the earthquake. Officials who were fighting the fires were given authority to begin blowing up buildings in order to stop the fire from jumping from building to building. Unfortunately, this strategy backfired when it was used in Chi-

San Andreas Fault

The San Andreas Fault Zone runs more than 600 miles (965 km), through the state of California, extending from the Mojave Desert in the south, through Indio (near Los Angeles), up to and beyond the San Francisco Bay area. It takes its name from San Andreas Lake, located in the San Andreas Valley, near San Francisco, which is one source of that city's water supply.

The San Andreas is a strike-slip fault. This means that the earth on either side of the fault line is moving in opposite directions. The threat of earthquakes varies in likelihood along the fault, being much lower in the south than up north in the Bay Area. This is because the southern portion of the fault line is constantly undergoing gradual movement, thus releasing strain along the fault and dissipating the energy that would otherwise need release through an actual earthquake. The interval between quakes along this part of the San Andreas is set at about 140 years.

In the San Francisco area, on the other hand, the fault is much more active. It is in this region that major quakes have occurred over the years, including the 1989 "World Series" earthquake, which originated in the nearby town of Loma Prieta and hit San Francisco during the playing of baseball's World Series there. There seems to be no natural mechanism for releasing energy along this part of the fault that is comparable to the situation in the south, and scientists believe that there is a 30 percent chance of another major earthquake occurring at any time during the next 30 years.

natown. One of the buildings destroyed on purpose in Chinatown contained mattresses. When the building was blown up, massive amounts of blazing debris was sent in the direction of surrounding wooden homes and buildings. Several other homes and buildings were set ablaze, causing major sections of Chinatown to burn to the ground.

In the aftermath of the earthquake and deadly fires the U.S. Army, San Francisco Red Cross, and the Relief Corporation provided recovery assistance. One of the issues that relief organizations had to fight during the recovery effort was discrimination against Asian immigrants. At the time, immigrants from Japan and China suffered discrimination and federal officials oversaw the relief effort to make sure that Asian refugees were treated fairly. Japanese immigrants, who feared that they would not receive adequate recovery assistance, formed the Japanese Relief Organization.

Chinatown, where the majority of Chinese immigrants lived, was left in a complete state of ruin after the fire. The Chinese government donated approximately $40,000 to the recovery effort and specifically stated that the funds were not to be used solely for the assistance of Chinese immigrants. The Chinese Merchants' Association also contributed funds to the recovery effort. A committee was established after the fire which was designed to assist Chinese immigrants. The committee decided that a brand new town was to be created for the former residents of Chinatown. However, the Chinese government disapproved of the plan to build another city. They insisted that Chinatown be rebuilt from the ground up. Government officials including the mayor of California agreed to the rebuilding plan, partly out of fear of disrupting trade relations with China.

It took approximately four years to rebuild San Francisco. In some respects the San Francisco earthquake of 1906 had a positive impact on the city. San Francisco now has very rigid building codes and construction laws, which served to contain the property damage and loss of life when the city suffered a powerful earthquake in 1989.

On October 17, 1989, San Francisco suffered its most powerful earthquake since the "Great Earthquake." The 1989 earthquake, which has been called the "Loma Prieta" earthquake or the "World Series" earthquake, occurred at approximately 5:04 P.M., during the third game of baseball's World Series, which was being played at Candlestick Park in San Francisco. The earthquake, which lasted approximately 15 seconds, measured 7.1 on the Richter scale and caused massive structural damage to the city. Property damage caused by the 1989 earthquake was estimated to be as high as $10 billion, making it the most costly earthquake in U.S. history. Although the property damage was enormous, the number of people killed or injured during the earthquake was relatively small. Experts believe that the strict building codes in San Francisco greatly minimized the amount of damage and loss of life caused by the earthquake. ◆

Tokyo-Yokohama Earthquake

SEPTEMBER 1, 1923

The Tokyo-Yokohama Earthquake of 1923 was the most devastating earthquake in Japan's history. The earthquake claimed the lives of 142,800 people. Although Japan has suffered several natural disasters throughout its history, the 1923 earthquake was by far the most deadly and de-

structive. The 1923 earthquake has also been referred to by historians as "The Great Kanto Earthquake." Kanto is a region in Japan in which Tokyo resides.

Japan lies within one of the most earthquake and volcano prone regions in the world. Two major plates meet beneath Japan, which causes an unusually high degree of seismic activity. (Seismology is the scientific study of earthquakes, specifically the amount of energy released by earthquakes.) The meeting of the Pacific and Asian plates has caused several major earthquakes in Japan's history. Major earthquakes have hit Tokyo on several different occasions throughout history including: 1633, 1703, 1792, and 1853. Before the 1923 earthquake the worst earthquake Japan suffered occurred in 1792, which claimed approximately 15,000 lives.

Japan's most destructive earthquake occurred in 1923 during which an estimated 142,800 people were killed. The Japanese not only have to contend with earthquakes and volcanoes, but tsunamis as well. A tsunami refers to a larger than normal wave of water that hits land after there has been a disturbance in a large body of water. The most devastating tsunami

Men and women clean up debris in the aftermath of the Tokyo-Yokohama Earthquake in 1923.

in Japan's history occurred in 1896 when it is reported that a 100-foot high wave crashed against the Japanese coast in Sanriku killing thousands of people. During the 1923 earthquake several large tsunamis were reported, however, the loss of life and property damage caused by the tsunamis was not significant.

On the morning of the earthquake, the temperature was warm and breezy. Tokyo had experienced rain and high winds which was not unusual for that time of year. Residents of Tokyo and Yokohama had no idea that the worst catastrophe in Japanese history was about to occur.

On September 1, 1923, at approximately 11:58 A.M. Japan was struck by a massive earthquake. The epicenter of the earthquake was near Sagami Bay, southeast of Tokyo. The **epicenter** of an earthquake is the point on the earth's surface directly above the point where an earthquake occurs. According to reports at the time the earthquake lasted approximately four to ten minutes. During the remainder of September 1, 1923, after the main earthquake, Japan suffered an estimated 200 **aftershocks**. In the days that followed Japan experienced nearly 1,000 aftershocks which compounded the destruction and death toll.

According to historians, the Tokyo-Yokohama earthquake of 1923 registered between 7.9 and 8.3 on the Richter scale. This, however, is only an estimate because the Richter scale had not been in existence at the time of the earthquake. The Richter scale, developed by Charles Richter in 1927, is a measure of the amount of energy released by an earthquake. An earthquake that measures 7.0 on the Richter scale is considered by experts to be a "major" earthquake, capable of serious damage and loss of life. The earthquake killed thousands of people, however, the fires that broke out in Tokyo and Yokohama after the earthquake were equally devastating.

Part of the reason that such an enormous number of fires broke out in Tokyo and Yokohama was because the earthquake struck near lunch time when many restaurants and homes had fires burning for the preparation of meals. The fires were responsible for numerous deaths in Japan. A bizarre burst of flames in Honjo and Fukagawa in Tokyo claimed the lives of 30,000 people. The group of refugees had gathered near a clothing factory to flee from the burning buildings when a tornado of flames descended upon them. The fires caused over 300,000 people to lose their homes. The earthquake destroyed nearly all of the fire fighting equipment Japan had at the time. Officials were therefore incapable of putting out the many fires that

---

epicenter the part of the earth's surface directly above an earthquake.

aftershock a minor tremor following the main shock of a larger earthquake.

blazed through wooden buildings and homes. Over half of the buildings in Tokyo caught fire after the earthquake. The earthquake also set off a series of landslides, some of which buried entire villages.

Japanese officials had an extremely difficult time managing the tragedy. Because the majority of water lines had been broken and the roadways and railways could not be traveled, it was nearly impossible to fight the raging fires. In addition the earthquake had severed all forms of communication in or out of Tokyo and Yokohama. The Japanese Army was forced to relay what had occurred to other parts of Japan. The day after the earthquake the Japanese government issued a statement indicating that it would seize all merchandise that it believed would be helpful for the relief effort. The government also immediately designated millions of dollars to help the earthquake and fire victims.

During the chaos that followed the tragedy there were reports of mistreatment toward Korean immigrants in Japan. Some Japanese citizens took their frustration out on Koreans by assaulting them and poisoning their drinking water. The Japanese government discouraged the behavior but eventually had to declare martial law to regain order. Governments declare martial law during severe states of emergency during which local affairs are taken over by the military until order is restored. The Japanese government issued a warning that anyone who was caught looting would immediately punished; many looters were shot in the aftermath of the earthquake.

Several countries contributed to the relief effort. As soon as the extent of the tragic earthquake was communicated ships began arriving to help the victims. The United States immediately donated $10 million to the relief effort. ◆

India Earthquake

MAY 1935

In May 1935, India experienced one of the most destructive earthquakes of the 20th century. The earthquake killed an estimated 56,000 to 60,000 people.

India is considered one of the most seismically active regions in the world. Seismology is the study of energy produced by activity beneath the earth's surface. Earthquake activity in India is believed to be the result of the movement two plates that lie beneath the country. India lies atop the meeting point of the Indian-Australian and the Eurasian plates. The meeting of these two plates, which formed the Himalayan Mountains, is believed to create massive amounts of energy which is released in the form of earthquakes. Scientists believe that the Indian plate is thrusting beneath the Himalayan Mountains which causes earthquakes in northeastern India.

Not surprisingly, India has a long history of destructive natural disasters. Earthquakes strike frequently in India and often claim numerous lives. Some of the most powerful and destructive earthquakes in history have occurred in India. One of the reasons so many lives are lost during Indian earthquakes is because of the large population density of the area; India has the world's second highest population. An earthquake that struck India on October 11, 1737, is said to have killed over a quarter of a million people. The 1935 earthquake killed approximately 60,000 people. In 1993 a massive earthquake killed an estimated 10,000 people. In 2001 another earthquake killed an estimated 30,000 people.

India has also suffered a number of other earthquakes throughout its history that were comparatively less deadly. In 1950 an earthquake that registered 8.5 on the Richter scale killed over 1,500 people. In 1988 over 600 people were killed in an earthquake that struck near Bihar. In 1990 another earthquake struck near the Uttarkashi hills which killed over 1,000 people. In 1997 an earthquake near Jabalpur killed another 1,000 people.

On May 31, 1935, at around 3:03 A.M., a massive earthquake struck near Quetta. Known as the "Great Quetta Earthquake," it occurred in the northwest region of India, in what is now Pakistan. The earthquake measured 7.5 on the Richter scale and killed an estimated 60,000 people. (The Richter scale, developed by Charles Richter in 1927, is a measure of the amount of energy released by an earthquake.) An earthquake that measures 7.0 on the Richter scale is considered by experts to be a "major" earthquake, capable of serious damage and loss of life.

The earthquake lasted approximately 30 seconds and was followed by several aftershocks that added to the death toll. Thousands of homes and buildings collapsed during the earthquake, crushing people as they slept. The earthquake occurred during the hottest time of the year in India, which made it difficult to tend to the thousands of people who had lost their homes.

Immediately after the earthquake people began searching through the rubble to rescue survivors. Roadways into and out of the city were cleared in order to transport the injured. Unfortunately the telegraph system was destroyed during the earthquake which made it difficult to communicate to other areas of India the extent of the damage and need for assistance.

Some researchers believe that India may be vulnerable to large amounts of deaths after natural disasters because of the way the country's infrastructure has been developed. Some observers believe that many of the deaths that have occurred in recent natural disasters in India could have been avoided. Because of the rapid population growth in India state officials may not have taken the necessary measures to enhance safety in major Indian cities. Many people in India live in very insecure homes made of brick or bamboo. In addition, many homes are built on soft soil which causes buildings to sink in a collapse easily when an earthquake hits.

Experts warn that India may have put itself at risk by building nuclear power plants in areas that are subject to earthquakes. Because of the massive amounts of property damage and loss of life caused by the Quetta Earthquake of 1935, India began creating and enforcing stricter building codes. Although India's building codes are among the strictest in the world, experts fear that the building codes may not be as rigidly enforced as they could be. ◆

Chile Earthquake

JANUARY 24, 1939

Chile has experienced many earthquakes throughout its history. The earthquake that struck the small South American country on January 24, 1939, was among the worst in its history. The earthquake lasted approximately three minutes and killed over 30,000 people.

Chile is a long, narrow country that runs along the western coast of South America. Chile experiences more earthquakes per year than any other country in the world. In addition to

In Chillan there were only a handful of buildings remaining after the massive quake.

earthquakes, Chile is also vulnerable to volcanic eruptions. One of the reasons that Chile experiences such an unusually large amount of earthquakes and volcanoes is its location above two major plates.

Chile lies above the meeting point of the Nazca and the South American plates (plates are large sections of the earth's crust). The plates meet near the Andes Mountains which extend the entire length of the country. The tension between the two plates causes large amounts of energy to be released in the form of earthquakes and volcanoes. Chile is also located along the eastern line of what is know as the "Ring of Fire," a large circle of land and sea in the Pacific Ocean that is known for its unusually high degree of earthquake and volcano activity.

On January 24, 1939, Chile experienced one of the most devastating earthquakes to occur in the twentieth century. Among the cities that were hardest hit by the earthquake were Chillan, Coihueco, and Concepcion. In Chillan there were only a handful of buildings remaining after the massive quake. In Concepcion approximately 70 percent of the buildings were destroyed, coal mines caved in, and several historic cathedrals were destroyed. Many of the people who were killed in the 1939 earthquake were children.

In 1960 Chile experienced another destructive earthquake. On May 21, 1960, at approximately 6:00 A.M. an earthquake that registered 7.7 on the Richter scale struck near Valdivia. The earthquake killed an estimated 1,300 people and injured 3,000 others. The earthquake caused approximately $550 million in property damages. A second earthquake struck the area the following day at approximately 3:00 P.M. The second earthquake registered 9.5 on the Richter scale. Both earthquakes set of a series of landslides and avalanches which caused massive property damage and loss of life. The earthquake that struck southern Chile on May 22, 1960, was the most powerful earthquake on record in history.

In addition to collapsing buildings from the earthquake, landslides, and avalanches, the people of Chile also had to contend with a massive tsunami after the 1960 earthquake. A tsunami refers to a larger than normal wave of water that hits land after there has been a disturbance in a large body of water. The tsunami that crashed into the shores of Chile was an estimated 30-foot-high wall of water. The tsunami hit the shores of Chile approximately an hour after the earthquake and smashed up homes and boats before carrying the debris back out to sea.

The 1960 earthquake also caused a 30-foot tsunami in Hawaii killing 61 people and a 36-foot tsunami in Japan that killed over 100 people. ◆

Alaska's Good Friday Earthquake of 1964

On March 27, 1964, a massive earthquake struck the southeastern coat of Alaska near Prince William Sound. The earthquake is best known for its power rather than the amount of death and destruction it caused. The Alaskan earthquake, often referred to as the "Good Friday Earthquake" because it occurred on the Christian holy day of Good Friday, was the most powerful earthquake in U.S. history. It was also the second most powerful earthquake to occur throughout the twentieth century. The largest earthquake on record was a 1960 earthquake that struck Chile.

According to seismology experts, Alaska is one of the most earthquake-prone states in the United States because it is one of the most seismically active areas in the world. Seismology is the study of energy given off due to disturbances beneath the earth's surface. As a result, Alaska has suffered several earthquakes and volcanoes throughout its history. In 1786 a destructive earthquake hit Alaska after the eruption of the Pavlov volcano. In 1812 another earthquake preceded by a volcanic eruption struck Atka Island. Powerful earthquakes have hit Alaska in 1857, 1861, 1878, 1883, 1896, 1911, 1912, and 1933. In 1946 a major earthquake in Alaska is said to have caused a tsunami in Hawaii which killed 170 people. In 1957 an earthquake of great magnitude churned 40-foot high tsunamis that caused massive property damage in Sand Bay, Alaska.

On March 27, 1964, at approximately 3:46 P.M., a massive earthquake struck the western coast of Alaska. The earthquake lasted approximately four minutes. The cause of the earthquake was the gradual movement of the Pacific plate into the North American plate which lay beneath Alaska. The earthquake was so powerful that it was felt throughout the entire state, parts of Canada, and through much of the state of Washington on the United States mainland.

Richter Scale

Developed in 1935 by Charles F. Richter, an engineer at the California Institute of Technology, the Richter scale is the measure by which scientists compare earthquakes, based on the amount of energy they release. As the scale numbers increase, they reflect an exponential, not numerical increase in earthquake power; each number on the scale stands for a 10-fold increase in power over the number preceding it. The least powerful earthquake that can be felt by humans measures 1.5 on the Richter scale; whereas a 4.5 quake can cause substantial damage, and a quake measuring 8.5 is devastating.

The strongest earthquake ever measured by the Richter Scale occurred just offshore of South America. The quake hit 9.5 on the scale, and caused thousands of deaths in Chile. In addition, the huge tsunami (a wave caused by the earthquake) killed many more, in places as far away as Hawaii, the Philippines, and Japan. Tsunami is a Japanese term: *tsu*, meaning harbor, and *nami*, meaning wave.

In the U.S., the largest earthquake occurred in Prince William Sound, Alaska, on March 28, 1964. Measuring 9.2 on the Richter Scale, the quake caused great destruction in more than 17 towns. The quake triggered a massive tsunami, which caused further damage along the coasts of Washington State, Oregon, California, and in Hawaii.

The earthquake registered 9.2 on the Richter scale. The Richter scale, developed by Charles Richter in 1927, is a measure of the amount of energy released by an earthquake. An earthquake that measures 7.0 on the Richter scale is considered by experts to be a "major" earthquake, capable of serious damage and loss of life. According to experts, the force of the 1964 Alaskan earthquake was approximately 2,000 times greater than the 1989 earthquake that hit San Francisco, California. The Alaskan earthquake caused 125 deaths and an estimated $300 million in property damage. The massive power of the earthquake was detected as far away as South Africa where disruptions in the levels of well water were noted.

An additional 16 people were killed as a result of the earthquake in Oregon and California. The areas affected by the earthquake included the Alaskan cities of Anchorage, Glennallen, Homer, Hope, Kodiak, Moose Pass, Seward, Sterling, and Valdez. Anchorage, Alaska, which was over 75 miles away from the earthquake's epicenter (point on the earth's surface beneath which an earthquake occurs), suffered the most property damage as a result of the earthquake. In downtown Anchorage, approximately 30 blocks of homes and businesses were damaged or destroyed by the earthquake.

After the earthquake, the coast of Alaska suffered a major tsunami. A tsunami is an abnormally large wave of water that hits land after there has been a disturbance in a larger body of water. The tsunami caused by the Alaskan earthquake sent massive amounts of water into the towns of Seward and Kodiak. In Kodiak a large portion of the city's fishing fleet was destroyed. According to the National Earthquake Information Center, 110 people were killed by the tsunami and 15 people were killed by the earthquake. Researchers believe that the Alaskan tsunami caused landslides as far away as California. Because of the tsunami many of Alaska's freshwater lakes were contaminated by salt water.

Because of the destructive force of the tsunamis after the 1964 Alaskan earthquake federal officials decided to set up a tsunami warning system near Alaska. The tsunami warnings system is a computerized warnings system that monitors the activity in the Pacific Ocean around the clock near Alaska. If major disruptions are recorded, warnings signals are sent electronically. ◆

Peru Earthquake

MAY 31, 1970

A massive earthquake devastated northern Peru on May 31, 1970. The earthquake was one of the deadliest natural disasters to occur in the twentieth century and the most devastating to ever occur in the Western Hemisphere.

Peru has suffered several destructive earthquakes throughout its history. Earthquakes in Peru are caused by the meeting of two plates beneath the earth's surface. The South American plate juts up against the Nazca plate, which runs along the western coast of South America. The earthquake that struck Peru in 1970 was the deadliest and most destructive earthquake in Peru's history. The earthquake killed approximately 66,794 people, caused between $500 million and $1 billion in property damage, and left an estimated one million people homeless. The earthquake destroyed or badly damaged approximately 152 small cities and another 1,500 rural villages in Peru.

On May 31, 1970, at approximately 3:23 P.M., a massive earthquake struck the western coast of Peru. The earthquake measured 7.8 on the Richter scale. (The Richter scale, developed by Charles Richter in 1927, is a measure of the amount of energy released by an earthquake.) An earthquake that measures 7.0 on the Richter scale is considered by experts to be a "major" earthquake, capable of serious damage and loss of life. The earthquake lasted approximately 45 seconds.

Chimbote, a small fishing town that lies on the western coast of Peru, was one of the cities hardest hit by the quake. Approximately 3,000 people were killed in Chimbote and several homes and nearly half of the buildings within the city were destroyed by the earthquake. The cities of Huaraz and Casma in northern Peru also suffered major damage as a result of the earthquake. In Huaraz an estimated 95 percent of the buildings were destroyed or badly damaged.

One of the most horrifying disasters caused by the earthquake was the destruction of the entire towns of Yungay and Ranrahirea. Yungay and Ranrahirea were virtually swept away by an avalanche that was caused by the earthquake. The towns were located at the base of a large mountain along the Andes, called Mount Huacaran. When the earthquake struck it caused a massive boulder to shake loose atop Mount Huacaran. The boulder moved swiftly down the mountain causing an avalanche of snow and ice to fall on top of Yungay and Ranrahirea. The towns were completed destroyed by the avalanche. The avalanche crushed an estimated 1,500 schools and 150,000 homes, forcing approximately 400,000 people out into the freezing cold. An estimated 20,000 people were killed by the avalanche.

One of the reasons the earthquake caused such an extreme amount of deaths is because of the time it took search and rescue teams to find survivors. When the earthquake struck it destroyed all methods of communication to other regions of Peru. In addition, when Peruvian officials learned of the tragedy many roads were blocked and their relief effort was poorly organized. This caused a delay in the organization of search and rescue teams. Many Peruvians died while trapped in the rubble or froze to death after losing their homes. A second reason why such an enormous number of people were killed is that the earthquake was not the only disaster Peru had to cope with. The earthquake set off other natural disasters including floods, landslides, and avalanches that caused massive property damage and loss of life.

Many of the homes that were destroyed during the earthquake were **adobe** homes. Adobe is made from clay and straw, and much softer than concrete. Although this material is less

adobe a brick or building material consisting of sun-dried earth and straw used in making adobe bricks.

expensive than concrete, it is relatively unstable. However, adobe homes have one advantage over conventional homes when it comes to earthquakes. Because adobe is much lighter than concrete, it is much easier to withstand the falling material than the much harder and heavier concrete. But some researchers believed that the existence of adobe houses in Peru increased the death toll because of their structural weakness.

The international community was quick to respond to Peru's needs. Nearly 60 countries helped Peru deal with the tragedy. The majority of the nations that contributed to the relief effort did so by providing direct support in addition to donations. According to the United States Agency for International Development (USAID) about $80 million was raised by foreign governments and private fund raisers to help Peru recover from the devastation. The United States was particularly generous with relief support, providing approximately $23 million worth of food, medical assistance, and supplies. The World Bank loaned Peru $65 million to help the country deal with the tragedy.

During the reconstruction period, the people of Peru held demonstrations in an effort to persuade the government to help develop the area rather than simply reconstruct it. The slogan of the political activists was "let us not reconstruct underdevelopment." The message to the government was that Peruvians were not happy with the standard of living in northern Peru, and wanted more than a rebuilding of the poor living conditions that existed before the earthquake. As a result the United States Agency for International Development (USAID) and the Peruvian government designated funds and created a program to redevelop the area with an emphasis on improving economic and social conditions. During the redevelopment period of the major changes made to the areas of northern Peru was that many of the adobe homes were replaced with conventional building materials such as concrete. ◆

Northern China Earthquake

JULY 28, 1976

On July 28, 1976, China experienced what has been described as one of the worst earthquake disasters in world history. The degree of property damage and lives

China has a long history of earthquakes.

lost qualifies the earthquake as the deadliest to occur in the twentieth century. The tragedy resulted in the death of over 242,000 people. About 165,000 people were badly injured by the earthquake. Although the exact number of people killed by the earthquake is unknown, some historians have placed the death toll over 500,000.

China has a long history of earthquakes. In 1920 China suffered an earthquake that was nearly as devastating as the one that shook Tangshan in 1976. The 1920 earthquake killed an estimated 200,000 people. An earthquake in 1556 is said to have killed over 800,000 people. According to earthquake researchers, one of the reasons that China is so prone to earthquakes is the movement of the Indian-Australian plate. This plate, which lies beneath the earth, extends across northern India where it meets the Himalayan Mountains in southern China. It is the force of the northern movement of the Indian-Australian plate that created the Himalayan Mountains. A second cause for major earthquake activity in China is something know as the "Ring of Fire." The Ring of Fire is a large circle of land and sea in the Pacific Ocean that is known for its unusually high degree of earthquake and volcano activity. The outer edge of the Ring of Fire lies on the eastern coast of China.

Before the earthquake struck Tangshan in July 1976, the city had been developing into a major mining and manufacturing city in China. The population of the city at the time of the earthquake had grown to exceed one million. During the days before the earthquake residents of Tangshan received several warnings and were educated on how to prepare for an earthquake and what to do afterwards. But when the earthquake struck, the majority of people in Tangshan were sound asleep and experts believe that the unfortunate timing of the earthquake added to the death toll.

On July 28, 1976, at 3:42 A.M., northeastern China was struck by a massive earthquake that measured 8.2 on the Richter scale. (The Richter scale, developed by Charles Richter in 1927, is a measure of the amount of energy released by an earthquake.) An earthquake that measures 7.0 on the Richter scale is considered by experts to be a "major" earthquake, capable of serious damage and loss of life. Approximately 16 hours after the first earthquake, China was struck by a second devastating earthquake that measured 7.9 on the Richter scale. The fault that shifted at the epicenter, the center of the earthquake, was approximately seven miles beneath the earth. Experts consider this shallow for an earthquake.

Faults in the Earth

Faults, in geology, refer to fractures in the earth's crust along which there are movements of the earth. These faults, and the movements that occur along them, are what cause earthquakes. There are many different types of faults, differentiated according to the way that the earth around them moves. In a *strike-slip fault*, the movement of the earth on one side of the fault is in the opposite direction of the earth on the other side. The San Andreas Fault is an example of this type.

A second type is known as a *dip-slip fault*. In this, a section of the earth moves downward relative to the earth on either side, which is simultaneously moving upward. A third type of fault is called a *detachment*, in which a wedge of earth is forced upward on a slant, and the earth lying above it is forced backward and downward. In a *reverse detachment*, the opposite occurs.

There are three major fault zones on earth. The first is the Circum-Pacific Seismic Belt, which gives rise to earthquakes in Alaska, the western coasts of the United States and Central and South America, New Zealand, New Guinea, the Philippines, and Japan. The second is the Alpide Zone, running from Java to Sumatra and encompassing faults in the Himalayas, the Mediterranean region, and out to the Atlantic Ocean. Finally, there is the Mid-Atlantic Ridge, which is a series of faults lying deep beneath the Atlantic Ocean.

There are other, less extensive fault zones throughout the world as well. One potentially dangerous fault region in the United States is the New Madrid Fault, which runs along the Mississippi River, where a major earthquake occurred in 1811. Another is the Tancheng-Lujiang (or Tan-Lu) Fault Zone in northeastern China, a strike-slip fault that was the site of a devastatingly powerful 8.2 earthquake in 1976.

It took only an estimated 10 to 16 seconds for the earthquake to release the majority of its destructive force. Within seconds of the earthquake, the majority of the homes and buildings in Tangshan were reduced to a pile of concrete and wood. The earthquake buried over 85 percent of the entire population of Tangshan in debris. Nearly one quarter of the entire population of Tangshan were killed by the earthquake. An additional 600,000 people were injured. The earthquake was so powerful that it destroyed portions of the historic Great Wall of China.

The city of Tangshan, which lies less than 100 miles southeast of the China's capital city of Beijing, suffered the most loss of life and property damage as a result of the earthquake. The city was in a complete state of ruin after the earthquake. Because the earthquakes occurred so close to the nation's capital, officials in China warned people in Beijing that they should leave their homes and prepare for another earthquake. Earthquakes are said to give off light when they first occur as a result of burning gasses that are released from beneath the earth's surface. The tremendous power of the earthquake is said to have given off a light from Tangshan, which was visible about 200 miles away.

The earthquake struck while several late night mining shifts were hard at work, unaware of what was about to occur. When the earthquake struck, hundreds of Tangshan miners were trapped beneath the ground. Although many of the workers were later rescued, many of them came to the surface only to learn that the earthquake had killed their families. Many people who died in the earthquake had little or no chance of survival. The earthquake struck in the middle of the night while most people were asleep. Many of the victims were crushed beneath their own roofs while they slept. Others laid trapped inside the fallen rubble with no hope of rescue until day break, which was too late for many.

As a result of their extensive experience with earthquakes, the Chinese government dedicated vast amounts of resources to the study of earthquakes and recovery techniques. Days before the earthquake, researchers in China communicated to public officials that conditions were right for a major earthquake. Officials in China sent a team of people to Tangshan to educate the local residents on how to best prepare for an earthquake. People were also warned to stay away from large auditoriums and movie theaters. In addition, earthquake and flood evacuation plans were put together. On July 25, Chinese officials were so certain that an earthquake was about to occur that they broadcast warnings to several communities three times a day and they began monitoring for an earthquake around the clock. Also on July 25, the government announced to residents of northeastern China that an earthquake could occur "any day now."

Many earthquake researchers have found that just before an earthquake hits animals begin to act strangely. This theory held true for the Northeastern China earthquake of 1976 as several different kinds of animals began to behave differently during the days leading up to the earthquake. There were reports that pigs began circling and ramming into their pens trying to escape, and chickens tried to escape from their coops. In addition, there were reports that weasels that normally slept during the day and hid from people were scurrying about during daylight hours in full view.

In the aftermath of the earthquake, China and the international community began pooling resources to help victims and search for survivors. China sent 100,000 troops to Tangshan to help dig out survivors and build shelters for those who had lost their homes to the earthquake. Recovery was particularly difficult for those who were badly injured during the earthquake. Because the hospitals were destroyed by the earthquake medical experts had to operate on victims outdoors without proper medical supplies. ◆

Guatemala Earthquake

FEBRUARY 4, 1976

In February 1976, Guatemala experienced the most destructive natural disaster in its history. A deadly earthquake hit the area killing an estimated 23,000 people.

Guatemala is a mountainous country in Central American that is vulnerable to earthquakes and volcanoes. Prior to the devastating earthquake of 1976, one of Guatemala's most destructive earthquakes occurred in 1902 in which over 2,000 people were killed. The April 18, 1902, earthquake occurred right around the same time as a massive volcanic eruption on Mount Pelée.

On February 4, 1976, at approximately 2:58 A.M. a major earthquake struck Guatemala. The earthquake killed approximately 23,000 people and injured an additional 70,000 others. The earthquake left an estimated one million people homeless. The earthquake registered 7.5 on the Richter scale and caused over $1 billion worth of property damage. The Richter scale, developed by Charles Richter in 1927, is a measure of the amount of energy released by an earthquake. An earthquake that measures 7.0 on the Richter scale is considered by experts to be a "major" earthquake, capable of serious damage and loss of life. The earthquake lasted for approximately 30 seconds and, in that time, brought down thousands of office buildings, homes, and apartment buildings.

The epicenter of the earthquake was approximately 20 miles south of Lake Izabeal. The epicenter of an earthquake is the point on the earth's surface directly above the point where an earthquake occurs. The capital city of Guatemala,

Guatemala City, was among the hardest hit regions in the country. The earthquake caused massive damage to Guatemala City's infrastructure, destroying the transportation and communications systems as well cutting off electricity and water in many regions of the country.

One of the reasons that the loss of life was so severe during and after the 1976 earthquake was the time the earthquake struck. Unfortunately, the earthquake struck while the majority of people in Guatemala were asleep. Many of the people who died in the tragedy were crushed beneath their own roofs as they slept. A second reason that so many lives were lost during the 1976 earthquake is related to the way homes and apartment buildings were built in Guatemala. Many of the homes that were destroyed by the earthquake were adobe homes, made from clay and straw.

Adobe homes are far less expensive than concrete homes, however they are also far less safe. The material is softer and there is less support near the roofs of adobe homes which makes them more prone to completely collapse when shaken by a violent earthquake. When adobe homes collapse during an earthquake there is very little chance that anyone trapped inside can survive. The absence of support causes the roof to crash straight down in a manner that covers the entire are of the interior.

Guatemala has experienced several destructive earthquakes since the tragedy of 1976. In October 1987, Guatemala suffered an earthquake that damaged several homes and apartment buildings. In September 1991, Guatemala sustained an earthquake which caused approximately 25 deaths and destroyed over 80 percent of the homes in the town of San Miguel Pochuta. In January 2001, an earthquake that occurred near the Central American country of El Salvador, killing nearly 1,000 people, caused major damage to Guatemala.

In the aftermath of the 1976 earthquake, the Guatemalan government gathered supplies and sent officials immediately to the most severely damaged areas. Many of the residents of Guatemala offered assistance to the residents of poorer areas who had lost their homes. People immediately began buying supplies in regions that withstood the earthquake and transporting them to the severely damaged areas. The United States offered assistance to its Central American neighbor almost immediately after the tragedy occurred. In addition, the U.S. Congress allocated $25 million to Guatemala to help the country's fragile economy. ◆

Central Mexico Earthquake

1985

On September 19, 1985, central Mexico suffered a devastating earthquake, estimated at being as powerful as the San Francisco earthquake of 1906. The massive earthquake registered 8.1 on the Richter scale. The Mexican government reported that approximately 5,000 people were killed in the tragedy. However, many observers believe that the earthquake killed nearly 9,000 people and injured over 30,000 others. An estimated one million people were left homeless after the tragedy. Twenty million people felt the earthquake in some degree. A day and a half after the earthquake, Mexico experienced a second earthquake, an aftershock, which registered 7.5 on the Richter scale.

Scientists had been monitoring the plates beneath the earth's surface off of the Mexican coast for a year before the earthquake. Some irregularities had been detected and scientists were suspicious that an earthquake could occur. Scientists had discovered that the Cocos Plate, which usually slides peacefully beneath Mexico, had stopped moving. When this happened, the researchers were concerned that tension was building, which could unleash a powerful earthquake.

However, people also believed that if an earthquake did occur, it would not affect heavily populated Mexico City. Because the activity of the Cocos Plate was approximately 250 miles from Mexico City, experts felt it would not pose a significant threat. Unfortunately, they were wrong. Even though Mexico City was a considerable distance from the earthquake's epicenter (the actual place where the plates shifted beneath the earth's surface) the force

The 1985 earthquake in central Mexico toppled buildings in heavily populated Mexico City.

of the shifting plates was powerful enough to cause massive death and destruction to the city. The regions that were closer to the center of the earthquake suffered far less loss of life because fewer people lived there. The main Mexican states that were affected by the earthquake were Jalisco, Guerrero, and Michoacan.

On the morning of September 19, 1985, the people of central Mexico had no idea that plates beneath the earth's surface were about to shift along the Pacific coast of Mexico. The earthquake occurred on the western coast of Mexico, beneath the Pacific Ocean. Although the number of lives lost was devastating, it could have been much worse. The earthquake struck at 7:17 A.M. At this hour, many people had not yet arrived for work and children had not arrived at school. Many of the buildings that caved in during the earthquake would have been filled with people had the earthquake happened an hour or two later.

Although many of the buildings that were damaged were sparsely occupied, the highways leading into Mexico City were crowded with people. The earthquake, which lasted approximately three minutes, caused tremendous damage to the highways in and around Mexico City, putting the early morning commuters in harm's way.

The earthquake was so powerful that its vibrations were felt as far away as Texas and Guatemala. In Mexico City, an estimated 500 to 800 buildings were destroyed or badly damaged during the earthquake, and 6,500 other buildings were damaged. The taller buildings were most heavily damaged during the earthquake. The total property damage from the earthquake amounted to $4 billion. The earthquake also produced a small tsunami on the west coast. A tsunami refers is an abnormally large wave of water that hits land after there has been a disturbance in a large body of water.

Mexico had already experienced 42 earthquakes that measured at least 7.0 on the Richter scale throughout the twentieth century. However, when earthquakes hit, they are never fully expected and the death and destruction that follow are outside the realm of human control. Thus, as hard as structural engineers tried to design buildings in Mexico City that were earthquake resistant, nothing could prevent the tall buildings from falling over. Many experts believe that one of the reasons so many buildings were damaged or destroyed in Mexico City relates to the land upon which Mexico City was built. Mexico

Seismic Waves

Seismic waves are waves of energy generated by the shock of an earthquake or explosion, and they cause the earth to shake, ripple, and vibrate. The waves travel along or near the surface of the earth, and take several different forms, defined according to where they occur and the direction in which they move, relative to their source.

There are two distinct types of seismic wave that occur on the surface of the earth. The first is the *Rayleigh wave*, in which the earth moves elliptically, outward from the point at which the shock occurs. Another type of surface wave, in which the earth moves perpendicularly to the direction of the fault that causes the shock. Such waves are called *Love waves*.

Two other seismic waves occur in the earth's interior. When the ground shakes back and forth along the path of the actual shock–along the earthquake fault, in other words–these are what scientists call *P-waves* (the P stands for pressure). If, however, the motion occurs as a back-and-forth shaking that is perpendicular to the direction of the fault, scientists term the movement *Shear-waves*, abbreviated to *S-waves*.

Seismic waves are measured by a seismograph, which records the vibrations produced by an earthquake. The simplest seismographs use a pen attached to a heavy weight that was hung like a pendulum over a stationary piece of paper. As the earth's vibrations were transmitted through the pendulum housing, the pendulum swings, making larger swings as the vibrations increased in intensity, and the pen traces the pendulum's movement across the paper. Modern seismographs accomplish this same feat with digital technology, and today there is a network of seismographic stations, set up in caves and vaults throughout the world, that constantly monitor the earth's seismic activity in hopes that someday we will be able to predict the next big quakes in time to reduce their damage and save lives.

City lies on ground that was once a lake. The soft sediment causes more severe shock waves when earthquakes hit, making it more difficult for large buildings to hold up.

One survivor had been buried beneath rubble for six days and seven nights before being rescued. She had been running toward a staircase to exit the building when it began to collapse. When she was finally pulled out of the wreckage, the rescue team was forced to amputate her leg in order to save her. Miraculously, a four-day-old infant who had been trapped in the collapsed hospital for nine days and eight nights was rescued.

The United States offered assistance to Mexico's recovery effort in a variety of ways. Several organizations immediately began raising funds. Several fundraising drives were put together in Texas, where the Hispanic population is high. In

Dallas, Texas, news flashes were broadcast frequently over the radio in Spanish to update those who were concerned about friends and relatives in Mexico.

Among the many groups that worked to provide immediate assistance to Mexico was the American Friends Service Committee (AFSC), an organization founded on the principles of the **Quaker** faith. According to newspaper reports at the time, AFSC decided that the most important form of assistance that the Mexican people required was cash to buy needed supplies. The reasoning behind this was that the Mexican economy had been struggling at the time and monetary assistance would be more beneficial than supplies because Mexico already had the resources to provide people with earthquake recovery supplies.

In response to the devastating loss of life and property damage caused by the Mexico earthquake of 1985 and an earthquake that hit San Diego, California, in July 1986, the United States and Mexico worked out a formal plan to combine their earthquake recovery efforts. The United States and Mexico put together a formal agreements in 1987 designed to assist one another in the recovery from future earthquakes. The agreements involved both nations expressing a commitment to help deal with earthquake recovery issues such as search and rescue help, medical assistance, and putting out fires. ◆

Armenia Earthquake

December 7, 1988

On December 7, 1988, Armenia was struck by a severe earthquake. The Armenian earthquake was the fourth strong earthquake to hit Asia in 1988 and was, by far, the most devastating. An estimated 25,000 people died in the earthquake and over 500,000 people were left homeless.

Armenia spent the majority of its history under the influence of a foreign government. Throughout much of the nineteenth and twentieth centuries Armenia was under Russian and Turkish control. It was not until 1991 that the small republic, located south of the Caucus Mountains in Asia, gained its independence.

Earthquake survivors in Armenia huddle around fires for warmth in 1988.

The population of Armenia at the time of the earthquake was approximately 3.3 million. When the earthquake struck there was no warning that a devastating tragedy was about to occur.

On December 7, 1988, at approximately 11:41 A.M., the earthquake struck near the border of Armenia and Turkey. The earthquake lasted for approximately 30 seconds and measured 6.9 on the Richter scale. (The Richter scale, developed by Charles Richter in 1927, is a measure of the amount of energy released by an earthquake.) An earthquake that measures 7.0 on the Richter scale is considered by experts to be a "major" earthquake, capable of serious damage and loss of life. The earthquake was not as powerful as other deadly earthquake that have occurred throughout history, however, it caused a series of landslides that resulted in massive property damage and loss of life. Four minutes after the main earthquake, an aftershock hit the area, causing many already badly damaged buildings to collapse entirely.

The three cities that were hardest hit by the earthquake were Spitak, Leninakan, and Kirovakan. Over one thousand buildings were destroyed in these cities. Nearly the entire town of Spitak was buried by the earthquake, killing about 16,000 residents. The city of Leninakan was also severely affected by the earthquake. Leninakan, a large industrial city in Armenia, lost the majority of its buildings to the earthquake. An image of a clock from a collapsed building in Leninakan poignantly showed the time 11:41, the exact time the earthquake struck. Thousands of Armenians who survived the earthquake slept outside in freezing conditions out of fear that aftershocks would cause further destruction. The city of Kirovakan was also severely affected by the earthquake. The time of the earthquake was particularly unfortunate for the people of Armenia. Many children were in school and office buildings were packed when the earthquake struck, instantly killing thousands of people in buildings that collapsed.

The scene after the earthquake was one of mass chaos. Thousands of people ran through the streets in an effort to escape the wreckage. People were rummaging through the rubble of fallen buildings in an effort to rescue trapped survivors. Hundreds of people gathered around fires caused by the earthquake in an effort to fight off the cold air. According to newspaper reports at the time, initial estimates were that between 50,000 and 100,000 people were killed during the earthquake. The earthquake affected an area of around 150 square miles. Hundreds of thousands of people were left without a home, leaving them defenseless against the cold winter climate. The northeastern border of Turkey was also affected by the earthquake. According to Turkish officials five people were killed and an estimated 400 homes were destroyed or damaged by the earthquake.

The Soviet Union responded immediately to the disaster sending medical supplies, surgeons, food, tents, blankets and other supplies to Armenia as soon as they learned of the disaster. The Soviet Union also set up a helicopter relief system to transport the injured from Armenia to nearby hospitals. At the time of the earthquake, Soviet President Mikhail Gorbachev had been visiting the United States. As soon as Gorbachev learned of the tragedy, he immediately made plans to return to the Soviet Union to lead the rescue effort.

Engineering played a major role in making the death toll so extreme. The Soviet Union used the same building practices throughout all of its republics, few changes or adjustments were made to fortify structures in earthquake-prone regions. When the earthquake and ensuing landslides struck regions of Armenia, many of buildings instantly collapsed.

At the time of the earthquake Armenia was still a part of the Soviet Union. In 1988 the **Cold War** was winding down, but relations between the United States and the Soviet Union were still tense. The Cold War was a period of tense relations between the United States and Soviet Union which lasted approximately from the end of World War II to 1991, when the Soviet Union collapsed. The Soviet Union had historically exercised strict control over the amount of information it shared with foreign countries. Out of a fear of appearing weak in the eyes of the international community, the Soviet Union often held back details regarding negative events. However, Gorbachev had been encouraging a policy of openness (called "Glasnost") at the time. Gorbachev therefore allowed much more exposure of the tragedy in Armenia than had previously been permitted.

The unfortunate tragedy in Armenia had a positive impact on relations between the United States and the Soviet Union. President Ronald Reagan and President-elect George H. W. Bush both called Gorbachev after the earthquake to offer their condolences as well as to volunteer assistance with the relief effort. The United States immediately sent member of the Disaster Dog Search and Rescue Team to Armenia to help the Soviet Union search for survivors. The U.S. Agency for International Development (USAID) led the effort to assist the Soviet Union with the Armenian earthquake disaster. ◆

Cold War period of history lasting from the end of World War II to approximately 1991 that the United States and Soviet Union were engaged in mutual suspicion and ideological differences that fell just short of military action and was without strong diplomatic relations.

Northern Iran Earthquake

JUNE 21, 1990

On June 21, 1990, Iran experienced the most deadly earthquake since 1976, when an earthquake in China killed approximately 240,000 people. Over 40,000 people were killed as a result of the earthquake in Iran, and approximately 100,000 others were injured.

Earthquakes occur on a regular basis in Iran, which is one of the most seismically active regions in the world. The area that was struck by the 1990 earthquake, Gilan, sits where two plates meet beneath the earth's crust. Prior to the 1990 earthquake,

A survivor of the 1990 earthquake in Iran sits despondently by what used to be her home.

Iran had experienced twelve earthquakes that measured 7.0 or greater on the Richter scale. An earthquake that measures 7.0 on the Richter scale is considered by experts to be a "major" earthquake, capable of serious damage and loss of life.

In September 1978, Iran experienced a devastating earthquake that killed an estimated 25,000 people. Some experts believe that the 1978 earthquake, which occurred in Tabas, was caused by nuclear testing that was being conducted in Siberia by the Soviet Union. Although experts could find no direct link between the nuclear testing and the Iranian earthquake, they were disturbed by coincidences between the two events. The earthquake occurred merely hours after the nuclear testing and the depth of the earthquake was unusually shallow, similar to the depth of the nuclear testing.

On June 21, 1990, at approximately 12:30 A.M., a massive earthquake struck northern Iran. The earthquake measured 7.7 on the Richter scale. (The Richter scale, developed by Charles Richter in 1927, is a measure of the amount of energy released by an earthquake.) The northern provinces of Gilan and Zanjan in Iran were the most severely damaged regions by the earthquake. Over 25,000 people were killed in Gilan. There were approximately 140 aftershocks following the earthquake which caused further death and destruction to the region.

An extraordinary number of people lost their lives in northern Iran in large part because the earthquake occurred in the middle of the night and most people were asleep. Thousands of people lost their lives when their homes collapsed on top of them; many of these homes were poorly built.

The scene after the earthquake was one of chaos and despair. Thousands of people were buried beneath the rubble of destroyed buildings. In Cyprus, an entire street of houses slid from its foundation. Approximately a half a million people were left homeless after the earthquake. Masked rescuers pulled body after body from the concrete and placed them on giant slabs of ice.

Because of their extensive experience in dealing with destructive earthquakes, Iran was well prepared to deal with the aftermath. The Iranian Red Crescent Society (IRCS), an organization similar to America's Red Cross, began helping earthquake victims immediately after the tragic event. The Red Crescent is so experienced in dealing with earthquake disasters that they informed the international community that they did not need any personnel sent the area to help. Iran also had 3,000 trained rescuers who were sent to northern Iran to search for survivors. Shortly after the earthquake Iran airlifted approximately 6,000 people from the northern provinces of Gilan and Zanjan.

Several nations of the international community contributed to the relief effort after the earthquake. The United Nations immediately sent supplies to the area. The European Union sent $2.4 million to Iran. The Canadian government donated $300,000 to Iran through its International Development Agency. France sent in a team of rescuers and search dogs as well as several tons of relief supplies. Some nations that contributed to the relief effort had historically poor relations with Iran. Among those countries were the United States, Great Britain, Iraq, and Israel. The U.S. Office of Disaster assistance pledged $225,000 in much needed supplies through the American Red Cross. Some analysts regarded this donation as unusually generous because, at the time, the United States believed that Iran may have been partly responsible for American hostages being held in Lebanon. Iran accepted donations from the United

Thousands of people lost their lives when their homes collapsed on top of them; many of these homes were poorly built.

States, which surprised some observers; Iran had refused U.S. assistance during previous disasters.

Political observers also believed it unusual that the British Government offered assistance. The relationship between Iran and Britain had been severed in 1989 when Iran's Ayatollah Ruhollah Khomeini ordered Muslims to kill British author Salman Rushdie. Rushdie wrote a book called *The Satanic Verses* that many Iranians considered insulting to their religion. Iraq, which had been at war with Iran for much of the 1980s, also offered sympathetic words and monetary support. Israel offered kind words and relief assistance to its historic enemy, however, Iran refused to accept any donations from Israel because of the historic political and religious tension between Jews and Muslims.

In October 1990, the World Bank decided to loan Iran between $200 and $300 million to help fund the reconstruction effort after the earthquake. The total amount of funds Iran needed for reconstruction was estimated to be $600 million. This marked the first time the World Bank agreed to loan Iran money since the 1970s. The World Bank had previously refused to participate in financial transactions with Iran because of the political policies advanced by Iran's former leader, Shah Reza Pahlavi.

After the earthquake, speculation among political analysts was that relations between the United States and Iran would improve out of necessity. The United States has had an uneasy relationship with Iran in the past. In the 1950s the United States supported the rise to power of Shah Mohammed Reza Pahlavi. However, the Shah's regime became increasingly repressive toward its citizens. As a result the Shah was replaced by **Ayatollah** Ruollah Khomeini in 1979. Under Khomeini's rule 66 American diplomats were taken hostage from November 4, 1979 to January 20, 1981. Relations between the United States and Iran never fully recovered from this event.

In 1990 Iran's president, Hashemi Rafsanjani, and religious leader Ayatollah Ali Khamenei agreed to accept monetary aid from the United States. Both leaders were criticized by some Iranian groups who did not want any assistance from an historic enemy. Some observers believe that the United States was attempting to persuade Iran to help free American hostages that were being held in Lebanon at the time. However, the United States made it clear that the donations it made to the earthquake recovery effort was not politically motivated. The United States donated the funds with "no strings attached." ◆

Kobe Earthquake

On January 17, 1995, the most powerful earthquake to ever strike an industrialized city hit Kobe, Japan. The earthquake registered 7.2 on the Richter scale. (The Richter scale, developed by Charles Richter in 1927, is a measure of the amount of energy released by an earthquake.) An earthquake that measures 7.0 on the Richter scale is considered by experts to be a "major" earthquake, capable of serious damage and loss of life. The Kobe earthquake of 1995 claimed over 6,300 lives, however, it is better known for the amount of economic destruction it caused. Japanese officials estimated that the total cost of rebuilding the city would amount to nearly $150 billion.

Japan lies within one of the most earthquake and volcano-prone regions in the world. Two major plates meet beneath Japan which causes an unusually high degree of seismic activity. (Seismology is the scientific study of earthquakes, specifically the amount of energy released by earthquakes.) The meeting of the Pacific and Asian plates has caused several major earthquakes throughout Japan's history. The most destructive earthquake prior to the 1995 Kobe earthquake, occurred in 1923 during which an estimated 142,800 people were killed. The Japanese not only have to contend with earthquakes and volcanoes, but tsunamis as well. A tsunami refers to a larger than normal wave of water that hits land after there has been a disturbance in a large body of water. The most devastating tsunami in Japan's history occurred in 1896 when it is reported that a 100 foot high wave crashed against the Japanese coast in Sanriku killing thousands of people.

Although earthquakes occur regularly in Japan, researchers did

A section of an overpass in Kobe, Japan shows the force of the 1995 earthquake.

not believe that Kobe was in great danger of an earthquake at the time of the disaster. Kobe rarely experienced even minor tremors, unlike other areas of Japan. Therefore, the amount of resources that Japanese officials dedicated to earthquake recovery and educating the public in Kobe was comparatively small. In 1995, the population of Kobe, Japan, was 1.5 million and the population of Osaka, Japan, the second largest industrial area of Japan, was 10 million.

Coincidentally, on the day that the earthquake occurred scientists and public officials had scheduled a conference designed to better educate the public and prepare Kobe for an earthquake. Not only was the earthquake unexpected, it occurred before dawn, a time when nearly the entire population were asleep. An estimated 6,300 people were killed during the earthquake and an additional 43,000 people were injured.

On January 17, 1995, at 5:46 A.M. a major earthquake struck near the city of Kobe, Japan. The earthquake lasted around 20 seconds. In that short period, an estimated 100,000 buildings collapsed or were destroyed and nearly 200,000 buildings were damaged. The earthquake left an estimated 300,000 people homeless during one of the coldest times of the year in Japan. One of the reasons that the amount of property damage was so severe in Kobe is the fact that the city is built on relatively soft land. The earthquake caused areas of the city to sink inward, which caused buildings to collapse. The roadways and railways leading in and out of the city were also badly damaged which made it more difficult for search and rescue teams as well as much needed supplies to get to the area.

In addition to the destruction of the transportation system the earthquake also severely damaged Japan's communication lines, electricity, gas, water, and sewer systems in and around Kobe. Adding to the city's misery, 20 seconds after the city had been shaken to a state ruin, a series of approximately 200 fires broke out. The majority of the fires occurred in the historical district of Kobe, where many of the homes were made of wood. Because of the amount of destruction to the city's infrastructure, fire fighters faced the problem of finding the fires, getting to the fires, and finding working water lines to fight the fires. As a result, many of the fires burned for two straight days, which resulted in the death of hundreds of people who were trapped in the rubble.

The majority of buildings that were destroyed during the Kobe earthquake of 1995 had been built long before the exis-

How to Survive an Earthquake

Scientists are not yet able to predict earthquakes–what can you do if the ground suddenly starts shaking? In the words of the Red Cross: "Drop, Cover, and Hold On!"

If you are caught in an earthquake, your first thought should be to get into a safe place: someplace where nothing can fall on you. Good choices when you are indoors would be under a desk or table, or in an interior doorway, where the support of the wall will shield you from falling chunks of ceiling. Cover your head, and hang on until the shaking stops. If you are in bed, stay there and protect your head with your pillow.

If you are stuck outdoors when a quake begins, the same principle applies. You want to stay away from things that can fall on you: buildings, trees, or utility poles. Drop to the ground, cover your head, and wait until the tremor subsides. If you are in your car, pull over to a clear space and stop. If you are in a tunnel or other area that is likely to collapse and unable to get to the exit in time, pull over to a supporting wall–it might shield you from the worst of the falling rubble.

If you live in a quake-prone area, advance preparation is a wise idea. In your home, bolt tall furniture to the walls to avoid them toppling during a quake. Make sure you know how to turn off the gas and electricity, so you can reduce the chance of fires. Make sure you have a fully charged fire extinguisher on hand, as well as flashlights and extra batteries.

Finally, remember that after the rumbling stops, you are still likely to experience aftershocks. These can occur hours and even days after the initial tremors. When they hit, remember: Drop, Cover, and Hold On!

tence of strict Japanese building codes were established. Many of the people who died in the earthquake lived in homes that were incapable of withstanding earthquakes. The homes that caused the most loss of life in Kobe were built with heavy roofs with very little support to keep roofs from caving in. After the earthquake Japanese engineers used different practices to rebuild homes, including constructing homes with lighter roofs and a greater amount of support to minimize the risk of injury if roofs cave in as a result of future earthquakes.

In the aftermath of the earthquake the city of Kobe, Japan, looked like it had just been through a devastating war. Thousands of buildings had completely collapsed or were severely damaged, sections of Kobe's highways were jutting up, twisted, or sunken in, and fires had broke out in several areas. The Japanese and American Red Cross organizations immediately contributed to the relief effort and raised over $300 million for Japanese victims. Japan received contributions to the recovery effort from around the globe. Several corporations also donated to the relief effort. Mitsubishi Motors, for example, donated over $1 million.

The Japanese government set up an emergency fund of approximately $10 billion, immediately after the earthquake to deal with the disaster. The government also arranged to have grants and loan money available for earthquake victims. Perhaps the most damaging aspect of the earthquake for Japan was the disruption of economic activity in the Osaka area, which amounted to approximately 20 percent of Japan's economic production. With the slowdown or complete shut down of several manufacturing businesses in Japan came massive unemployment. The economy in Kobe came to a complete halt which not only affected the immediate area, but also had an impact on the international economy. Japanese officials estimated that it would take years for the local economy in Osaka to recover from the earthquake.

Many of the people who lost their homes as a result of the earthquake were placed in temporary housing. The housing project helped many people get back on their feet after the earthquake, however, over 150 people died while living in the temporary housing units. Some people died because of disease, while others committed suicide after losing family members and friends to the earthquake. ◆

Turkey Earthquake

AUGUST 17, 1999

In the summer of 1999, a devastating earthquake struck western Turkey causing massive death and property damage. According to Turkish government reports, an estimated 17,000 people were killed by the earthquake and over 44,000 people were injured. An additional 250,000 people lost their homes as a result of the earthquake. The total amount of property damage caused by the earthquake was estimated to be $6.5 billion.

On August 17, 1999, western Turkey was hit by the earthquake. The earthquake measured 7.4 on the Richter scale and lasted approximately 45 seconds. The Richter scale, developed by Charles Richter in 1927, is a measure of the amount of energy released by an earthquake. An earthquake that measures

7.0 on the Richter scale is considered by experts to be a "major" earthquake, capable of serious damage and loss of life. The epicenter of the earthquake, or point on the earth's surface beneath which the earthquake occurred, was approximately seven miles southeast of the city of Izmit. Izmit is an industrial city located about 50 miles east of the historic city of Istanbul. The earthquake occurred along the North Anatolian fault line which has been the cause of several major earthquakes in Turkey's history.

The earthquake caused a massive fire at an oil refinery in Turkey. The fire, which was caused by explosions that were set off from the earthquake, lasted for several days. The fire at the Tüpras refinery in the city of Korfez caused more economic damage than loss of life. The refinery was surrounded by concrete structures which prevented the fire from spreading out of control. Tüpras refinery accounted for about one-third of Turkey's oil production.

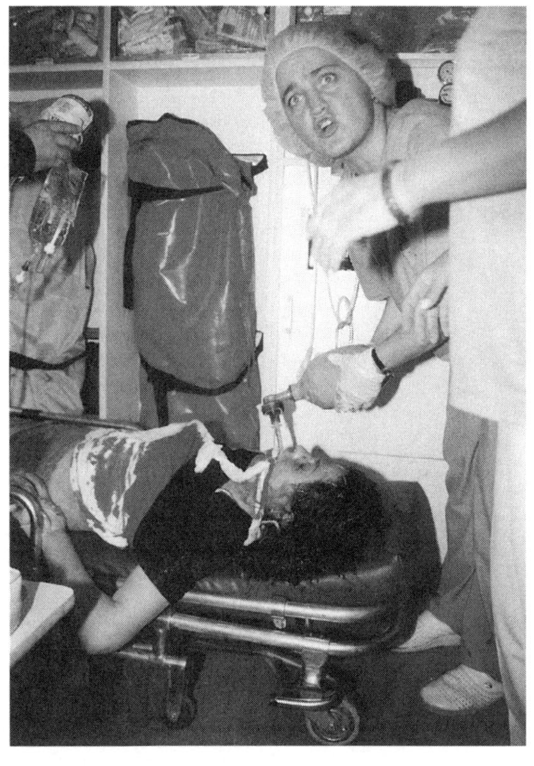
An emergency medical team tends to a victim of the 1999 earthquake in Izmit, Turkey.

Thousands of buildings collapsed during the earthquake. Many of the buildings that gave out due to the force of the earthquake were five stories high or larger. The buildings that collapsed were thought to be earthquake resistant. One reason that the destruction to buildings in Turkey was so severe is because the fault line ran through industrialized cities. However, experts who reviewed the buildings after the earthquake believe that the buildings were not structurally sound. In addition, many of the buildings were built along known fault lines which, researchers believe, should have been avoided. Researchers also found that many of the buildings that completely collapsed were built recently.

The Turkish Red Crescent, an organization similar to the Red Cross, led the relief effort in Turkey providing tents, blankets, bedding, and meals. The Red Cross contributed to the relief effort by providing approximately $150 million in supplies such as food, shelter, water sanitation, and medical assistance.

One year after the earthquake thousands of Turkish people were still forced to live in tents.

Organizations, governments, and volunteers did their best to treat earthquake victims after the earthquake, however, many Turkish residents were critical of the effort put forth by their government. One year after the earthquake thousands of Turkish people were still forced to live in tents. Many residents also complained that the homes destroyed during the earthquake were poorly built resulting in unnecessary deaths.

Turkey suffered a second major earthquake in 1999, three months after the earthquake that devastated Izmit. In November an earthquake that measured 7.2 on the Richter scale struck near Duzce killing an estimated 845 people and injuring over 5,000 others. In November 1999, the World Bank announced that it would be loaning over $750 million to Turkey to help it rebuild from the 1999 earthquakes. According to researchers a major earthquake could strike Istanbul in the near future. Experts believed that it would take years for Turkey to recovery from the economic damage caused by the earthquake.

Earthquake experts have found that the conditions along Turkey's western coast, located above the North Anatolian fault line are very similar to the conditions in San Francisco, California, which lies above the San Andreas fault. Both areas contain buildings that run along the fault lines and both countries have strict building codes for construction in the area. According to experts, one of the most important differences between the regions is that in California, the strict building codes are more rigidly enforced. This makes buildings more likely to withstand major earthquakes. Experts who studied the damage caused to Izmit, Turkey have a better understanding how a major earthquake could impact the infrastructure of San Francisco. ◆

Taiwan Earthquake

SEPTEMBER 21, 1999

On September 21, 1999, the island of Taiwan, off the coast of mainland China, experienced a major earthquake. The 1999 earthquake was one of very few major earthquakes that occurred throughout Taiwan's history. The earthquake which occurred near the city of Taichung and shook the nation's capital of Taipai, measured 7.6 on the Richter scale. (The Richter scale, developed by Charles Richter in 1927, is a measure of the amount of energy released by an earthquake.) An earthquake that measures 7.0 on the Richter scale is considered by experts to be a "major" earthquake, capable of serious damage and loss of life.

On Monday afternoon at approximately 1:47 P.M., on September 21, 1999, a massive earthquake hit central Taiwan. The amount of property damaged caused by the earthquake came to an estimated $9.2 billion. About 82,000 housing units were badly damaged or destroyed by the earthquake. An estimated 2,400 people were killed during the earthquake and nearly 10,000 others were injured. The epicenter of the earthquake, the point on the earth's surface where the earthquake occurred, was near the county of Nantou in central Taiwan. The city that was hardest hit by the earthquake was Taichung.

According to earthquake researchers, Taiwan's 7.6 magnitude earthquake was unusual. According to experts, earthquakes usually occur hundreds of miles beneath the earth's surface. Taiwan's earthquake occurred a little over one mile below the surface. In addition, according to experts, the earthquake happened in an area where researchers believed one was unlikely to occur.

The earthquake destroyed over 10,000 apartment buildings which caused an estimated 100,000 people to become homeless after the earthquake. Some residents of Taiwan believed that the buildings they lived in that collapsed during the earthquake had been poorly built. A year after the earthquake, many residents of Taiwan began taking legal action. People in Taiwan believed that construction workers had deliberately taken money-saving shortcuts when they built the homes and apartment buildings in central Taiwan and violated governmental building codes.

Although it seemed clear that construction workers had violated safety codes, the government had yet to convict anyone as of 2000. Some observers believe that the reason that the construction companies were not prosecuted is because they could not be found. It is a common practice for construction companies to dissolve immediately after they complete a project in order to avoid legal action and taxes.

A volunteer organization by the name of Tzu Chi immediately began providing assistance to the earthquake victims. The woman who founded the organization, Master Cheng Yen, a

The amount of property damaged caused by the earthquake came to an estimated $9.2 billion.

Buddhist nun, had built a charitable reputation through her heroic volunteer work in Taiwan. Thousands of Tzu Chi volunteers arrived in the destroyed communities even before the government. Taiwan was also helped by the international community in the aftermath. Twenty nations offered assistance to Taiwan immediately after the earthquake including the United States, Japan, France, Russia, Singapore, and China.

During the recovery effort, China was particularly generous to Taiwan. Taiwan and China have historically had a stormy relationship. In 1949, Taiwan was taken over by Chang Kai-shek, the former leader of China who had been ousted when Mao Zedong came to power. Under the leadership of Lee Teng-hui Taiwan has been moving away from Chinese rule, toward democracy and capitalism. China considers Taiwan to be a province of China that broke away from its rule but is still, technically, the property of China. Taiwan, however, resists Chinese intervention into its political affairs.

Some political analysts suspect that China's President, Jiang Zemin, was politically motivated in offering generous amounts of assistance to Taiwan during its time of need. China's Red Cross offered Taiwan over $150,000 in cash and supplies after the earthquake and Zemin told the Taiwan government that China was willing to assist in any way the could. Prior to the earthquake political relations between China and Taiwan had been faltering. Taiwan President, Lee Teng-hui had taken steps toward securing formal independence from China. In response, China sent warships and conducted military exercises near Taiwan in an effort to persuade Taiwan to think otherwise about independence. China has made public statements in recent years that it would use force to prevent Taiwan from trying to formally break from China.

After the Taiwan earthquake, officials in Taiwan admitted that the rescue efforts could have been better organized. Officials in charge of the recovery efforts were criticized for not having a centralized management team to oversee the search and rescue efforts. They were also criticized for not having experts such as translators and engineers as well as the necessary equipment on hand to assist with the relief effort. According to some observers, the government of Taiwan wasted the entire first day of the recovery effort because they were poorly organized. Taiwan officials claimed that one of the reasons that their relief efforts were poor was the fact that major earthquakes rarely occur in Taiwan. Taiwan therefore had little experience in dealing with major natural disasters.

The economic losses due to the earthquake were hard on Taiwan. Not only did Taiwan have to face the challenging prospect of rebuilding areas that were affected by the earthquake, the country also lost money because of the products and services that were shut down after the earthquake. Taiwan, one of world's largest producers of computer products, provides numerous electronic items that service large U.S. companies such as Compaq, Hewlett Packard, and Dell. The earthquake caused several semiconductor manufacturing companies to cease production. In addition, Taiwan companies had to deal with power outages after the earthquake that also hampered production. Taiwan estimated that hundreds of millions of dollars would be lost in microchip production as a result of the earthquake. ◆

India Earthquake

JANUARY 26, 2001

January 26 is Republic Day in India, a national holiday on which the nation celebrates its independence from Great Britain and honors its constitution. That morning in 2001, many people settled down in front of their television sets with a cup of tea to watch the nation's annual military parade.

At the same time, in the western Indian town of Anjar near the border with Pakistan, about 400 children who normally would have been in school were walking in a procession through the narrow streets of the town, singing patriotic songs. Suddenly, at 8:46 the ground started to shake violently. The houses and high-rise buildings on either side of the street began collapsing like cardboard boxes. The ruins of the buildings rained down on the children, and 45 seconds later the street was nothing but a pile of smoking rubble. None of the children buried beneath the rubble survived.

In less than a minute, western India, primarily the western Indian state of Gujarat, had suffered one of the most devastating earthquakes in the nation's history. The epicenter of the quake, which measured 7.9 on the Richter scale–classifying it as a "major" earthquake–was about 12 miles north of the coastal

The Asian subcontinent is prone to large earthquakes, for India is the site of the most massive collision of continents on earth.

town of Bhuj, though tremors could be felt as far away as Bangladesh and Nepal in the north and Madras in the south. The quake was the worst to hit India in over half a century, and the last time an earthquake of such intensity hit Gujarat was in 1819. Bhuj, with a population of about 150,000, was the hardest hit. Nearly every building in the town was either destroyed or badly damaged. Power and telephone lines were taken out, and relief efforts were hampered because roads, bridges, and rail lines were destroyed. To help the injured, military transport planes carried doctors and medical supplies into the area. Because the town's only hospital was badly damaged, doctors had to operate in tents on a military airbase. Many of the wounded were carried in handcarts to the airbase by friends, neighbors, or relatives.

As officials surveyed the wreckage in the hours immediately following the disaster, they feared that the death toll would reach as high as 2,000. It turned out, though, that 2,000 was a serious underestimation. As the days passed, the death toll was repeatedly revised higher and higher. In all, about 15,000 people were killed in the quake, though officials feared that the number could continue to rise as victims were dug out of the rubble–a process that could take months. In addition to the dead, over 61,000 people were injured and some 600,000 were left without homes. In the meantime, as 200 aftershocks shook the region, thousands more slept outside in tents and on mattresses lining the streets, afraid to go into their homes. Officials estimated that the cost of rebuilding could reach $5.5 billion.

Two major factors contributed to the devastation. The first was geography. The Asian subcontinent is prone to large earthquakes, for India is the site of the most massive collision of continents on earth. About 60 million years ago, the Eurasian and Indo-Australian tectonic plates came together along what is now India's northern border. Neither plate yielded to the other, and the intense pressure that resulted formed the Himalayas. The impact between the two plates continues, and satellite photos show that the Himalayas are still rising. West Gujarat is particularly vulnerable, for it lies near the so-called Allah Bund, or Wall of God, fault, along which a major earthquake was recorded in 1956. All of India, however, has suffered large earthquakes in recent years. In 1999 a 6.8 earthquake hit Utter Pradesh, killing 110; in 1998 a 6.6 quake hit Bihar, killing nearly 1,500; in 1993 a major quake struck the state of Maharashta, killing 10,000; in 1991, 2,000 were killed when a 7.0 quake hit northern India.

The other factor contributing to the devastation was poor enforcement of Indian building codes. Multi-story buildings in the region are supposed to be built to withstand major earthquakes, but many builders and contractors simply ignore the codes. In the major industrial town of Ahmadabad, with a population of over 4 million, some buildings were entirely flattened, while others **adjacent** to them that were built to code were not even cracked.

adjacent immediately next to.

Amid such devastation, numbers tell only part of the story. The real story in any natural disaster is the suffering and heroism of individual people and communities. One of the most compelling of such stories concerned the Swami Narayan School in Ahmadabad. Thirty-nine students were studying in the building when the quake hit. The building, which was hastily constructed, had opened just four months before and was now nothing more than a pile of ruins. Guided by the cries of those buried in the rubble, workers struggled desperately to find survivors; some used sledgehammers, while others clawed at the ruins with bloody hands. News photos showed a slender arm, draped in a violet scarf, protruding from a pile of rubble. Four survivors were found, but at least 24 victims remained buried, beyond the reach of rescuers.

The international community was quick to offer help to India. Turkey and Taiwan, which each suffered a massive earthquake in 1999, sent rescue teams with dogs and equipment. At least 20 countries, including the United States, as well as the International Red Cross and World Relief, sent food, blankets, and emergency supplies. Even hostile Pakistan, which has fought three wars with India since 1947, sent relief planes with blankets, tents, and food. Said the Pakistani foreign minister, "The desperate situation transcends political differences." ◆

Volcano Eruptions

Thira Eruption

1500 B.C.

The eruption of Thira (historically spelled Thera) which occurred around 1500 B.C. is one of the most historic volcanic eruptions to ever occur. The massive explosion that came from Thira almost completely destroyed the island, and all who lived on it.

The Thira eruption is believed to have wiped out the Minoan civilization. Thira was located on an island between Greece and Turkey in the Mediterranean Sea. Before the catastrophic eruption of Thira, the Minoan Civilization thrived on the island of Crete. The Minoan Civilization was one of few civilizations that flourished during the Bronze Age near the Aegean Sea. The Bronze Age was a period in history following the Stone Age, in which man began using metals. The Bronze Age lasted from approximately 6500 B.C. to 1000 B.C. and was followed by the Iron Age.

The area in which the Minoan Civilization existed, and where Thira erupted, was previously called Santorini. Santorini is the largest active **caldera** in the world. A caldera is a massive crater in the sea which is usually circular and created by the explosion of a volcano's peak. Several eruptions have occurred in Santorini since the destructive eruption of 1500 B.C. In 1649 the residents of Santorini were forced to evacuate after an eruption. In 1650 an earthquake as well as a volcanic eruption occurred. Eruptions also occurred in 1866, 1925, and 1939, each of which produced lava flows.

The Minoan Civilization, which lasted from approximately 3000 B.C. to 1100 B.C., was the most advanced of its time. The

caldera a crater with a diameter much larger than that of the volcanic vent formed by the collapse of the central part of the volcano.

153

civilization was named for King Minos, who was a Greek king of Crete and son of Zeus according to Greek mythology. According to some historians, after the eruption of Thira in 1500 B.C. the Minoan Civilization was almost completely destroyed. The society went into steep decline and never recovered from the tragic eruption.

According to Greek legend the eruption of Thira created the fictional continent of Atlantis beneath the sea; the continent was destroyed in one day and sunk beneath the water. Plato wrote about Atlantis and described it as located just beyond the Pillars of Hercules. The Atlantic Ocean was named for the fictional underwater continent of Atlantis and many have been fascinated by Atlantis and several researchers have actually made expeditions in search of the lost continent.

Many scholars believe that the Thira eruption was several times more powerful than that of Krakatoa, which was one of the most powerful eruptions in history. Researchers often compare the eruption of Thira to that of Krakatoa because of their similarities including the massive tsunamis that each eruption caused.

Historians believe the massive eruption of Thira created enormous tsunamis throughout the eastern part of the Mediterranean Sea. A tsunami refers to a larger than normal wave of water that hits land after there has been a disturbance in a large body of water. The tsunamis created by the Thira eruption of 1500 B.C. flooded many of the shores of Crete and are believed to have contributed to the demise of the Minoan Civilization. ◆

Vesuvius Eruption

79 C.E.

I n the year 79 A.D., a massive volcanic eruption in southern Italy destroyed the cities of Pompeii and Herculaneum. Mount Vesuvius is perhaps the most famous volcanic eruption in world history. An estimated 16,000 people are believed to have died in the tragedy.

Mount Vesuvius is the only active volcano in Europe. It is located in southern Italy near the city of Naples. Three major Roman cities were destroyed in the eruption of 79 A.D.: Hercu-

With Mt. Vesuvius in the background, the ruins of Pompeii remain as a large tourist attraction.

laneum, Pompeii, and Stabiae. In 1709 researchers discovered the ancient Roman city of Herculaneum. In 1748 researchers discovered the historic city of Pompeii, which had been completely buried by the volcanic eruption. The discovery of the cities was a major finding for historians and archaeologists, because it allowed them the opportunity to learn vast amounts about Roman culture and society. The volcanic ash from the eruption preserved much of what existed of the ancient Roman cities. Although scientists continue to unearth the ancient cities, their findings have provided enormous amounts of historical information about the Roman Empire such as the way homes and buildings were constructed, the type of art people enjoyed, and the way people went about their daily lives.

The city of Pompeii was situated about one mile away from Mount Vesuvius. At the time of the eruption Pompeii was one of the more advanced cities of Rome. The streets were paved and many of the homes were two stories high, which was an indication of the wealth the city produced. The people of Pompeii had little fear of Mount Vesuvius because it had shown no signs

For about three days, the volcano launched out rocks and spewed lava.

of eruption for several hundred years. In 62 A.D. Pompeii suffered a major earthquake that destroyed many of the buildings in the thriving city. But the people of Pompeii rebuilt the city shortly afterward and the city resumed its rapid development.

On August 24, 79 A.D. a major volcanic eruption occurred at Mount Vesuvius. The volcano sent giant pieces of rock on the cities Herculaneum and Pompeii. Shortly after the eruption the area surrounding Mount Vesuvius became black from all of the ash that came pouring out of the volcano. Thousands of people managed to flee from the eruption, however, an estimated 16,000 people lost their lives. Many of the people who died after the eruption are believed to have been killed by the massive outpouring of poisonous gases from the volcano. For about three days, the volcano launched out rocks and spewed lava. After the third day of erupting, the city of Pompeii was completed buried in ash, lava, and rock from the volcano.

Scientists who studied the remains of people from Herculaneum after the excavation of the city came to new conclusions. Before the remains were discovered, it was believed that the people who lived near the volcano died from suffocation before their bodies were burned by the material emitted from the eruption. Scientists now believe that many of the people were burned to death instantly. After studying the bodies, some researchers concluded that the heat from the volcanic ash was approximately 750 degrees Fahrenheit. The ash and vaporous gas that poured down on the people of Herculaneum as well as Pompeii, scientists believe, would have killed people in a matter of seconds.

After the disaster of 79 A.D., Mount Vesuvius again erupted in 1036, 1049, and 1139. The eruption of 1036 caused lava to pour out of the mountain, but no deaths were reported. Mount Vesuvius began erupting again around 1500, and in 1631 a major volcanic eruption caused severe damage and loss of life in surrounding cities. Several small towns were devastated by lava and mudflow from the eruption. An estimated 4,000 people died in the tragedy. Violent eruptions have also occurred in 1767, 1779, and 1872. Mount Vesuvius has erupted in more recent years, however, the damage and loss of life has been less severe. Notable eruptions have occurred in 1906, 1913, and 1944. The 1906 eruption resulted in approximately 100 deaths in the city of San Giuseppe.

Each year thousands of tourists travel to the excavated city of Pompeii. ◆

Mount Etna Eruption

In 1669 a massive eruption occurred at Mount Etna in southern Italy. The 1669 eruption is one of the most famous volcanic eruptions in history. An estimated 20,000 people were killed in the tragedy. It is known not only for the death toll and destruction caused by the eruption, but the efforts made by the local people to save the city of Catania.

Mount Etna is located on the eastern coast of Sicily, an island to the south of mainland Italy. Etna is one of the most famous volcanoes in the world and its name comes from a Greek word meaning, "I burn." According to Greek legend, Mount Etna was the workshop of Hephaestus, the Greek god of fire. Another Greek legend held that Mount Etna was the home of Cyclopes who were former blacksmiths said to be forging thunderbolts beneath Mount Etna for Zeus. Several historic authors have written about the volcano including Virgil, Hesiod, Pythagoras, and Thucydides.

Lava, or molten rock that pours out of volcanoes, has flowed out of Mount Etna on several different occasions throughout history. **Geologists** who have studied the mountain contend that there is evidence to suggest that Mount Etna was active as long as 2.5 million years ago. The earliest record of an eruption from Mount Etna occurred in 1169 B.C. An estimated 15,000 people were killed in the 1169 eruption. The 1669 eruption, however, is the most well-known and documented of Mount Etna's eruptions.

After the 1669 eruption, the mountain erupted again in 1755. This eruption caused flooding in the cities below the mountain when the heat from the lava expelled by the volcano melted snow and ice near the top of the mountain. In 1852 an eruption at Mount Etna produced a massive outpouring of lava which covered approximately three square miles of land at the base of the mountain. In 1928 an eruption from Mount Etna buried the town of Mascali. In more recent years the volcano has erupted in 1971, 1983 and 1992. According to researchers, Mount Etna has erupted an estimated 135 times throughout history.

On Friday, March 8, 1669, an earthquake occurred near eastern Sicily. On March 11, Mount Etna exploded, sending rock and lava several miles into the air. The explosion sent a shower of hot volcanic material on top of several small villages

geologist an individual who studies rocks and rock formations.

at the base of the mountain. The area below the mountain was heavily populated at the time because the material produced by volcanoes creates excellent soil for farming. The eruption that occurred on March 11 lasted approximately four months and completed destroyed 12 towns at the base of the mountain. The city of Catania sustained the most damage and loss of life.

A group of 50 people from Catania attempted to save the city when they saw the lava flowing from the mountain. They began digging a trench around the city which they hoped would divert the flowing lava away from the city. Initially, their plan worked as the lava began streaming into the trench they constructed. However, eventually the trench became filled with lava and the fire-hot substance resumed its slow descent toward the city. Historians believe that this may have been the first time in history that people attempted to divert the flow of lava. The volcanic eruption killed an estimated 20,000 people.

In 1983 officials in Italy attempted to divert the flow of lava after another eruption from Mount Etna. Dynamite was used to blast a path away from the local towns. In February 1992, an eruption from Mount Etna threatened the residents of Zafferana. In 1992 the Italian government invited the United States to work on an experiment designed to divert the flow of lava from Mount Etna. The experiment was called "Operation Volcano Buster." A team of volcano experts and military personnel blasted a passageway near the mountain and used helicopters to drop concrete into the area to block the flow of lava. Experts believe the operation was, in large part, a success.

Since the major eruption of 1992, experts have been closely monitoring the volcano. Mount Etna erupted again in 1998, threatening the city of Catania. Some experts believe that a major eruption could occur in the near future. If another volcano occurs in the future that threatens the safety of Sicilians near the mountain, Italian officials are prepared to take the same action they took in 1992. ◆

Mount Tambora Eruption

April 1815

The Mount Tambora eruption of 1815 was one of the most powerful and deadliest volcanic eruptions in world history. An estimated 92,000 people were killed as a result of the eruption. The majority of deaths were caused by starvation. The eruption released so much volcanic material that it had an impact on the climate around the world for an entire year.

The eruption of 1815 occurred on Java, an island in the Pacific Ocean which is part of Indonesia. At the time of the eruption, the islands of Indonesia were a colony of the Dutch. Indonesia did not become an independent nation until 1949. Java lies within what is known as the "Ring of Fire." The Ring of Fire is a large circle of land and sea in the Pacific Ocean that is known for its unusually high degree of earthquake and volcano activity.

Dutch colonists on the island believed that the Tambora volcano was **dormant**. In 1814, however, the mountain began releasing small amounts of vapor and ash. On the evening of April 5, 1815, Tambora exploded in a massive volcanic eruption. The volcano exploded again on April 11 and 12. The power of the explosion could be heard nearly 900 miles away on the island of Sumatra, which is also part of modern day Indonesia. Ash from the volcano rained down as far as 800 miles away from Tambora. The series of eruptions blew nearly a mile of rock off of the top of the peak of the volcano. Approximately 12,000 people were killed in the areas around Java after the volcano.

dormant temporarily without action but with the capability to resume or begin activity.

Shortly after the volcanic eruption a tsunami crashed into the island of Java causing further death and destruction. A tsunami is a larger than normal wave of water that hits land after there has been a disturbance in a large body of water.

The Tambora eruption sent an estimated 1.7 million tons of volcanic material into the air. Scientists believe that the tiny pieces of ash that were sent in the air caused temperatures to drop around the world. The temperature of the earth dropped so severely the following year that 1816 became referred to as the "Year Without a Summer." Scientists believe that the Tambora eruption played an important role in the drop in temperatures the following year, however, many scientists are not fully convinced that the volcano was the sole cause of the climate changes.

This is only a slight exaggeration of the climate changes that took place in 1816. The drop in temperatures had a major impact on agricultural production throughout the northern hemisphere. The winter months of 1816 were not unusually cold, but the spring and summer months were extremely cool. Snowfalls occurred in Europe during the summer months of

June, July, and August in 1816. So many crops failed as a result of the lack of sunlight that farmers were forced to slaughter their animals and some people in Europe and Canada were forced to eat rats to survive. France, which had just concluded the Napoleonic Wars, was one of the most severely affected countries by the famine. ◆

Cotopaxi Eruption

JUNE 1877

The Cotopaxi Eruption of 1877 is known for the enormous amount of flooding caused. Cotopaxi is Ecuador's most famous volcano and its 1877 eruption killed an estimated 1,000 people.

Ecuador is located on the western part of South America and is bordered by Colombia to the north and Peru to the east. The western coast of Ecuador borders the Pacific Ocean. The Andes Mountains run north and south through the country. Cotopaxi is part of the Andes Mountains. Ecuador was ruled by the Spanish Empire until 1830 when it gained its independence.

Cotopaxi is the second highest mountain in Ecuador (an estimated 19,348 feet). Until 1986, when a volcanic eruption occurred atop Chile's Tupungato, Cotopaxi was the highest active volcano in the world. Cotopaxi has erupted several times throughout history; eruptions have been documented as early as 1532 and 1533. However, scientists believe that eruptions may have occurred thousands of years ago. Cotopaxi has erupted approximately 50 times since 1738, and an eruption in 1744 is believed to have been heard over 500 miles away. The last time that Cotopaxi erupted is believed to have been 1942.

Minor earthquakes occurred near the mountain in 1976, however, the quakes did not cause an eruption. Ecuador has a very warm climate throughout the year because it lies so close to the Equator. Despite the warm temperatures, Cotopaxi has a large amount of ice and snow at its peak because its enormous height. It was this snow and ice on the mountain that caused the majority of property damage and loss of life after the 1877 eruption. Centuries ago, the people of Ecuador worshipped Co-

Mt. Cotopaxi

topaxi as if it were a god. The Inca people are also believed to have worshipped the mountain. Historians believe that an eruption from Cotopaxi in 1534 protected the people of Ecuador from Spanish invaders, who were not accustomed to seeing volcanoes and ran in terror when the volcano erupted.

The Cotopaxi eruption in June 1877 produced such an enormous amount of ash that the city of Quito, Ecuador's capital city, went completely dark at 8:00 A.M. The lava that poured out of the volcano caused the ice and snow atop the mountain to melt and was sent streaming down the mountain, flooding approximately 50 to 100 miles of land around the volcano.

The melting of the snow and ice produced what is known as a **lahar**. A lahar is a landslide of mud and volcanic material that rushes down the mountain after an eruption. The lahar completely destroyed Latacunga, a town located approximately 27 miles from the mountain. Many residents of Latacunga were killed instantly by the massive mudflow that swept through the town. The flow of muddy waters of the lahar was so powerful that approximately 18 hours after the eruption, the lahar

lahar a flowing mass of water and volcanic debris.

streamed 200 miles away to the town of Esmeraldas, near the Pacific Ocean.

The town of Latacunga has been destroyed by volcanic eruptions from Cotopaxi on two other occasions prior to the 1877 disaster (in 1742 and 1768). Today there is far less snow and ice on top of Cotopaxi. However, scientists believe that if Cotopaxi were to erupt again there is a strong possibility that Latacunga would be devastated by another lahar. ◆

Krakatoa Eruption

AUGUST 27, 1883

On August 27, 1883, a massive volcanic eruption occurred on the island of Krakatoa in Indonesia. The Krakatoa eruption was one of the deadliest volcanic eruptions in history. An estimated 36,000 people were killed in the tragedy.

Krakatoa is an island that is part of Indonesia. The island is located between the larger Indonesian islands of Java and Sumatra. Krakatoa lies within what is known as the "Ring of Fire." The Ring of Fire is a large circle of land and sea in the Pacific Ocean that is known for its unusually high degree of earthquake and volcano activity.

At the time of the 1883 eruption, the islands of Indonesia were a colony of the Dutch. Indonesia did not become an independent nation until 1949. Before the volcano erupted there were no people living on the island of Krakatoa. The island consists of three volcanoes. Scientists believe that a massive volcano occurred on the island at approximately 416 A.D. Another eruption occurred in 1680, however, little damage was reported.

There was little evidence that anything was brewing beneath the island of Krakatoa during the years before the eruption. On May 20, 1883, the people of nearby Sumatra and Java were alerted to the possibility that a volcano on Krakatoa could occur when a series of explosions came from the island. After the explosions, vapor and ash began streaming from the top of the Krakatoa mountain. Sumatra and Java are two larger of

Indonesia's approximately 13,600 islands. The capital of the Indonesia, Jakarta, lies on the northern coast of Java. Between May 20, 1883, and the massive eruption of August 27, 1883 a series of more violent explosions occurred.

The people of Java and Sumatra, however, who were approximately 30 miles away from the island, did not believe they were in danger until an earthquake beneath Krakatoa rattled the Indonesian islands on August 26, 1883. The next day, a series of five explosions occurred on Krakatoa in a massive eruption. The explosions were so loud that they were heard approximately 3,000 miles away on the island of Rodriguez. The eruption sent ash flying into the air an estimated 15 miles high. The eruption was so powerful it virtually wiped the island off of the face of the earth. Approximately two-thirds of the entire island on the north side was blown into the sea. Although several people were burned to death on the island of Sumatra, the majority of people who died from the eruption drowned in the massive tsunamis caused by the eruption.

The power of the Krakatoa eruption created massive tsunamis that crashed into the coastlines of Java and Sumatra. A tsunami is a larger than normal wave of water that hits land after there has been a disturbance in a large body of water. The tsunamis created by the eruption were reported to be over 100 feet high in some areas. When the waves came crashing into Java and Sumatra, several small villages were destroyed. In a town called Karang Antoe, which was miles away from shore, a gigantic wave wiped out an estimated 3,000 people.

In 1927 a minor eruption occurred on Krakatoa which was called the "child of Krakatoa." Following the eruption, scientists studied the island in an effort to determine what caused the massive eruption. They concluded that an enormous amount of pressure built inside the mountain due to vapor that was released from **magma**. Magma is molten rock beneath the ground; when it emerges from the earth it is converted into lava. In 1960 a group of researchers investigated Krakatoa in an effort to learn more about the causes of tsunamis. Experts believe that volcanic eruptions cause the temperature to drop for several years after an eruption. The drop in temperature is a result of ash particles that get caught in the air and obstruct the rays of the sun.

Krakatoa became active again from 1959 to 1963; however no major eruptions occurred. In March 1994, the vol-

The eruption was so powerful it virtually wiped the island off of the face of the earth.

magma molten rock material within the earth that eventually results in a rock formation when it cools.

cano began erupting again and continued for approximately one year. None of the volcanic activity since the massive eruption of 1883 has caused serious damage or destruction to Indonesia. ◆

Mount Pelée Eruption

May 5, 1902

The Mount Pelée eruption of 1902 was the most deadly and destructive volcanic eruption to occur in the Caribbean. The eruption completely buried the town of St. Pierre in Martinique, killing nearly everyone in the town. The total number of people killed in the eruption was estimated to be 28,000.

Mount Pelée is located on the island of Martinique. Martinique, which lies on the eastern side of the Caribbean Sea, has been governed by France since 1946. The land on the island is extremely fertile in large part because volcanic material creates soil that is ideal for crops. The French enslaved the people of Martinique early in the 1600s and used them to produce sugar until the middle of the nineteenth century. Today Martinique's economy is still dependent upon sugar production, in addition to rum and tourism.

Volcanic activity in the Caribbean Sea is a result of tension created by the meeting of two plates beneath the earth's surface. The South American plate meets with the much smaller Caribbean plate beneath Martinique. The tension between the two plates creates large amounts of energy beneath the earth's surface which is released in the form of earthquakes and volcanoes.

The people who lived near the volcanic mountain in St. Pierre

Mount Pelée during its 1902 eruption

had grown accustomed to occasional activity around Mount Pelée. In 1889 Mount Pelée began releasing large amounts of ash and vapor. In April 1902, regular mild eruptions began occurring at Mount Pelée. On May 5, 1902, water that had formed near the top of the mountain, called a "crater lake," was forced out by an eruption. The water caused flooding along the River Blanche near St. Pierre killing 23 people at a sugar plant. This event, in addition to another nearby eruption that killed 1,700 people on the island of St. Vincent, stirred people's fears in St. Pierre.

People began leaving St. Pierre out of fear that a massive eruption was about to occur. However, the government of France sent local troops to the region to calm people and prevent them from fleeing the area. However, people were still frightened and began leaving in larger numbers. In an effort to convince people that Mount Pelée was safe, the governor moved to the area with his wife. On May 8, 1902, a massive eruption occurred sending ash and lava down the side of the mountain. Within approximately two minutes from the time of the eruption the entire city of St. Pierre was destroyed. All of the clocks in St. Pierre had stopped at around 7:52, showing that this was the time the town was destroyed.

The eruption destroyed approximately eight square miles around Mount Pelée. Only a handful of people in the entire town survived the tragedy. Nearly 28,000 people died after the eruption. One of the known survivors was a prisoner by the name of Joseph Surtout. Surtout survived because he was locked in a dungeon, concealed beneath the hot volcanic material that coated the city. He remained in his cell for four days until his cries for help were answered. Another known survivor was a shoemaker by the name of Leon Comprere-Leander who lived far enough away to escape harm.

The city of St. Pierre after the volcanic eruption was in a state of complete ruin. Homes and buildings were burned and the carbonized remains of people were everywhere. The majority of people who were killed by the eruption in St. Pierre were burned to death. Rescuers who came to the area after the eruption found bodies scattered all around. Some bodies were badly burned while others were only slightly so. The volcanic eruption also destroyed several ships that were docked near St. Pierre. Members of the crew were killed and ships were burned. On May 20, 1902, another eruption oc-

> **The majority of people who were killed by the eruption in St. Pierre were burned to death.**

curred, however, by this time St. Pierre had already been destroyed.

In 1929 Mount Pelée began showing signs that it was going to erupt. This time local officials evacuated St. Pierre and the surrounding areas. The volcanic activity that began in 1929 lasted for approximately three years but never produced the amount of destructive outpouring that occurred in 1902. ◆

Mount St. Helens Eruption

MAY 18, 1980

The state of Washington contains two of the most well-known volcanoes in the United States, Mount St. Helens and Mount Rainer. Mount St. Helens is located near Portland, Oregon, and Mount Rainer is located near Seattle, Washington. Beneath the state of Washington the continental land mass meets the Juan de Fuco plate, creating the potential for earthquakes and volcanic eruptions. The tension between the two land masses, which lie beneath the Pacific Ocean, create a large amount of energy that is released in the form of earthquakes and volcanoes.

Mount St. Helens was named by the explorer George Vancouver who named the mountain after his friend, Baron St. Helens. Native Americans had earlier named the mountain "smoking mountain," and "Lady of Fire." Mount St. Helens had been active in the nineteenth century. Minor eruptions occurred between 1830 and 1857, but the mountain became dormant for 123 years before violently erupting in 1980. Mount St. Helens had become a popular vacation area prior to the eruption. However, on March 20, 1980, Washington experienced a minor earthquake. Then on March 27, Mount St. Helens began to give indications that it was not completely dormant after all. A small explosion occurred at the peak of the mountain causing vapor and ash to pour out. The volcano began discharging ash and rock and the grounds around Mount St. Helens shook as if a minor earthquake had occurred.

On April 7, 1980, Mount St. Helens began trembling and a bulge was detected on the north side of the mountain. The bulge suggested that the mountain was filled with magma near the top and was trying to find a way out. Magma is molten rock

Active Volcanoes in the United States

Mount St. Helens is only one of many active volcanoes in the United States. In fact, the nation ranks third in the world, behind only Indonesia and Japan, in the number of active volcanoes within its territory. A full 10 percent of all the earthquakes occurring during the last 10,000 years happened in what is now the United States.

Most of America's volcanoes are on the Aleutian Islands and Hawaiian Islands, the Alaskan Peninsula, and in the Cascade Mountain Range in the Pacific Northwest. One of the world's largest volcanoes is Mauna Loa, on the island of Hawaii. The Hawaiian volcanoes as a group erupt frequently, but they are less dangerous than the Alaskan and Cascade Range volcanoes because the eruptions consist largely of simple lava flows, and the people who live near their slopes generally have ample time to move to safety.

The Alaskan and Cascade Range volcanoes, on the other hand, erupt less frequently, but when they erupt they do so suddenly and with explosive force. One or two of Alaska's volcanoes erupts every year, but most are far from settled areas and pose little danger to people. The most dangerous ones are found in the Cook Inlet region, near human settlements. Here is where the Redoubt Volcano erupted four times during the twentieth century, the last time in 1989, and Mount Augustine has been erupting with increasing regularity over the past 100 years.

The world's largest eruption to occur during the twentieth century occurred at Mount Novarupta, another Alaskan volcano. Novarupta blew its top in 1912, and some of the deposits it left behind were still hot enough to boil water four years later.

In addition to Mount St. Helens, the Cascade Range volcanoes include Mount Baker, which last erupted in 1976, and Lasser Peak. Mount Ranier, which has been silent since the 1400s, is still considered active and dangerous. To date it only produces periodic flows of mud, but scientists believe that a true eruption could occur at any time. Beyond the Cascade Range, there are a few other areas of volcanic unrest in the United States, including the Long Valley Caldera of California and the Yellowstone Caldera in Yellowstone Park, Wyoming.

beneath the ground; when it emerges from the earth it is converted into lava. Researchers believed that the volcano could erupt at any time. Two days later the governor of Washington, Dixy Lee Ray, declared a state of emergency and the National Guard was called in to prevent people from getting too close to the volcano.

One resident of the area (a man named Harry Truman) refused to leave his home. Truman lived five miles from the volcano, but the 83-year-old man was convinced that the volcano would not hurt him. However, he was killed when his home was covered by rock and debris moments after it erupted.

The sound of the explosion was so loud that it could be heard as far away as Canada and California.

On May 18, at 8:30 A.M., Mount St. Helens exploded, releasing ash, rock, and lava. The eruption occurred at the same time as an earthquake that registered 5.1 on the Richter scale hit the area. The Richter scale, developed by Charles Richter in 1927, is a measure of the amount of energy released by an earthquake. An earthquake that measures 7.0 on the Richter scale is considered by experts to be a "major" earthquake, capable of serious damage and loss of life.

When Mount St. Helens erupted, the mountain blew apart on its north side. The force of the eruption was so powerful that over 1,300 feet of rock at the top of the mountain were blow off. Before the eruption, Mount St. Helens stood approximately 9,664 feet high and after the eruption the mountain was 8,364 feet high. The eruption lasted for about nine hours, during which the mountain blasted out over 500 tons of volcanic ash. The rock and debris from the explosion covered an area of nearly eight miles. The sound of the explosion was so loud that it could be heard as far away as Canada and California. The Mount St. Helens eruption killed 57 people, however as many as 43 others were reported missing after the event.

The number of lives lost as a result of the 1980 Mount St. Helens eruption was not as large as other historic natural disasters. However, the eruption caused an enormous amount of property damage. Some estimates suggest that the property damage caused by the volcano was more an $1.5 billion. In addition, the volcano destroyed over 150 square miles of forest that could have been used for logging. The volcanic eruption set off a massive avalanche which caused flooding and damage near Toutle River and Lake Spirit. The avalanche of rock, ice, and mud traveled at speeds between 70 and 150 miles per hour, destroying everything in its path. The volcano erupted again in April 1982, but it caused very little damage.

Mount St. Helens was converted into a gigantic laboratory after the eruption. The U.S. government converted Mount St. Helens into a national monument. Approximately 4 million people visit Mount St. Helens each year to tour the historic site. Scientists come from around the globe to study the effects that the eruption had on the atmosphere and environment. One of the things that has surprised scientists is the growth of life in the area after the eruption. Several different life forms have made a new home out of the mountain. Researchers believe that within a century's time the area around the volcano will be as full of life as it was prior to the eruption.

In the mid-1980s researchers concluded that a major earthquake was likely to occur in the Pacific Northwest in the near future. Although Washington has experienced several minor earthquakes throughout its history a destructive earthquake has not yet occurred. Scientists also believe that Mount St. Helens will erupt again in the future. However, researchers are not certain when another eruption will occur. ◆

El Chichon Eruption

MARCH–APRIL 1982

In March 1982, El Chichon erupted along the eastern coast of Mexico in the Sierra Madre Mountains. The eruption killed an estimated 187 people. The amount of death and destruction caused by the eruption was not as severe as other historic volcanic eruptions, but the El Chichon eruption was significant because it was the first volcanic eruption in which scientists using modern equipment were able to study the effects of a major eruption on the atmosphere.

El Chichon is a volcano in Mexico that is part of the Sierra Madre mountain range. Prior to the 1982 eruption El Chichon was an unknown and relatively inactive volcano. There are no prior records of a major eruption ever occurring at El Chichon.

On March 28, 1982, at 11:32 P.M. El Chichon began erupting, causing serious property damage to the surrounding areas and an estimated 187 deaths. The eruption forced many local residents to flee their homes because of the amount of volcanic material that was expelled. The eruption forced officials to close several roads as well as the airports. In addition a significant amount of damage to cocoa, coffee, and banana crops was caused by the ashfall following the eruption. According to government estimates the amount of damage caused to crops was about $55 million. The ash also affected the livestock on the island. The animals could no longer eat the grass because it was contaminated by the volcanic material.

On March 29, 1982, a minor earthquake on the eastern side of the volcano killed 10 people and injured approximately 200 others who had taken refuge in a church. The next day, at approximately 9:00 A.M. a second, less severe, eruption occurred.

The eruption on El Chichon was the first major eruption in which scientists were able to study the direct impact of a volcanic eruption on the atmosphere.

The volcano continued erupting periodically through April 11, 1982. A massive eruption on April 4 sent large rocks flying from the mountain which crushed several homes.

After the eruption thousands of people who had lived in six different villages around the volcano became stranded on El Chichon. The ash from the volcano made it difficult to locate survivors. The Mexican government sent in troops to try to find the survivors, many of whom were fleeing from the eruption. On April 10, 1982, some of the peasants who had been stranded for 11 days were spotted by helicopters conducting a search around the volcano for survivors. The Mexican government rescued over 60,000 people after the El Chichon eruption.

The eruption on El Chichon was the first major eruption in which scientists were able to study the direct impact of a volcanic eruption on the atmosphere. The research conducted after the El Chichon eruption was heavily debated among experts. Scientists who studied the event found that the particles released by the eruption traveled around the earth in approximately 20 days. Researchers also found that the atmosphere was 140 times more dense than it was after the Mount St. Helens eruption of 1980. Shortly after the eruption, scientists believe, the temperature in the northern hemisphere slightly decreased. Researchers believe that this was the result of several million tons of ash that were sent into the atmosphere by the eruption.

When ash is trapped in the atmosphere it blocks the sun's rays to the earth, causing temperatures to drop. Researchers conducted experiments after the Mount St. Helens eruption of 1980 and the El Chichon eruption of 1982 to see if the materials emitted by volcanic eruptions blocked rays of light. After shining laser beams at the clouds of volcanic ash coming out of the volcanoes, scientists found that the volcanic material substantially blocked the light.

The most dramatic instance in which temperatures dropped as a result of a volcanic eruption occurred in 1816. After the Tambora eruption of 1815 in Indonesia, scientists believe temperatures dropped dramatically the following year causing major crop failure and consequently starvation. The year after the Tambora eruption has been referred to as the "Year Without a Summer." Some scientists suspect that the El Chichon eruption of 1982 may have caused severe climate changes in 1983. Although not all scientists agree with this theory, it is believed that the ash produced from El Chichon, which stayed in the atmosphere until 1985, did have some impact on global temperatures. ◆

Nevado del Ruiz Eruption

NOVEMBER 13, 1985

The 1985 eruption of Nevado del Ruiz was the deadliest and most destructive volcanic eruption ever to occur in South America. The eruption resulted in the deaths of over 25,000 people.

Nevado del Ruiz, located in central Colombia, is one of many active volcanoes located along the Andes Mountains. It is the northernmost volcano in South America. Nevado del Ruiz erupted in 1595 and 1845; however neither of these eruptions caused serious damage or loss of life. One of the features that makes the Nevado del Ruiz volcano potentially deadly is the large of amount of snow and ice that rest near the peak of the mountain. When magma, or molten rock, begins to rise up the mountain due to pressure beneath the earth it causes the snow and ice to melt. The melting snow and ice can cause mudflows below the mountain. This is what occurred in the 1985 tragedy. The town of Armero, which was the most severely affected by the 1985 eruption, had been built atop the remains of a mudflow that covered the area after an eruption in 1845.

There were signs that the volcano was going to erupt in January 1985, when the volcano began emitting vapor and ash. In September 1985, a small eruption melted the ice that had formed atop the mountain, causing avalanches. On November 13, 1985, researchers warned government officials in Colombia that the town of Armero would be in grave danger if the volcano erupted. Unfortunately, the Colombian government did not take action to evacuate people in Armero. The people of Armero were told to remain in their homes.

The November 13th eruption was one of the deadliest eruptions of the twentieth century. The eruption caused a "lahar," a landslide of mud and volcanic material that rushes down the mountain after an eruption. The lahar destroyed the town of Armero, Columbia. At 9:00 P.M. the ash from the volcano caused ice and snow to melt on the mountain sending a giant mudflow toward the town of Armero. The melted snow and mud from the volcano flooded into the Lagunillas River and began racing toward Armero. At 11:00 P.M. a wave of muddy waters crashed into the town killing thousands of people.

Many of the people who died in the volcanic flood had already gone to bed for the evening. According to people who survived the tragedy, when the volcano erupted there were radio broadcasts instructing people to remain calm and not to be concerned about the eruption. The few people who managed to survive the tragedy saw the flood coming and ran to higher ground. People who witnessed the volcano said they saw flames flying through the air. Flood from the Lagunillas River caused the majority of deaths after the volcanic eruption. According to reports at the time, floodwaters came crashing into Armero in 50 to 60 foot waves.

The floodwater washed away everything in its path including trees, homes, and cars. People who left their homes to escape the flood were immediately swept away by the rushing water. According to those who survived the tragedy, the waters that rushed through Amero were initially cold. However, as the volcano emitted more molten rock, the water began heating up. According to some witnesses, boiling water eventually began pouring into Armero. An evacuation plan for Armero had been formed by officials in Colombia in the event that the Nevado del Ruiz erupted. Unfortunately, the plan had not been put into operation when the volcano erupted on November 13.

After the Nevado del Ruiz tragedy, the town of Armero was not rebuilt. What remains of the small town lies uninhabited today. The Nevado del Ruiz continued erupting for years after the massive 1985 eruption. Another major eruption occurred in 1992, however, no major injuries or property damage were caused. ◆

Fires

Fire of Rome

64 C.E.

The fire of Rome was one of the most famous events in the history of Ancient Rome. The fire occurred during the period of the Roman Empire's development known as "Pax Romana," or Roman Peace. The ruling emperor at the time of the fire was Nero, who many historians believe was one of the cruelest rulers of Ancient Rome. Nero's reign as emperor followed that of Claudius in A.D. 54. Nero, who was 16 years old when he became emperor, is reported to have committed or ordered several serious crimes, such as the murder of Claudius' son, Britannicus; the murder of his own mother, Agrippina; and the murder of his wife, Octavia.

According to legend and some historical sources, Nero himself set the fire of A.D. 64 that devastated the city. Although it is unknown how the fire actually started, Nero took advantage of the tragedy to rid himself of a powerful enemy, the Christians. Nero blamed the fire on the Christians and unleashed a series of persecutions against Christians in the years that followed. Following the fire, Nero placed large tax burdens on the people of Rome which ultimately led to a revolution. When the Roman Army turned against Nero, he committed suicide in A.D. 68.

At the time of the fire, Rome was poorly built. The city was an unorganized maze of streets and alleyways. Rome was **haphazardly** reconstructed this way after it was invaded by the Gauls in 391 B.C. Gaul was an ancient nation that included parts of western Germany, France, Belgium, and northern Italy. Although Nero's reign after the fire was tyrannical, he is given credit for reconstructing Rome into a stronger and more efficient city

At the time of the fire, Rome was poorly built.

haphazard without thought or sufficient planning.

175

Nero is depicted playing his lyre as Rome burns, though some historians contend he was not even in the city during the fire.

tenement an apartment building or house meeting the bare minimum standards of safety, comfort, and sanitation, usually occupied by poorer citizens of larger cities.

kithara an ancient Greek stringed instrument simliar to a lyre, though larger.

with wider roads and more open spaces. Nero was also believed to be fond of Greek art and liked to think of himself more as an entertainer than a statesman. During his rule he encouraged creative expression in arts such as theater, poetry, painting, and architecture.

There were many poorly maintained **tenement** buildings (crowded apartment buildings) that made Rome vulnerable to a disastrous fire. When the fire began, there was no way of putting it out. The fire lasted for several days and nights, killing countless people, destroying countless homes, eventually laying waste to two-thirds of the entire city.

The fire broke out in several different areas of Rome, which adds merit to the theory that the fire was deliberately set. When the fire began, people crammed into the streets and alleyways in chaos and fear. Some men tried to help others whose homes had caught fire, others attempted to steal goods from unsuspecting citizens. As the fire progressed a huge gust of wind fed the blaze, expanding its path of death and destruction. At this point even those who were looking for homes to plunder began running for safety. Many people who managed to escape the fire were trampled or suffocated in the streets. The exact number of Romans killed by the fire is unknown.

Legend holds that in the midst of the fire, Nero climbed atop his palace roof in harpist clothing and began to sing and play a stringed instrument called a **kithara**. This image of Nero playing a "fiddle" while much of Rome burned to the ground is consistent with how historians have depicted the emperor over the years.

However, contemporary scholars such as Richard Holland have raised doubts about Nero's demon-like reputation. Historians have pointed out that ancient Christian writers may have exaggerated Nero's cruelty in retaliation for Nero blaming the

Great Fire of Rome on Christians. In addition, historians point out that although Nero had his mother killed, it may have been partly justified. They contend that Nero's mother, Agrippina, consistently plotted behind Nero's back while he was emperor, and could not be trusted. Some historians even suggest that Nero was not even in Rome at the time of the fire, but Nero was miles away in his summer villa. Historians also point out that Nero did not kill nearly as many people as earlier emperors Caligula, Claudius, and Julius Caesar.

Princeton historian Edward Champlin presents a different view on Nero and the Great Fire of Rome. Champlin believes that Nero probably did start the fire but for reasons other than raw cruelty. Champlin suggests that Nero's quest to be remembered as an emperor that rebuilt Rome drove him to burn down the city. By setting an uncontrollable fire, Nero gave himself the opportunity to rebuild the city as he saw fit. Although historians disagree on whether Nero started the fire as well as his motives, they do agree on one point: the city that replaced the burned remains of Rome was much stronger than that which existed before the fire. ◆

> **Historians point out that although Nero had his mother killed, it may have been partly justified.**

Great Fire of London

On September 2, 1666, London, England, suffered the beginnings of a devastating fire that destroyed the majority of the city. Remarkably, historical documentation has only directly linked six deaths to the fire. However, historians suspect that a greater number of deaths actually occurred. The Great Fire of London in 1666 was not the first time the city had been hit by a huge fire. In 1084 a devastating fire killed 3,000 people. Another fire in 1633 burned down several homes near London Bridge.

The fire of 1666 began on Pudding Lane at a bakery, and raged for five straight days destroying homes, businesses, and churches. The fire burned down an estimated 13,200 homes, 44 businesses, and 87 churches including St. Paul's Cathedral. An area of one and one half by one half mile (approximately 435 acres) was burned to the ground. Nearly 100,000 people were

This lithograph by Sir Christopher Wren depicts the fire of London in 1666.

left homeless. One of the reasons the fire was so destructive is that nearly all of the structures in the entire city were made of wood.

The cause of the fire was linked to Thomas Farynor's bakery shop. Farynor was one of the king's bakers who, some historians believe, forgot to wet down the stove before going to bed. One of his servants awoke to the smell of smoke and alerted Farynor. The fire spread rapidly as sparks landed on hay in the stable of a nearby hotel on Fish Street Hill, which caused the Church of St. Margaret to catch fire. Moments later both Pudding Lane and Fish Street Hill were blazing. The fire was further fueled by a warehouse on Fish Street Hill that stored alcohol—wine and brandy—and oil. The fire then quickly spread to Thames Street. At 8:00 A.M. on September 2, 1666, about six hours after the fire began, the fire was spreading across London Bridge.

At this point London officials made an effort to stop the fire. A royal command was issued to begin tearing down homes. In the absence of fire-fighting resources and water, a last resort method of trying to contain a fire was to tear down homes that lay in the direct path of the flames. This could bring a halt to the fire by essentially creating a dead end; the fire would be unable to continue jumping from house to house. However, the first attempts to end the fire in this fashion failed.

Those attempting to tear down the houses (called "trained bands") accidentally fueled the fire by tearing down homes that were already close to the fire. Later, in a state of desperation, town officials decided to use gunpowder to tear down homes. The fire was finally extinguished at Holborn Bridge. Yet just when Londoners began to feel a sense of relief, the fire sparked up again and began moving toward Westminster. This time the Duke of York immediately ordered the destruction of houses to stop the fire.

When the city was rebuilt, architects used bricks and stone almost exclusively. The chief architect responsible for rebuilding the city was Sir Christopher Wren who rebuilt St. Paul's Cathedral, a widely admired building and a popular tourist attraction today. When the city was rebuilt many of the business people who lived in London were afraid to move back to the city. As a result, many merchants began setting up trading squares west of the city in what became Bloomsbury and Mayfair. However, merchants eventually began moving back into the city helping to convert what was once a mound of ashes into a thriving industrial metropolis.

Although the king's baker is blamed for the Great Fire of London, other factors laid the groundwork for disaster. Both the weather and a lack of fire-fighting preparation were equally to blame for the amount of devastation London suffered in 1666. That summer was exceptionally hot and unusually little rain had fallen. By September many of the rivers and streams had dried up, leaving little water with which to fight the fire. However, even if water were available, there was no organized fire-fighting strategy in place for the 130,000 people who lived in London at that time.

Prior to the Great Fire of London, England did not have a government-sponsored fire-fighting program. In 1600 London began developing programs to fight fires, most of which were sponsored by the Church of England. However, the fire of 1633 demonstrated that the fire-fighting mechanisms that were in place were completely ineffective. After the fire, changes were made in the interest of fire safety. When the city was rebuilt,

Both the weather and a lack of fire-fighting preparation were equally to blame for the amount of devastation London suffered in 1666.

London officials forced all buildings to be made of brick or stone. In addition, by 1700 several insurance companies had been created in response to the large number of people who were put in debtors prison because of the Great Fire of London. In 1707, Parliament passed a law requiring every parish to contain a horse-drawn fire-fighting unit, equipped with hoses, ladders, and buckets. ◆

Great Chicago Fire

OCTOBER 8, 1871

On October 8, 1871, Chicago suffered one of the worst fires in United States history. The fire jumped from house to house engulfing the city. Before the fire ended, four and one half square miles (2000 acres) of Chicago had been burned to the ground. An astounding 17,500 buildings were destroyed by the massive fire that raged for 30 hours straight. A tremendous stroke of luck helped extinguish the fire; heavy rainfall smoldered the flames as it reached Diversey Street. An estimated 300 people were killed by the fire, 100,000 people were left homeless, and $200 million in damage was caused. At the time of the fire, the population of Chicago was around 330,000.

After a summer with very little rainfall in the Midwest, the city of Chicago, which contained many buildings made of wood, was vulnerable to a disastrous fire. In addition, the city's streets, sidewalks, and bridges were all made of wood. Between July and October of 1871, only one inch of rain had fallen on Chicago. Several small fires had broken out in Chicago in the weeks before the Great Chicago Fire.

The fire began in a small barn on DeKoven Street, owned by the O'Leary family. There is a popular legend that a cow owned by the O'Learys kicked over a lantern, which started the fire in the hay-filled barn. This theory, however, has since been dismissed by historians and now passed on only as myth. In fact, the Chicago City Council passed a resolution on October 28, 1997, which freed the O'Learys (and their cow) of any blame for the fire. Some have argued that a milk thief knocked over a lantern while thieving in the O'Leary barn while others contend that arsonists started the fire. Despite these theories and ideas, the exact cause of the fire has never been discovered.

Some historians believe that a man by the name of Daniel "Peg Leg" Sullivan deliberately started the fire. Sullivan was the first person to spot the O'Leary barn on fire. When he saw the fire, he claimed to have hobbled to the O'Leary home and warned them before running through the streets yelling for help. In 1995 Richard F. Bales, a Chicago Title Insurance lawyer, looked into Sullivan's story 124 years after the fire. Bales took it upon himself to read through historical records from the fire for a period of two years and found several inconsistencies with Sullivan's testimony. After reviewing the layout of the homes in the area Bales discovered that Sullivan could not have been standing in front of a home next to the O'Leary's (as he claimed) and had a clear view of the fire. Another home as well as an eight-foot high fence would have blocked his view. In addition, there is no record that anyone ever heard Sullivan warning them.

A man stands in what was left of the Fifth National Bank in Chicago following the fire of 1871.

Another man named Lee Sullivan (who is not related to Daniel "Peg Leg" Sullivan) saw the fire from his home on Clinton Street and ran over to a drugstore to pull the alarm. However, when he tried to get the key from the drugstore owner, the owner refused. The owner explained that he had just seen a fire truck pass by and assumed that the authorities were already aware of the fire. This unfortunate decision caused a delay in sounding the fire alarm. This delay may have resulted in greater loss of life and property damage than otherwise might have occurred.

The fire that began in the O'Leary barn was fueled by a 30 mile per hour wind that hit the city from the southwest. The fire was blown to the north and east by the wind, gaining momentum with each gust. The blaze had gathered so much force that it spread across the Chicago River. It then began moving toward the county courthouse, engineered to be fireproof. Instead, the courthouse bell tower caught fire causing the 5,000 pound bell to come crashing down on the building. The fire proceeded to burn the courthouse building down from the inside. The mayor of Chicago, Roswell B. Mason, was in the courthouse at the time as were several prisoners. The inmates screamed and pounded on their jail cells begging to be set free. The less dangerous prisoners were released and the more dangerous criminals were escorted out by guards just before the courthouse was engulfed in flames.

A legend has been passed down regarding the tragedy that took place in the courthouse building. It is believed that the mayor had issued an order to release all of the prisoners who were trapped in the courthouse building in order to save their lives. In 1998 the great-great-granddaughter of Mason, Elizabeth Trowbridge Wild, discovered a piece of paper in a family scrapbook that contained a message written by the mayor. The piece of paper read, "Release all prisoners from jail at once, keeping them in custody if possible." Wild donated the historical relic to the Chicago Historical Society. Historians confirmed that the handwriting on the paper matched that of the Chicago mayor, which instantly converted the long-held legend into historical fact.

Ironically, the O'Leary home was not affected by the fire and has since been replaced by the Chicago Fire Academy. A large statue of a flame stands in front of the Academy, to commemorate the events. Another irony of the Great Chicago Fire of 1871 is that Chicago ultimately benefited from the tragedy. City engineers and architects learned from historic mistakes and rebuilt Chicago into one of the greatest industrialized cities in the world.

In memory of the tragedy that occurred in Chicago in 1871, the U.S. Fire Administration holds a national fire prevention day. The event, which is designed to raise public awareness about hazards of fire, was started in 1922. The Fire Administration distributes important safety information during Fire Prevention Day. For example, each year more people are killed by fires than by all natural disasters combined and having a smoke detector in the home doubles your chances of surviving a fire. Today one can take a bus tour of Chicago while listening to an historical narrative of the disaster. ◆

The Great Peshtigo Fire

OCTOBER 8, 1871

In the words of one scholar, "The Great Peshtigo Fire was, and is, the worst fire in the history of the United States, taking more lives than the next two fires combined."

Yet this horrific **conflagration**, which incinerated more than one million acres of farms, forests, and small towns in Wisconsin and upper Michigan, has been relegated to the back pages of history because of a surreal coincidence: it happened on October 8, the same day in 1871 as the Great Chicago Fire that has assumed almost mythic proportions in the American historical imagination. Devastating as it was, however, the Chicago fire, which took some 250 lives, pales in comparison to the firestorm that howled through the settler towns and open country of the upper Middle West, leaving some 1,500 corpses in its path.

The fire was preceded by a three-month drought so severe that on the morning of October 8, many **congregants** in Peshtigo, a small Wisconsin logging town, were praying for rain. In the surrounding timberland countless ponds, bogs, and creeks had simply disappeared, while the Peshtigo River, the main source of water and means of transportation in the area, was at a perilously low level. The grasslands and woods had become bone-dry tinder.

The dry spell presented some advantages, however, chief among them the opportunity for additional land clearing. The land-clearing technique of the time typically left a quarter of the tree along with piles of sawdust and waste called slash. This parched environment needed only a small spark to create a big problem, especially given common local practice of heedlessly setting small fires to clear logging debris. Many such fires erupted throughout the summer but proved a mere nuisance, along with periodic wildfires of unknown origin.

Local lore has it that on the evening of October 8, railroad workers set fire to some timber to clear land for track work. The resulting brushfire leaped out of control and ballooned into a deadly inferno, buoyed by a surge of hot winds. As the blaze began to spread, it cut telegraph wires, cutting off communication between towns.

conflagration a large, diasastrous fire.

congregants church-goers.

This engraving depicts people fleeing burning houses during the 1871 fire in Peshtigo, Wisconsin.

stygian extremely foreboding, dark, or gloomy.

maelstrom a powerful and sometimes violent whirlpool of activity which draws in objects within a given radius.

At around 8:30 P.M. that night, the townsfolk of Peshtigo were unsettled by a dull roar in the distance. The sound then sharpened into what witnesses compared to a large discharge of artillery as the ravenous flames approached the towns. After an initial stand by the local firefighters, the townspeople were in full retreat toward the river as the fire seemed to feed on itself in a **stygian** frenzy, throwing off firewhirls that tore off treetops. The smoke and exploding marsh gases made breathing all but impossible.

The gathering energy of the conflagration created a veritable cyclone of flame. Although the winds were blowing in the range of only 15-30 miles per hour, the force of the galloping fire generated fire winds of nearly 80 miles per hour, demolishing barns and houses and hurling heavy wagons like toys. In the words of one historian, "The peculiar physics of mass fire had multiplied its fury into a **maelstrom** of energy equivalent to the chain reaction of a thermonuclear bomb. There was no defense for the populace but flight."

But on this night there was no exit for many as falling ash and embers ignited clothing and hair, severely blistering those who were not killed. Some ran frantically into buildings that collapsed on them. Some survived by lying down in the middle of clearings, others by submerging themselves in local rivers, ponds, and the nearby Green Bay, although even some of those escapees drowned because of the difficulty of keeping one's head above water in the superheated air. Many local residents were burned beyond recognition. According to some estimates, nearly half of the blighted town's population perished in the blaze, which skirted Green Bay but raced on to other towns as it fanned out over 1.2 million acres, including parts of Door and Kewaunee Counties. The total damage estimate of $169 million was the same as that for the great Chicago fire.

In 1963 the town opened the Peshtigo Fire Museum next to the Peshtigo Fire Cemetery, which holds the remains of several hundred victims of one of the fiercest natural calamities in American history. ◆

Iroquois Theater Fire

DECEMBER 30, 1903

The Iroquois Theater fire of December 30, 1903, was the most lethal conflagration in Chicago history, the second worst in the history of the United States, and the fourth worst among recorded blazes in the world. Its death toll of 602 far surpassed the 250 casualties of the Great Chicago Fire of 1871 and the 490 who perished in the Cocoanut Grove nightclub fire in 1942.

When it opened in November 1903, only a month before the deadly blaze, the Iroquois Theater was a font of civic pride among Chicago's politicians and civic boosters, a lavish symbol of the city's prosperity and thriving popular culture. The six-story entertainment palace, located on 24-28 Randolph Street, was richly **appointed** with marble and mahogany and was touted as a "virtual temple of beauty" that deployed the latest engineering techniques to render it immune to fire. In reality the buildings owners had cut corners on fire protection despite the lengthy chronicle of devastating blazes that had afflicted theaters throughout the United States and Europe. The chief hazards at the Iroquois were the huge canvas scenery backdrops

appointed decorated and equipped.

that were not only decorated with dangerously inflammable oil paints but were also hung near the hot stage lights. Additional safety measures lacking in the Iroquois were a contingent of firemen strategically located around the stage area and adequately provisioned with extinguishers and water hoses; and an asbestos curtain to shield the audience from the spread of fire from the stage.

On December 30, 1904, a gleeful holiday audience packed the ornate showplace to see a matinee performance of the musical comedy Mr. Bluebeard, starring the beloved **vaudevillian** Eddie Foy, Annabelle Whitford, and a huge supporting cast of singers, dancers, and extras. The theater's rated seating capacity was 1,724, but that afternoon's show had packed in enough standees to bring the attendance to around 1,900. The first act proceeded without a hitch, and after a brief intermission, the second act began as scheduled, at about 3:15 P.M. Several minutes into the act, a stagehand noticed that one of the suspended canvas scenery flats was resting against a hot lighting reflector and had begun to smolder and then ignite. He tried to reach out to snuff the small flame, but it was just out of his reach.

Soon the flames started surging up a velvet curtain. The fireman on duty tried to suppress the fire with his only equipment, two tubes of a patented fire suppressant called Kilfyres. This powder proved impotent against the galloping flames, which were now racing to envelop other props and the overhead electrical lighting, which now began to shower the stage with sparks.

As the flaming scenery began to fall on the cast members, they ran off the stage toward the rear exits. Foy asked the orchestra to continue playing and came forward to reassure the increasingly anxious crowd. At Foy's behest the stage manager began to drop the supposedly fireproof asbestos curtain, but it jammed on a lighting fixture or inadequate tracks on its way down. (The curtain was eventually destroyed by the fire, and later testimony revealed that it had not been made of asbestos after all.) Meanwhile, as the panicked cast members streamed out through the rear exit, the inrushing air, unobstructed by any protective curtain, pushed the flames into the auditorium.

Pandemonium erupted among the audience as the hall was quickly engulfed in fire. As Foy later remembered it, "A sort of

vaudevillian individual actor who participated in vaudeville, a stage performance consisting of acting, singing, and dancing.

cyclone came from behind. And there seemed to be an explosion." With the stage beginning to fall apart, the audience stampeded for the 27 exits but found more than half of them barred by iron gates. The first arrivals at the exits were trampled to death by the wave of frantic humanity surging behind them. The ushers were of no use since they had never been through a fire drill. As the frantic crowd turned toward the main exits, still more people were trampled to death.

As the trampled and suffocated corpses piled ten high near the windows and doors on the stairwell area, others jumped to their death from an alley fire escape. Those who jumped later survived only because they hit the dead bodies lining the pavement rather than the concrete beneath. Others died as they leaped from the balcony to the orchestra section of the theater.

The death-dealing panic lasted fifteen minutes, time enough to take the lives of 577 people; an additional 27 succumbed to their injuries in the following days. The coroner's **inquest**, which was featured on the front pages of newpapers throughout the country, exposed criminal negligence on a vast

The charred remains of the Iroquois Theater

inquest official investigation.

scale among the theater's management and the city officials, many of whom had been coaxed into ignoring flouted fire regulations with the promise of free seats to upcoming performances. **Indictments** were brought against the theater's managers, the building owners, and Mayor Carter H. Harrison, but the charges were eventually dropped. The only jail sentence was meted out to the tavern owner who opened his doors as a temporary morgue and then proceeded to filch valuables from the corpses. None of the victims ever managed to win a penny in legal damages.

The Iroquois catastrophe prompted a renewed concern with citywide fire safety. In the ensuing weeks all the city's theaters, public halls, and churches were closed pending a thorough fire-safety inspection, and a new, more exacting, and more strictly enforced fire code was enacted.

The ill-fated Iroquois was able to repoen the following year, rechristened the Colonial Theater. It was demolished in 1926. ◆

The Triangle Shirtwaist Company Fire

MARCH 25, 1911

The Triangle Shirtwaist Company was a garment **sweatshop** in lower Manhattan, just east of Washington Square Park, in the vicinity of what is now the New York University campus. On March 25, 1911, it was the scene of a catastrophic fire that took the lives of 146 garment workers, making it New York's worst factory blaze ever. It was one of the worst disasters to afflict a group of workers since the advent of the Industrial Revolution. The indignation that ensued from the incident imparted fresh impetus to fire-safety and worker-protection laws and spurred support for the union movement.

The Triangle Shirtwaist Company was a typical sweatshop of the early twentieth century, when the labor movement and government regulation of business were still weak and **germinal** phenomena in the United States. Owned by Isaac Harris and

Max Blanck, the company turned out women's tailored shirts that were assembled on the top three floors of the ten-story Asch building by the company's 500 female employees—mostly Jewish and Italian immigrants between the ages of 13 and 33. They worked long hours under unsanitary and unsafe conditions for an average of $6 a week, a woefully meager sum even when adjusted for inflation to current dollar values. Most of the exit doors were kept locked to enforce worker discipline, and the only fire protection was 27 buckets of water and a single, creaky fire escape.

At 4:45 P.M. on March 25, 1911, the sounding of the company bell meant the end of another workday. As the women workers assembled their belongings, someone yelled "Fire!" For reasons that have never been clearly pinpointed, flames had begun to sprout from a rag bin on the eighth floor, and several workers tried to douse them with the available buckets of water, but to no avail. Within minutes the entire eighth floor was engulfed in flames that fed eagerly on the abundant cotton fabrics. The 275 women on the floor bolted for the only exits: the two passenger elevators and the stairway. In their panic to escape, the door to the stairway was temporarily slammed shut. As one worker, Celia Saltz, later recalled, "All I could think was that I must run to the door. I didn't know there was a fire escape. I even forgot that I had a younger sister with me. The door to the staircase wouldn't open. We pushed to the passenger elevators. Everybody was pushing and screaming. When the car stopped at our floor, I was pushed into it by the crowd. I began to scream for my sister. I had lost her. I had lost my sister." Celia passed out in the elevator, and when she awoke, lying on the floor of a nearby building, the first thing she saw was her sister's face bending over her.

The elevators, which held only 10 people each, made enough trips to the eighth floor to vacate nearly all of its workers, many of whom emerged staggered gasping onto the street, their clothing smoldering or partially burned. Most of the workers on the tenth floor managed to escape as well.

The workers on the ninth floor were not as fortunate. The flames had raced upward and enveloped most of the ninth floor, where most of the additional 300 workers now struggled to escape from the rapidly igniting piles of cotton fabric. At first the women stampeded to the east stairway, but it was an impassable tower of flame. They then raced to get to the west stairway and

Female garment workers in New York City in 1961 sit before a poster depicting the victims of the 1911 Triangle Shirtwaist fire.

passenger elevators, but the door was locked, and the elevator was slow in coming to their aid. The frantic women began to hurl themselves down the elevator shaft and out the ninth-floor windows, all of them hurtling to their death. In addition, those seeking to escape by the rear fire escape were killed when the creaky structure collapsed under their weight.

By now Pump Engine Company 20 and Ladder Company 20 had arrived, but their life nets, like the blankets of the volunteer good samaritans, simply ripped apart when struck by the force of three or four bodies at once. Moreover, their ladders were useless, extending only to the sixth floor, and the stream of water from their hoses reached only the seventh story. A gathering crowd of thousands gasped in horror as the bodies of desperate young women piled up on the street. One survivor, Pauline Cuoio Pepe, was 19 years old at the time. She later recalled, "It was all nice young Jewish girls who were engaged to be married. You should see the diamonds and everything. Those were the ones who threw themselves from the window. What the hell did they close the door for? What did they think we were going out with? What are we gonna do, steal a shirtwaist? Who the heck wanted a shirtwaist?" By the time the smoke cleared, 146 workers had died.

The public revulsion over the abysmal working conditions at the factory prompted the governor to appoint an investigative panel within a month of the fire. The Factory Investigating commission was headed by New York Senator Robert F. Wagner, Alfred E. Smith, and Samuel Gompers, the president of the American Federation of Labor. Five years of hearings and fact-gathering led to the passage of important factory-safety legislation. Several months after the blaze the New York City government established the Bureau of Fire Regulation, which enhanced the fire department's powers to enforce fire-safety rules in factories. The tragedy proved to be a turning point in promoting the idea of government safety regulation of private enterprise in the United States. ◆

The Cocoanut Grove Nightclub Fire

NOVEMBER 28, 1942

The inferno that swept through Boston's Cocoanut Grove nightclub on November 28, 1942, taking 492 lives, was the deadliest nightclub fire and one of the worst disasters of any kind in American history.

The lethal conflagration stands in sobering contrast to the boisterous carousing with which the night began. America was at war, and on that Saturday night the popular supper club was jammed with more than 1,000 revelers, twice the facility's legal maximum occupancy. To accommodate impatient patrons, the club had set up extra tables in various open spaces, even on the dance floor, and thus blocked aisles that would be needed to assure safe exit in case of an emergency.

But the club's fire preparedness was sorely lacking in many other respects as well, all of which were curiously overlooked just a week earlier during an inspection by Lieutenant Frank Linney of the Boston Fire Department, who pronounced the facility to be in "good condition," with "a sufficient number of exits" and a "sufficient number of fire extinguishers." In reality, the premises were an open invitation to disaster. To enhance its simulated tropical allure, the owner had liberally **festooned** the club with notoriously flammable artificial palm trees, rattan tables and chairs, and fabric wall hangings and canopies. A number of crucial exits were camouflaged by the dense plastic vegetation, and many of the doors were locked or even welded shut to deter those who might try to sneak out without settling their bill. Moreover, the club's management preferred to hire low-wage and thus inexperienced and ill-trained staff.

On the evening of November 28, in the middle of the Thanksgiving holiday weekend, the club was packed with the locals, **G.I.s** eager for a few hours of fun before moving on to foreign battlefields, and a sizable retinue of Boston College football fans fresh from that afternoon's big game with Holy Cross. At around 10:00 P.M., amid the noisy high spirits, a bulb went out in one of the club's aritifical coconuts in the basement Melody Lounge. The employee assigned to replace it was among the club's numerous illegalities on that night–a 16-year-old high school football star and honor student named Stanly Tomazewski who was two years below the minimum age for working in a nightclub. To see what he was doing, Tomaszewski lit a match. Having replaced the bulb, he blew out the match, not noticing it had contacted a plastic palm that had begun smoldering. Soon it was on fire, spreading rapidly through the bar area and igniting the draperies. The horrified teen dashed out of the building through a kitchen door.

As thick toxic smoke blackened the room, more than a hundred panicked customers converged on the single staircase exit, but the lengthening tongues of flame trapped many in a fiery tomb. The fire was spreading so rapidly that the upstairs diners remained oblivious to the emergency until an escapee from the Melody Lounge streaked across the room screaming, her hair on fire. Before the diners had a chance to move, the inferno overwhelmed the room and killed all the customers. Patrons in other areas jammed the revolving door, rendering it useless after the first few people had escaped. The adjacent emergency doors were bolted shut, trapping scores of people inside the blazing building.

Amid the deadly pandemonium, a few acts of clear-headed heroism stand out. Henry W. Bimler, a waiter, calmly escorted

Survivors attempt to assist victims of the Cocoanut Grove fire in November, 1942.

two frantic woman to the kitchen's walk-in refrigerator, where they remained safely insulated from the blaze. The bandleader, Mickey Alpert, made several rescue missions back to the burning buildling and emerged with badly burned hands. Marshall Cook, a chorus dancer, broke a second-floor window through which 35 entertainers and stagehands made it safely to the roof of the next building. A former naval officer and ex-fireman named Joseph Lawrence Lord was passing by. He broke a window and plunged in to rescue people. He later recalled, "The smoke was choking and thick, but no different really than any fireman meets during many a fire. I crawled along on my hands and knees and then bumped into . . . three women and two men, and one by one, I dragged them to the window I had jumped through. I hoisted them up on the sill and then yelled. . . . Firefighters gave me a hand and pulled them through the window to safety."

A Red Cross nurse's aid remembered the air of panic that hindered rescue efforts. "I had to knock down two survivors with **jujitsu** because they got out of hand. I questioned a girl who

jujitsu an art of weaponless fighting emphasizing the use of throws, holds, and paralyzing strikes to disable an opponent.

National Fire Protection Association

The National Fire Protection Association, today headquartered in Quincy, Massachusetts, is an international, non-profit agency that began in 1896 with the efforts of an MIT engineer and a handful of insurance executives. Today it boasts a membership of almost 70,000, and supports its programs entirely through the sale of fire prevention materials produced by the association.

Back in the late nineteenth century, John Ripley Freeman, recently graduated from MIT, became a factory inspector, working with insurance underwriters to assess policy claims and coverages. He had a lively interest in technological advancements, particularly in areas that related to his employment, so he was up-to-date on improvements that had been made in sprinkler systems designed for factories. He realized that buildings using sprinkler systems suffered far fewer fire losses than non–sprinklered factories, and began pushing for insurers to encourage the use of these devices by offering reduced insurance premiums.

In 1871, Freeman's message took on a greater urgency, when the devastation of the Great Chicago Fire stunned the nation. By 1896, Freeman had managed to convince most of the large insurance companies that national fire standards were a good idea both for public safety reasons and for their own corporate profits.

In the early 1900s, Freeman and several insurance executives drew up a series of safety codes required in any building covered by insurance. Along with demanding that sprinklers be installed, the group worked out a set of electrical standards and several other safety requirements as well. Soon, however, the group recognized that all these safety standards would be of little use if the public was not involved in the fire-safety effort.

In May of 1911 a NFPA member group, the Fire Marshall's Association of North America, sponsored the first Fire Prevention Day. In 1920, President Woodrow Wilson showed his support of the idea by declaring the day a national event, and in 1922 the day was extended to a full week. During the week, local schools and other public institutions participate in projects designed to illustrate fire safety and fire prevention issues, and work at reducing or eliminating fire hazards in the home, school, and workplace.

was pretty high on liquor, and she said she didn't know there was any trouble until the smoke grew heavy. . . . I gave artificial respiration three times . . . and shock treatment once."

These valiant efforts nothwithstanding, 491 people–nearly half the club's patrons that night–died in the blaze, and only 100 escaped injury-free. Boston Hospital took in 130 patients and 300 corpses, the largest influx of trauma victims ever to descend on an American emergency room.

In the aftermath of the fire, theater fire-code regulations were extended to nightclubs, including mandatory sprinkler systems, clearly demarcated exit signs, and strictly enforced occupancy limits. The club's owner, Barnett Welansky, was convicted of manslaughter on April 15, 1943.

The shuttered, charred remains of the Cocoanut Grove were finally demolished in 1944. ◆

The Beverly Hills Supper Club Fire

MAY 28, 1977

The inferno that destroyed the Beverly Hills Supper Club in Southgate, Kentucky, on May 28, 1977, was one of the worst disasters in U.S. history; among nightclub fires, its toll of 165 deaths and 164 injuries was exceeded only by the 1942 Cocoanut Grove nightclub fire in Boston, which claimed 491 lives.

The original Beverly Hills nightclub was a marvel of opulence when it opened in 1937, sprawling over 17 lush acres on the west side of U.S. 27 in Southgate. The costly operation enjoyed mixed success over the years, and after several changes of ownership, it closed in 1961. It reopened briefly in 1969 but then was again shut down by new owners for extensive renovations. While under reconstruction, a major fire destroyed much of the structure, which was rebuilt and reopened in 1971, when the *Cincinnati Enquirer* reported that the new management had failed to remedy "10 major safety defects outlined by the state," among them faulty access to stairway enclosures and exits, which had not received a full inspection by the state fire marshall. Nevertheless, state officials vouched for the safety of the renovated club.

Shortly after a new, larger showroom was opened in 1974, a small fire was triggered by a short circuit in the club's main electrical control board. Despite that sign of potential electrical overload, still another show room was added in 1975, and in January 1977 a state-mandated fire inspection found that "in case of emergency, evacuation should be no problem with existing exits."

Within the facility's walls, the decades-old aluminum wiring was beginning to smolder because of electrical overload.

That assessment received a ghastly refutation only four months later, on the night of May 28, 1977. The boisterous Memorial Day crowds began to gather early that Saturday. By 8:30 in the evening the main nightclub show room and several private parties were in full swing. The Greater Cincinnati Choral Union were in the midst of their annual dinner and fashion show in Crystal Rooms 1, 2, and 3, while rooms 4, 5, and 6 accommodated the revelers of the Afghan Hound Club of Southwestern Ohio. At the other end of the grounds, glasses were raised in various tributes at the Savings & Loan League of Southwestern Ohio and Northern Kentucky.

As guests filed out of a wedding reception in the Zebra Room on the club's ground floor, they were bemoaning the room's excessive warmth, speculating that the air conditioning must be malfunctioning. But something far more dire was amiss. Within the facility's walls, the decades-old aluminum wiring was beginning to smolder because of electrical overload. It was not until twenty minutes later, however, at 8:50, that a reservations clerk first noticed the acrid aroma of smoke. Following the scent to its source, she opened the doors of the empty Zebra room and saw a thick, scalding fog of smoke. She later commented, "All I saw was smoke. Hot, hot, hot. It singed my hair." She ran to a nearby bartender, who raced to the room with a fire extinguisher. But by then the room was engulfed by flames.

A call went out to the fire department, and the evacuation effort began as flames raced darted out of the Zebra Room and up the main stairway, rendering it impassable for the 200 people in the second-floor Crystal Rooms. All but two survived by filling out through the kitchen exits. As a 1978 account in the *Fire Journal* put it, "In the early stage of the fire, there was evidently little panic. Despite the confusion, employees managed to warn patrons, . . . and patrons began to leave the building. Except the patrons in the Cabaret Room."

The Cabaret Room, at the other side of the sprawling structure, was packed to more than twice its legal occupancy limit of 511 as the eager customers awaited the night's main attraction, crooner John Davidson. At roughly 9:00 P.M., a busboy, alarmed by the failure to notify the patrons of the emergency, took to the stage to announce that a minor fire had started, and he asked that the patrons begin to vacate the room. Some simply thought it was part of the opening comedy act, while others rose and proceeded toward the exits.

Protecting Yourself During a Fire

Many of the deaths that occur during fires happen because people are caught by surprise and react in panic. There are ways to increase your chances of survival, however, if you take the time to familiarize yourself with your surroundings and plan ahead.

First and foremost, make certain that you always know where the exits are, whether you are at home or in a public place. Try to imagine at least two escape routes, should a fire break out. Check for the location of a fire alarm or, lacking one, a telephone. At the first sign of a fire, tell yourself to stay calm, then try to make your way to the alarm or the phone to report the situation to the fire department.

Avoid elevators, and especially avoid crowds of people rushing the exits–a great many fire-related deaths are actually caused when people are trampled while trying to escape. If you need to open a door, test it for heat first by touching the frame, knob, and the door itself with the back of your hand. If they are hot, don't open it; there are probably flames on the other side. Even if they are cool, open the door slowly, and be ready to slam it shut again if you see smoke rushing toward you.

If you cannot exit through a door, seal smoke out by stuffing all cracks with cloth or tape. If the room you are in is already filling with smoke, get down so that your face is no more than a few inches above the floor. If possible, wet a cloth and hold it over your mouth and nose to filter out the smoke. Find your way to an external window, and open it from both the top and bottom, so that smoke will circulate out of the room. If escape is impossible, stay by the window and try to signal for help, but do not break the glass, because flames on the outside of the building can easily jump into the room with you.

Meanwhile the inferno was rushing down the corridor from the Zebra Room and burst into the Cabaret Room. As one survivor recalled, "I looked over my left shoulder, and I heard a big whoosh sound. There was flame and smoke, and it just rolled into the room and it was the blackest smoke I'd ever seen . . . If you could just take oil and just get it to roll in midair, then that was the way the smoke was." Within minutes the room was a giant column of flame, and the frantic patrons stampeded toward the exits, trampling the less agile and speedy along the way as the temperature in the room soared to 2,000 degrees Fahrenheit. Scores of people died on the spot from inhaling smoke and the toxic gases spawned by the burning of plastic seat cushions. The banquet captain later recalled seeing dozens of such bodies that bore not a trace of fire or smoke. "They looked like they were asleep because they were clean," he said. The final death toll was 165.

In February 1978, a grand jury was empaneled to investigate possible crimes related to the fire. The following August the grand jury found no criminal negligence and laid the lion's share of the blame on the patrons of the Cabaret Room, noting that "even though notified to evacuate, [they] failed to react and remained seated until the conditions of the room itself indicated the need to exit. By this time in some instances it was too late." In February 1979, a special prosecutor reached a similar conclusion, stating that "nothing is to be gained from additional efforts to pursue criminal prosecution in connection with the fire."

culpability fault; responsibility for a wrong or injury.

Various independent investigators have reached far different conclusions about **culpability** for the disaster. The National Fire Protection Association found numerous code violations such as lack of exits and faulty construction materials. Additional factors were the lack of sprinklers and the obsolete, fire-prone aluminum wiring, which has since been banned by the state authorities.

The various civil suits filed in connection with the fire resulted in $50 million in awards to 281 plaintiffs. ◆

Indonesian Forest Fires

1997–1998

At 1.43 million hectares, Indonesia trails only Brazil as a preserve of precious rainforests. It shares with Brazil the quandary of how to balance the commercial imperatives of loggers and farmers with maintaining the integrity of this critical component of the world's ecological balance. Throughout the 1990s the Indonesian rainforest was in constant danger from the small land-clearing fires started by local farmers. Because of an extended drought in 1997 and 1998, these fires raced out of control, raging throughout the islands of Java, Kalimantan, Sumatra, Sulawesi, and Irian Jaya. The heavy smoke from these blazes darkened the skies and poisoned the air throughout Southeast Asia, most notably in Malaysia, Singapore, Bruei, and Thaliand, and less severely in the Phillipines and Australia.

The first sign of trouble in the past decade was the vast conflagrations that consumed more than 500 square kilometers of the tropical forests of Kalimantan and Sumatra in September

and October 1991. These fires were attributed to the highly flammable debris carelessly scattered by overzealous loggers, whose heavy influence in political circles has shielded them from close government regulation. According to a study by the World Resources Institute, barring government intervention Indonesia's forest will shrink by 12 percent by 2010; many environmentalists consider this a conservative estimate.

In 1997 the outbreak of uncontrolled blazes in Indonesia reached unprecedented and alarming proportions. On September 25 of that year, the Indonesian government declared a national disaster. When the ensuing efforts of the National Disaster Management Coordinating Board proved unequal to the **herculean** task of bringing the fires under control, the regime in Jakarta issued an appeal to the international community to furnish resources and personnel to fend off impending environmental calamity.

Thanks to the exertions of Indonesia's resident United Nations Coordinator, the international body sent a United Nations Disaster Assessment and Coordination Team (UNDAC)

An airplane dispenses water in an attempt to contain a forest fire in Indonesia.

herculean extraordinary strength, power, and stamina; a reference to the mythical Greek hero Hercules.

to Indonesia on September 27 to help in managing the fire-fighting teams and in coordinating the work of the government and international NGO's (non-governmental organizations).

The fires raged the remainder of 1997, ravaging some 7,500 square kilometers in Indonesia and claiming 262 lives. Over the following three months the dense smoke and haze originating in Indonesia began to cause severe air pollution in Malaysia and Thailand and spread far enough to affect 70 million people in six countries. Throughout Southeast Asia, economic activity was drastically hampered as businesses and schools were forced to shut down and tourism plummeted. According to the World Wide Fund for Nature, the sun was so thoroughly eclipsed by the haze that for nearly a month no shadow appeared in land areas encompassing 20 million people.

abate to put an end to; nullify.

The 1997 fires finally began to **abate** with the onset of the monsoon season in December. Because of the skewed weather patterns engendered by El Niño, the monsoons, which normally prevail until April, were less of a deterrent than had been hoped. The rainy season in El Kalimantan lasted only until January, after which the fires regained their momentum, and by April 1998 the fires returned to their peak 1997 levels, consuming 1,830 square kilometers, nearly 1 percent of the land mass of the province, including 30 percent of the Bukit Suharto eco-forest, 23 percent of the Kutai National Park, and large swaths of private plantations. The blazes also endangered the health of the population, engendered dangerously high levels of atmospheric carbon dioxide, and threatened the region's precious biodiversity.

Because of the continuing ineffectuality of the Indonesian government's intervention, in February 1998 the environmental ministers from the nine-member Association of South East Asian Nations (ASEAN) issued an urgent appeal for international aid. Another UNDAC team arrived in late March 1998 to coordinate international aid efforts. In addition, the UN secretary general appointed Klaus Töpfer, the executive director of the United Nations Environmental Program (UNEP), to coordinate the international response to the emergency.

One of Töpfer's first initiatives was bringing the matter before the Admistrative Committee on Coordination (ACC), meeting in late March in Geneva, Switzerland. The ACC pledged its full resources to helping Indonesia contain the fires.

Late in April Töpfer traveled to Jakarta to meet with Indonesian President Suharto and members of his cabinet to plan an international assistance campaign and to urge the government to implement tighter regulations governing the use of land-clearing fires.

These various efforts resulted in a campaign to help Indonesia obtain better firefighting equipment and implement more extensive and rigorous training programs for firefighting personnel. In Jakarta UNDAC also established a Joint Technical Coordination Group on Fire Fighting to work on an ongoing basis to integrate the efforts of the Indonesians and outside governmental and nongovernmental agencies. In late April 1998 firefighting authorities from all over the globe assembled in Geneva to discuss the most effective ways to help the Indonesians fight existing fires and prevent future ones.

Since 1998 the fires in Indonesia's rainforests have abated, but the government is far from having established firm control over the land-clearing blazes set by local farmers. Shortly after the fires had receded, Indonesia's Environment Minister, Sarwono Ksusmaatmadja, told reporters, "This has something to do with the survival of our agribusiness. So I hope this time we make doubly sure that this won't happen again. Otherwise, we'll be out of business forever." ◆

Northern Brazil Fires

1997–1998

"The world's tropical forests are disappearing, but it is not easy to understand the complexities of how this is happening." These ominous words, written by the environmental scientist Johann G. Goldammer in *Science* magazine, took an a special urgency in 1997 and 1998, when vast swaths of the tropical forests of Brazil and Indonesia succumbed to uncontrolled conflagrations.

By March 1998 the fires in Brazil consumed 1.5 million acres of highland **savannah**, pasture, and virgin forest, an area equivalent to the whole of Southeast England. Most of these blazes were set intentionally to clear land in the savannah country, and they then spread to the forest areas. The most

savannah a tropical grassland marked by scattered trees and drought-resistant undergrowth.

The 1998 fires destroyed 22 percent of Roraima's farmland.

dengue fever an infectious disease caused by a virus and marked by severe joint pain, rashes, and headaches.

severely afflicted area was the northern state of Roraima, where the effects of a prolonged drought and El Niño combined to create a disaster of unprecedented proportions. Moreover, as pasture land dried up, the water turned stagnant, becoming a breeding ground for mosquitos that spread malaria and **dengue fever** to many small communities, especially those of the Yanomami people. In some of their villages the rate of malaria contraction was 80 percent during the drought.

Despite these afflictions, the Indians and small farmers clung stubbornly to their traditional practice of burning small areas to prepare fields for cultivation despite the drought conditions that make each such minor blaze the potential starting point of an epic wildfire. This practice is necessitated by the weak soil of the Amazon, which must be fertilized by a layer of ash. Some environmentalists estimate that this slash-and-burn technique lays waste to 2,000 square miles of Brazilian rain forest each year.

There is evidence that some of the fires were set by large landowners as a means of pressing for forgiveness of agricultural loans obtained from local banks. Whatever the immediate cause, the 1998 fires destroyed 22 percent of Roraima's farmland, nearly four percent of the state's total area, resulting in homelessness for more than 6,000 people and disrupting the agricultural livelihood of nearly 200 indigenous communities, most of them Yanomami. In some manner some 90 percent of the 40,000 Indians in Roraima were directly or indirectly affected by the blazes.

Most scientists believe that such widespread fires are likely to recur unless the Brazilian government can manage to change the agricultural folkways of local farmers and apply the brakes to pell-mell commerical development of rainforest areas. Daniel Nepstad, a forest ecologist with the Woods Hole Research Center in Massachusetts, views Roraima as a prototype of the potential disaster awaiting the entire Amazon because of the lush diversity of its plant life.

Some carbon-dating evidence indicates that there have been no less than four vast, natural "burn-offs" in the past two millennia, with the last one having occurred in about 1600. But the 1998 fires were possibly the worst since then. In a March 1998 interview, Philip Fearnside, a scientist at the National Institute of for Amazon Research, told a reporter, "People want to treat this like a nature disaster, like an earthquake or tidal wave,

---

El Niño

El Niño was first recognized in the nineteenth century, when fisherfolk along the Pacific Coast of Ecuador and Peru noticed that the fish had apparently disappeared from their usually rich anchovy fishing grounds. At the same time, unusually heavy rains, accompanied by severe flooding, occurred. This proved to be a recurring event, happening every few years in the weeks just before Christmas. In honor of the date of its occurrence, the locals called the phenomenon "El Niño," which means "the (Christ) Child." Today the name refers to the larger weather system that causes this phenomenon, and scientists are now aware that El Niño is a global-scale climate change phenomenon, responsible for a wide variety of disastrous occurrences throughout the world.

The weather system known as El Niño originates over the ocean in the tropical Pacific region. Here, under normal conditions, a large pool of warm water forms and is pushed westward by the trade winds, then circulates back to its starting point. During this cycle through the sea, the pool gradually dissipates its excess heat.

Every 3-5 years, however, the trade winds are unusually weak. Pools of warm water remain stalled in the eastern and western Pacific, gradually increasing in size and temperature. The increased water temperature kills the small marine life of the area, removing the food source for many animals and larger fish in the region. As a result, migratory patterns are disrupted as hungry predators leave their normal feeding grounds to search for new prey.

The unusually high temperatures generated in the growing pool of water have other effects as well. They disrupt normal weather patterns throughout the world, generating heavy rains in some areas, drought in others. With these abnormal weather conditions, new problems arise. In Ecuador and Peru, El Niño brings heavy rains and flooding, resulting in diseases from contaminated water and infections borne by increased rat populations. El Niño was one very real cause of the drought that afflicted Brazilian forests in 1998, rendering them highly flammable and thus contributing to the great forest fires of that year.

where nothing can be done. But it's not just El Niño, there are economic and social factors that also have an impact."

The United States agency responsible for monitoring Amazon deforestation, the National Space Research Institute, reports that 12 percent of the 2 million square miles of the Amazon have been cut down by farmers and loggers, thus fostering conditions for more frequent and more severe fires. Ademire dos Santos, the chief of Brazil's Environmental Protection Agency in Roraima, is hopeful that the 1998 fires will spur preventive action. He told a reporter, "I think this will be a lesson. They used to say tropical rain forest doesn't burn. Now, they can see it does. If we don't move away from this archaic [slash-and-burn] agriculture, we are risking other tragedies." He is not so sure, however, that environmental awareness will be easy to sell to the poor indigenous farmers who rely on traditional farming methods for their meager subsistence livelihood.

One hopeful direction is alternative agriculture–growing fruit trees, rubber and Brazil nuts rather than traditional crops. Another possiblity is sustainable logging–a method akin to crop rotation that allows various areas to recover from previous **depradations**. The World Wildlife Fund has already collaborated with the Brazilian government in carrying out some experiments in sustainable logging.

Despite these encouraging remedial efforts, there is a growing concern among environmentalists that the loss of the world's tropical forests–a real possibility that would be an incalculable blow to the earth's ecological balance–is proceeding faster than the sense of urgency about the problem. ◆

depredations plunderings and waste of resources.

Dongdu Disco Fire

DECEMBER 25, 2000

Although Christmas is not an official holiday in mainland China, many younger people celebrate it. In Luoyang, an ancient Chinese capital city located just south of the Yellow River in the province of Henan, several hundred young people decided to celebrate Christmas in 2000 by attending a special evening party at the Dongdu Disco.

The disco, located on the fourth floor of a commercial building in a shopping center in an older part of the growing city, was dimly lit and packed with people; later reports said that over 400 tickets had been sold to the event. But what began as a night of holiday revelry would end for most in horror.

At about 9:35 P.M. a fire broke out in a furniture shop in the basement of the building. Although flames reached only the first floor, clouds of thick, billowing smoke filled the stairwells and trapped the partygoers on the fourth floor. As people began to realize that they had no escape route, panic broke out. Some managed to leap from windows, while others hung in the window openings, too frightened to jump. Later, it was learned that several victims left urgent cell phone and beeper messages with

As people began to realize that they had no escape route, panic broke out.

family and friends, pleading for help. Firefighters were called, but by the time they were able to bring the fire under control at about 12:45 A.M., it was too late, and the grizzly task of recovering the bodies of victims—most of whom had died of smoke inhalation—began.

Over the next hours rumors spread that as many as 700 people had died, but the official Chinese news agency put the final death toll at 309. Dozens of people were treated for smoke inhalation at local hospitals, but no exact count of survivors was available. While most of the victims were partygoers, a few were construction workers who had been doing renovation work on the building at the time. (It is a common practice in China for construction crews to work around the clock.) Among deaths caused by fires in China, the death toll at the Dongdu Disco was second only to that of a 1977 fire that killed 694 people in Xinjiang.

Like many disasters, particularly those involving human fallibility, this one did not have to happen, and in the days that followed, many citizens in the community expressed anger with public officials, believing that the tragedy was the result of government incompetence and corruption. Their belief was not without foundation, for the privately-run dance hall was operating illegally. The glass-fronted building, a maze of shops and narrow corridors, was constructed in the 1980s, and while it had foam fire extinguishers, it had no sprinkler system, fire alarms, or smoke alarms. Residents of the building said that the owners had promised to improve safety, but no action had been taken—despite repeated warnings from public officials about inadequate fire-fighting systems. In fact, the building had a history of safety violations that extended back at least three years; in 1997 local officials had listed it as one of the 40 most dangerous commercial buildings in the province. Just a week before the fire it had failed a safety inspection. Though officials had canceled the building's license to lease space, the managers continued to rent out the fourth floor as a disco, and other businesses in the building leased space without legal contracts.

Compounding these problems, the disco had no emergency exits and only two regular exits, one hidden behind a bar. Witnesses also said that exits to the building were blocked by boxes of merchandise; others said that exit doors were locked. In short, once the fire started and smoke began to fill the building, the hundreds of Christmas-night partygoers were doomed.

In the days that followed, many local citizens took part in uncharacteristic protests against local officials. One group of protesters, for example, climbed onto a traffic police podium in the middle of a busy Luoyang intersection and unfurled a banner that read "Justice for the Dead of 25.12," referring to the date of the fire, December 25. Other protesters filled the surrounding streets, blocking traffic. Uniformed police charged the podium and tore down the banner, and paramilitary police were called to break up the protest. One elderly man pounded his fists against the window of a police truck; others held photos of family members killed in the fire; a distraught woman wagged her finger in the face of a city official sent to negotiate with the protesters. Web sites fueled rumors about the tragedy and alleged that officials were covering up the tragedy. Many citizens were upset by how slowly emergency services responded; one witness claimed that an hour after fire trucks arrived, firefighters had been able to find only a weak trickle of water to fight the flames.

Faced with mounting public discontent, Chinese premier Zhu Rongji vowed that those responsible for the blaze would be severely punished. His statements were met with skepticism, for safety had been a chronic problem in many of China's public buildings, and many building owners and managers either ignored safety regulations or, in some cases, bribed corrupt local officials to look the other way. To counter public unrest, the Chinese Ministry of Public Security released an urgent circular ordering that all discos and dance halls operating without a license or fire-control systems be closed immediately and that all hotels, shopping malls, hospitals, and schools be inspected for fire dangers. Unfortunately, many such circulars had been published in the past, with little effect.

The question that remained for investigators, though, was what caused the fire. Chinese police announced that approximately 20 people were under surveillance for their possible role in the tragedy, including managers of a Taiwan company that owned the building. On December 27, they announced that they had arrested four welders who had been working on renovations in the building. According to the police, sparks from a welding operation accidentally ignited the fire, but the welders fled without raising any alarm. ◆

Shipwrecks

Sultana

The explosion of the steamboat *Sultana* on April 27, 1865, was the worst maritime disaster in American history and one of the most lethal in the history of the world, taking 1,547 lives, exceeding the *Titanic's* death toll of 1,512. Nearly all of the victims were **emaciated** Union soldiers who had been liberated from Southern prisoner-of-war camps and were heading North to rejoin their families. Yet the disaster received very little notice at the time and has receded as a footnote to history, largely because it occurred shortly after the assassination of President Abraham Lincoln.

emaciated dangerously thin; wasting away.

The *Sultana* was a typical sidewheel steamboat of the era. Originally built in 1863 to serve as a cotton transport, the 1,719-ton steamer ran a regular route on the Mississippi River between New Orleans and St. Louis. During the Civil War the ship functioned primarily as a troop transport for the Union Army.

Soon after the end of the war, the *Sultana* was summoned to Vicksburg, Mississippi, to pick up a large contingent of recently released Union prisoners of war. The ship was long overdue for basic maintenance. The ship steamed out of New Orleans on April 21, 1865, carrying about one hundred cabin passengers. When it arrived in Vicksburg on April 24, a routine inspection revealed a severe leak in the ship's boilers and departure was held up while the boilers were repaired. During the delay an additional contingent of released Union prisoners showed up, impatient to make the journey home. As high in spirits as they were frail of body, the homeward-bound surged onto the creaky vessel in numbers that far exceeded the *Sultana's* rated capacity

The boat disintegrated under the terrible force of the blast, and hundreds of sleeping soldiers were killed instantly.

of 376. Although no precise figure is available, most reliable scholarly accounts put the total passenger count at 2,000 to 2,300. The bodies were tightly serried into every available square foot of space on deck, in the cabins, and in the hull.

The *Sultana* struggled upstream against an unusually strong current on a journey that was scheduled to end at Cairo, Illinois. At the stop in Memphis, Tennessee, the boat's boilers were found to be leaking again. After another hasty repair, the boat pulled out late at night on April 26, 1865, battling so strong a current that one of the ship's officers commented, "I'd give all the interest I have in this steamer if we were safely landed at Cairo."

Several hours later, about 10 miles north of Memphis, the ship's failing boilers finally gave. No longer able to contain the steam's pressure, they exploded with such force that the explosion was heard back in Memphis; the accompanying fireball lit up the sky for miles around. The boat disintegrated under the terrible force of the blast, and hundreds of sleeping soldiers were killed instantly. Those not killed by the explosion drowned in the icy currents of the river.

There were a few freakish exceptions to the general carnage. One man was propelled 200 feet by the blast but landed in the river and was able to swim to safety on the bank. Three others were blown into the water while still clinging to a piece of the deck; it floated all the way back to Memphis, where the men were rescued. But these were the rare grace notes in a roar of fire and death.

The ensuing fire consumed the remains of the steamer. According to one man who survived by latching on to a fragment of the upper deck, "On looking down and out in to the river, I would see men jumping from all parts of the boat into the water until it seemed black with men, their heads bobbing up and down like corks, and then disappearing beneath the turbulent waters, never to appear again."

As the burning remains of the ship drifted out of control, dozens of dazed and maimed men remained on board. Some of them were able to seize hold of doors of fragments that kept them afloat in the water. Torn between incineration and drowning, many desperate men clung to the remnants of the hull until the last possible moment. One witness recalled, "The men who were afraid to take to the water could be seen clinging to the sides of the bow of the boat until they were singed off like flies. Shrieks and cries for mercy were all that could be heard; and that awful morning reminded me of the stories of doomsday of my childhood."

The 500-600 survivors that dotted the shoreline were transported to Memphis hospitals, where some 200 of them perished shortly thereafter. For several days barges set out to retrieve bodies and returned loaded with charred and bloated remains. Although official estimates of the total death toll vary, many scholars place the number in the range of 1,700. Yet that unprecedented catastrophe received little notice in the nation's press, still preoccupied with the assassination of Abraham Lincoln and its aftermath. The nation's worst maritime disaster barely registered in the national consciousness and has remained a footnote to history. ◆

General Slocum

June 15, 1904

The worst disaster ever to befall New York City on a single day was the fire aboard the paddleboat *General Slocum* on June 15, 1904, which took the lives of 1,021 people who had set out for what they believed would be a serene Sunday cruise followed by an idyllic picnic.

Named for the Civil War hero Henry W. Slocum, the doomed vessel had accumulated a dubious safety record in its 13-year life, running aground six times and suffering four collisions. Yet it remained a profitable and popular boat, with its spacious 235-foot length and luxurious accommodations. Only a month before its final disaster, the *Slocum* had been certified as safe by officials of the U.S. Steamboat Inspection Service, who somehow managed to overlook its old lifebelts, balky fire pump, frayed hoses, or the layers of paint that had effectively welded the lifeboats to the side of the steamer.

Unaware of these hazards, the St. Mark's Evangelical Lutheran Church, a congregation on New York's Lower East Side that served the local German community, chartered the *Slocum* for the its annual Sunday-school maritime outing to the Locust Grove Picnic Ground on Eaton's Neck. The students' families, as always, invited relatives from all over New York for

The remains of the *General Slocum* as it sinks following a terrible fire that killed 1,021 people.

a festive family-reunion atmosphere. On the sunny morning of June 15, 1904, the 1,331 passengers, most of whom were women and children, eagerly boarded the aging steamer, oblivious to the somber omens of the the conflagration that lay ahead: the three barrels of glasses were put aboard the ship packed in hay and stored in the forward cabin despite prohibitions against sailing with loose hay; the 35 member crew made up mostly of novices who had had little or no emergency training.

The boat pulled out at 9:20 A.M. to festive music and dancing on the deck. But only 16 minutes later, a fire began to spread from the storage locker area, where the hay was stowed. As the ship passed Astoria, a boy frantically accosted a deckhand and shouted, "Mister, there's smoke coming up one of the stairways." The deckhand opened the door of the storeroom, and the hay in the barrels ignited into deadly flame. The captain, first informed of the fire by a frenetic young boy, at first dismissed it as a prank.

Meanwhile, the deckhand grasped at the first object he could find to throw on the leaping flames. Unfortunately, he grabbed two bags of charcoal. Several more critical minutes elapsed while the first mate consulted with the engineer before they finally called the captain and activated the fire hose. But the ancient hose disintegrated at the first rush of water.

Finally apprised of the gravity of the fire, Captain William Van Schaick decided to bypass the hazardous gas plants on the Queens and Bronx shores and push ahead another one and a half miles to the sandy beach of North Brother Island, near the current location of LaGuardia Airport. Meanwhile desperate passengers, many with their garments aflame, jumped overboard without life preservers, many of which were affixed immovably to the ceiling by mesh wire. One of the survivors recalled, "Some of them we could not budge, and others pulled to pieces and spilled the crumbs of cork all over our heads." The lifeboats, bonded to the side of the boat by successive layers of paint, were never launched.

When the ship finally ran aground, it was still in deep water. Dozens of panicked passengers and crew clambered down the rails to escape the inferno. One survivor, 14 years old at the time, recalled that "my father told me to jump, but I could not get my hand off—it was baked on the rail with the paint." She finally managed to wriggle free and jump into the water. "I had to be careful to clear the paddlewheel, as people were being caught [in it] and died; so I tried to jump out far enough, and I struck a rock and broke all my front teeth."

The horror of the episode was compounded by a group of **craven** onlookers ashore who stripped some of the dazed and incapacitated victims of their valuables while they awaited medical attention or demanded money to pull people out of the water.

craven fainthearted and lacking in courage or bravery.

The disaster took 1,021 lives. An official investigation ruled that the fire was ignited by a cigarette or match thrown carelessly among the barrels. An inquest jury indicted the captain, first mate, officers of the steamboat company, and a steamboat inspector. Only the captain, however, was found guilty, on a variety of charges: failing to conduct fire drills, hiring unqualified crew members, and not maintaining critical safety equipment such a pumps, fire hoses, life jackets, and life boats. He received a sentence of 10 years in prison but was released on parole after serving three and a half years.

The crippled ship was salvaged for service as a barge and finally sank off the shore of Atlantic City in 1911. ◆

Titanic

April 14–15, 1912

gargantuan overly large and outsized.

hull the frame or body of a ship exclusive of sails, yards, and masts.

The ocean liner *Titanic* was the technological summit of its time, the early-twentieth-century equivalent of a space station or supercomputer. Here was a vessel that inspired awe not only for its **gargantuan** dimensions and lavish accommodations but also for its claimed immunity to the hazards of nature. In the *Titanic* the cruel whims of the sea had at last met their match, most notably in the form of a double-bottomed **hull** with 16 watertight compartments that would keep the ship afloat even if four were flooded, an unthinkable contingency.

The *Titanic's* 53,000 metric tons of weight and 882 feet of length made it the largest ocean liner of the era, and its exquisite appointments and lavish facilities made it the most splendid: it featured a theater, a variety of elegant restaurants, a reading and writing room, a gym, a barber shop, a swimming pool, a miniature golf course, ballrooms, and first-class cabins of unparalleled size and sumptuousness. The *Titanic* promised a dazzling voyage for those who could afford it: the top price for first-class passage was $4,350 (about $50,000 in 2001 dollars). Its superabundance in nearly every particular was marred by one fatal deficiency, born of overconfidence: it carried lifeboats for only half of the ship's passenger capacity of 2,200.

Thus provisioned, on April 10, 1912, the *Titanic* set out from Southampton, England, on its much-heralded maiden voyage, bound for New York City. The ship's first-class passenger list was a roster of the elite of Anglo-American high society, politics, and industry, including the mining tycoon Benjamin Guggenheim; John Jacob Astor, Major Archibald Butt, Isidor Straus, the head of Macy's department store, and his wife, Ida; Mrs. Margaret Tobin Brown, the Colorado socialite later lionized as the "Unsinkable Molly Brown"; and the British aristocrats Sir Cosmo and Lady Duff Gordon.

Mindful that the *Titanic's* management company, the White Star line, hoped to set a speed record on its first crossing, the ship's captain, Edward J. Smith, maintained a brisk pace on the first few days on the high seas, averaging 550 miles per day. Everything seemed to be proceeding splendidly; Second Officer Charles H. Lightoller reflected the high spirits in the following diary entry:

"It was clear to everybody on board that we had a ship that was going to create the greatest stir British shipping circles had ever known. Each day, as the voyage went on, everybody's admiration of the ship increased; for the way she behaved, for the total absence of vibration, for her steadiness even with the ever-increasing speed, as she warmed up to her work."

All during the day on Sunday, April 14, the *Titanic* had begun to receive telegraph reports of approaching icebergs. At noon, it received this message: "Greek steamer *Athenai* reports passing icebergs and large quantities of field ice today." At 9:30 P.M. another such warning arrived from the *Mesaba*: "Much heavy pack ice and a great number of large icebergs." That last message was never sent to the bridge because the ship's chief radio operator, Jack Phillips, was overhwhelmed with requests for personal messages to be sent on behalf of the ship's passengers.

Nevertheless, Captain Smith had had ample warning of the danger that lay ahead, yet he unaccountably failed to reduce the ship's speed or post additonal lookouts. At 11:40 P.M., Seaman Frederick Fleet, peering out from his 50-foot perch, noticed a hulking white object looming ominously in the distance, and the

The prow of the *Titanic* lies at the bottom of the Atlantic Ocean.

Titanic was heading directly toward it. He rang out the warning bell and called the bridge to announce, "Iceberg ahead." Less than a minute later, a mild shudder rippled through the great ship's **starboard** side as it grazed the side of the ice floe.

The impact was so mild that it failed to rouse some of the sleeping passengers. One first-class traveler recounted the moment in these words: "[It was] as though someone had drawn a giant finger all along the side of the boat." A science teacher in second class portrayed it as "nothing more than what seemed to be an extra heave of the engines . . . no sound of a crash or anything else . . . no jar that felt like one heavy body meeting another."

Yet the *Titanic* had been mortally wounded. The short encounter with the iceberg had left six seemingly slight gashes in the ship's steel hull, but they were sufficient to puncture and flood six watertight compartments and thus doom the fabled vessel. Later **metallurgical** tests revealed that the ship's steel was overly brittle and thus prone to fracture because of an excess of slag used in its manufacture.

The crew quickly became aware that the ship had at most a few hours left and began organizing the evacuation. Initially the first-class passengers greeted the news with bemused incredulity and seemed more concerned with extracting their valuables from the bursar than with leaving the warmth of a luxury liner for a tiny lifeboat adrift in the frigid darkness of the open sea. When the first lifeboat was lowered at 12:45 A.M., it was less than half full. John Jacob Astor helped his wife into a lifeboat and graciously retreated when he was told that only women and children could enter it. Ida Strauss decided that she would not avail herself of the safety of a lifeboat. "No," she said. "I will not be separated from my husband, As we have lived, so we will die." She offered her warm coat to her maid, Ellen Bird, who proceeded to the lifeboat alone.

As the bow of the ship slipped beneath the water at 1:00 A.M., the urgency of the situation became clear, and the pace of lifeboat launchings quickened accordingly. As that frantic hour wore on, Jack Phillips kept up his stream of SOS messages, adding, "Women and children on boats. Cannot last much longer." Benjamin Guggenheim stood stoically on the deck with his valet, respendent in full evening attire. He told a woman waiting to board a lifeboat, "We've dressed up in our best, and are prepared to go down like gentlemen."

At 2:20 A.M., the *Titanic's* boilers exploded; the ship went into a vertical position and then slipped quietly beneath the icy waters as the desparate screams of the stranded—most of whom were **steerage passengers**—rang out across the waters. As the lifeboats splashed in the desolate darkness and silence, none of the survivors knew if an SOS had been received or if they would ever be rescued. At about 4:00 A.M. the lights of the *Carpathia* appeared on the horizon, and it immediately set to work hoisting the 700 survivors from their lifeboats. Of the 2,200 people on board, 1,513 had perished. Many more lives might have been spared if another ship, the *Californian*, only 10 miles from the *Titanic* at 11:40, had been alerted to its plight. But the *Californian's* radio operator had shut off his receiver and retired for the night just before the moment of impact.

steerage passengers passengers on a ship paying the lowest fares and given subpar accommodations.

The inquiry following the disaster noted the insufficiency of lifeboats and the captain's heedlessness in maintaining full speed in the face of repeated iceberg warnings. To prevent another such catastrophe, an International Convention for Safety of Life at Sea was convened in London in 1913 and established binding regulations that included lifeboat space for all passengers; mandatory lifeboat drills; and 24-hour radio watches on all ships.

The wreck of the *Titanic* was found in 1985 and has since been throrougly examined through the use of unmanned submersible vessels. The grand ship's tragic story has assumed the proportions of legend, recounted in dozens of books, a Broadway musical, and three major motion pictures, the most recent of which, *Titanic* (1997), was the most expensive and highest-grossing film ever made. The film's worldwide popularity helped to remind a new generation that even the most advanced technology is but a ragged **supplicant** before the imperious powers of nature. Perhaps Charles Lightoller, the ship's second officer, said it best in testimony before a Congressional inquiry: "I don't think I'll ever feel secure of anything again." ◆

supplicant helpless person or thing in the face of awesome power.

Empress of Ireland

MAY 28, 1914

More than two years after the sinking of the supposedly unsinkable *Titanic* staggered the imagination of the world, another luxury liner met a similarly grim fate, costing nearly as many lives but with far less fanfare. Perhaps because the *Empress of Ireland* was smaller, less lavish and renowned than the White Star's doomed **flagship**, its violent end has occasioned few books and no blockbuster films. But its shockingly rapid demise—it sank in only 14 minutes from the moment of impact—remains one of the most devastating if underreported of modern maritime disasters.

Roughly two-thirds the size of the *Titanic*, the *Empress of Ireland* was a two-stack, twin-acre steamer that measured 550 feet long and weighed 14,000 tons. Along with her sister ship, the *Empress of Britain*—both built and run by the Scottish Fairfield Shipping Company—the vessel had spent several profitable years on the route from Liverpool, England, to Quebec, Canada, a journey she typically accomplished in six days thanks to a then-impressive average cruising speed of 20 **knots**. Although not among the elite of the day's ocean liners, *Empress of Ireland* nonetheless was appointed with the luxuries that were typical of that era's floating palaces. As one writer described the ship, "She was a special ship with appointments comparable to the *Lusitania*. For examples, her first-class dining room was 65 feet wide, 58 feet long, and had leather upholstery, guilded woodwork, sculpted ceilings, cut-glass ceilings, cut-glass fixtures, and an atrium that went up two levels to a music room."

At 4:27 P.M. on May 28, 1914, the *Empress of Ireland* set out from Quebec on it first trip of the summer season and the last of its career. Early the next morning, after the ship had traveled serenely through 200 miles of the St. Lawrence River, the *Empress's* skipper, Captain Henry Kendall, spotted another ship three miles away, heading toward it. Henry Kendall steered sharply northward to give the other ship a wide berth, but the oncoming vessel—the Norwegian coal ship *Storstad*—soon disappeared into a swiftly descending fog bank.

Exactly what happened next is shrouded in an equally thick fog of conflicting stories about botched maneuvers, confusing signals, and faulty judgments. Several minutes after entering the fog bank, thinking he had properly altered course to skirt danger, the *Storstad's* chief officer was suddenly confronted by the sight of the *Empress's* starboard profile. His desperate reversal of engines was far too little, too late as the *Storstad* plowed into the *Empress*, tearing a huge gash that triggered a massive onrush of water into the liner's boiler rooms. Within minutes the *Empress's* starboard side sank nine feet, thrusting dozens of shocked passengers into a fatal plunge into the river's icy waters. The power failed within three minutes, leaving hundreds of terrified crew and passengers to grope in the darkness. The

Empress slipped below the water's surface in only fourteen minutes, enough time to launch only seven of the ship's forty lifeboats. A hasty SOS was for naught–1,012 people perished, 840 of them passengers still in their beds.

All three countries involved in the catastrophe launched official probes into its causes. The Canadian Court of Inquiry heard the account of Captain Kendall, who survived to testify that he had been stopped for eight minutes in the fog at the time he was struck by the *Storstad*. Captain Thomas Andersen also testified, but offered a less detailed account since he was not at the bridge at the moment of impact. The British inquiry was led by Lord Mersey, who had also investigated the sinking of the *Titanic*. Mersey laid the blame on the officer steering the *Storstad* for having failed to consult his captain and ask for instructions when the fog descended. The Norwegian Maritime Court absolved the *Storstad's* officers of any responsibility.

Subsequent investigators have noted that Kendall's claim to have stopped does not square with the physical evidence of the impact. They further note that Kendall had not closed all his watertight compartments, a standard safety procedure under fog conditions.

Although the *Empress of Ireland* plunged quickly to its watery grave, the *Storstad* lived to sail again. After being impounded briefly for the investigation, it was repaired and resumed service under Captain Andersen. But the *Storstad*, too, met a violent end not long after, when it was struck by a torpedo from a German submarine. Although the ship was lost, all those aboard survived. ◆

Eastland

July 24, 1914

On the morning of July 24, 1914, a joyful boating excursion for employees of the Western Electric Company turned into a catastrophe as the lake passenger steamer *Eastland* listed and rolled over, taking 844 of the 2,572 excursionists to their deaths. It remains the largest death toll of any disaster in the history of Chicago.

Completed in 1903 by the Michigan Steamship Company, the *Eastland* was intended chiefly for passenger runs on the

Smaller boats attempt to rescue survivors of the *Eastland* catastrophe along the Chicago River on July 24, 1914.

capacious capable of carrying a great deal of material; having an abundance of space.

ballast a weighty substance or object used to control the draft and improve the stability of a ship or the ascent of a balloon.

heavily traveled 77-mile Lake Michigan route between Chicago and South Haven, Michigan. Eventually the steamer also plied the waters of Lake Erie, shuttling passengers between the Ohio cities of Sandusky and Toledo. After changing hands several times, the vessel became the property of the St. Joseph-Chicago Steamship Company in June 1914, after which it returned to its initial service between Chicago and various towns in northern Indiana and southwestern Michigan.

The **capacious** *Eastland* stood four decks high and was 269 feet long. Its relatively narrow width–36 feet–enabled it to cruise at up to 22 miles per hour, earning it widespread renown as one of the faster steamers on the Great Lakes. From its inception, however, it experienced alarming mishaps that cast a shadow over its reputation for seaworthiness. In the summer of 1904, while heading for Chicago with a load of some 2,500 passengers, the boat began listing sharply to the starboard side and righted itself only after passengers were moved away from that side of the ship and water was added to the **ballast** tanks. Two years later another such listing incident occurred, again presumably because of passenger crowding on the ship's starboard side.

Although these two incidents spawned reservations about the *Eastland's* stability, the steamer amassed thouands of hours of safe and trouble-free operation over the years. To dispel any rumors to the contrary, The Eastland Navigation Company, which owned the ship from 1909-1914, took out a newspaper ad in 1910 in which it offered $5,000 to anyone who could prove that "the *Eastland* is not a seaworthy ship, or that she would not ride out any storm or weather any condition that can arise on either lake or ocean." The ship's unblemished record over the ensuing four years seemed to vindicate the owner's claim. In 1915 the ship's new owners made changes that probably raised its center of gravity and thus compromised its stability; nevertheless the remodeled *Eastland* passed a mandatory U.S. government inspection on July 4, 1915, at which time its maximum passenger load increased to 2,500.

None of the passengers seemed alarmed by what seemed like mild swaying.

The Western Electric Company rented the *Eastland* and six other ships for its annual company picnic outing, a cruise to Michigan City, Indiana, for which 7,000 tickets had been sold. Because the renovated *Eastland* and the *Theodore Roosevelt* were the most modern and renowned of the six ships in the company's chartered fleet, they attracted the most passengers. By 6:30 A.M., the two ships began taking on passsengers at their moorings on the south side of the Chicago River. Within 10 minutes the *Eastland* began to list to the starboard side, so the boat's engineer had the ballast tanks filled on the **port** side to right the ship, which leveled out 10 minutes after the first tilt.

port left side of a ship or plane looking forward; the right side is starboard.

As passengers resumed streaming onto the ship, it began leaning to the port side, so the engineer ordered a partial filling of the ship's starboard ballast tanks, which again briefly righted the *Eastland*. With the ship fully loaded by 7:10 A.M., it once again began to lean to port, so the water was released from that side's ballast tanks. After a temporary aggravation of the port list, the ship leveled temporarily but soon resumed such a pronounced port tilt that water began sloshing into several port-side openings. None of the passengers seemed alarmed by what seemed like mild swaying.

The passengers concentrated on the port side for a better view of the launch. Just as the gangplank was withdrawn at around 7:25, the port-side tilt became so bad that passengers were redirected to the starboard side to restore the ship's balance. However, the flow of water onto the port side rendered the adjustment futile, and by half past the hour the tilt was an alarming 45 degrees. By now any object not bolted down was sliding and crashing about, and a sense of panic began to grip the crowded decks. Passengers began to crawl out of passageways on the starboard side as the Eastland kept tilting so far to port that it finally came to a full rest on that side.

The lucky passengers were those who had managed to scramble to the safety of the starboard side or who managed to stay afloat in the water when dislodged from the overturned ship. Hundreds of others were less fortunate. In the words of one surviving passenger,

"I shall never be able to forget what I saw. People were struggling in the water, clustered so thickly that they literally covered the surface of the river. A few were swimming; the rest were floundering about, some clinging to a life raft that had floated free, others clutching at anything that they could reach–at bits of wood, at each other, grabbing each other, pulling each other down, and screaming! The screaming was the most horrible of all."

Despite the frantic rescue efforts of nearby boats, hundreds of people had been pulled under by the *Eastland's* fatal imbalance while others were trapped in the boat as the water rose faster than rescuers could reach them. In all 844 people perished in the disaster–841 passengers and three crew members.

After the ship was finally set upright nearly a month later, it was acquired by the Illinois Naval Reserve, which made enough safety modifications to allow its use as a training ship, rechristened the U.S.S. *Wilmette*. It was finally decomissioned in 1945 and two years later was sold to a salvager for scrap metal. ◆

Lusitania

May 7, 1915

The name *Lusitania* survives in posterity as one of the causes of the United States' entry into World War I. A British passenger ship, it was torpedoed off the coast of Ireland on May 7, 1915, by a German submarine and sank in 20 minutes, taking 1,198 people to their deaths, including 128 Americans. The incident galvanized anti-German and pro-British sentiment in the United States as "Remember the *Lusitania*!" became a rallying cry in the nation's newspapers.

One of the fastest and most luxurious ocean liners of its day, the *Lusitania* had been in transatlantic cargo and passenger service since 1906. When the *Lusitania* set out from New York for its return journey to Liverpool, England, the German government had already issued a warning, widely publicized in the American and international press, that because British liners were suspected of transporting war materials, they were fair game for German submarines. Despite the recent sinking of several British merchant ships by German U-boats off the south coast of Ireland, the *Lusitania* felt confident of its ability to evade attack because of its exceptional agility and speed for a vessel of its imposing size (32,000 tons).

These incidents had prompted the British Admiralty to issue a warning to the *Lusitania's* captain, William Turner, to avoid the area on his return journey and to execute sudden, evasive changes of course–zigzagging–to throw off any would-be pursuers. Curiously, Turner ignored nearly all of the admiralty's guidelines. As he neared the Irish coast, he was more concerned about patches of fog than German submarines, so he actually slowed down instead of speeding up. In addition, he sailed perilously close to the shore–where U-boats were wont to hunt their prey–instead of the deeper open waters. Moreover, he eschewed zigzagging in the belief that evasive action was warranted only after the actual sighting of a submarine. He was, however, steering the ship farther from the shore than it had gone on several previous trips during the war. A veteran merchant captain, Turner was evidently inclined to rely more on intuition than orders from distant bureaucrats. Others have pointed out that the perilous conditions called for more than mere advice and warnings–a destroyer escort, they argue, was called for under the circumstances.

On the afternoon of May 7, 1915, as the Lusitania lumbered off the Irish coast south of Queenstown, it came within the

The top photo shows the *Lusitania* while the bottom portrays a German U-139 submarine emerging from the water.

sights of of German U-boat officer Walther Schweiger. Apprised that the giant liner was probably carrying *munitions*, Schieger took aim and dispatched a single torpedo, which struck its target, exploding on contact and piercing the *Lusitania's* hull on the starboard side. Passengers aboard the ship described that first explosion variously as "a peal of thunder," a "dull, thudlike sound," or "like a million-ton-hammner hitting a steel boiler a hundred feet high and a hundred feet long."

As water surged into the first and second boiler rooms, the boat shuddered and listed from side to side. There soon followed a second, even more massive explosion, the cause of which remains a source of controversy among scholars. Some argue that it might have been hit by a second or even third torpedo, while others contend that the blast originated from within the ship. But supporters of the latter thesis disagree about whether the trigger was the ship's own boiler room or its suspected cargo of munitions. Although the official records show a cargo of platinum, bullion, diamonds, and precious gems, such items were never discovered in the wreckage. Many scholars believe that hidden in bales of fur and boxes marked "cheese" were copious supplies of three-inch shells and countless rounds of rifle ammunition. As one historian has noted, if the ship did carry such materiel, it would have constituted "a **contraband** and explosive cargo which was forbidden by American law and . . . should never have been placed on a passenger ship."

Whatever the source of that convulsion, it proved fatal to the *Lusitania*, which sank within 18 minutes, taking 1,198 people to their deaths. Thanks to the captain's **alacrity** in issuing an SOS, help still managed to arrive in time to rescue 764 passengers. The magnitude of civilian loss of life sparked indignation throughout the world, especially in the United States, which lost 128 of its citizens in an attack on an unarmed civilian vessel that the United States government deemed to be "contrary to international law and the conventions of all civilized nations."

Diplomatic tensions between the United States and Germany neared the breaking point over the incident, which was one of the most significant factors in mobilizing American popular opinion in favor of U.S. intervention in World War I. President Woodrow Wilson sent three sharp notes to the German government demanding **reparations** and a cessation of U-boat attacks on nonmilitary vessels. Although it refused to accept re-

---

contraband goods being shipped illegally.

alacrity promptness.

reparations payments by one entity to another for past transgressions or offenses.

sponsibility for the incident, the German government did agree to make reparations and to end U-boat harassment of merchant and military ships. Despite this **modus vivendi**, the sinking of the *Lusitania* set U.S.-German relations on a collision course that resulted in American entry into the war. ◆

modus vivendi Latin phrase for compromise.

Mont Blanc Explosion

DECEMBER 6, 1917

The largest preatomic explosion in history took place on December 6, 1917, just off the shore of Halifax, Nova Scotia. The horrific blast was triggered by a fire aboard the French transport ship *Mont Blanc*, loaded with munitions and explosives earmarked for the battlefields of Europe. After a collision with the Belgian steamer *Imo* sparked the blaze, the *Mont Blanc's* crew abandoned ship and allowed her to drift perilously close to shore. When the deadly cargo detonated, the cataclysmic explosion took some 1,900 lives, injured thousands more, and wiped out half the city of Halifax.

The Mont Blanc was a small French ship (3,000 tons) ferrying arms to the Allied armies during World War I. On the fateful morning of December 6, 1917, the vessel was steaming out of Halifax Harbor to join its military escort, a necessity given the ship's deadly cargo: in the holds and on deck were 35 tons of **benzol**, 300 rounds of ammunition, 10 tons of gun cotton, 2,300 tons of **picric acid** (a poisonous, explosive yellow crystalline solid used in explosives, dyes, and antiseptics), and 400,000 pounds of dynamite.

benzol a mixture of benzene and other aromatic hydrocarbons.

picric acid a toxic explosive yellow crystalline acid used in high explosives, as a dye, or in medications.

Another ship, the Belgian steamer *Imo*, came within sight of the *Mont Blanc* as the two ships traveled through the Narrows leading away from Halifax. The *Mont Blanc* had failed to hoist the red flag indicating an explosive load, but the ship did manage to establish contact with the *Imo*, which signaled her intention to bear to the port side, close to the shoreline town of Dartmouth. The *Mont Blanc*, meanwhile, sent a signal that it planned to pass to the *Imo's* starboard side. Both ships were very close to the Dartmouth shore, and the *Mont Blanc* had slowed to a near stop.

Unexpectedly, however, the *Imo* decided to stay on course instead of swerving aside. The captain of the *Mont Blanc* then believed it necessary to veer toward port so the ships could pass on each other's starboard flanks. Then both ships, in an excess of caution, decided to reverse engines to further slow their encounter. But that maneuver caused the *Imo* to drift right and collide with the *Mont Blanc*. The bow of the *Imo* plowed into the *Mont Blanc* hold that bulged with load picric acid, stored just beneath the deck's supply of benzol. The resulting chemical spark immediately sprang into deadly flame as the *Mont Blanc's* crew scrambled for lifeboats and shouted warnings about the possibility of impending disaster.

The blazing vessel drifted back toward Halifax, grazing a pier that immediately went up in flames. The Halifax fire department was by now stationed by the nearest hydrant, waiting for their opportunity to approach the craft. Unfortunately, there was also ample time for hundreds of spectators to gather by the banks and by windows to witness the fiery spectacle. At 9:05 A.M., just 20 minutes after its impact with the *Imo*, the *Mont Blanc's* lethal cargo finally detonated in a blinding, deafening flash of such force that windows were smashed over a 50-mile radius and shock waves were felt nearly 300 miles away. The ship's hull was shattered into tiny missile fragments, and its cannon barrel and anchor shank were each propelled more than two miles from site of the explosion.

The casualty totals were commensurately grim: 1,900 deaths and 9,000 injuries, including 1,000 cases of blindness or eye damage from flying glass. The entire north side of Halifax–some 325 acres–was leveled. The city's hospitals and emergency facilities were able to attend to only a fraction of the wounded and dying. The city was further traumatized by a blizzard the following day that paralyzed emergency efforts under a blanket of 16 inches of snow.

Relief aid was speedily dispatched from all over the world–$18 million from Canada, $5 million from Great Britain, and nearly $1 million from the state of Massachusetts, which also offered invaluable volunteer manpower through its Masachussetts-Halifax Relief Committee, a gesture commemorated ever since in Halifax's annual donation of a Christmas tree to Boston.

The dazed city gradually reassembled the pieces of its shattered community life. In only two months 3,000 residences were rebuilt and repaired and hundreds of temporary apartments constructed for those made homeless by the blast. An entirely new community arose as 328 new houses were built from cement blocks called hydrostones. The neighborhood has since become known as Hydrostone and remains one of the loveliest areas of Halifax.

The city pays tribute to the victims of the disaster every December 6 at 9:00 A.M. with a memorial service near the site of the explosion that nearly destroyed a city. ◆

Kiangya

In one of the worst maritime disasters of the twentieth century, the Chinese steamer *Kiangya*, carrying more than 3,000 passengers, exploded and sank near Shanghai, China, on December 3, 1948, claiming as many as 2,800 lives.

The *Kiangya* was a 2,100-ton steamship owned and operated by the China Merchants' Steam Navigation Company. Although the ship was rated to carry a maximum load of 2,250 passengers, at the time of the disaster, it was packed well beyond that figure with refugees who were fleeing from China's bitter civil war between the Nationalist forces of Chiang Kai-Shek and the Communist forces under the command of Mao Zedong. The refugees were seeking haven in Ningpo, a port city located in Cehkiang Province, approximately 200 miles south of Shanghai.

The ship was about 50 miles south of Shanghai when a blast ripped a huge hash in its stern, destroying the radio room and the electrical system. The ship sank so rapidly that there was no time to dispatch lifeboats, although many passengers survived by donning life jackets and leaping into the icy waters of the China Sea. Initial government statements attributed the explosion to communist **saboteurs**, but it later emerged that the cause was a Japanese mine left over from World War II.

The death toll has never been established precisely because no one really knows how many passengers were aboard the ship. Most estimates, however, place the passenger count between 3,000 and 4,000. Newspaper reports gave conflicting accounts of the number of survivors as well. On the day of the explosion, Associated Press (AP) wire dispatches reported that rescue vessels had picked up some 700 survivors. The following day, however, a spokesman for the Cina Merchants'

saboteurs those engaging in the sabotage of an operation or entity in a criminal fashion.

Steam Navigation Company said that there were nearly 1,000 survivors, 26 of whom had been seriously injured. Radio reports from other ships indicated that additonal survivors had been found. The final AP dispatch on the disaster, datelined April 19, reported the government's claim to have recovered 1,217 bodies from the hull of the steamer, but an indeterminate number of passengers were believed to have drowned in the sea after having jumped from the sinking ship. Hence death-toll estimates have varied widely, ranging from 1,200 to 3,000. ◆

Toya Maru

SEPTEMBER 26, 1954

The 1954 wreck of the Japanese ferry *Toya Maru* was responsible for as many deaths as the 1912 sinking of the *Titanic*, yet the later disaster received only modest press attention in the West and has since receded into obscurity everywhere but Japan.

The train ferry *Toya Maru*, a service of Japan's National Railways, operated between the city of Hakodate, on the Japan's northern-most island of Hokkaido, and the city of Aomori, on the north of Honshu, the country's main island. Plying the waters of the Tsugaru Straits on September 26, 1954, the ferry was overwhelmed by a typhoon that led to a failure of the boat's engines. With the crew's control of the vessel at a minimum, it managed to hobble into the harbor at Hakodate only to smash into a reef, after which it rolled over and sank rapidly. Packed beyond its rated capacity, the ship was carrying some 1,300 passengers at the time of the disaster.

Rescue teams raced immediately to the scene of the wreck. The Japanese Coast Guard and the U.S. occupation forces conducted an exhaustive search for survivors, deploying 36 craft of the Japanese Maritime Safety Force, patrol boats, minesweepers, and landing craft. These vessels were supplemented by two U.S. Navy ships and planes from U.S. bases throughout Japan. Rescuers immediately made the grim discovery of 500 bodies trapped inside the hull of the ferry. The protracted search yielded no additional survivors beyond the 171 passengers rescued on the night of the disaster.

The Japanese government launched an immediate investigation into the cause of the wreck. Initial suspicions focused on crew error, since the Central Meteorological Observatory reported that it had issued severe storm warnings to the ship's point of origin at Hokkaido. Within days of the disaster, newspapers published editorials questioning the wisdom of proceeding with the journey under those conditions.

Three days after the accident the Japanese cabinet ordained that the government-owned National Railways would be responsible for financial compensation to the families of the victims of the wreck, including the 57 U.S. Army and Air Force personnel who were among the dead. The compensation rates were set at $1,388 for each adult death and $835 for each child.

On September 30, a legislative committee investigating the incident issued its preliminary findings. The panel of inquiry, made up of parliamentary representatives from all of Japan's five major political parties, absolved the weather service, citing its timely report of the violent weather. The committee did find fault with the ship's captain, Koichi Kondo, for having departed from standard maritime procedure in a heavy storm, which calls

Ships gather around the *Toya Maru* after it capsized during a typhoon.

for dropping anchor well offshore and then heading into the surf with any available engine power. Instead, the *Toya Maru's* captain anchored the ferry just short of the beach, where the anchor chain broke in the turbulent surf and the waves thrust the ferry onto a reef. ◆

Andrea Doria

JULY 25–26, 1956

Launched in 1953, the *Andrea Doria* was the pride of the Italian Line's postwar fleet of transatlantic cruise ships–the fastest, sleekest, most luxurious, and, seemingly, the safest. With a hull divided into eleven water-tight compartments, the *Andrea Doria*, like the *Titanic*, was deemed unsinkable. Like the *Titanic*, it sank on the high seas after a collision. Unlike the *Titanic*, however, the *Andrea Doria* was felled not by an iceberg but by another luxury liner, the *Stockholm*, on a fog-shrouded night. The most provident contrast to its ill-starred predecessor was the relatively modest death toll–46 passengers on the *Andrea Doria* and five crewmen on the *Stockholm*. The survivors numbered 1,660.

With its three outdoor swimming pools–one for each class of service–its generous display of serious artworks in its public rooms, and its opulent first-class cabins, the *Andrea Doria* was among the most sought-after of the more than 50 ocean liners that carried passengers between Europe and America in the mid-1950s. It also boasted the day's most technologically advanced navigational and radar equipment. Combined with her watertight compartments that in theory would prevent a list of more than 15 degrees under any imaginable circumstances, the *Andrea Doria* seemed an impregnable fortress of elegant modernity.

On the evening of July 25, 1956, the *Andrea Doria* was on the final leg of a nine-day voyage from Genoa to New York as it serenely steamed toward Nantucket Island. At about the same time the eastbound *Stockholm* was heading home to Sweden. The *Andrea Doria's* Captain, Piero Calamai, ordered the ship to head directly for the Nantucket Lightship–the mouth of New York Harbor–at about 10:20 P.M. The two ships were still well out of the range of each other's radar. Concerned about the

dense fog enveloping his ship, Captain Calami sounded his foghorn regularly. The *Stockholm* sailed under clear skies without any reason to believe that it was headed for a hazardous fog bank.

The *Stockholm*'s captain, H. Gunnar Nordenson, was trying to save time by sailing well north of the prescribed route for eastbound ships, into the teeth of busy sea lanes normally reserved for incoming ships. Nevertheless, the captain was content to leave the ship's steering to his 26-year-old third officer, Carstens-Johannsen. The *Andrea Doria* picked up the *Stockholm* on its radar at 10:45 P.M., while the ships were still 17 miles apart but heading directly at each other. Calami was unconcerned, however, believing that there was ample time for both ships to adjust course to skirt any danger. The *Stockholm* picked up the *Andrea Doria* with only 12 **nautical miles** separating the two vessels. Calami began to veer south as Carstens performed calculations that he thought would place him at a safe distance from the approaching blip on his radar.

But each man made precisely the wrong assumptions, for when the two ships–traveling at a combined clip of 40

The *Andrea Doria* begins to list after colliding with the Swedish ship *Stockholm*.

nautical mile unit of distance used for air and sea navigation based on the length of a small arc of a large circle of the earth; a unit equal to 6076.115 feet.

knots—came into view of each other when only two miles apart, they were locked into a deadly convergence. Carstens issued a hasty order to turn sharply to starboard. But Calamai had already decided to turn in the same direction. With only a mile between them, Carstens finally saw the *Andrea Doria* clearly enough to realize that the ships were on a collision course. The giant vessels were now locked helplessly in what would prove to be a deadly embrace.

At 11:10 P.M. the *Stockholm's* bow ripped into the *Andrea Doria's* starboard hull plates, shredding seven of its decks and wounding the ship to its keel. At that moment many of the ship's 1,134 passengers were still enjoying late-night entertainment, but many had already gone to bed. It was they, tucked serenly away in their plush, cozy cabins, for whom the mortal impact struck with the most horrifying impact. A New York attorney, Walter Carlin, had just left the bedroom area to brush his teeth when he was knocked to the ground, as he heard the blood-curdling screech of metal on metal. He staggered back to the cabin to see his wife sucked through a hole and into the sea.

Camille Cianfarra, a reporter for *The New York Times*, watched in horror as his daughter, Joan, and his stepdaughter, Linda Morgan, were jolted through a gap and into the lapping waves. Camille was soon pinned by jagged metal and quickly bled to death. Only his wife, Jane, appeared to have been spared. Thure Peterson, who had been hurtled into the next cabin, fought frantically to save his wife and another woman, Jane Cianfarra, both pinned down under metal wreckage. As the ship listed ominiously, Cianfarra was finally freed, but Peterson remained so badly entangled that only heavy machinery would free her. Finally, at 4:20 A.M., as the last lifeboats were launching, Peterson turned to her husband and whispered, "Oh, darling, I think I'm going. I'm going." After watching his wife die, a dazed and despondent Peterson leaped into one of the last two lifeboats.

Mortally wounded, the Andrea Doria began to list alarmingly as the captain sent out desperate distress signals, knowing that his lifeboats could accommodate only 1,044 of the ship's 1,706 passengers. Although the *Stockholm*, still seaworthy, took on many of the *Andrea Doria's* passengers, disaster was avoided by the timely arrival of the venerable *Ile de France*, which came within 400 yards of the sinking Italian vessel and ended up with the lion's share of those rescued.

Believing that her entire family had perished, a desolate Jane Cianfarra returned to New York. Linda Morgan's name had appeared on every list of the disaster's victims. But miraculously, Linda Morgan had been thrust onto the deck of the *Stockholm* and delivered to a New York hospital to recover from her injuries. When her father, the newscaster Edward P. Morgan, heard that his daughter was safe, he rushed to her side and called his first wife, Jane, also recuperating at a nearby hospital. He told her, "Something's happened that some people call a miracle, and I'm with her now."

Eleven hours after the collision, the last inch of the *Andrea Dorea* slipped beneath the waves of the Atlantic–at exactly 10:09 A.M. on July 26. Forty-six of the boat's 1,706 passengers had died. Because the ship sank so slowly, the *Ile de France* had time to steam to the rescue and avert a disaster on a scale comparable to that of the *Titanic*. ◆

Tampomas **II**

Indonesia is a sprawling **aggregation** of some 16,000 islands, so ferry service is the lifeblood of travel among the scattered segments of the nation. Unfortunately, many of the ferries are ill-serviced, delapidated, and overcrowded, posing a chronic danger to travelers between the islands. In the past decade alone the country has suffered two deadly ferry accidents: the worst, the sinking of the *Cahaya Bahari*, claimed nearly 500 lives in June 2000. Up until then the Indonesia's gravest maritime disaster was the wreck of the ferry *Tampomas II* in January 1981, in which nearly as many people perished.

The *Tampomas II* was a relatively new member of Indonesia's ferry fleet in 1981, having entered service only 10 years earlier under Japanese ownership. It was later purchased by the government-owned shipping company, Pelni Shipping Corporation. Its vessels were notorious for carrying only the barest minimum of safety equipment in order make room for the maximum number of passengers.

On January 27, 1981, the 6,139-ton interisland vessel, with a passenger load of 1,054, had covered most of a 1,000-mile journey from the Indonesian capital of Jakarta to Ujung Pandang, a

aggregation a body, group, or mass of units or parts loosely associated with each other.

port city in Celebes. As the boat approached the halfway point between Surabaya in east Java and the southern tip of Borneo, it burst into flames. The precise cause of the blaze has never been pinpointed, but investigators have pointed to a possible explosion in the engine room or a fire in one of the 166 automobiles being hauled by the ship.

Shortly after the outbreak of the fire, the ship began to list badly and then started sinking rapidly. With no time to launch lifeboats or life rafts, hundreds of passengers donned lifejackets and jumped into the sea. Because the ship was so far from the nearest shore, helicopter rescue was not feasible. A ship in the vicinity, the *Sangihe*, rescued 149 people; the other survivors were picked up by two Indonesian minesweepers and another unidentified vessel. An additonal 13 rescue vehicles persisted in the search over the ensuing days, tossing rubber boats into the sea in the hope that survivors might see them and swim toward them. But no more survivors were found past the first 24 hours after the accident. When the search efforts were suspended, there were 87 confirmed dead and 355 passengers and 25 crew still missing and presumed dead. There were 670 survivors. The total death toll might even have been considerably higher because many passengers were traveling without tickets and were thus omitted from official passenger counts.

Among the survivors was the ship's master, Captain Rivai, who severely criticized the Pelni company for chronically rushing ships into service between trips without allowing sufficient time for basic maintenance. He claimed to have filed complaints about **shoddy** maintenance many times in the past, but his warnings had always been ignored. ◆

shoddy clumsily or hastily put together.

Dona Paz

December 20, 1987

One of the worst maritime disasters of the century and the worst in Philippine history occurred on December 20, 1987, when the passenger ferry *Dona Paz*, packed with nearly 3,000 passengers, collided with an oil tanker, burst into flames, and sank, claiming at least 1,600 lives.

The 2,215-ton *Dona Paz* had departed from the Leyte island port of Tacloban, 375 miles southeast of Manila, which was its destination. The ferry's official capacity was 1,424, but most first-hand observers believe the vessel was packed with at least twice that many holiday travelers, many of whom had managed to find their way on board without tickets and so did not show up on official passenger lists. One survivor said the vessel was so crowded that some cots were shared by four people and that many hundreds were seated on the floors throughout the three-level ship.

At 10:00 P.M. on December 20, 1987, the *Dona Paz* collided with an oil tanker, the *Victor*, which was heading for Masbate Island with a 8,300-barrel load of oil. Most of the *Dona Paz's* passengers were asleep at that hour and were jolted into terrified consciousness by the severe impact and simultaneous explosion. In the words of one survivor, Paquito Osabel, "I went to a window to see what happened, and I saw the sea in flames. And I shouted to my companions to get ready, there is fire. The fire spread rapidly and there were flames everywhere. People were screaming and jumping. The smoke was terrible. We couldn't see each other, and it was dark. I could see flames, but I jumped."

Alodia Bascal, 18 at the time, recalled the panic that erupted on board after the explosion. "People were screaming and running," she said. "Then all of a sudden there was smoke everywhere." Her father also survived the disaster, but her grandfather and uncle perished.

Another survivor was Almario Blong, a fisherman, who was among those roused from sleep by the collision. "When I woke up," he told a reporter, "The ship was on fire and so I jumped." As he tried to swim away from the flames, he passed many bodies of those already consumed by the fire. "The sea was in flames," he recalled, "and many burned to death." Another fisherman, Pamilo Culalia, was on the ferry's third deck when awakened by the blast of impact. "I was still shaken by the noise when I saw my father-in-law jump into the sea." He instinctively followed suit without pausing to look for his brother, his 14-year-old daughter, or his 10-year-old niece. After swimming to a safe distance, he looked back at the the ship. "I saw the ship in flames and I wanted to kill myself. But God shook me and woke me." After swimming for more than two hours, he and his father-in-law were thrown life preservers and picked up by a passing ship.

The coast guard's initial inquiry into the disaster indicated that some of the ship's officers were watching television or drinking beer at the moment of impact. One survivor testified that only one **apprentice** officer was on the bridge at the time of the disaster, when the ship was making its way through the busy shipping lanes of the Tablas Strait, 110 miles south of Manila off Mindoro Island.

Only 24 passengers and 2 crew members were rescued. Depending on how many people were actually aboard the ship, the death toll might have been as high as 3,000. The president of the Philippines, Corazon C. Aquino, issued a statement describing the accident as "a national tragedy of harrowing proportions" and called on her more fortunate countrymen to come to the aid of mostly poor families affected by the disaster (wealthier Philippines mostly travel by air and seldom use the ferries). She added, "Our sadness is all the more painful because the tragedy struck with the approach of Christmas."

One grieving man told a reporter, "My parents–my mother–was on the boat and is maybe dead. I loved them. But this is life. Filipinos live in permanent insecurity." He reflected that the disaster seemed to hark back to an earlier time of overcrowded, unregulated passenger ships. "This accident came from the nineteenth century. It should not happen now." ◆

Exxon *Valdez*

MARCH 24, 1989

The gravity of most maritime disasters is usually gauged by the number of human fatalities. One of the deadliest naval disasters in modern history–the 1989 spill of 11 million gallons of oil from the Exxon *Valdez* with Bligh Reef into Prince William Sound, Alaska–caused not a single human death or injury, yet the death toll was staggering: 250,000 seabirds, 2,800 sea otters, 300 harbor seals, 250 bald eagles, up to 22 killer whales, and countless billions of salmon and herring eggs. It was an environmental **holocaust** that so violently devastated the bay's delicate ecosystem that a decade later only two of the area's 22 species have fully rebounded.

The Exxon *Valdez* was part of a transporation system that had, up until then, achieved an unblemished record in carrying some 2 million barrels of oil each day from the North Slope fields to the Gulf Coast markets. The very long-term success of the operation bred an overconfidence that was reflected in the operation of the Exxon *Valdez* on the day of the disaster.

The tanker, under the command of Capt. Joseph Hazelwood, started out from the Trans Alaska Piepline terminal at 9:12 P.M. on March 23, 1989. The chief wheelhouse officer was William Murphy, a highly skilled ship's pilot hired expressly to guide the 986-foot vessel through the Valdez Narrows. Murphy's mission accomplished, he turned the wheelhouse over to Capt. Hazelwood, who ordered his **helmsman**, Harry Claar, to steer the vessel clear of the shipping lanes to circumvent the icebergs in the area. Hazlewood then turned the pilothouse over to Third Mate Gregory Cousins, leaving him with explicit orders about when and where to initiate the return to the shipping lanes. By now Robert Kagan had taken over the steering, and he and Cousins unaccountably failed to execute the ordered return to the shipping lanes soon enough. By the time Cousins issued the right rudder command to turn toward the shipping lanes, the ship's response was sluggish. He then ordered harder action on the rudder, again with minimal response.

By now Cousins knew the ship was in serious trouble and phoned Hazelwood to report the problem. At 12:04 A.M., March 24, while the two men were talking on the phone, they felt the initial impact with Bligh Reef, which the helmsman, Robert Kagan, described as a "bumpy ride" and Cousins as "six very sharp jolts." Hazelwood, who had been drinking, returned to the pilothouse and struggled in vain to dislodge the ship from the reef. At 12:26 A.M., the captain radioed the Valdez traffic center and reported the problem with these words: "We've fetched up, ah, hard aground, north of Goose Island, off Bligh Reef, and ah, evidently leaking some oil and we're gonna be here for a while and, ah, if you want, ah, you're so notified."

"Some oil" turned out to be a horrific hemmhoraging of 257,000 barrels, some 38,800 metric tons, or enough oil to fill 125 Olympic-sized swimming pools, the largest spill in the history of

The Exxon *Valdez* anchored in oil-strewn water

helmsman ship's crewmember responsible for steering.

the United States and the 34th largest in the history of the world. It is, however, widely considered to be the most environmentally destructive, given the pristine natural surroundings in which it occurred. The resulting pollution affected 1,300 miles of shoreline, of which 200 miles were heavily or moderately soiled. The original oil slick extended for some 460 miles, all the way to the village of Chignik on the Alaska peninsula.

Exxon spent four summers and $2.1 billion on the cleanup, employing some 10,000 people on the vast undertaking, whose **efficacy** is still questioned by many environmentalists. A variety of techniques were employed: hot water, soon abandoned because it was as destructive to some fragile organisms as oil; high-pressure cold water hosing and spraying of beaches; mechanical devices such as backhoes and other heavy machinery to churn up oil beneath the surface; bioremediation, a form of fertilization to foster the spread of microorganisms that head hydrocarbons, a method that worked best on lightly oiled beaches; and chemical solvents, although these were used sparingly.

Cleaning the animals was a still more painstaking task. Oil degrades fur and feathers and destroys their insulating function, thus exposing the animals to **hypothermia**. Other animals ingested the toxic oil while trying to clean themselves or while eating other oiled animals. In many cases such ingestion leads to rapid death; in others, long-term physiological damage such as liver dysfunction or blindnesss. Squads of veterinarians and volunteers did their best to clean the animals, often with the aid of mild liquid dishwashing soap. More than 10 years after the spill, only two of the 23 harmed species have made a full recovery.

Although Exxon claims that all of the major damage from the spill has now been overcome, most scientists disagree. Molly McCammon, the executive director of the Exxon *Valdez* Oil Spill Trustee Council, told a reporter in 1999, "Exxon will tell you that there was no injury, or if there was injury it was very short. I think we have documented very well that there has been substantial, significant injury to a number of species over time, and that a number of those haven't recovered." A resident of Prince William Bay, fisherman Ron Anderson, gave the same reporter an even more succinct assessment. "Is it clean? It's antiseptic. There's nothing that lives there anymore."

Exxon's voluntary cleanup efforts were deemed woefully inadequate by the general public as well, who were angered and scandalized by the apparent ineptitude that had led to the debacle. In a ruling on October 9, 1991, a U.S. District Court imposed a $150 million fine on Exxon, the largest financial penalty for an environmental violation, although $125 million of that sum was forgiven because of Exxon's cleanup efforts. Of the remaining amount, the North American Wetlands Conservation Fund received $12 million and the Victims Crime Fund $13 million. Exxon further agreed to pay $100 million in criminal restitution charges to the federal government and the state of Alaska. The oil firm also was required to pay out $900 million, in ten annual installments, to settle civil claims.

Those outlays were minor compared to the civil penalty imposed by a federal court jury in September 1994: $5 billion in **punitive damages** to Alaskan fishermen, natives, and property owners, the largest such fine ever imposed on a corporation. The incident also led to more stringent regulation of oil transport. The U.S. Congress passed the Oil Pollution Act of 1990, which mandated stricter supervision of oil tank vessels, owners, and operators. In 1990 Alaska issued its final report on the wreck of the Exxon Valdez. It concluded, in part,

> "No human lives were lost as a direct result of the disaster . . . Indirectly, however, the human and natural losses were immense—to fisheries, subsistence livelihoods, tourism, wildlife. The most important loss for many who will never visit Prince William Sound was the aesthetic sense that something sacred in the relatively unspoiled land and waters of Alaska had been defiled. Industry's insistence on regulating the *Valdez* tanker trade its own way, and government's incremental accesssion to industry pressure, had produced a disastrous failure of the system."

As for the Exxon *Valdez* itself, the repaired tanker now transports oil across the Atlantic Ocean under its new name, the *Sea River Mediterranean*. The state of Alaska passed a law permanently barring it from entering Prince William Sound. ◆

punitive damages monetary reward for damages over and above the normal compensation a plaintiff would receive to further punish a defendant for a serious wrong.

Salem Express

DECEMBER 16, 1991

In one of the worst maritime disasters in Egyptian history, 462 passengers on the ferry *Salem Express* died in December 1991 when the ship struck a coral reef and sank in the Red Sea.

The *Salem Express* was a 4,771-ton ferry that began life as the *Fred Scamaroni* in 1976, the product of the French shipbuilders

Constructions Navales et Industrielles de la Mediterrane, based in Le Seyne. The ship was briefly renamed *Nuits Saint George* before assuming its final identity as *Salem Express*, under the ownership of the Egyptian Samatour Shipping Company in Alexandria.

The *Salem Express* hauled passengers and automobiles between Egypt and Saudi Arabia. Hassan Moro, a highly regarded seaman, a former instructor at the Egyptian Naval Academy was appointed captain of the *Salem Express* in 1988, and developed an intimate knowledge of the ship's 450-mile route beween Safaga and Jeddah. In order to reduce the trip by by two hours, Moro preferred to approach Safaga by threading a path between the Egyptian shore and the Hyndman Reefs that lie south of the city. Nearly all the other ships tried to avoid the treacherous reefs by taking the more time-consuming route farther from the coastline, sailing to the north of Panorama Reef and thus remaining safely in deep water until they arrived in the port of Safaga (this slower route later became mandatory), which lies 293 miles southeast of Cairo.

On December 16, 1991, the *Salem Express* departed Jedda in calm weather, carrying 578 passengers and 72 crew by official count; many survivors of the wreck claimed that the ship actually carried twice that number. But at night heavy rains and gale-force winds began to rock the vessel. Capt. Moro tried to stay as close to the coastline as possible to lessen the impact of the storm on the ship, especially for the unfortunate passengers traveling on deck. At around midnight the ship came into the vicinity of the Hyndman Reefs, but because of the poor visibility and the ship's eastward variance from its normal course, it struck the southernmost reef, trearing a hole in the starboard side of the hull. The impact dislodged the bow's car doors, flooding the car deck. The double onrush of water caused a severe starboard tilt. In less than 20 minutes the ship sank on its starboard side in 30 meters of water.

Bereft of either life jackets of lifeboats, the frantic passengers leaped into the turbulent waters. Most of them succumbed to hypothermia and exhaustion. Amazingly, 180 survivors were able to swim safely to shore in the shark-infested waters. Because the reported death toll of 462 is based on the official passenger count, many suspect that the wreck claimed close to twice that many lives.

A number of smaller vessels within view of the disaster were prevented from attempting a rescue effort by the violent storm.

One seaman who watched the ferry's approach commented, "One moment she was there, and the next she was gone!"

The wreck of the *Salem Express* has become a ghoulish tourist attraction for Red Sea deep-sea divers. ◆

Neptune

Feburary 17, 1993

At least 500 people–and possibly twice that many–perished in the wreck of the Haitian ferry *Neptune* in February 1993.

Transportation in Haiti, the poorest country in the Western hemisphere, is always a rudimentary affair. Maintenance of public transportation vehicles is a luxury rather than a mandated necessity as it is in wealthier countries. The *Neptune*, a 39-year-old converted freighter, turned out to be a tragic example of this neglect. The rusted, 163-foot, triple-decked ferry plied the waters between Port-au-Prince, Haiti's capital, and Jérémie, a small town near the western end of Haiti's southern peninsula.

On February 17, 1993, the creaky old ferry embarked from Jérémie on its regular 18-hour, 220-mile run to Port-au-Prince. Although approximately 800 tickets had been sold for the trip, the passenger-accounting process was far from rigorous, so an many as 2,000 people might have been packed onto the boat, along with its typical cargo overload of charcoal, agricultural produce, and livestock. Most of the passengers were poor peasants from Jérémie who routinely traveled to the markets of Port-au-Prince. The ferry has always been the most popular means of making the trip because of the wretched condition of the roads and the chronic fuel shortages that render bus service more of a promise than a reliable reality.

Survivors of the wreck and the boat's captain, Benjamin St. Clair, gave essentially the same account of the cause of the wreck. As the ship approached the capital's port, a driving rainstorm sent hundreds of passengers running from the open deck to the tarpaulin-covered portion of the boat. Because the ferry was overloaded with cargo, the shift in weight caused a severe list, and the boat began taking on water. As panic set in among the passengers, their frantic scurrying caused a pronounced **oscillation** that

oscillation continued movement from side to side.

There were no lifeboats or life jackets aboard the craft, so passengers were forced to swim for their lives.

resulted in more water coming aboard, and the boat finally began to sink.

There were no lifeboats or life jackets aboard the craft, so passengers were forced to swim for their lives. The U.S. Coast Guard dispatched five cutters and several aircraft to assist the Haitian government in the search for survivors. The government was able to account for 285 survivors, some of whom had clung to floating animal carcasses or bags of charcoal for up to 31 hours before before they were able to paddle or drift to shore. Many survivors put the passenger count at nearly 2,000, but a co-owner of the ferry, Carmin Magloire, placed the total at 900. Because the actual passenger count remains a matter of conjecture, no precise death toll was ever reported, although anywhere from 500 to 1,000 people likely perished in the disaster.

In the wake of the tragedy, many students of Haitian history pointed out that the neglect and incompetence that engendered the sinking of the *Neptune* was typical of the dire impoverishment of nearly every aspect of Haitian life. In the words of Michel-Rolph Trouillot, a Haitian anthropologist who was teaching at Johns Hopkins University at the time of the accident, "The notion of government-provided services has never reached the majority of the Haitian population, and it is certainly no the sense that the Haitian ruling classes have of the role of government." A U.S. Coast Guard official told a reporter, "We've seen that boat overloaded like that so many times and just shaken our heads. To anybody who cared, it was a disaster just waiting to happen." ◆

Estonia

SEPTEMBER 28–29, 1994

In one of the worst ferry diasters in history, the Swedish-Estonian vessel *Estonia* filled with water and sank in the Baltic Sea in September 1994, killing nearly 1,000 people. At a news conference following the disaster, the Swedish prime minister, Carl Bildt, said, "It is a human tragedy beyond belief, and most certainly the worst human disaster that has affected my country for at least a century."

Built in West Germany in 1980, the *Estonia* began life as *Viking Sally* under the management of the Sally Line, one of

Europe's largest ferry companies. In 1992 it was acquired by Est-line, a joint Swedish-Estonian venture that renamed the ship the *Estonia* and sailed it under an Estonian flag. The six-deck, 515-foot ferry, which could hold 2,000 people and 460 automobiles, was known for its capacious and comfortable facilities, which included a **smorgasbord**, an indoor pool, and a bar area featuring live music and dancing. Although the vessel had had no previous safety problems, an informal safety inspection conducted several hours before the fatal voyage revealed slight imperfections in the seals that ringed the bow doors though which cars and buses entered and left the ferry. A Swiss official said, however, that "the overall impression that the Swedish surveyor got was that it was generally a well-kept ship." The official added that he did not believe that a seal problem alone would have leaked enough water to cause the kind of sudden and catastrophic flood that sank the *Estonia*.

On September 28, the *Estonia* made its usual evening departure from Tallinn, the captial of Estonia, for its regular overnight run to Stockholm, the capital of Sweden. It was carrying 1,049 people, including 70 civilian Swedish police workers who had been attending a seminar, 21 teenagers from a Bible school, 56 retirees on a group tour, and many dozens of Swedes who had spent the day shopping and sightseeing in Tallinn. The ship first began to encounter noticeable roughness at about 8:30 P.M., when the bar band stopped playing because of the heavy swaying of the ship. By midnight, when most of the passengers were asleep in their cabins, the storm had grown more severe, with the ship heaving in what survivors said were 20-foot waves. When water began to engulf the interior of the boat, a distress call went out at 1:24 A.M. The boat sank less than half an hour later.

The sudden torrent overwhelmed the unwary crew and the defenseless, sleeping passengers. Einar Kukk, the ship's second mate, told a reporter, "Many people didn't wake up in time. Some had been drinking and so were not in the best condition to cope." He added, "The noise woke me up. I could feel the ship was listing. I ran up on deck, put on a life vest, and gave vests to others. There were lots of rafts in the water. One had turned completely over, and we were three people lying on top. One was a completely naked man in his fifties. We spent six hours on there."

Another survivor, Hannu Seppanen of Finland, recalled, "One thing you really heard were the screams of women out in

The sudden torrent overwhelmed the unwary crew and the defenseless, sleeping passengers.

smorgasbord a lunch or dinner buffet with a variety of foods and dishes; a heterogenous mixture.

the sea. The screams of women." Another survivor awakened by the flood was Paul Barney, from England, who told a reporter, "The boat lurched really severely. I was thrown off my bed and things started to slide in the cabin. I tried to make my way up to the exit, but that got harder as the ship started to list more and more." Finally reaching the top deck, Barney found no life jackets. He managed to crawl onto a lifeboat with 11 others, five of whom perished during the seven-hour ordeal of bouncing on the cold, rough seas. "Hope was beginning to disappear because the weather got really severe," Barney recalled. There were seven-and eight-foot waves coming over us. Every time we got slightly warmer, we got drenched again."

Interviewed from his hospital bed in Turku, Finland, Andrus Maidre, a 19-year-old Estonian survivor, told a reporter, "Some old people had given up hope and were just sitting there crying. I also stepped over children who were wailing and holding onto the railing." At one point a group of Swedes formed a human chain on the deck so that life jackets could be passed to people who had landed in the water without them. One Swedish passenger, Rolf Sorman, survived by clambering onto an upside-down life raft. He recalled that as he helped others aboard the raft, "There was an Estonian girl. I tried to hold on to her, but my fingers were so stiff. She went down into the water when a big wave came over the boat."

There were only 126 survivors, most of whom were rescued by helicopters dispatched simultaneously by Sweden, Finland, and Estonia. Nearly all were suffering from hypothermia.

Studying the wreckage with underwater video equipment, the official board of inquiry concluded that the cause of the disaster was failure of the ship's huge front cargo door, which had "completely separated from the rest of the vessel" following a failure of its locks. ◆

Cahaya Bahari

June 29, 2000

Indonesia is a sprawling aggregation of some 16,000 islands, so ferry service is the lifeblood of travel among the scattered segments of the nation. Unfortunately, many of the ferries are ill-serviced, delapidated, and overcrowded, posing a chronic danger to travelers between the islands. An especially tragic instance was the sinking of the *Cahaya Bahari* on June 29, 2000, a creaky, wood-hulled vessel that was loaded down with 500 passengers, twice its prescribed load, many of them desperate refugees from **sectarian** violence on the far eastern Maluku islands who were seeking a haven on the island of Sulawesi. Only 10 people survived the wreck.

sectarian limited in character or scope; partisan.

The ship left the Malukus carrying 198 passengers and crew as well as 290 Christians fleeing from the Christian-Moslem fighting that had flared over the previous 18 months, taking the lives of more than 2,500 people throughout the Maluku islands. The refugees were natives of the village of Duma on the Maluku island of Halmhera, where Muslim vigilantes had murdered more than 180 Christians on May 19, 2000, in the worst episode of the religious strife.

Although 90 percent of Indonesia's quarter billion people are Muslim, the population of the Maluku Islands is split evenly between Muslims and Christians. The unrest was triggered in January 1999 by a fight in the central marketplace of Ambon, an incident that many local observers believed to be an intentional provocation. Efforts to deploy the military to suppress the violence were unavailing, since the soldiers merely ended up taking up arms for one of the two religious factions. According to an observer from Human Rights Watch, speaking at the time of the ferry tragedy, "Soldiers have broken ranks and joined the fighting as partisans, and, as a result, Indonesian troops right now have virtually no crediblity in areas where a neutral force is most desperately needed."

The rising tide of violence between the Christian and Muslim communities was propelled in party by the arrival of more than 2,000 armed militia of the Islamic Laskar Jihad organization. As the Maluku governor commented at the time, "It is a very complicated, very big problem, because national poitics is involved. The Laskar Jihad is connected to some political elite, because they come to Ambon without anybody stopping them. . . ."

Whatever the precise cause of the upsurge in religious fantaticism, thousands of refugees had been streaming out of the islands over the preceding year to escape the spasms of unchecked *vigilante* violence. For months the ferries from Ambon and other Maluky islands were operating under unsafe and overcrowded conditions to accommodate the demand.

With each new outbreak of killings, the small ports on the islands became choked with frantic families clamoring to board one of the outbound ferries. Such was the scene at Ambon on June 29 when the *Cahaya Bahari* pulled into port. According to one reporter, "They pushed and jostled in a panic to board the battered ferry, witnesses said, fleeing a massacre in which up to 200 of their fellow villagers had been killed. They were the lucky ones, mostly women and children as well as more than 30 wounded survivors, cramming aboard the *Cahaya Bahari*, nearly doubling its licensed load to almost 500 passengers." Once it was packed beyond its capacity, the ship began its journey to Manado, the capital of nearby North Sulawesi province, which is some 1,500 miles northeast of Jakarta, the capital of Indonesia.

At 1:00 P.M., several hours into its passage, the ship reported that it was taking on water. That was the last communication from the ferry, which at that point was roughly 40 miles from the nearest shore. Naval search parties set out on a rescue mission but found no trace of the ship over the following three days. A few hours before the search mission was to be called off, a fishing boat found 10 survivors of the wreck clinging to debris in waters close to the tiny islet of Karakelong, which is about 120 miles northeast of Manado, a port city on Sulawesi Island where the search operation had been based.

According to the head of Indonesia's National Search and Rescue Agency's monitoring center, the six men and four women were in poor condition, suffering from extreme dehydration and exhaustion and severe sunburn. The survivors reported that the *Cahaya Bahari* had capsized and sunk after taking being buffeted by huge waves and taking on water because of sudden storm of the island of Sulawesi.

When the news of the boat's fate reached the dozens of anxious relatives maintaining a hopeful vigil at Manado airport, there were sobs of grief and shock. John Girobus, whose mother perished on the boat, told a reporter, "Until now we had been praying that the ship was still afloat. Now we know that it has sunk and only a few people have been rescued. Everyone is very worried about their families."

At the Vatican, Pope John Paul II spoke of his "great sorrow" for the victims, of whom he said, "I pray that the Lord grant them their eternal reward, and I invoke with all my force peace and security for those islands tormented by violence." ◆

Kursk

On August 12, 2000, one of the world's largest nuclear submarines, the Russian *Kursk*, sank during a naval exercise in in the Berents Sea, triggering a protracted worldwide media drama of agonizing suspense over the fate of the 118 crew members.

The nuclear-powered *Kursk* was a behemoth–twice as long as a Boeing 747, the *Kursk* boasted a displacement was 14,700 tons on the surface, 24,000 tons on the surface. The ship carried 24 Granit-skimming cruise missiles with conventional or nuclear warheads and 28 torpedoes. On the August 12 mission the *Kursk* carried no nuclear warheads. Because of the dire financial straits of the Russian government, the ship was reported to have been lacking in other essential equipment as well–according to a Russian newspaper, the *Kursk* was operating without emergency backup batteries.

The ship's commander, Capt. Gennady Lyachin, had commanded the ship for a year before the fateful day, and he was proud of the Kursk's safety record. After the ship's first outing on October 19, 1999, Lyachin boasted to reporters, "There wasn't one emergency alarm on the ship." Shortly before the *Kursk's* last mission, its crew had been ranked as the best submarine crew of the northern fleet.

The submarine set out on August 10, 2000, on what the Russian government believed would be a vindication of its boasts. At 11:28 A.M. the sub was cruising within 60 feet of the surface with its **periscope** up when he radioed the task force commander for permission. What followed was not the sound of surging torpedoes but rather a quick jolt of an explosion, followed within a second by a an enormous, deafening blast that registered at 3.5 on Richter scales 2,000 miles away. The blast, which one seismic-research station measured the explosive force as equvialent to two tons of dynamite, ripped apart the double-hulled forward section of the vessel, instantly flooding between two and four of the ship's ten compartments.

Lyachin and his fellow officers in the command center were likely to have been killed within seconds by the torrent. Some of the men were likely trapped stationed behind the thick,

periscope a tubular instrument on a submarine containing lenses and mirrors by which an observer sees a field of view otherwise blocked.

watertight walls protecting the ship's nuclear reactors, but with the ship sent into a nosedive by the inundation of water and still propelled forward by the engines, it doubtless slammed to the floor of the ocean with such force that the impact would likely have killed those who had not already drowned. It is possible that some did survive both the flooding and the impact, since **sonar** devices picked up morse-code tapping from the stern sections of the boat, but those survivors faced an agonizingly slow demise, beyond the reach of rescue teams and enduring temperatures of 5 degrees celsius and pounding headaches as the carbon dioxide built up in the suffocating confines of the craft. They would no doubt be tantalized by the sound of the minisubs maneuvering futilely to free the men. After August 14, the tapping stopped. In the words of Ilya Klebanov, the Russsian deputy prime minister who headed the commission of inquiry on the disaster, "The majority of the crew were in the part of the boat that was hit by the catastrophe that developed at lightning speed." Klebanov surmised that most of the men probably died "within two minutes or less."

The Russian Northern Fleet commander, Adm. Vyacheslav Popov, unaccountably attempted no radio contact with the *Kursk* for 11 hours after the explosion, perhaps having assumed that the explosions did not emanate from the sub. Although he issued a rescue alert, he did not dispatch any vessels until 11:00 P.M., nearly 12 hours after the disaster. The Russian government's reaction to Western offers of assistance was an equally puzzling rebuff, perhaps motivated in equal measures by stubborn national pride and by fears that inviting assistance from the West would compromise elements of their **proprietary** nuclear technology.

The Russians' rescue efforts were hampered by high winds and rough seas, which thwarted attempts to attach a Kolokol diving bell on a submersible rescue craft to the wreck's sternside escape hatch. After five days of futile efforts, the Russians finally accepted help from Norway, which dispatched fifteen deep-sea divers to the scene, and Great Britain, which send an LR5 minisub designed expressly for such a rescue mission. The gestures seemed largely symbolic, since the estimated 72-hour oxygen supply had long since run out. When a Russian minisub finally reached the sub's escape hatch later in the week, it was so badly mangled that no attachment was possible. A U.S. naval officer doubted that American assistance would have turned the tide. "Sure, we might have done better than the Russians," he said, "but given the conditions out there, that would mostly have been luck."

The cause of the explosion remains a matter of speculation. The Russians first claimed that there had been a collision with another vessel, even though no other ships in the area reported any impact or damage of any kind on that day. The Russians eventually dropped that doubtful hypothesis and focused on the likelihood of an explosion of some of the ship's weaponry, a thesis echoed by Western analysts who attributed the blast to one of the ship's own torpedo missiles to a high-pressure air tank. Many Western military experts contended that in the underfunded and ill-equipped Russian Navy, such a catastrophe was inevitable.

The sinking of the *Kursk* proved a temporary political setback for Russia's president, Vladimir Putin, who refused to return from his Black Sea vacation to address the emergency. After four days of mounting public indignation, Putin finally traveled to the port city of Vidyayevo, the *Kursk's* home base. After meeting with some 500 of the crew's grief-stricken relatives, he told reporters, "I have a great feeling of responsibility and guilt for this tragedy." He then declared a national day of mourning and announced a financial settlement—each victim's family received $10,300, the equivalent of a decade's worth of wages for a Russian naval officer.

On May 14, 2001, Klebanov announced that the *Kursk* would be raised from the sea by September 20, 2001. Klebanov was in charge of the Russian government's investigation commission looking into the accident. Although many were quite obviously interested in any answers the sunken ship might have been able to provide, some of the families of the crew members were reluctant to see the *Kursk* lifted from the water, indicating that it would be preferable to follow the naval tradition of burying the dead at sea. ◆

Western military experts contended that in the underfunded and ill-equipped Russian Navy, such a catastrophe was inevitable.

Air Disasters

Hindenburg

MAY 6, 1937

Sports fans are familiar with the site of the Goodyear blimp hovering peacefully over major sporting events, promoting the tire company's products to a national television audience while providing spectacular aerial views of the stadium below. Now a promotional novelty, blimps were once the chief airborne rival to cruise ships for transatlantic crossings–until May 6, 1937, the day the German airship *Hindenburg* burst into flames while attempting to land at an airfield in New Jersey.

In the early part of the twentieth century blimps were usually called airships or zeppelins. Initially built chiefly for military applications such as bombing and surveillance, these giant **oblong** tubes of lighter-than-air gas became most popular as a means of halving the five to six days it took an ocean liner to cross the Atlantic Ocean. The later models were equipped with luxury accommodations such as gourmet dining rooms, plush sleeping cabins, and elegant lounges. The state-of-the art in airship service was the German-built *Hindenburg*, which outstripped all its rivals not only in opulence but also in size: it weighed 240 pounds and was 300 yards long.

The *Hindenburg's* chief drawback was the highly flammable hydrogen gas that, pumped into the behemoth's rubbery skin, kept it afloat in the sky. The only alternative lighter-than-air filling for the giant tube was the far safer, nonflammable gas helium, but it was available from only five natural-gas fields, all of them in the United States. Recalling Germany's airship raids over Britain during World War II, the U.S. government forbade

oblong a shape deviating from a square, circular, or spherical form by elongnation in one dimension.

253

the export of helium to Germany. Hydrogen, however, had worked well for the *Hindenburg's* esteemed predecessor, the *Graf Zeppelin*, which debuted in 1928 and carried 18,000 passengers on 144 transatlantic crossings during its eight years of service.

Notwithstanding this outstanding safety record, the management of the Hindenberg took no chances with sources of fire during its flights. Passengers were barred from bringing aboard matches, cigarette lighters, or even children's toys that might give off sparks. "We Germans don't fool around with hydrogen," said the *Hindenberg's* chief steward.

After nearly a year of successful crossings, the Hindenburg inspired unquestioned confidence in the safety of its operation under the command of its chief pilot, Captain Max Pruss, who had been flatteringly profiled in *Collier's* magazine in 1937. According to the article, "Only a stroke of war or an unfathomable act of God will ever mar this German [airship's] . . . passenger record."

By 1937 the *Hindenburg's* landings in the United States had become so commonplace that they attracted only local newspaper and radio coverage, along with the awestruck gawkers who had never seen a flying object of such immensity. On May 6, 1937, as the *Hindenburg* floated toward the landing field at Lakehurst, New Jersey, strong headwinds and thunderstorms delayed the airship's descent. It finally received landing clearance at 7:00 P.M. Among those on hand for the arrival were the 92-member ground crew, friends and relatives of the passengers, an Associated Press photographer, and Herbert Morrison, a radio reporter for radio station WLS in Chicago.

It appeared to be a thoroughly routine descent as the airship hovered 200 feet off the ground, drifting ever closer to the landing tower. The first person to notice that something might be amiss was a ground-crew worker, W. W. Groves, who was directly beneath the Hindenburg. He recalls seeing a small spark, "like static electricity," that leaped across the underside of the blimp. "Look!" exclaimed Groves to his coworker, and at that moment a fireball rose with terrifying suddenness into the evening sky. An observer from a more distant prospect recalled the moment as "a faint pink glow in the lower center of the ship . . . like some thick silvery fish with a rosy glow in tis abdomen. It began small and pale, and spread redder and larger." The giant fireball reduced the airship to ashes within sixty seconds, killing 13 passengers, 22 crew members, and one ground worker.

Miraculously, there were survivors. One witness recalled seeing "fire everywhere, rushing, sweeping its way through the pitiful crumpling wreckage. It was not possible that anything should be alive in that inferno. Yet men leaped out." One was Joseph Spah, a professional acrobat who smashed one of the ship's windows, clung to a metal bar on the outside of the ship until the intense heat forced him to let go, and then walked away from a 40-foot fall with only a broken heel. Even more miraculous was the escape of Werner Franz, a 14-year-old cabin boy, who was in the underbelly of the aircraft when it exploded into flame. Believing he was doomed, he commenced praying when a water tank above him burst, spraying enough water to douse the flames around him and allowing him to flee the ship unharmed.

The official investigation of the disaster by the U.S. Bureau of Air Commerce concluded that "a small amount of explosive mixture [hydrogen] in the upper part of the ship could have been ignited by . . . [an] electric phenomenon like a ball of lightning." Many observers disputed the bureau's conclusion, noting that the *Hindenburg* had waited for the storms to pass before attempting to land. Noting the rapidly rising world tensions of the era, they suspected that the crash resulted from an act of sabotage directed against the Nazi regime in Germany. Whatever the cause, the fireball ended not only the *Hindenberg* but also the entire era of lighter-than-air passenger carriers, which were deemed too dangerous and unwieldy, especially given the progress in airplane technology at the time.

Through countless newsreel and documentary retellings, the tragic fate of the *Hindenberg* has attained iconic stature, along with the sinking of the *Titanic*, among the humbling failures of modern humanity's technological **hubris**. The lesson rings out with each replaying of Herbert Morrison's live radio report to the listeners of WLS in Chicago:

"Oh, oh, oh! . . . It's burst into flames! Get out of the way, please! It is burning, bursting into flames and is falling. . . . Oh! This is one of the worst. . . . Oh! It's a terrific sight. . . . Oh! It's crashing . . . bursting into flames, and it's falling on the mooring mast and all the folks between us. This is terrible. Oh, the humanity and all the passengers. . . . This is the worst thing I've ever witnessed. . . . This is one of the worst catastrophes in the world." ◆

Whatever the cause, the fireball ended not only the *Hindenberg* but also the entire era of lighter-than-air passenger carriers.

hubris exaggerated self-confidence or pride that usually results in retribution or tragedy.

Pan Am Flight 1736 and KLM Flight 4805

On March 27, 1977, an airport bombing that diverted several flights to another landing site, a fog-shrouded runway, and an accumulation of small misunderstandings between the pilots led to the deadliest airline disaster in history, a collision between two 747 jumbo jets at Los Rodeos airport (then called Santa Cruz), Tenerife, in the Canary Islands, which claimed 583 lives.

The year-round warmth and splendid beaches of Spain's Canary Islands have long been a magnet for European and American tourists seeking an exotic respite from the wearying blasts of winter. Two such plane loads of vacationers–one from Los Angeles, the other from Amsterdam–were scheduled to land at Los Palmas, a major airport serving the islands, in March 27, 1977. Both planes, however, were diverted to the smaller Los Rodeos air field at Tenerife after a terrorist's bomb led to a temporary shut-down of Las Palmas.

Both diverted planes were Boeing 747 jumbo jets that had made long flights. But the exasperated crews and passengers had no choice but to endure this unforeseen detour in their vacation plans. KLM flight 4805 had left Amsterdam that morning at 9:31 with 235 mostly young passengers and a crew of 14. They touched down at Los Rodeos four hours later, piloted by Captain Jacob Veldhuyzen van Zanten, one of KLM's most experienced and respected pilots and its chief training pilot for 747s.

Pan Am flight 1736 had originated in Los Angeles the previous evening and had been delayed there and at a refueling stop in New York. Its crew was under the command of Captain Victor Grubbs, at age 57 one of Pan Am's most accomplished veteran pilots. The plane's mostly elderly complement of 380 passengers, booked for a 12-day Mediterranean cruise aboard beginning the next day, were understandably exasperated at the news of the diversion after 13 hours of travel. Nevertheless, the plane had no choice but to proceed to Los Rodeos, where it landed 35 minutes after the KLM flight.

While lined up with the growing contingent of diverted aircraft, KLM Captain van Zantent became concerned about the adequacy of his fuel supply and requested permission to refuel for the return trip to Amsterdam. This procedure entailed moving a fuel tanker onto the runway. Nevertheless the Los Rodeos air traffic controller (ATC) granted the request.

Shortly after the planes landed their crews heard the news that Las Palmas had reopened, and the *queue* of smaller diverted planes began maneuvering around the refueling KLM 747 to continue their journeys. The Pan Am 747, however, did not have enough room to taxi around its Dutch counterpart, so the American plane was obliged to wait out the refueling process before taking off.

By the time the refueling ended at 4:30 P.M., a thick blanket of fog had settled over the airport, reducing visibility to roughly 700 feet. The KLM crew was granted permission to backtrack down runway 12 to a taxiing exit onto the other runway, 30, proceed to the end of it, and then turn back onto 12 for takeoff. Meanwhile, with the fog so dense that the ATC could not see the runway, the Pan Am plane was told to taxi down runway 12 and then turn onto runway 30 at exit 3 to make way for the KLM plane's takeoff.

The ATC was asking the Pan Am crew to take exit C3, which was normally not used by jumbo jets. So Grubbs thought he meant exit C4, the third exit for jumbo jets, which was farther down the runway. As the Pan Am jet lumbered toward its mistaken exit, the KLM jet was poised at the opposite end of runway 12, impatient for takeoff clearance. The Dutch crew ran through its pre-takeoff checklist, and then Captain van Zantent begins to move the plane forward. His first officer shouted, "Wait. We don't have clearance," prompting van Zantent to hit the brakes and order the first officer to verify the clearance authorization. The following conversation ensued:

KLM: KL4805 is now ready for takeoff. We're waiting for our ATC clearance.

ATC: KL4805. You are cleared to the Papa beacon. Climb to and maintain flight level 90. Right turn after takeoff. Proceed with heading 040 until intercepting the 325 radial from Las Palmas VOR.

This clearance was meant as a post-takeoff instruction, not as a clearance to take off. As the first officer read back the ATC instructions, the ever-impatient van Zantent again began to throttle ahead for takeoff. The KLM responded, "Roger, sir, we are cleared to the Papa beacon, flight level 90 until intercepting the 325. We're now at takeoff." But the ATC mistakenly interpreted this to mean that the KLM plane was merely at takeoff position, not that it was taking off, so the ATC responded, "OK. Standby for takeoff. I will call you." But only the OK registered with the KLM crew–they evidently did not hear the follow-up qualification. The KLM began speeding down runway 12, directly in the path of the Pan Am 747, which had not yet made its exit turn.

Twenty seconds into the ill-fated takeoff, the KLM flight officer heard the rest of the exchange, which indicated that the Pan Am jet was still on the runway. He asked van Zantent, "Did he not clear the runway then?" And van Zantent answered, "Oh, yes."

At that moment the Pan Am's Captain Grubbs saw the lights of the KLM racing toward his craft at 180 miles per hour. He shouted, "There he is! Look at him!" The Pan Am's first officer cried out, "Get off! Get off! Get off!" as Grubb frantically tried to push his plane out of the way. But it was too late. Van Zantent saw the Pan Am plane and tried to go airborne prematurely to avoid the impact; although his plane rose slightly, it still sliced off the top of the Pan Am 747, hurtled through the air for another 500 feet, and then smashed to the ground in a fireball, killing all those aboard.

As fires and explosions erupted throughout the remains of the Pan Am plane, 70 people managed to escape death by leaping out of the inferno to safety, but nine of them died later.

Subsequent investigations by Dutch, American, and Spanish authorities reached predictably conflicting conclusions about the cause of the disaster. The Dutch faulted Grubbs for missing the proper exit and remaining on the runway too long. The Americans focused on the ambiguous clearance instructions issued by the Spanish ATC. The Spanish probers assigned primary blame to the KLM crew for having failed to clarify the clearance instructions. ◆

Japan Air Lines Flight 123

AUGUST 12, 1985

The deadliest airline disaster involving a single plane occurred on August 12, 1985, when Japan Air Lines flight 123, a Boeing 747SR, crashed into Mount Otsuka, near Tokyo, causing 520 deaths.

The doomed aircraft was a Boeing 747SR (Short Range), which was intended for use on heavily traveled shorter routes. Because of its smaller fuel tanks, it could accommodate up to 550 passengers in its structurally reinforced fuselage. The evening of the ill-fated flight was the eve of an important Japanese holiday, when people traditionally travel home to gather with their families. The plane was thus carrying a near-capacity load that evening: 509 passengers and a crew of 15. After arriving from a previous flight, the aircraft refueled at Tokyo's Haneda airport and took on a fresh flight crew. The commander of the plane was 49-year-old Captain Masami Takahama, a 19-year veteran of the airline and a training pilot with 12,500 hours of experience as a pilot.

Flight 123 proceeded down the runway for takeoff at 6:12 P.M. for its 215-mile flight to Osaka. Six minutes after takeoff, the plane radioed the airport with a request for permission to take a more direct route to Osaka, which was granted. Then, 13 minutes into the flight, with the aircraft at its cruising altitude just off the coast southeast of Mt. Fuji, the Tokyo air-traffic controller (ATC) noticed an emergency signal from the aircraft, followed by a voice transmission: "Tokyo . . . JL123. Request immediate . . . ah . . . trouble. Request return back to Haneda . . . descend and maintain flight level 220." The ATC granted the request and gave the vector for the return route to Haneda.

But the ATC noticed that instead of following the prescribed vector, the plane seemed to be adrift. The ATC issued revised directions to the hobbled plane, but it again seemed unable to follow the recommended course. The unresponsive crew was evidently preoccupied with regaining control of the **recalcitrant** aircraft, so the ATC radioed a message that their further exchanges should be in Japanese to relax the unnerved crew and thus facilitate communication. The plane was now veering inland, in the direction of Mt. Fuji, and managed to dispatch the following message to ATC: "Ah . . . the R5 [cabin] door is broken. Ah . . . we are descending now." By this time, the messages were being forwarded instantaneously to Japan Air Lines headquarters so that company engineers could assist the pilots in righting the troubled jet.

Still streaking eastward, the jet had descended to an altitude ot 13,500 when the crew radioed, "JL 123, JL123 uncontrollable!" The ATC asked the pilot to make a right turn back toward Haneda, but the plane veered left instead, dropping to 6,800 feet, which placed in harm's way of the area's many

The doomed aircraft was a Boeing 747SR (Short Range), which was intended for use on heavily traveled shorter routes.

recalcitrant difficult to control or manage.

mountains. The crew then managed to regain a safer altitude of 13,000 feet and asked the ATC for a verification of its precise location; they were told that the plane was 45 miles northwest of Haneda as the plane veered rightward and downward to 8,400 feet before disappearing from the ATC radar screens. At that moment the plane slammed into the lower slopes of Mount Osutaka; miraculously, four people survived the fiery crash.

Subsequent investigation revealed that the cause of the crash had nothing to do with an improperly latched cabin door, which had been the crew's assumption. The truth emerged from a photograph of the crippled, meandering aircraft that was snapped by an amateur photographer in a mountain village. It showed that the aircraft had lost much of its vertical fin and tailcone; a large section of the former was later discovered floating in Sagami Bay. Other fragments of the plane's tail section were found scattered about the countryside, all of which indicated substantial pre-crash damage of some sort.

The most revealing evidence came in the form of the eyewitness testimony of one of the survivors, an off-duty flight attendant who told of an abrupt decompression in the rear of the craft that caused severe oscillations in the plane's course and corresponding fluctuations in engine thrust. Inspection of the wreckage indicated that right after the decompression, the plane's hydraulic control systems completely failed.

The investigators attributed the decompression to a rupture of the rear pressure bulkhead. Their hypothesis was confirmed when a close examination of the bulkhead revealed a riveted splice that had originated in a faulty repair protocol at Boeing seven years earlier that reduced the bulkhead's resistance to metal fatigue by more than half. ◆

Challenger Space Shuttle Explosion

JANUARY 28, 1986

The launch of the *Challenger* space shuttle was a double milestone in the history of the United States space program. Not only was it the the twenty-fifth shuttle flight, but it was also the first time that an ordinary American citi-

zen–Christa McAuliffe, schoolteacher and mother of two–had participated in a space launch as part of the U.S. government's projected "citizens in space" program. At noon on January 28, 1986, a rapt nation huddled before countless TV screens to witness the momentous liftoff. The craft soared gracefully toward the heavens for 73 seconds and then erupted into a ball of flame and smoke and disintegrated before tens of millions of horrified viewers. With the countless videotape replays of the diaster over the ensuing days and weeks, the *Challenger* disaster became a defining moment of national self-examination and reassessment of the methods and goals of the U.S. space program.

By the time of the *Challenger* launch, space shuttle flights had become so commonplace that the three major television networks had ceased covering them live. But an unprecedented wave of publicity preceded the *Challenger* liftoff because of the inclusion of Christa McAuliffe, who had been selected out of tens of thousands of applicants to represent ordinary American citiznes as America's first nonprofessional to accompany a team of astronauts into Earth orbit. The 37-year-old McAuliffe was a highly regarded high school social studies teacher who seemed

The crew of the
Challenger.

the ideal choice to galvanize an interest in space studies among America's youth. The very embodiment of the successful modern woman, McAuliffe became an overnight celebrity, the subject of countless admiring news features and interviews. Her presence on the *Challenger* returned the shuttle program to the forefront of American media attention.

No mere public-relations ornament, McAuliffe was assigned important experiments as a payload specialist alongside her colleagues on that diverse and impressive *Challenger* crew, whose other members were Francis Scobee, an air force pilot who commanded the mission; Judith Resnick, a mathematics whiz assigned primarily to taking photos of Halley's comet while aboard the craft; Ronald McNair, the second African American to travel into space, who held a doctorate in physics from MIT and was aboard as a mission specialist; Michael Smith, a navy pilot; Ellison Onizuka, an aerospace engineer and the first Asian American assigned to a space mission; and Gregory Jarvis, an air force satellite communication specialist.

The eagerly awaited *Challenger* mission had been hounded by technical difficulties and weather problems that resulted in several postponements of the launch date. On one such occasion the crew sat strapped in their capsule for for five hours only to face another rescheduling. The next attempt, on January 28, 1986, came on a morning that was freakishly cold for the normally balmy climes of Florida. By 6:30 A.M. the mercury had plunged to 27 degrees Fahrenheit. With icicles forming on the launch pad, NASA dispatched three separate ice inspection teams, all of whom pronounced the vehicle safe for launch.

The *Challenger's* internal instrumentation showed that the right booster was especially cold, calling into question the reliability of the booster's O-rings at such low temperatures. In fact, the previous day, two men who had played a key role in designing the rocket boosters had argued vehemently for another postponement of the launch: Roger Boisjoly, a senior engineer at Morton-Thiokol, the firm that built the mission's solid-rocket boosters; and his boss, Bob Ebeling. On the evening of January 27, the two men spent six hours on a teleconference with NASA officials in which they insisted that an O-ring failure was a very real danger in such cold weather.

The men pressed the point that no such rocket had ever been launched below 53 degrees Fahrenheit, and even that temperature, claimed Boisjoly, had damaged joints during a launch a year earlier. As the engineer later explained to a reporter, "When solid rocket boosters leak, they explode." The job of preventing that falls to two quarter-inch rubber O-rings that expand with the heated metal during a launch and prevent the escape of hot gasses that might trigger an explosion. As Boisjoly went on to explain, "On the day *Challenger* lauched, it was very cold, and when the temperatures dropped the rubber O-rings became harder and less pliable. Hard O-rings move slower and they seal less effectively. There might only be a fraction of a second's difference, but that is enough to separate success from total disaster."

Boisjoly seemed to be winning his case on the open conference call, but the pressure from NASA was so intense that when a Morton-Thiokol vice-president went off line for five minutes to confer privately with NASA officials, he returned to announce that the management team was going to overrule the engineering team and give the company's formal assent to the launch to accommodate NASA's evident wishes, perhaps reflecting impatience from their patrons higher up in the governmental hierarchy.

The next morning Ebeling invited Boisjoly to watch the launch from his Morton-Thiokol office. Boisjoly recalled, "[Ebeling] grabbed my arm and asked me to come in and watch the launch. At first I told Bob, 'No, I don't want to see the launch.' I knew what was about to happen, and I just did not want to see the failure." With further coaxing, Boisjoly sat in Ebeling's office and watched the same images that flashed through tens of millions of living rooms, workplaces, and classrooms on that frigid Florida morning of January 28. As the countdown reached T minus five seconds, the two men grasped hands, expecting the worst. They were elated when *Challenger* lifted successfully off the launch pad. Boisjoly later recalled, "I turned to Bob and said, 'We've just dodged a bullet,' because it was our expectation that it would blow up on the pad."

But 73 seconds into the flight their unheeded warnings flashed into ghastly reality as the *Challenger* disintegrated in a maelstrom of flame and smoke. There were no survivors. Some experts have contended that the crew was conscious during the fatal descent into the waters of the Atlantic Ocean.

The shocked nation was subjected to endless analyses, replays, and what-ifs during its prolonged ritual of mass-media mourning for the doomed crew. President Ronald Reagan paid the astronauts tribute at a nationally televised memorial service. He said, in part, "The future is not free, the story of all

Some experts have contended that the crew was conscious during the fatal descent into the waters of the Atlantic Ocean.

human progress is one of a struggle against all odds. We learned again that this America was built on heroism and noble sacrifice. It was built by men and women like our seven star voyagers who answered a call beyond duty."

The disaster occasioned much soul-searching and internal reform at NASA, which included major supervisory staff changes, more rigorous launch-clearance protocols, and an overall re-examination of safety procedures. On the other hand, Roger Boisjoly, stigmatized as a whistle-blower, has found few offers of employment since resigning from Morton-Thiokol in the wake of the *Challenger* disaster. After several years of emotional torment, he is now at peace with himself. As he told a reporter on the 15th anniversary of the ill-fated launch, "I beat myself up for a long time over what happened on that night. Maybe I hadn't done enough. Maybe I should have gone home and called *The New York Times* or something. Well, I don't beat myself up anymore. If I couldn't convince the guys on the inside who had all the technical data, how would I have convinced total strangers?" ◆

Iran Air Flight 655

July 3, 1988

United States prestige in the world was staggered in July 1988 when a Iranian commercial airliner, mistaken for an F-14 fighter jet, was shot down by the navy cruiser U.S.S. *Vincennes* in the Straits of Hormuz, killing all 298 people on board. Faces went ruddy with embarrasment in Washington and with rage in the Middle East, where many critics cited parallels with the Soviets' 1983 downing of a Korean Air Lines Boeing 747, which claimed 269 lives.

The incident was a tragic boiling over of the simmering tensions between the United States and Iran in the geopolitically critical region of the Persian Gulf. On July 3, 1988, the *Vincennes* was patrolling the Straits of Hormuz when a helicopter from the ship took fire from three small Iranian boats at 10:10 A.M. A half hour later the *Vincennes* was engaged in combat with three armed Iranian speedboats, of which it sank two and damaged the third. As that battle progressed, the *Vincennes's* sophisticated Aegis radar system indicated that a high-speed aircraft was approaching the ship. The plane seemed to fit the profile of an F-14 fighter; a crew member quickly perused commercial flight schedules to avoid a costly mistake, and he found no commercial flights due to pass over the ship at that time. Unfortunately, he had failed to consider that Iran Air's Flight 655, a commercial Airbus, packed with 298 passengers and crew, had left 17 minutes late.

At that point the *Vincennes's* harried commander, Capt. William C. Rogers, attempted to establish communication with the approaching jet, which he claimed emitted both military and civilian signals. After seven attempts at communication went unanswered, the *Vincennes* sent radio warnings to the plane that it must change its course, but again there was no response. Two minutes later, at 10:51, the jet was within two miles of the *Vincennes.*

Fearing for the life of his men but preferring to err on the side of caution, Rogers radioed his commanding officer, Admiral Anthony Less, for permission to fire on the approaching jet. Less gave his approval, and at 10:54 Rogers sent another flurry of warnings to change course; at about that time, the Iranian Air pilot was conversing with the air-traffic controller and failed to pick up Rogers's warnings—the Iranian pilot's last recorded words were as follows: "I am at level one-two-zero (12,000 feet), climbing to one-four-zero (14,000 feet)," to which the controller responded, "Goodbye, have a nice flight." At that moment Rogers ordered the firing of two surface-to-air missiles, one of which scored a direct hit and blew the plane out of the sky.

At a press conference following the incident, the Chairman of the Joint Chiefs of Staff, Admiral William Crowe, dismissed comparisons to the Korean Air Lines incident, pointing out that Flight 655 had happened upon a combat zone. He further contended that U.S. restraint had cost its soldiers' lives in May 1987, when an Iraqui missile hit the U.S.S. *Stark,* killlling 37 U.S. sailors. Crowe said, "A decision was made early in the commitment to give our commanders sufficient latitude to protect their people . . . They do not have to be shot at before responding. Throughout our involvement in the Persian Gulf, the Iranian government has repeatedly threatened and fired upon U.S. forces."

As soon as the news of the disaster reached the Iranian airwaves, massive spontaneous demonstrations broke out in the streets of Tehran and elsewhere in the country, with enraged

After seven attempts at communication went unanswered, the *Vincennes* sent radio warnings to the plane that it must change its course.

mourners shouting, "Death to Reagan!" and "Revenge, revenge!" Iran's President Seyed Ali Khamene'i denounced the United States as the "arch-Satan," and called the incident "one of the biggest crimes of the war." Ayatollah Ruhollah Khomeini called for sabotage of "American financial, political, and military targets everywhere," inciting his people to "go to the war fronts and fight against America and its lackeys." The incendiary oratory notwithstanding, no military retaliation was forthcoming from Iran, then preoccupied with its hostilities with Iraq and far too weak militarily to survive a confrontation with U.S. armed might.

Despite the U.S. rationale of self-defense in a combat zone, unsettling questions persist. How could the *Vincennes'* $600 million Aegis radar system, the most advanced in the world, and highly skilled technicians who were operating it have failed to distinguish between a commerical airliner and an F-14 fighter jet? Despite Rogers claims that Flight 655 was emitting military as well as civilian signals, a subsequent investigation showed that only civilian signals were emanating from the aircraft. How to account for the mistaken reading? The Pentagon's own investigators attribute the error to "stress, task fixation, and unconscious distortion of data." Moreover, the Airbus was in regular communication with the control tower, yet the *Vincennes* failed to monitor these conversations.

While acknowledging the crew's serious and fatal errors, Secretary of Defense Frank Carlucci abided by the report's judgment that "no disciplinary or administrative action should be taken against any U.S. naval poersonnel associated with this incident." Admiral Crowe concluded that "Captain Rogers acted reasonably and did what his nation expected of him in the defense of his ship and crew." An essayist in *Time* magazine reflected at the time that this generous **absolution** was likely to be of "little consolation to the survivors of those who died on Flight 655 or to the collective American conscience." ◆

absolution forgiveness; a pass.

PanAm Flight 103

December 21, 1988

At 6:25 P.M. on December 21, 1988, PanAm Flight 103, which had originated in Frankfurt, Germany, took off from London's Heathrow Airport with a total of 259 passengers and crew members aboard. The flight path of the

plane, a Boeing 747-121, would take it over the British Isles and the North Atlantic Ocean on its way to New York City. About 21 minutes later, at 6:56, the plane leveled out at 31,000 feet. Seven minutes after that an air traffic controller transmitted the plane's final oceanic clearance but received no acknowledgment from the aircraft. In the meantime the plane completely dropped off the air traffic control radar screens.

The nose section of the destroyed PanAm 103

What air traffic controllers and others later learned was that at 7:02 and 50 seconds, PanAm Flight 103 had violently exploded in midair. The wreckage rained down on the town of Lockerbie, Scotland, killing 11 people on the ground. The impact of the crash was so strong that the British Geological Survey recorded what appeared to be a seismic event–an earthquake–measuring 1.6 on the Richter scale. Most of the wreckage hit the ground in a residential area called Sherwood Crescent at the southern edge of Lockerbie, creating a crater 155 feet wide and 196 feet long and demolishing 21 residential buildings. Other portions of the plane fell into the countryside east of town, and bits of the wreckage were scattered farther to the east over a distance of nearly 80 miles. Within hours journalists flooded the scene and transmitted the first views the public had of the still smoking wreckage. Within days, the quiet town Lockerbie, Scotland, became known around the world.

Responsible for determining the cause of the crash was the United Kingdom's Air Accident Investigation Branch, or AAIB. The AAIB quickly began the grisly task of painstakingly re-assembling the nearly four million pieces of the wreckage, often having to sift through bags of mud and debris to find bits of the plane. From their reconstruction of the plane the investigators determined that the cause of the disaster was an explosion, which in turn was caused by a so-called IED, short for "intentional ex-plosive device." In other words, PanAm 103 was brought down by a bomb. The investigation centered on a Toshiba radio/cas-sette recorder that had been packed into a brown suitcase placed in the cargo hold of the plane. Within that cassette recorder were the remains of a timing device that apparently detonated the bomb. The central question that emerged from the investigation, of course, was: Who planted the bomb?

Dozens of theories emerged in answer to this question. One theory was that the bomb had been planted by renegade mem-bers of the U.S. intelligence community, who were in effect as-sassinating a whistle-blower who was on the jumbo jet. Others, including some victims' families, tried to tie the explosion to the government of Iran, arguing that Iranian hard-liners were bent on vengeance for an incident in July 1988, when the U.S. cruiser *Vincennes* shot down an Iranian plane with 290 passen-gers aboard. Others focused on the crude barometric timing de-vice, which, it happened, matched similar devices found in an October raid by German police on a militant Palestinian stronghold. Still others thought that the plane was accidentally shot down because it flew too close to an area where military training exercises were being conducted. But in November 1991, after a three-year investigation, the Lord Advocate, Scot-land's chief law-enforcement officer, issued a warrant for the ar-rest of two Libyans, Al-Amin Khalifa Fhimah and Abdel Baset al-Megrahi, who were alleged to have ties both to the Libyan intelligence service and to Libyan Airlines in Malta.

What followed was the diplomatic task of extraditing the two suspects from Libya, a task made particularly difficult be-cause of the virulent anti-Western sentiments of Libya's ruler, Colonel Muammar Gadaffi. Gadaffi argued for nearly eight years that the suspects could not receive a fair trial in a Scottish court. In spite of sanctions by the United Nations, Gadaffi refused to turn the suspects over until 1998, and then only after the UN secretary general, Kofi Annan, and South African leader Nelson Mandela intervened. Authorities agreed to Gadaffi's condition that the trial be held in a neutral third country. Accordingly, in 1998 the Netherlands agreed to set aside a former air force base named Camp Zeist as the site of the trial. The verdict was announced in February 2001. Based on over 10,000 pages of testimony from 235 witnesses, the three-judge panel of Scottish judges found al-Megrahi guilty but found the evidence insufficient to convict Fhimah.

The trial attracted widespread notice because of its international implications. The prosecution argued that the accused men were acting under the orders of Colonel Gadaffi himself, whose motive, according to this theory, was to seek revenge for a U.S. bombing raid on Tripoli in 1986. During that raid, which was conducted from British airbases, Gadaffi's adopted daughter was killed. The defense, in contrast, argued that the raid had been carried out by an extreme militant faction of the Popular Front for the Liberation of Palestine, with aid from the governments of Syria and Iran. The court, however, refused to offer an opinion on any of these wider issues. Its decision instead focused on a number of pieces of evidence: Al-Megrahi had traveled to Malta on December 20, 1988, under a false name. There he purchased clothes from a Maltese shopkeeper who identified him and said that he seemed indifferent to what he was buying. The clothes and the bomb, concealed in a suitcase, were placed aboard an Air Malta flight to Frankfurt, Germany, and transferred to Flight 103. Finally, al-Megrahi had an association with Edwin Bollier, an electronics expert from Zurich, Switzerland, who, prosecutors said, had manufactured the timer for the bomb.

The verdict is unlikely to close the case entirely for as of February 2001, the question remained open about whether the Iranian government would pay compensation for the victims' families. ◆

The trial attracted widespread notice because of its international implications.

Xiamen Airlines Flight 8301

October 2, 1990

Early October is a busy time for travel in China. October 1 and 2 are national holidays, and the traditional Mid-Autumn Festival is celebrated on October 3. As in the

Shortly after the plane took off, a young man holding a bouquet of flowers walked toward the cockpit.

United States over Thanksgiving, many people travel to attend family reunions, and the airports are jammed. One of the busiest Chinese airports is Baiyun Airport in Guangzhou, just across the border from Hong Kong.

At 6:57 on the morning of October 2, 1990, a Boeing 737-247 took off from Xiamen in southeastern Fujian province for a short, 230-mile flight to Guangzhou, one of a number of internal routes the airline operated. The plane, with 93 passengers and nine crew members aboard, was one of 26 Boeing 737s operated by Xiamen Airlines, a semiautonomous unit of the Civil Aviation Administration of China (CAAC) and one of the nation's newer airlines.

Shortly after the plane took off, a young man holding a bouquet of flowers walked toward the cockpit. It was later speculated that the two security guards on the plane believed he wanted to offer the flowers to the crew as a holiday token, so they allowed him through. His "bouquet," though, was deadly, for once inside the cockpit, the man opened his jacket. Strapped to his chest were 15 pounds of explosives. He ordered all crew members except for the pilot out of the cockpit and demanded that the plane fly to Taiwan, where the hijacker presumably would have found political asylum. (It should be noted that although China's dozen or so airlines have a good safety record, Chinese officials are notoriously tight-lipped about air accidents in their country, particularly if they involve foreigners or a crime. They are also hesitant to make public any criticisms they might have of airline procedures. Thus, details about the accident remain sketchy and sometimes contradictory.)

The captain tried to reason with the man, whom Chinese officials later identified as 27-year-old Jiang Xiaofeng, described as a "ruffian" and an "active criminal." The captain told the man, correctly, that the plane did not have enough fuel to get all the way to Taiwan, and as a compromise he offered to fly to Hong Kong. In one version of events, the hijacker would not listen and believed that the plane was on its way to Taiwan. In another version, he accepted the pilot's proposal and believed that the plane was headed to Hong Kong. Supporting the second version was the fact that apparently the CAAC had given the pilot clearance to land "at any airport within or outside China's borders, including Taiwan, " and he was given permission to land at Hong Kong for refueling before going on to Taiwan.

The plane, however, was headed to neither destination. It continued on its path to Guangzhou and circled the Baiyun Airport for about 40 minutes. When the hijacker realized he had been tricked, he either detonated the explosives or tried to wrest the plane's controls away from the pilot; it's not clear which, for some witnesses claimed to have seen an explosion before the plane hit the ground, while others said that they did not see an explosion until after the plane touched down. Either way, the plane hit the ground hard and was out of control as it careened at a high rate of speed into a holding area. Its starboard wing sliced into the **fuselage** of a parked China Southwest Airlines Boeing 707, which was empty except for the captain, who was performing preflight checks.

Unfortunately, also in the path of the runaway jet was a China Southwest Airlines Boeing 757 filled with passengers and awaiting takeoff clearance for a flight to Shanghai. The Xiamen 737 collided with the port wing and the upper center of the 757's fuselage. At that point it turned upside down, engulfed by a ball of flames, before coming to a halt. Reports differ about the number of casualties, but both *Time* magazine and the Aviation Safety Network said that 128 died, including 82 on the Xiamen plane and 46 on the ground; AirDisaster.com, an aviation safety Web site, puts the number at 132. It was China's worst reported air disaster and the third reported civilian hijacking in China in recent years; the last had been in 1988, when two armed men diverted another Xiamen 737, also on its way to Guangzhou, to Taiwan.

The time of the accident was 8:30 A.M. Word of the disaster first came out at about 9:00, when Hong Kong aviation officials were informed that the Baiyun Airport was closed but not told why. The airport was opened six hours later, but only to international flights. In the meantime the area around the crash was cordoned off, and diplomats, journalists, and others were kept firmly away. The CAAC did not make its first official comments about the disaster until a week later, when a CAAC official said that the disaster "revealed problems" at the airport and with Xiamen Airlines that would be addressed. The official also said that "The companies concerned are making serious efforts to deal with its aftermath" and went on to say that the nation's aviation staff were being reminded that safety regulations were "formulated in accordance with the principle of putting safety first." The official did not respond to questions about why the runway at Baiyun was not cleared as the Xiamen plane circled for 40 minutes. While the bulk of the responsibility for the disaster lay obviously with the hijacker, loss of life in one of the world's worst air piracy accidents could have been reduced if ground procedures had been different and the runway had been cleared. ◆

China Airlines Flight 140

APRIL 26, 1994

China Airlines Flight 140, which originated in Taipei, Taiwan, was en route to Nagoya, Japan, on the evening of April 26, 1994, with 256 passengers and 15 crew members aboard. After an uneventful flight, the plane was making a routine landing on Nagoya International Airport's runway 34 when it crashed just past 8:15 P.M.

The final moments of Flight 140 should have been as uneventful as the rest of the flight had been. The plane, one of six Airbus A300-600Rs flown by China Airlines, was state of the art and virtually new; it had been delivered in January 1991, and had accumulated only 8,550 flight hours in 3,910 flight cycles. Until that date, none of the 162 Airbus 300-600Rs in service at that time had ever crashed (although seven Airbus planes had crashed in the preceding decade). Its landing gear were down and locked, and no maintenance issues with the plane had been recorded. The weather was clear with only a slight breeze, and the pilot, Captain Wang Lo-chi, was a veteran. He reported no problems on his final approach.

After passing the airport's outer marker about eight miles from the airport at 8:12, Wang was given landing priority and clearance to land. A little after 8:15 he told the tower that he was "going around"–that is, that he was pulling up from the landing and was going to fly around the airport to try again–but he did not say why. The tower acknowledged and told him to stand by for further instructions, but that was the last communication between the plane and the tower. The tower sounded the crash alarm at 8:15 and 47 seconds.

A number of persons on the ground witnessed the crash. They said that they saw the aircraft in a nose-up attitude and rolling to its right. Investigators later confirmed that the aircraft had rolled about 40 degrees and hit the ground about 300 feet to the right of runway 34. While some witnesses believed that the plane's right wing hit the ground first, the fact that the plane's horizontal stabilizer separated from the plane led investigators to conclude that the plane's tail had to have struck the ground first. This would be consistent with eyewitness reports of the plane's nose pitching up. After the plane hit the ground, the fuselage slid about 150 feet before erupting in a series of explosions; because the plane was carrying enough fuel to return to Taipei, it was almost totally destroyed from post-crash explosions and fire. Wreckage was spread over 1,000 to 1,200 feet. Miraculously, seven passengers, all from the mid-cabin area, survived.

With advances in technology, one frequently hears the expression that a modern airliner is so sophisticated that it can "fly itself." The crash of Flight 140 shows that humans—and human error—still have a major role to play in aviation. For what happened to Flight 140 was a series of avoidable missteps that effectively neutralized some of the plane's automatic systems. It crashed because the crew mistakenly activated the plane's TOGA (takeoff/go-around) lever, misjudged the plane's trim, and attempted to execute procedures that contradicted the logic of the plane's automated safety systems.

In essence, the crew was forced to choose between allowing the plane to fly on automatic pilot or flying the plane manually. Instead, the crew chose a halfway approach, probably because the plane had moved to a nose-up attitude as a result of the mistaken TOGA command, which was defeating their efforts to bring the plane's nose down. Put simply, the crew was simultaneously telling the plane to pull up and to land—like a horseback rider kicking a horse forward and pulling back on the reins at the same time. The plane's systems chose to pull up, but without enough thrust to keep the plane in the air. The plane rapidly lost airspeed, though the crew managed to gain a little altitude and speed seconds before the crash. But when the plane stalled at 790 feet, its speed dropped to 78 knots and it rolled to its right and crashed. If the captain had noticed that the TOGA indicator light was on, he probably could have saved the aircraft even in its final seconds. Instead, the cockpit voice recorder showed that the captain grew increasingly frustrated as the plane failed to respond as it should have.

In July 1996, the Japanese Aircraft Accident Investigation Committee split the responsibility for the crash between the pilots and Airbus Industrie, the manufacturer of the plane. They

The crash of Flight 140 shows that humans–and human error–still have a major role to play in aviation.

concluded that the crew was not adequately trained in the use and operational characteristics of the A300's autopilot, that they responded badly when the plane was out of trim, and that the captain should have taken over control of the plane from the first officer earlier. But the committee also pointed to what they regarded as design flaws in the A300, specifically the position of the autopilot's TOGA lever beneath the throttle. The committee, whose findings were endorsed by the U.S. National Transportation Safety Board, also said that Airbus needed to study the workings of the automatic flight system, perhaps redesigning it in a way that would consider pilot reactions. In the committee's view, the system was too complicated, especially in emergencies. They also argued that airline manufacturers should standardize specifications of automatic flight systems to make training easier and more uniform.

The crash of Flight 140 was the second crash of a China Airlines jetliner in six months. In November 1993, a Boeing 747 crashed while landing at Hong Kong, though no one was killed. In response to the crash of Flight 140, the airline revamped its flight training procedures and contracted with Germany's Lufthansa airlines to provide consulting services for flight operations and aircraft maintenance. Despite these efforts, China Airlines experienced tragedy less than four years later when another Airbus, Flight 676, crashed on landing in Taipei, Taiwan, leaving 204 dead. ◆

American Airlines Flight 965

DECEMBER 20, 1995

At 6:34 on the evening of December 20, 1995, American Airlines Flight 965 was cleared for takeoff from the Miami International Airport. The plane climbed to a cruising altitude of 37,000 feet en route to the Alfonso Bonilla Aragon International Airport at Cali, Columbia.

At 9:03 local time, Flight 965 made contact with the air traffic control center in Bogota, Columbia. Twenty-three minutes later, the Bogota center cleared the flight to descend to 24,000 feet. American Airlines ground control then told the pilots that they could expect to land to the airport's north, on Runway 01.

Tragically, the plane never arrived at Cali, for at 9:41 it slammed into the ground near the summit of El Deluvio Mountain, a 12,000-foot peak. Aboard were 163 passengers and crew; miraculously, four passengers survived the crash, which left 159 dead. At the time it was the deadliest U.S. jetliner crash since terrorists blew up PanAm Flight 800 over Lockerbie, Scotland, in 1988.

The preholiday flight should have been uneventful–as it was until the final six minutes. At the time American Airlines had one of the best safety records in the business. The plane, a Boeing 757, had a record of nearly flawless safety performance. The pilot, Nicholas Tafuri, and the co-pilot, Don Williams, were experienced. The weather around Cali was good, with only scattered clouds at 1,700 and 10,000 feet. So why did the plane fly into a mountain?

Shortly after the accident, American Airlines' chief pilot, C. D. Ewell, stated, "The accident reminds us that aviation, while not inherently dangerous, is terribly unforgiving of any inattention to detail." Flying into the Cali airport in particular demands any flight crew's complete attention because in making their approach pilots have to negotiate a dark, mountainous corridor for some 70 miles. But what the cockpit voice recorder of 965 showed during the final 30 minutes of the flight was a great deal of inattention on the part of the flight crew, including idle conversation about snacks and about flight attendants' work schedules. Further, the crew failed to conduct an "approach briefing," a standard procedure during which the crew reviews its speed, altitude, and other important navigation checks. This was an especially significant oversight because antigovernment **guerrillas** in Columbia had knocked out one of the Cali airport's radar stations three years before.

Compounding the problem was confusion after control of the flight was switched to Cali approach controller Nelson Rivera Ramirez. (Some investigators speculated at first if Ramirez's English was poor, the result might have been some sort of fatal miscommunication; in fact, his English was quite clear, though Ramirez himself confessed that while his technical English was good, his command of the language was not good enough for him to challenge the crew on what he interpreted as "illogical" replies that "made no sense.") What first seemed to distract the crew was the controller's offer to allow the plane to land directly from the north rather than circle for a landing from the south. Tafuri took the controller up on that

The preholiday flight should have been uneventful–as it was until the final six minutes.

guerrillas individuals who engage in irregular warfare tactics, especially as members of an independent unit.

For over a minute the crew did not notice that the plane was making a long, arcing turn.

offer after Williams, who was flying the plane at the time, told him, "Yeah, we'll have to scramble to get down. We can do it." Williams then deployed the plane's "speed brakes," or the flat panels on top of the wings that rotate up and help with rapid descents.

Further confusion arose when the controller asked the crew to report when they passed the ground radio navigation point called Tulua. Several times the controller said "Report Tulua," but he got no response. For a minute and a half, the pilot flipped though papers trying to find the radio codes for Tulua. In the meantime, however, the plane had passed Tulua, unknown to the crew. So when the pilot entered the Tulua code into the plane's flight management computer, the plane responded by making a long left turn to return to Tulua. For over a minute the crew did not notice that the plane was making a long, arcing turn. At one point Williams asked, "Uh, where are we?" Tafuri responded, "Let's go right to, uh, Tulua first of all." "Yeah, where we headed?" asked Williams.

By now the plane was 86 seconds into its turn and headed toward the mountains. At this point Williams turned off the flight management computer and reprogrammed the autopilot to begin a right turn. But for another 25 seconds the pilots did not know where they were in relation to Tulua. Williams asked:

"So you want a left turn back around to ULQ [the Tulua code]?"

Tafuri responded, "Nawww . . . Hell no, let's press on to . . ."

"Well, we're, press on to where, though?" said Williams.

The plane was still descending, and after the pilots made first a left turn and then a right turn, a mountain was between the plane and the airport. The pilots, clearly confused about where exactly they were, engaged in conversation about what to do next and wondered what had happened to Tulua. The conversation was interrupted by a loud warning from the ground proximity warning system. Williams disconnected the autopilot and began an emergency climb. But according to the plane's flight data recorder, he failed to retract the speed brakes, depriving the plane of crucial lift. Thirteen seconds after the ground warning system sounded, and as Williams was gunning the engines, the plane slammed into the mountain.

The question of whether or not American Airlines was guilty of "willful misconduct" was important one for the firm.

Under the existing international aviation treaty, which would govern damage claims made by the families of Colombian citizens aboard, such claims are normally limited to $75,000 per person–unless willful misconduct can be proved. In that case, families of the victims can sue for much greater damages. In September 1997, a federal judge in Miami, Florida, ruled that American Airlines was in fact guilty of willful misconduct. In his ruling he stated, "The undisputed facts . . . simply leave no room for a reasonable jury to find that the pilots' deliberate decision to continue to descend the aircraft from an off course position at night, in an environment known for high terrain, . . . was anything other than an act of willful misconduct." ◆

ValuJet Flight 592

MAY 11, 1996

Perhaps no airline disaster in recent years has focused public attention on airline safety as much as the crash of ValuJet's Flight 592.

The afternoon weather was virtually perfect on the afternoon of May 11, 1996, when the DC-9 left Miami, Florida, for a routine two-hour hop to Atlanta with 110 people on board. Yet just minutes after taking off, the pilot radioed air traffic control that the plane needed to return to Miami. Then, at approximately 2:15, the plane suddenly dove 7,500 feet in just 40 seconds and crashed nose first into the muck and sawgrass of the Everglades just west of the city. At the moment of impact, the plane was traveling at a speed of 500 miles per hour. The 57-ton jetliner left a black hole in the Everglades half the size of a football field.

For the next month, divers attempted to recover not only the plane's debris but the remains of the people who perished in the crash. To say that the task was difficult would be an understatement. The divers had to wear special gear to protect themselves from the perils of the swamp. Eventually, backhoes had to be brought in to dig through the muck. But the force of the impact was so great that little of the plane was left, and what was left was buried in the mud and grass. By the time the search was called off on June 10, only 75 percent of the plane was recovered and the remains of only 36 of the victims were found.

Robert Francis of the National Transportation Safety Board stands alongside wreckage from ValuJet Flight 592.

Early in the investigation that followed, authorities strongly suspected that only an explosion of some sort–perhaps a bomb–could have caused the plane to crash so suddenly. But on May 30 the National Transportation Safety Board (NTSB) released details about the plane's final moments based on information from the plane's cockpit voice recorder. Their key finding was that six minutes after take-off the crew heard an unidentified noise. Shortly afterward panicked voices could be heard from the cabin reporting a fire. Moments later those voices fell silent.

When the investigation was complete, the NTSB identified the source of the fire: The plane had been illegally transporting used oxygen generators. These generators, which are installed above passenger compartments to provide oxygen in case of cabin depressurization, had been removed from another ValuJet plane and loaded into the DC-9 to be transported back to the airline's headquarters in Atlanta. They were labeled as empty, but they were not, and the safety caps that normally would be put on out-of-commission generators were missing. Falling pressure in the plane's cargo hold triggered the chemical reaction that produces oxygen–a reaction that also produces intense heat, which caused the generators to ignite. Because the plane did not have smoke detectors in its cargo hold, the flight crew did not know of the fire. Otherwise, they might have been able to return to the Miami airport in time. Instead, the fire spread to the cabin. Autopsy reports showed that many if not all of those aboard died from inhaling toxic fumes before the plane hit the ground.

The fallout from the ValuJet disaster was wide-ranging. Initially, both the U.S. secretary of transportation, Federico Peña, and the head of the Federal Aviation Administration (FAA), David Hinson, declared that the airline company was safe. Yet at the time of the crash, ValuJet was in the middle of a 120-day FAA safety review, and an FAA report prepared before the crash indicated that the airline had recently had eight aborted take-offs and unscheduled landings. The report further said that ValuJet had "ineffective (maintenance) control and procedures." Among the FAA's findings were 34 violations, including delayed maintenance, failure to repair jammed landing gear, cabin doors that would not lock, and an inoperative weather radar system on one plane. Suddenly, Americans began to wonder whether they could trust the federal government's oversight of the airline industry. Their uneasiness was compounded by the spectacular crash of TWA Flight 800 near New York in July of that year. By the end of the year, both Peña and Hinson had left their jobs and the FAA's safety chief, Anthony Broderick, had resigned under pressure. Some observers believed that the FAA was criminally negligent in its oversight of ValuJet.

The crash also affected both ValuJet and the airline industry. Prior to the crash, the airline had been doing well. Its planes were full, its stock price was strong, and in less than three years it had expanded to 31 cities with 51 planes. But within a week it had cut the number of its flights in half and investors in the company began to lose money. Eventually the airline was shut down for 15 weeks, and in 1997 it merged with AirTran Airways and flew under that company's name. In the meantime, the value of investments in other small, low-cost airlines tumbled as investors began to question whether such airlines were safe.

The ValuJet crash led to the nation's first criminal trial in connection with a commercial jet crash. The defendants in the trial were SabreTech, Inc., which was ValuJet's maintenance firm, and two of its employees. They were charged with mishandling hazardous materials and, more seriously, with conspiracy. Prosecutors argued that the employees had knowingly mislabeled the oxygen generators as empty. In December 1999, a Florida jury acquitted the company and its employees of the conspiracy charge but did find them guilty of the less serious charge of mishandling hazardous materials. In October 2000, a U.S. district court ordered the company to pay $2 million in fines and restitution to victims' families. This fine, combined with an FAA fine of $2.25 million levied in 1998, effectively put SabreTech out of business.

As a result of the ValuJet crash, the FAA added hundreds of new inspectors, many of them assigned to oversee start-up

Suddenly, Americans began to wonder whether they could trust the federal government's oversight of the airline industry.

airlines. The agency also banned oxygen generators from cargo holds and required fire detectors and fire extinguishers in the holds of all airplanes–a step that the NTSB first recommended in 1988. ◆

TWA Flight 800

On July 17, 1996, the residents of Long Island, New York, were enjoying a warm summer evening. Some were strolling along the beach on the island's south shore, while others were sitting in waterside restaurants with a tranquil view of the Atlantic Ocean.

Suddenly, at 8:31 P.M., many of the beachcombers noticed a huge orange fireball out over the water. As they watched it plummet into the ocean, they realized with horror that they had just witnessed the midair explosion of an airplane. Later, as the rest of the nation watched scenes of the burning debris on television, Long Islanders would learn that they had seen the crash of TWA Flight 800, a Boeing 747 headed out over the North Atlantic. The plane had taken off from New York City's John F. Kennedy Airport at 8:15 with 230 people aboard, among them 16 American teenagers headed for Paris, the plane's destination, with their French club. The plane climbed until it reached 13,700 feet, when it broke apart and began to fall. At 8,500 feet it erupted into a fireball and 24 seconds later hit the water, leaving wreckage scattered over a five-square-mile area 10 miles off the coast of Long Island and 40 miles east of New York City.

Within hours, helicopters hovered over the scene and a circling C-130 transport plane dropped flares to help rescuers from 40 Coast Guard vessels search for survivors. What they found were only charred remains. The following day, divers arrived on the scene to begin the underwater salvage effort. On July 25 they discovered the plane's "**black boxes**," which investigators hoped would explain the crash. The task they began that night–finding and assembling as much of the wreckage as they could–would require 10 months and 10,000 staff-hours to complete.

In the summer of 1996 the American public was already uneasy about air travel. In May of that year, ValueJet Flight 592

black box the in-flight voice recorders of the pilots and crew of airline flights.

had crashed in the Florida Everglades, killing all 110 people aboard. Like TWA Flight 800, the ValuJet plane seemed to have fallen inexplicably from the sky; neither weather nor pilot error seemed to have been a factor in either crash. This new disaster once again caused the public to wonder how safe air travel was if an airliner can just explode and fall from the sky. For the second time in a little over two months, federal investigators were faced with the problem of trying to find the cause of a major air disaster.

The answer came on August 21, when investigators confirmed that there was an explosion in the plane's center fuel tank. The best answer investigators were able to offer about the source of the explosion was that volatile fuel vapors had built up in the fuel tank and an electrical spark caused them to explode. They based their conclusion not only on **forensic** evidence from the plane but also on the fact that in May mechanics had discovered a fuel leak in a Boeing 737-200 that they believed was caused by electrical arcing. Investigators of TWA Flight 800 concluded that a similar kind of electrical arcing probably ignited the vapors in the plane, causing it to explode.

TWA 800 was painstakingly reconstructed to try to determine the cause of the accident that claimed 110 lives.

forensic belonging to or suitable to courts of law or to public disuccsion and debate.

National Transportation Safety Board

The crash of TWA Flight 800 brought widespread public attention to a 30-year-old independent agency that had previously been largely unknown: the National Transportation Safety Board (NTSB). Founded in 1967 with funding from the Federal Department of Transportation, the NTSB is charged with the task of investigating civilian aviation accidents to determine their causes and develop preventive measures that could prevent future occurrences of such accidents. In 1975 the agency severed its ties with the government, becoming fully independent.

Since 1967, the NTSB has investigated more than 110,000 aviation accidents involving U.S. planes, both in the United States and abroad. The board's work goes on 24 hours a day, 365 days a year. Whenever an aviation accident occurs, an NTSB investigation team is sent to the crash site to survey the damage and recover evidence that can help explain what happened, including the on-board flight recorders and pieces of wreckage. Investigators analyze the direction in which the fusilage metal is bent or the pattern of debris on the ground in order to piece together a picture of what may have happened just prior to the accident.

The NTSB's second mission, preventing future accidents, is equally important. Each year it files safety recommendations and publishes a Ten Most Wanted list of improvements that it deems most urgent. Over the years, the NTSB has issued nearly 12,000 recommendations, including improvements such as the use of less explosive fuel mixtures and suggestions for better fusilage design. However, as an independent agency, the NTSB cannot force the airlines to accept its recommendations. Instead, it relies upon public support and industry cooperation.

The NTSB's need to work closely with the airlines to get their cooperation, and its slow, methodical approach to investigating crash-sites, has sometimes sparked public disapproval and charges of insensitivity to the families of crash victims. In response, the NTSB affirms its commitment to airline safety, and states that its procedures are designed to provide the most detailed analyses of aviation accidents possible, and thus to ensure a steady improvement in safety in the skies.

This conclusion, however, failed to put to rest alternate theories about the disaster. Many people believed that something more sinister was at work and that the U.S. government was covering it up. Within days of the crash, these theories began to circulate, many of them over the Internet. One was that a bomb in the plane had exploded. But another theory, which began to develop a kind of life of its own in the public imagination, was that the plane had been shot down by a missile. This theory was based on claims by eyewitnesses that just before the plane blew up, an object that looked like a missile intercepted the aircraft. Some linked the missile to terrorists, but others had a different, more troubling explanation: that the plane had been accidentally shot down by the U.S. Navy during a top-secret training exercise. These rumors were fueled on March 12, 1997, when Pierre Salinger, press secretary during the Kennedy administration and a former ABC News correspondent, published a report in which he said that he was "totally sure" the aircraft was hit by a Navy missile. He based his claim on an air traffic control radar tape that showed a blip heading toward the plane just before it exploded. In November 1997, Ian Goddard, who had co-authored a report on this theory with Salinger, retracted the claim, calling it "reckless and a mistake." Salinger, though, refused to join him in the retraction.

To investigate these and other possibilities, the Federal Bureau of Investigation (FBI) stepped into the National Transportation Safety Board's probe of the crash. The FBI conducted a 16-month investigation, interviewing 7,000 people who touched or had access to the plane both at JFK Airport and in Athens, Greece, where the flight originated. In November 1997, the FBI closed its investigation, saying that the bureau could find no evidence of criminal wrongdoing. It dismissed the "Navy missile" theory as "Internet gossip," and the NTSB said that the "missile" on the radar tape was a Navy plane flying 7,000 feet above Flight 800. In response to claims of eyewitnesses that they saw something that looked like a missile speeding toward the plane, investigators concluded that what they saw was a trail of fire left by fuel leaking from the plane.

In response to the crash, the NTSB focused its attention on the electrical systems of the nation's commercial air fleet. The following fall the board issued an "airworthiness directive" requiring airlines to immediately inspect the wiring in older 747s. Then in April 1997, the board recommended design changes in the wiring of 747s and other planes. Despite these steps, the families of many of the crash's victims launched a campaign to have the nation's aging 747 fleet grounded. ◆

In November 1997, the FBI closed its investigation, saying that the bureau could find no evidence of criminal wrongdoing.

Saudi Arabian Airlines Flight 763/Kazak Airlines Flight 1907

NOVEMBER 12, 1996

At 6:33 P.M. on November 12, 1996, Saudi Arabian Airlines Flight 763, a Boeing 747 carrying 300 passengers and 12 crew members, took off from the Indira Gandhi International Airport in New Delhi, India, bound for Dhahran and Jiddah in Saudi Arabia. Most of the passengers were Indians traveling to jobs in Saudi Arabia or Muslims making the traditional pilgrimage to Mecca. After takeoff, New Delhi air traffic control authorized the plane to climb to 14,000 feet. The pilot acknowledged the transmission.

At about the same time Kazak Airlines Flight 1907 was approaching the New Delhi airport en route from Shymkent in the former Soviet republic of Kazakhstan. The Ilyushin Il-76, a Russian-manufactured cargo plane, had been chartered by a company in neighboring Kyrgyzstan, and most of the 28 passengers and 10 crew members aboard were Kyrgyz. As it made its approach, air traffic control authorized the plane to descend to 15,000 feet. Like the pilot of the Saudi plane, the pilot of the Kazak plane acknowledged the transmission.

Both pilots were informed that they were headed toward each other on the same flight path, but at different altitudes. Both were instructed to "report when in sight" of the other aircraft. After the Kazak pilot reached 15,000 feet, the control tower informed him of the location of the other plane, saying, "Identified traffic 12 o'clock reciprocal. Saudi Boeing 747, 14 miles. Report [when] in sight." The Kazak pilot replied, "Repeat how many miles." The tower repeated that the plane was 14 miles away, then soon afterward said that it was 13 miles away. The Kazak pilot acknowledged both messages.

What followed was a minute of silence–followed at 6:40 by the third worst airline disaster and the deadliest midair collision in history as the two planes collided about 60 miles west of the New Delhi airport. The pilot of an American C-141 U.S. Air Force transport plane bringing supplies to the U.S. Embassy in New Delhi witnessed the crash from an altitude of about 20,000 feet: "We noticed out of our right hand a large cloud lit up with an orange glow, from within the clouds. The glow intensity of the cloud became dimmer and the two fireballs descended and became fireballs on the ground" about a minute later. The Kazak plane crashed near the small village of Birhod. Witnesses that saw the Saudi plane descend said that the pilot seemed to have maintained some control of the aircraft and guided it away from populated areas to a field near the village of Charkhi Dadri, seven miles from the Kazak plane, where it plowed a trench about 60 yards long and 15 feet deep into a farm field.

Local residents rushed to the scene to offer assistance and search for survivors, but it soon became clear that no one could have survived the crash. The crash site of the 747 was a particularly gruesome scene, as the charred remains of many of the victims lay scattered with twisted pieces of metal over a wide area. Three people were still barely alive, but all died at hospitals a short time later. The final death toll was 349, surpassing the 176 killed in a midair collision over Yugoslavia in 1976. (The total of 349 indicates a discrepancy in the total number of persons reported to have been aboard the two aircraft.) No one on the ground was killed.

What followed was considerable speculation about the cause of the accident, especially since midair collisions are extremely rare. Some pilots who fly in and out of Indian airports wondered whether there was miscommunication between air traffic control and one or both of the pilots, saying that it was often difficult to understand the English-language instructions radioed to them by controllers. Indian officials, though, were quick to defend air traffic control operations, insisting that they conformed to international flight safety standards. Aviation experts pointed out that the **altimeter** on Russian-built Ilyushin Il-76s is calibrated in meters rather than feet. Pilots at the helm of many older Soviet-bloc planes have to rely on a chart to convert feet into meters, increasing the possibility of a mistake. Still others noted that the Ilyushin Il-76 plane was not equipped with a modern radar system that would have alerted the pilot if the plane was in the path of another plane. More modern jetliners are equipped with what is called a Traffic Alert and Collision Avoidance System, or TCAS, which queries other planes about their altitude and direction and warns the pilot if another plane is too close.

Accompanying this speculation, too, was a great deal of finger-pointing. The Indian media rushed to blame Kazak

> **It soon became clear that no one could have survived the crash.**

altimeter an instrument which measures altitude in an aircraft and registers atmospheric pressure occurring with changes in altitude.

Airlines, a state-run company with an aging fleet, heavy debt, and a poor safety record–though records later indicated that the Kazak plane may have been only four years old and was in good technical condition.

The Indian Air Traffic Controllers' Guild leapt to blame the New Delhi airport. They pointed out that all takeoffs and landings at the airport occur along a single flight corridor, with planes flying in opposite directions on the same path separated by as little as a thousand feet in altitude. For years pilots and controllers had been saying that the lack of other routes into and out of the airport created a safety hazard. This hazard, combined with an antiquated radar system and the fact that New Delhi airport traffic had doubled in the previous five years, was a recipe for disaster. In the meantime, Indian officials pointed the finger of blame at two targets. One was neighboring rival Pakistan, which had recently closed an air traffic control center near India's Punjab region. The other was the United States, which, officials claimed, had held up a Federal Aviation Administration project to upgrade the New Delhi airport's radar facilities under a contract with the Raytheon Corporation. At the time of the accident, the radar upgrade was not complete. With some inconsistency, Indian officials also defended their 1970s-vintage radar systems.

After an investigation, the Airports Authority of India pinned the blame for the crash on Kazak Airlines, concluding that the Kazak plane failed to maintain the altitude assigned to it by air traffic control. The plane was assigned a flight level of 15,000 feet but flew below that level into the ill-fated Saudi airliner. ◆

Korean Air Flight 801

August 6, 1997

Korean Air Flight 801, a regularly scheduled passenger flight, departed from Kimpo International Airport in Seoul, South Korea, at 9:53 in the evening on August 5, 1997. The plane, a Boeing 747-300 carrying 237 passengers and 17 crew members, was en route to Guam, a U.S. territorial island in the western Pacific.

Until its final few minutes the flight proceeded uneventfully. About 240 nautical miles northwest of the A.B. Won

Guam International Airport in Agana, Guam, just after 1:00 A.M. on August 6, the first officer made initial contact with the Guam Air Traffic Control Center and Radar Approach Control. As the flight descended from 41,000 feet over the next 40 minutes, it maintained regular contact with the air traffic control center. Following normal procedures used when landing on Guam, the plane descended in a series of steps designed to enable it to stay above the high terrain that surrounded the island airport. But at 1:42, as the plane was making its final approach to runway 6 Left, an approach made more difficult by gusting winds, heavy rain, and reduced visibility, it slammed into a mountain about three miles southwest of the airport.

Emergency response at the crash site was hampered by a number of factors. First, the air traffic controller did not immediately realize the plane had crashed. Then, emergency vehicles were blocked by a fenced gate that encircled the property where the accident occurred. They then had to follow a narrow road that was blocked by a broken pipeline and vehicles that had been damaged when they were struck by the plane. By the time help arrived at the scene, the plane had been destroyed not only by its initial impact with the ground but by the post-crash fire. Of the 254 persons aboard, 228 were killed. Miraculously, 23 passengers and three flight attendants survived the crash–the third worst airline accident ever on U.S. soil.

The crash of Korean Air Flight 801 was classified as a "controlled flight into terrain," the deadliest kind of crash because the crew was taking no steps to avoid a crash or to minimize its effects: they virtually flew the plane into the ground. The question that everyone wanted answered, of course, was why? Although weather conditions were not ideal, they were not unmanageable or particularly dangerous. Nothing went wrong with the plane itself. Further, the crew of Flight 801 had a great deal of experience. The pilot, a 10-year Korean Air veteran, had had almost 3,200 flight hours in the Boeing 747, over 1,700 hours as captain. The first officer had over 4,000 flight hours, and the flight engineer had over 13,000 total flight hours, 11,000 as a civilian flight engineer. In addition, both the pilot and the first officer had recently undergone training for landing at the Guam airport in a 747 during nighttime, visual-flight-rules conditions. And yet, despite the crew's training and experience, "pilot error" was listed as the official cause of the crash after the National Transportation Safety Board completed its investigation in 1998.

Emergency response at the crash site was hampered by a number of factors.

The crew essentially ignored these readings and failed to call them to one another's attention.

glideslope landing instrument on an aircraft that indicates the angle of a plane's descent.

Examination of the plane's cockpit voice recordings showed that there was confusion in the cockpit. Crew members were questioning one another about the state of the instrument landing system, particularly after failing to acknowledge an air traffic controller's warning that Guam had no operating **glideslope**. This is a component of the landing system that shows pilots whether they are descending at the correct angle. There was an alternative instrument that the flight crew could have used, but it is clear from the cockpit voice recorder that the crew could not decide whether or not the glideslope was working. For example, at 1:39, after clearing the plane to land, the air traffic controller said "glideslope unusable." Shortly thereafter, the flight engineer can be heard asking, "Is the glideslope working?" to which the captain responded, "Yes, yes, it's working." Moments later one of the crew members said, "Check the glideslope if working." Pilots are supposed to acknowledge important information, and a flight crew is supposed to monitor and crosscheck one another to maintain what experienced pilots call "situational awareness"–a clear sense of what is going on around them. The crew of Flight 801, perhaps as a result of fatigue, failed to maintain situational awareness.

Additionally, after the crew adopted a plan to descend into the airport in a series of steps, they ignored airline procedures and failed to notice when the plane had reached the minimum approved altitude for each step. Standard landing procedures called for the plane to descend to no lower that 2,000 feet until 1.6 miles from the VOR (the radar on the outer edge of the airport approach). Then the plane was to descend to no lower that 1,440 feet until reaching the VOR. After crossing the VOR the plane could descend to its "minimum descent altitude" of 560 feet. Yet flight data shows that the plane began to descend when it was five miles from the VOR and descended rapidly through the 2,000 and 1,440-foot altitudes until it struck rising mountain terrain just west of the VOR. In the last seconds before the crash, an onboard radar device called the ground-proximity warning system repeatedly gave altitude readings showing that the plane was dangerously close to the ground. The crew essentially ignored these readings and failed to call them to one another's attention as they went through a routine prelanding checklist. Compounding the problem was the fact that the Federal Aviation Administration had taken out of operation the airport's "minimum safe altitude warning system" (MSAW).

When Flight 801 was attempting to land, it was following the procedures used in "non-precision landings," or landings made without the use of land-based navigational aids. Since 1988, 38 airliners have crashed as a result of "controlled flight into terrain." Thirty-five of those 38 crashed during non-precision landings. As a result of the crash of Flight 801 and others, the airline industry is re-examining pilot training and the elimination of certain non-precision landing procedures. ◆

Garuda Airlines Flight 152

SEPTEMBER 26, 1997

Each year an average of 25 airplanes throughout the world–airliners, commuter planes, and air taxis–crash for no apparent mechanical reasons. According to the *Washington Post*, these types of crashes represent about 80 percent of all air disasters. Members of the air industry have even given this type of crash its own name, "controlled flight into terrain," or CFIT, usually pronounced "cee-fit." This type of crash is usually the deadliest kind of air disaster, for the pilot normally has no reason to take any action to avoid a crash or minimize its effects–the pilot essentially flies the fully operational plane into the ground or water. Because of the prevalence of CFITs, the Flight Safety Foundation, a worldwide organization dedicated to aviation safety, has even appointed a special task force to study them and reduce their incidence.

The 222 passengers and 12 crew members on board Garuda Airlines Flight 152 on September 26, 1997, were all victims of a controlled flight into terrain. On that date the twin-engine Indonesian Airbus A-300 was flying from the Indonesian capital of Jakarta to Medan, on the northern tip of Sumatra, Indonesia, about 870 miles away. The plane was scheduled to arrive in Medan at about 2:30 P.M. local time. But at 1:55 P.M. it crashed into a mountain near the village of Buah Nabar in the Sibolangit district south of Medan, about 20 miles short of the airport runway. None of the passengers or crew, who were almost all Indonesian nationals, survived.

Crash investigators initially speculated that the plane may have gone down because of poor visibility. The plane was flying in a smoky haze caused by hundreds of forest fires that had been devastating southeast Asia in recent days. Those fires disrupted air service in much of the region, causing several airports to shut down. Sumatra was one of the worst affected islands.

Poor visibility may have been a contributing factor in the accident, but a transcript of the conversation between the captain and the air traffic controller at Polonia Airport in North Sumatra suggests that the fatal cause of the crash was confusion about which direction the plane should have turned to begin its final descent for landing. Medan is on Sumatra's coast, where it overlooks the Strait of Malacca and is protected by mountains rising to the southwest in the general direction from which the plane was flying. Any pilot flying into Medan has to negotiate mountainous terrain to make the approach. The pilot also has to ensure that the plane maintains the proper altitude to stay above any rising terrain. Flight 152 crashed into a mountain because it did not follow the correct flight path into the airport and may have been flying too low.

As the plane was making its approach, the pilot–Captain Hance Rahmowiyogo, a 20-year veteran with more that 12,000 flying hours–expressed concern about whether the plane was at a high enough altitude. After establishing an initial heading into the airport, he said to the controller, "Confirm we are cleared from a mountainous area." The controller replied: "Affirm sir. Continue turn left on heading 215." Heading 215 would be roughly to the southeast. Later, the controller again addressed the pilot: "GIA 152, turn right heading 046; report established localizer."

This instruction meant that the plane should make a right turn to a northeasterly direction. The instruction also meant that the pilot should inform the controller when he had established contact with a radio beacon that would guide him to the airport.

What follows is the portion of the conversation that contains the key to the crash:

Pilot: Turn right heading 040, GIA 152 check established.

Controller: Turning right sir.

Pilot: Roger 152.

Controller: 152 confirm you're making turning left now?

Pilot: We are turning right now.

Controller: 152, OK you continue turning left now.

Pilot: A [pause] confirm turning left? We are starting turning right now.

Controller: OK [pause] OK.

Controller: GIA 152, continue turn right heading 015.

Ten seconds later the pilot screamed "Allahu akbar," an Arabic exclamation meaning "God is great" that is often uttered by Muslims at emotional moments. Seconds later the plane slammed into a mountain.

What the transcript shows is that the air traffic controller inadvertently told the pilot to turn right–into a mountain–rather than left to make the sweeping turn toward the northeast that would have aligned the plane with Runway 5. In the confusion, the controller told the pilot to continue making a right turn when the plane should have been turning to the left. In flat terrain with good visibility, such an error might have been easily correctable. But under the conditions that faced Flight 152, the confusion about the direction of the plane, combined with the smoke and haze enveloping the island, was fatal. ◆

China Airlines Flight 676

FEBRUARY 16, 1998

China Airlines Flight 676 originated at Dempasar-Ngurah Rai Airport in Bali, Indonesia. Most of the 196 people aboard the jumbo jet were returning home to Taiwan from vacations on the resort island. The plane was a twin-engine A-300 made by Airbus Industrie in Toulouse, France, and delivered to the airline in December 1990. The plane had accumulated just over 20,000 hours of flight time and 8,800 flights.

As the plane was making its approach into Chiang Kai-Shek Airport in Taiwan in heavy fog and light rain, something went seriously wrong. Citizens of a residential area surrounding the airport reported that at about 8:05 in the evening, they heard a loud explosion, followed by a series of smaller explosions, and the evening sky lit up. One resident reported looking out the front windows of his apartment and seeing an airplane seat, a piece of carry-on luggage, sandals, and a chunk of twisted metal on the street. Lying on the ground across the street was a badly burned human body.

What they learned later was that Flight 676 had hit the ground several hundred yards short of runway 05/23L, clipped the top of a retaining wall separating the airport from nearby houses, then skidded through several homes before coming to rest in a rice paddy and bursting into flames. Soon firefighters were on the scene, rushing from house to house trying to douse flames and combing through the smoldering debris looking for survivors. Seats from the plane littered the ground, and the smell of burning jet fuel and rubber filled the humid night air. The only portion of the jetliner that was recognizable was the tail section, and many local residents found bits of metal and debris, as well as body parts, in their gardens.

All 196 people aboard, plus seven on the ground, were killed, making the crash the deadliest in the history of Chiang Kai-Shek Airport. Because of the force of the crash and the subsequent explosion, many of the dead could not be identified without DNA analysis. Among those killed in the crash were Sheu Yuan-dong, who was governor of Taiwan's central bank, and three other high-ranking financial officials, who had been attending a meeting of Asian central bankers in Bali. To calm the nation's financial markets, the government conducted an emergency meeting to appoint his successor to the post.

The crash was a setback for China Airlines, the national airline of Taiwan. In 1994 China Airlines Flight 140, also an Airbus A-300, exploded and burned during an aborted landing in Nagoya, Japan, killing 264 people. Prior to that disaster, four other China Airlines planes had crashed during the preceding eight years. As a result of these accidents, the airline had embarked on an extensive safety campaign, including pilot retraining. In the light of this latest disaster, the Taiwanese Civil Aeronautics administrator, Tsai Tuei, resigned to take moral responsibility for the crash. Taiwanese television showed scenes of an airline official **kowtowing**, or kneeling and touching the ground with his forehead, before a woman who had lost a family member on the flight.

Initially, it was believed that the cause of the crash was poor weather. Because of the fog and rain, the pilot of the aircraft had trouble with his approach. According to an airline spokesman, he reported that he was unable to see the runway as he made his approach and asked to come around again for another try. It was immediately after asking for another try, a "go-round," that the pilot lost contact with the tower. But despite the poor weather conditions, visibility was about 3,300 feet, or 1,300 feet more than the minimum required for landing.

In the weeks that followed the accident, investigators, including the Taiwan Civil Aeronautics Administration (TCAA) focused less on the weather and more on the aircraft's high angle of approach to the airport. In July 1999, the TCAA (with the support of the U.S. National Transportation Safety Board and Australia's Bureau of Air Safety Investigation) concluded that pilot error caused the crash. When the flight was about six miles from the airport, it was about 2,000 feet too high. During the flight's final approach, the plane never descended below 1,300 feet, and its landing gear remained retracted. Air traffic control gave the captain an altitude warning, but, according to the TCAA, he failed to take corrective action. He then applied full power for a miss-approach go-around but failed to monitor the plane's pitch-up angle for 14 seconds after gunning the engines. The airplane climbed more than 1,000 feet, then stalled at an altitude of 2,751 feet. From there it fell to the ground about two nautical miles away from the airport runway, hitting the ground tail first in a slight nose-up attitude. Put simply, the pilot was too high during his approach, and as he pulled up to try the landing again, he stalled the airplane.

Despite blaming pilot error for the crash, the TCAA also cited the culture of China Airlines and its need to enhance pilot training. Following the 1994 crash in Nagoya, which also resulted from a missed-approach, go-around maneuver, the airline instituted a number of changes in the Airbus A-300 autopilot design. Some pilots, however, believed at the time that this technical solution was not necessary and that the reason for the 1994 crash, like that of the 1998 crash, was simple pilot error. Today, China Airlines struggles to restore its reputation in the air travel community. ◆

Swissair Flight 111

September 2, 1997

About 20 miles southwest of Halifax, Nova Scotia, lies picturesque St. Margaret's Bay and the tiny coastal town of Peggy's Cove. Few people living outside of Nova Scotia would ever have had reason to even hear of Peggy's Cove before September 2, 1997.

That day, at about 10:30 P.M. Atlantic Time, Swissair Flight 111 plunged into the waters of the Atlantic Ocean six miles offshore from Peggy's Cove, killing all 214 passengers and 15 crew members aboard. The jumbo jet had taken off from New York's John F. Kennedy International Airport about an hour earlier, bound for Geneva, Switzerland. Within hours of the crash, Peggy's Cove became the center of futile efforts to rescue any survivors, then of efforts to salvage the wreckage of the plane, which was scattered over a 30-square-mile area in 190-foot waters.

At the time of the crash, the plane was attempting to make an emergency landing at the Halifax Airport, about 10 miles north of the city. According to the airline, the pilot reported problems very early in the flight and was directed to try to land at Boston's Logan Airport. The pilot, though, elected to continue flying in the direction of Halifax, 400 miles to the northeast. Then about 16 minutes before the crash, the pilot radioed controllers at the Moncton, New Brunswick, air traffic control center, declaring "Pan Pan Pan," an international distress signal short of an emergency. The pilot went on: "We have smoke in the cockpit, request deviate immediate right turn to a convenient place." The controller suggested Halifax, and the pilot agreed. At that time, the plane was flying at an altitude of 33,000 feet and was about 70 nautical miles southwest of Halifax. The plane immediately began descending at a rate of about 3,000 feet per minute and leveled off 30 miles away from the airport at an altitude of about 10,000 feet, hoping to give flight attendants time to prepare passengers for an emergency landing.

To this point, the pilot appeared to have control of the plane. But after discussion with the air traffic controller about dumping fuel and making an arcing turn to approach the airport's runway from the southwest, the situation deteriorated, though it remains unclear why. About 90 seconds after the plane leveled off, the pilot contacted air traffic control: "We are declaring an emergency. We are starting to vent now. We have to land immediately." Forty-four seconds later the pilot made a last, unintelligible transmission. The plane then began a five- to six-minute, 9,700-foot death spiral into the ocean. As the plane began to fall, air traffic radar lost contact with its transponder and picked up only "primary" echoes from the plane about eight miles south of Peggy's Cove. The silence of the transponder, which identifies the plane and transmits information about its altitude to air traffic controllers, suggests that the plane lost electrical power.

The airliner was a Douglas MD-11, a plane similar to the older three-engine DC-10 and the world's only modern wide-cabin airliner powered by three engines. The plane, which entered service in 1990, is 200 feet long and normally can carry 285 people, although it can be reconfigured to seat up to 410. The plane used to be built by the McDonnell Douglas Corporation, but Boeing took over production when it purchased McDonnell Douglas in 1997. Boeing announced plans to stop production of the MD-11 because it proved unpopular with airlines, though freight carriers such as Federal Express liked the plane because of its size and 7,500-mile range. One of FedEx's MD-11s crashed while landing in Newark, New Jersey, in July 1997, though the crew was able to escape before fire destroyed the plane.

Because there was a fire in the plane, the Federal Bureau of Investigation (FBI) and the Federal Aviation Administration (FAA) immediately suspected that the plane was transporting hazardous materials. Still fresh in their minds was ValuJet Flight 592, which had caught fire and crashed into the Florida Everglades in May 1996. The investigation of that accident determined that the plane was illegally carrying decommissioned oxygen generators, which started the fire. However, as investigators recovered and reassembled Flight 111's wreckage–a process that took over a year–they came to a different conclusion. Focusing on the forward area of the aircraft, they found melted aluminum electrical wires with melted copper and charred or missing wire insulation. They also learned that many smaller parts of the plane were discolored as a result of heat exposure. Though investigators have not been able to say precisely what caused the crash, they announced in November 1998 that they suspected that a fire in the forward area of the plane damaged cables that controlled the plane's systems.

The crash of Swissair Flight 111 focused attention on the insulation that is used on the world's 12,000 passenger jets, for tests determined that that insulation–similar to material used in walls and ceilings of homes–can burst into flame at high temperatures. Prior to the crash, the aviation administration in China recommended testing of the insulation after an MD-11 fire in Beijing in 1995. In September 1997, Boeing recommended that the insulation used in the MD-11 and other McDonnell Douglas planes be replaced. That year, too, the FAA recommended that manufacturers initiate new, more stringent testing procedures for the insulation they used. As a result of the Swissair crash, the FAA in October 1998 recommended that the insulation in all planes be replaced with a new, more heat-resistant variety, but the agency did not consider the fire threat serious enough to issue an "airworthiness directive" that would have made the change mandatory. Although the FAA has no authority over Swissair, the company began to replace the insulation in its planes that year, sharing the cost of the retrofit with Boeing. ◆

EgyptAir Flight 990

OCTOBER 31, 1999

At about 1:52 A.M. on October 31, 1999, EgyptAir Flight 990, a regularly scheduled flight from New York City to Cairo, Egypt, went into a fatal dive and plunged into the Atlantic Ocean 60 miles south of Nantucket Island, Massachusetts, 28 minutes after takeoff. The plane was a Boeing 767 model 366ER, a stretched and extended-range version of the basic 767. A search-and-rescue operation was launched, but it was soon clear that none of the 217 passengers and crew members on board, including 100 Americans, survived in the 250-foot waters.

By December 21 the National Transportation Safety Board (NTSB) completed the first phase of its effort to recover the wreckage. A second recovery effort was completed on April 3, 2000. In total, investigators found about 90 percent of the airplane, including the vital cockpit voice recorder (CVR), which recorded the conversation that took place at the plane's controls just before the crash.

The NTSB took the lead in conducting the post-crash investigation, but Egyptian investigators were also closely involved. Over the next months the two parties came to sharply different conclusions about the cause of the crash. At issue was liability, for if the plane crashed as a result of mechanical failure or faulty maintenance, then the families of the non-U.S. victims, mostly Canadians and Egyptians, could seek compensation in the United States by suing Boeing, or possibly the company responsible for maintenance work on the plane. If, on the other hand, the crash was the result of the actions of the crew, then victims' families would have to look to EgyptAir for compensation.

The days, weeks, and months following the crash of Flight 990 became the stuff of a novel of international intrigue. Conspiracy theorists hinted darkly that the plane was brought down by the Israelis, and they speculated that an Israeli jet that took off in the area shortly before Flight 990 might have had something to do with the crash. Others suggested that a terrorist was responsible. The Egyptians, however, scoffed at these theories and offered a less dramatic one of their own: analysis of metal from the wreckage showed that rivets in the control system of the plane's elevators, which allow movements up and down, were sheared in opposite directions. This would mean that a jam in the controls pushed the plane into its fatal dive into the ocean. In other words, the crash was caused by mechanical failure.

But in August 2000, the NTSB released 1,700 pages of documents that they said supported a dramatically different explanation: that co-pilot Gamil Batouti deliberately put the plane into its dive. Based on information provided by the Federal Bureau of Investigation (FBI) and the contents of the cockpit voice recorder, they argued that Batouti was having emotional and psychological problems and that he crashed the plane in an act of murder-suicide.

The FBI reports focused on Batouti's behavior at a hotel in New York City just before the crash. According to their investigation, Batouti there may have exposed himself to two teenage girls, stalked female hotel guests, and made passes at hotel maids. One informant told the FBI that Batouti had offered her $100 to come to his room the night before the crash.

More important, however, were the contents of the cockpit voice recorder (CVR) and the eerie events that took place in the plane's cockpit in the 10 minutes before the crash. At about 1:40 Batouti, a member of the relief crew for the long flight, came into the cockpit and insisted that the man then flying as copilot take a break and get some sleep. Batouti then conversed with the pilot, Captain Ahmed El Habashi, until about 1:48, when the captain excused himself to use the rest room.

At 1:48 and 30 seconds the CVR recorded a human voice saying something unintelligible; Arabic-speaking interpreters said that the words were "control it." English-speaking investigators said that they heard "hydraulic." But at 1:48 and 40 seconds, just before a series of unexplained clicks and thumps, Batouti said faintly "Tawakalt ala Allah," a common Arabic phrase meaning "I rely on God." Batouti would calmly utter this expression a total of 14 times during the plane's final minutes.

At 1:49 and 45 seconds, the plane's autopilot was cut off, apparently by hand; three seconds later, Batouti again said "I

> **Co-pilot Gamil Batouti deliberately put the plane into its dive.**

mantra a mystical formula of incantation; a repeated phrase or set of words.

rely on God." At 1:49 and 50 seconds the engines were reduced to idle and the plane's elevators began pushing the plane into a dive. Three seconds after that Batouti began rhythmically repeating "I rely on God," though he showed no signs of heightened emotion or stress.

Twelve seconds into the dive, the captain, now back in the cockpit and clearly distressed, said "What's happening? What's happening?" Batouti continued his **mantra** as the plane lost 5,000 feet of altitude, descending to 30,000 feet. Twelve seconds after that, the plane's elevators split in different directions. While the cause is unclear, U.S. investigators said that the split may indicate that Batouti and the captain were struggling for the controls of the plane. At almost the same time, fuel to the plane's two engines was cut off, shutting them down. El Habashi then said, "What is this? What is this? Did you shut the engines?" As the plane plummeted toward the ocean, the only other thing that Batouti said was "It's shut." In the meantime, the captain can be heard imploring Batouti to "Pull. Pull with me," as he attempted to pull the plane out of its dive. He briefly succeeded when the plane reached 15,000 feet, but after climbing to about 25,000 feet the plane plunged again and hit the water just before 1:52. To investigators, who submitted the CVR tape to voice analysis, the fact that the captain was clearly under extreme stress but Batouti remained calm suggests that the co-pilot was acting deliberately.

Egyptian officials sharply disputed the conclusions of the U.S. investigators. Nevertheless, on January 25, 2001, EgyptAir accepted liability for the crash in a U.S. district court, meaning that they would be responsible for the compensation of the victims' families. The company, though, reserved the right to sue other parties, including Boeing, in the event later information supported their belief that the plane crashed because of a mechanical failure. ◆

Industrial Accidents

Grandcamp Explosion

I n the spring of 1947, Texas City, Texas, was a booming Gulf of Mexico seaport town of about 18,000 people. While much of the rest of the United States was mired in a post-World War II recession, Texas City, which is located near Galveston and Houston, was a boomtown. Along the waterfront there was plenty of work for longshoremen and for workers in the chemical plants and oil refineries that stood near the wharf.

On the bright, cool morning of April 16, 1947, the townspeople of Texas City were headed to work. One of the worksites was Pier O in the harbor, where the French ship S.S. *Grandcamp* was docked. The ship was a "Liberty" ship bound for Europe, one of many such vessels that delivered vital supplies to the war-torn nations across the Atlantic. This ship already contained cargo consisting of twine, oil-field machinery, drill stems, and peanuts. At Texas City it had stopped to pick up an additional item—2,300 tons of **ammonium nitrate**.

Ammonium nitrate is a crystalline powder that in peacetime is an excellent source of nitrogen for crops. During the war, however, it had acquired another use—as an explosive in demolition bombs. It packs so much punch that in 1921 it had caused an explosion and fire in Germany that killed 600 people and injured 2,000. Nearly 50 years later just three tons of it in the back of a parked truck would be enough for an anti-government terrorist named Timothy McVeigh to destroy the federal building in Oklahoma City, Oklahoma.

ammonium nitrate a colorless crystalline salt used in fertilizers and explosives.

At about 8:00 that morning the hatch on the number 4 hold of the *Grandcamp* was opened so that **stevedores** could continue loading the fertilizer. Minutes later, a fire started in the hold of the ship–started, it was speculated, by a discarded cigarette. Workers on the ship tried to douse the fire with jugs of drinking water, then with fire extinguishers, but without success. Soon, clouds of smoke were rising from the ship–a sight that was nothing new in Texas City. The town's residents were used to industrial fires, which had become a form of theater for them, and many times in the past they had gathered to watch fires in the town's oil refineries. This morning many of them gathered to watch the peach-colored smoke, which many later described as "pretty," rising from the *Grandcamp*.

Volunteer firefighters were called to try to extinguish the fire; by 8:45 they were spraying water on the ship's deck, but the deck was now so hot that the water simply vaporized. Ship's officers ordered that the hatches be battened down in an effort to use the ship's fire-smothering steam system to put the fire out. But instead of putting the fire out, the heat and pressure produced a combustible gas that eventually blew the hatch covers off, sending more smoke skyward. Soon, a carnival atmosphere began to take over in the town. Schoolchildren cut classes to go down to the wharves; people gathered along the edge of a firewall to watch the smoke; the chief of security at the Republic Oil Co. refinery took carloads of people to watch the fire, and the company's top managers ran out to catch rides with him. At the nearby Monsanto Chemical Co., people gather in the drafting room, which had a good window view of the smoke.

However, what started as just another fire, a commonplace occurrence in an industrial town like Texas City, quickly turned into horror–and the worst industrial accident in U.S. history. At 9:12, as efforts to extinguish the fire continued to be unavailing, the ammonium nitrate in the *Grandcamp* exploded. The devastation caused by the explosion was almost unimaginable. As a mushroom cloud rose 2,000 feet into the air, many members of the community believed that the United States had been attacked with an atomic weapon. The blast, heard 150 miles away, knocked two airplanes out of the sky and shattered windows throughout the city and up to 25 miles away. Chunks of steel flew through the air; the *Grandcamp's* 3,000-pound anchor was found two miles away. Many of these pieces of steel landed on nearby houses and businesses; others landed on pipelines and storage tanks, igniting secondary explosions.

Hundreds of people were killed instantly, including the ship's crew, many of the curious onlookers, all but one member of the volunteer fire department, and 145 shift workers at the Monsanto plant just across the pier.

As if the initial disaster weren't bad enough, a second major explosion rocked the town just 16 hours later. The *High Flyer*, another ship docked at Texas City, was down for repairs, but its hold was loaded with 961 tons of ammonium nitrate. When the *Grandcamp* exploded, the *High Flyer* was torn from its moorings and came to rest against a third ship, the *Wilson B. Keene*. The initial explosion tore the hatches off the *High Flyer*, but no fire had been detected. But when city official learned that ammonium nitrate was aboard the ship, they gave orders to tow the ship away from the port. Unfortunately, the ship would not budge; it was probably stuck on debris from the *Grandcamp*. After flames were spotted aboard the *High Flyer*, an alarm sounded and the waterfront was cleared. Like the *Grandcamp*, the *High Flyer* exploded; many of those who had been injured in the initial blast and evacuated for medical treatment to nearby Galveston could see their town lit up in the dark as though it was daytime. Again, the blast set off a string of secondary explosions, igniting crude oil tanks, a grain elevator, warehouses on the piers, and the *Wilson B. Keene*. Fortunately, though, there was little loss of life because of the time of day and the evacuation.

The residents of Texas City spent the next week trying to put out the fires—and bury the dead. All told, 468 people were confirmed dead, but a hundred people were listed as missing, and the remains of 63 people never identified were buried in a mass grave at the edge of town. Thirty-five hundred people suffered injuries, many of them from flying pieces of metal and broken glass. ◆

Three Mile Island Nuclear Power Plant Accident

MARCH 28, 1979

The issue of nuclear power has divided Americans for decades. Proponents of nuclear power argue that the world is running out of fossil fuels, and that burning

Three Mile Island
Nuclear Generating
Plant near Harrisburg,
Pennsylvania.

coal and petroleum products pollutes the environment. Nuclear energy, it is argued, is the cheapest, cleanest way to provide for the nation's large and ever-growing energy needs. Opponents maintain that nuclear power, and particularly nuclear power plants, are inherently unsafe, and that a serious accident at a nuclear power plant could result in a disaster of unimaginable proportions.

The debate reached a new level around 4:00 in the morning on March 28, 1979. On that day an unlikely sequence of mechanical failures and human error at the Three Mile Island nuclear power plant near Harrisburg, Pennsylvania, scuttled the nuclear power industry in the United States. More than two decades later, the phrase "Three Mile Island" continued to symbolize for many people the fear they felt about the dangers of nuclear power generation.

The accident that would have such far-reaching effects began in the non-nuclear section of the plant. There, the main feedwater pumps stopped running because of either mechanical or electrical failure. The result was that feedwater–the water supplied to the nuclear generator that boils and becomes steam, providing the driving force for the power generator–was not getting to the reactors. And without enough water to cool them, the reactors began to overheat. As a result, first the turbine, then the nuclear reactor automatically shut down. But in the meantime, pressure in the nuclear part of the plant began to increase, so a "pressurizer relief valve" opened. The valve should have closed when enough pressure was released, but it did not, and faulty instrument readings led plant operators to believe that the valve had in fact closed. The open valve caused pressure to continue to drop in the system. Then, compounding the problem, a water-level indicator told operators that the system was full of water–as it should have been–when it was not. Not knowing that the valve was stuck, operators stopped adding water to the system.

In the meantime, yet another problem appeared. Forty-two hours before the accident, the emergency feedwater system was tested. Because of human error, a valve that was supposed to be reopened at the end of the test was left closed, preventing the emergency feedwater system from operating until about eight minutes into the accident.

What this bizarre sequence of failures meant was that not enough water was present to cool the nuclear reactors. The situation was not unlike that of a car that has a radiator leak; without enough coolant in the system, the engine begins to overheat. In fact that is what happened at Three Mile Island. The nuclear fuel overheated to the point that some of the metal tubing that contained the nuclear pellets reacted with water to a form a hydrogen bubble above the reactor core. The pressure from this bubble prevented cooling water from circulating throughout the core. The result was that two or three hours into the accident, the reactor was severely damaged. Temperatures in the reactor reached 5,000 degrees, and the plant came within 30 minutes of a large-scale meltdown that assuredly would have cost lives and caused billions in property damage.

Though no "meltdown" took place, in the sense that overheated fuel did not breach the containment vessel to the ground below, there was significant damage and the iron and concrete of the reactor building were contaminated with radiation. Additionally, low levels of radioactive gas, mostly in the form of xenon, were released into the air. Some people feared that the "hydrogen bubble" would cause an explosion, but this did not happen. Nonetheless, the governor of Pennsylvania ordered the evacuation of small children and pregnant women within a five-mile radius of the plant on March 30. He also suggested that people living within 10 miles of the plant stay indoors and keep their windows closed. The people of Pennsylvania did not know how close they came to a disaster of unimaginable proportions.

The accident at Three Mile Island was the worst nuclear disaster in the history of the United States. Nonetheless, no one was either killed or injured as a result of the disaster, and according to the Nuclear Regulatory Commission, the health effects of the disaster were minimal. According to the NRC, the average dose of radiation that 2 million people in the vicinity of the plant received as a result of the accident was 1 *millirem*—in contrast to the 6 millirems that a person would receive from a set of chest X rays and the 100 to 125 millirems that everyone in that region gets from natural "background radiation"—including from cosmic rays and the breakdown of naturally radioactive elements. The NRC further concluded that no adverse effects on human, animal, or plant life nor to food, soil, water, milk, and the like could be traced to radiation contamination.

In spite of these and similar reports, the disaster at Three Mile Island inhibited the nuclear power industry in the United States. This process was no doubt hastened by the release that year of a major motion picture, *The China Syndrome*, that depicted a nuclear accident eerily similar to that at Three Mile Island. Many demonstrations against the use of nuclear power followed the accident, culminating in an anti-nuclear rally in New York City attended by 200,000 people. Many antinuclear activists disputed the NRC's claims that the health effects of the disaster were minimal. After 1985, construction on nuclear power plants came to a virtual standstill and the public turned away from nuclear power—despite the promise of the 1950s that nuclear power would be so inexpensive that it would be "too cheap to meter." Today, the reactor at Three Mile Island is permanently shut down, the cooling system decontaminated, and most of the reactor's components dismantled and shipped to a low-level nuclear waste-disposal sight. It should be noted that the TMI disaster affected the plant's reactor number 2; reactor number 1 was unaffected.

As a result of the accident at Three Mile Island, sweeping changes were made in emergency response planning, reactor operator training, plant engineering, radiation protection, and the like. It's safe to say that the nuclear industry is one of the most heavily monitored and regulated industries in the world, and despite some noteworthy accidents like that at Three Mile Island, its safety record and ability to deliver clean energy with no air pollution or acid rain has been admirable. However, Three Mile Island exposed the dangers of nuclear power, delaying nuclear fission as an alternative to fossil fuels for the nation's energy needs. ◆

Bhopal Poisonous Gas Leak

DECEMBER 3, 1984

About four miles outside the center of Bhopal, India, Union Carbide India Ltd. (UCIL), a subsidiary of the American corporation Union Carbide, operated a pesticide manufacturing plant that, in late 1984, employed about 630 people. The plant had begun to make a common household pesticide called SEVIN in 1969. One of the chemicals used in producing SEVIN is methyl isocyanate, commonly referred to as MIC. Throughout the 1970s the plant imported MIC from a Union Carbide sister plant in West Virginia, but in the late 1970s UCIL added a production unit to make its own MIC. The MIC production plant at Bhopal was based on the design of the West Virginia plant. For 15 years the production process at Bhopal went smoothly–until disaster struck.

Describing the events that linked the name "Bhopal" with catastrophic industrial accidents is fairly simple. At about 11:30 P.M. on the evening of December 2, 1984, workers at the plant notified their supervisors when they noticed that MIC was leaking from one of three 15,000-gallon storage tanks. (One of the tanks was always kept empty to use as reserve storage in case of an emergency.) Over the next hour or so nothing could be done to stop the release. Then at about 12:45 A.M. on December 3, workers noticed that pressure in the tank was increasing rapidly until it opened one of the tank's safety release valves. Before the situation could be stabilized, 40 metric tons of the toxic chemical had been released into the atmosphere, raining death and disability on the city's 900,000 residents, including a large community of squatters just outside the boundaries of the plant.

The accident was a major catastrophe by any standards. Although estimates of the number of deaths and injuries vary, it is generally believed that about 2,000 people died and up to

The entrance to the
Union Carbide plant in
Bhopal, India

100,000 were injured. The International Medical Commission
on Bhopal estimated that as of 1994 about 50,000 people remained partially or totally disabled as a result of the accident,
most with damage to their respiratory systems. The accident
also did significant damage to livestock and crops.

In addition to ongoing health problems in those affected by
the accident, the Bhopal disaster left behind two legacies. The
first was the passage of legislation designed to help prevent a
similar catastrophe in the United States. In 1986, in the wake
of Bhopal and a 1985 gas leak at the Union Carbide West Virginia plant, Congress passed the Emergency Planning and
Community Right to Know Act, empowering the Environmental Protection Agency (EPA) to help states and communities
develop accident contingency plans and to ensure that the
public is given information about hazardous materials in their
locales. Further, in 1990, Congress reviewed a number of chemical incidents that had occurred in the United States, comparing them with Bhopal. Congress concluded that many of these
incidents could have been as disastrous as those at Bhopal and
that existing U.S. programs to prevent such accidents were in-

adequate. Thus, in the Clean Air Act Amendments of that year, Congress passed a number of provisions to prevent chemical accidents. One provision established of the U.S. Chemical Safety and Hazard Investigation Board to investigate and report on the causes of domestic chemical incidents.

The second major legacy of Bhopal was **litigation**–which was still ongoing at the turn of the century. Initially, both Union Carbide and the government of India conducted investigations of the accident, but both were parties to the lawsuit that was filed on behalf of the victims, so they were unable to agree on very much. For example, both agreed that the accident was caused by water, which had gotten into the tank and caused a violent chemical reaction. However, Union Carbide and the Indian government were unable to agree on how that happened, nor were they able to agree on whether Union Carbide was responsible for the plant's design, maintenance, and safety procedures. (On May 10, 1988, Arthur D. Little, Inc., after conducting an independent investigation, concluded "with virtual certainty" that a disgruntled employee had introduced water into the tank with a water hose.) The Indian government argued that Union Carbide was actively involved in the design of the plant and that it intentionally cut back on safety features. Union Carbide, on the other hand, contended that although it had provided the basic design of the plant, UCIL was responsible for safety and maintenance of the plant and that the Indian government had sole regulatory oversight.

In 1985 India passed legislation establishing the Indian government as the sole representative for people seeking compensation from the accident in American courts, where 145 suits had been filed on behalf of 200,000 plaintiffs. In 1986 the U.S. District Court of Southern New York, ruling in favor of Union Carbide, moved the trial to India. The trial ended in February 1989 when the Supreme Court of India ordered Union Carbide and UCIL to pay a total of $470 million in damages to the government of India. The two companies complied 10 days later. The issue seemed to be settled, but in 1990 a new government in India sought to reopen the case, hoping to increase the amount of the settlement. A similar effort was made by Bhopal activists in August 2000. Neither effort was successful.

Though Union Carbide was the target of intense criticism, especially by environmental activists, fairness demands recognition that the company took immediate steps to mitigate the damages caused by the disaster. The day after the accident the

The second major legacy of Bhopal was litigation.

litigation action in a court of law; a case before a court.

company sent technical advisers to India and paid for medical equipment to help the local medical community. By April 1985 the firm had contributed $7 million to a disaster relief fund. In early 1986 Union Carbide and UCIL agreed to donate $10 million for a hospital to aid the victims in Bhopal; ground was broken for the new hospital in 1995, and the building was completed in 1999. Meanwhile, in 1987 the company provided another $4.6 million to help victims of the Bhopal disaster. ◆

Chernobyl Nuclear Power Plant Explosion

APRIL 26, 1986

The worst fears of those who have expressed concern and opposition to the development of nuclear energy were realized on April 26, 1986. On that date an explosion shredded reactor number 4 at the Chernobyl nuclear power plant in the Ukraine, one of the republics of the former Soviet Union, releasing massive amounts of radiation that left huge tracts of land in the Ukrainian and Belorussian republics uninhabitable for generations to come.

The Chernobyl nuclear power plant, just outside the town of Pripyat, was one of the largest plants in the Soviet Union. The plant, which was located 11 miles northwest of Chernobyl, 10 miles from the border between the Ukraine and Belorussia, and 70 miles north of the Ukraine's capital city of Kiev, began operating in the 1970s. Reactor number 1 came online in 1977, number 2 in 1978, number 3 in 1981, and number 4 in 1983. Each of the four reactors could generate 1,000 megawatts of electricity, and together they provided about 10 percent of Ukraine's electrical power. At the time of the accident, two additional generators at the plant were under construction.

The accident took place in the early-morning hours of April 26, 1986. Reactor 4 was operating at very low capacity during a planned shutdown, during which operators were intending to conduct some tests. The reactor's design, however, made it very unstable at low power levels. To make matters worse, plant personnel were careless about safety precautions during the test. Suddenly there was a power surge, causing two

The Chernobyl nuclear power plant

explosions that destroyed the reactor core and blew a large hole through the roof of the reactor building. Fed by fires and the heat of the reactor core, a strong updraft carried radioactive debris up to a height of over half a mile. The result was a catastrophe by any standard: It is estimated that before clean-up crews were able to bring the situation under control some two weeks later, between 100 and 150 million curies of radiation–primarily in the form of radioactive isotopes of **iodine** and **cesium**–were released into the atmosphere. To put that figure in perspective, it takes about five curies of radiation for topsoil to be considered seriously contaminated.

As was typical of the Soviet Union during the Cold War years, officials at first did not release any information about the explosion–either to the world or to residents living near the site of the catastrophe. But prevailing winds carried radioactive fallout across Belorussia into Poland and Sweden, where heightened radiation levels were detected. Finally, Soviet authorities were forced to acknowledge the accident and brought it to the world's attention during an evening news broadcast on April 28, then in newspaper reports on April 30. Many observers

iodine a nonmetallic halogen element usually obtained as weighty, shiny blackish gray crystals and used in photography, medicine, and analysis.

cesium a silver-white element of the alkali metal group that is the most electropositive element known.

believe that the Chernobyl disaster contributed to the breakup of the Soviet Union because it forced government officials to be less secretive (as they had been, for example, in the wake of a major accident at a nuclear weapons plant in the Ural Mountains in 1957).

In the days and weeks after the explosion, workers arrived in an attempt to contain the damage. They dropped 5,000 metric tons of shielding material, consisting of lead, boron, sand, and clay, onto the reactor. They constructed a concrete foundation under the reactor to keep groundwater from being contaminated. Finally, they built a concrete-and-steel shell, a "sarcophagus," over the damaged reactor to keep radioactive materials from escaping. Twenty-nine workers died from acute radiation poisoning during the cleanup.

The first evacuation of the area began about 36 hours after the accident. The first evacuees were the 35,000 residents of Pripyat. Beginning on May 3, a larger 1,100-square-mile area, which included parts of Belorussia, was evacuated. But as those monitoring the situation determined that ever larger areas were "seriously contaminated," an additional 50,000 people were evacuated from Belorussia in 1986 and 1987, then another 30,000 between 1991 and 1993 and 50,000 from the Ukraine between 1991 and 1996. In sum, more than 200,000 people were permanently evacuated from their homes.

The most serious environmental effect of the catastrophe was the contamination of topsoil, destroying important farmland. Of nearly equal severity was the threat to both surface water and groundwater. In some of the most heavily contaminated areas, such as the area around Pripyat, all topsoil and vegetation was stripped and buried, all wells were sealed, and surface water was prevented from draining into the Dnieper River system, which provides Kiev's water supply. Belarus (which changed its name from Belorussia after the breakup of the Soviet Union) was perhaps the hardest hit. Half, or nearly 11,000 square miles, of the area described as "seriously contaminated" lies in Belarus, and as a result of contaminated soil, the country lost nearly 20 percent of its farmland.

The health effects of the catastrophe have been more difficult to measure; some increase in the death rate was attributable to poor nutrition, and some to the fact that over time a half a million workers participated in the cleanup effort, and thus were exposed to high levels of radiation. It seems clear, though, that one type of cancer–thyroid cancer in children–can be attributed directly to fallout from Chernobyl. In one region of Belarus, for example, the rate of thyroid cancer in children increased 22-fold from 1986 to 1990 compared to 1981 through 1985.

In response to the accident, international organizations contributed to an effort to improve the safety of so-called RMBK reactors–the type of reactor used at Chernobyl. This reactor design is considered less safe than other designs (such as those used in the United States and Europe) because the reactors have no containment shell, the graphite blocks used to control fission are flammable, and excess steam in a reactor's core can cause the nuclear reaction to increase. Despite these efforts, the nuclear power industry of the Soviet Union, then of its successor nations, was seriously damaged by the Chernobyl catastrophe. Opposition to nuclear power, particularly in Ukraine, intensified until in 1990 the Ukrainian parliament declared a moratorium on nuclear plant construction (though that nation lifted the **moratorium** in 1993 because of severe electrical shortages). The parliament also voted to permanently shut down the Chernobyl plant within five years, but continuing electrical shortages led to repeated postponements of the closure. Finally, in 1996 the so-called Group of Seven, or the world's major industrial nations, pledged $300 million to continue cleanup work at Chernobyl and to decommission the plant. Finally, in December 2000, the plant was totally shut down. ◆

moratorium a legally authorized period of delay in the performance of a legal obligation or payment of debt.

The following authors contributed the new articles for **Macmillan Profiles:** *History's Most Devastating Disasters:*

William Kaufman
Paul Kobel
Mike O'Neal
Erica Wetter

Additional Resources

GENERAL

Abbot, Patrick Leon. *Natural Disasters.* McGraw College Division, 1998.

Alexander, David. *Confronting Catastrophe: New Perspectives on Natural Disasters.* Oxford University Press, 2000.

Alexander, David. *Natural Disasters.* Kluwer Academic Publishers, 1993.

Baehre, Rainer K., ed. *Outrageous Seas: Shipwreck and Survival in the Waters Off Newfoundland, 1583-1893.* IMcGill-Queen's University Press, 1999.

Barnes, Jay, and Neil Frank. *Florida's Hurricane History.* University of North Carolina Press, 1998.

Beryl, Frank. *Plane Crashes: An Illustrated History of Great Air Disasters.* Bell Publishing Company, 1981.

Farrington, Karen. *Natural Disasters: The Terrifying Forces of Nature.* Random House, 1999.

Frater, H. *Natural Disasters: Cause, Course, Effect, Simulation.* Springer Verlag, 1997.

Harris, Stephen L. *Agents of Chaos: Earthquakes, Volcanoes, and Other Natural Disasters.* Mountain Press Publishing Co., 1990.

Langley, Andrew. *Great Disasters.* Olympic Marketing Corporation, 1986.

Longshore, David. *Encyclopedia of Hurricanes, Typhoons, and Cyclones.* Facts on File, Inc., 1998.

McGuire, Bill. *Apocalypse: A Natural History of Global Disasters.* Continuum International Publishing Group, Inc., 2000.

Newson, Lesley. *Devastation! The World's Worst Natural Disasters.* DK Publishing, 1998.

Olesky, Water. *Nature Gone Wild.* Julian Messner, 1982.

Parker, D. J., ed. *Floods.* Routledge, 2000 [two volumes].

Ritchie, David, and Alexander E. Gates. *The Encyclopedia of Earthquakes and Volcanoes.* Facts on File, 2001.

Rosenfeld, Jeffrey P. *Eye of the Storm: Inside the World's Deadliest Hurricanes, Tornadoes, and Blizzards.* Perseus Press, 1999.

Smith, Howard E., Jr. *Killer Weather: Stories of Great Disasters.* Dodd, Mead, 1982.

Smith, Keith, and Roy Ward. *Floods: Physical Processes and Human Impacts.* John Wiley & Son Ltd., 1998.

Sparks, R. S. J., et al, eds. *Volcanic Plumes.* John Wiley & Son Ltd., 1997.

Steinberg, Theodore. *Acts of God: The Unnatural History of Natural Disasters in America.* Oxford University Press, 2000.

Stewart, Stanley. *Air Disasters: Dialogue From the Black Box.* Hippocrene, 1986.

Sweeney, Karen O'Connor. *Nature Runs Wild: True Disaster Stories.* F. Watts, 1978.

Vogel, Carole Garbuny. *Nature's Fury: Eyewitness Reports of Natural Disacters.* Scholastic Paperbacks, 2000.

Wade, Nicholas, ed. *The Science Times Book of Natural Disasters.* Lyons Press, 2000.

Waltham, Tony. *Catastrophe: The Violent Earth.* Crown, 1978.

Zebrowski, Ernest. *Perils of a Restless Planet: Scientific Perspectives on Natural Disasters.* Cambridge University Press, 1997.

VIDEORECORDINGS

Air Disaster, Acorn Media, 1996.

Air Disasters, Vol. 1: The Facts, Fox Lorber, 1997.

Amazing Video: Natural Disasters, E-Realbiz Com, 1997.

Earthquake: Death & Destruction, Madacy Entertainment, 1997.

Extreme Disasters: Infernos of Distruction, Unapix, 1999.

Extreme Disasters: Nature's Deadly Force, Unapix, 1999.

Eyewitness - Natural Disasters, Dorling Kindersley, 1997.

History's Greatest Shipwrecks Box Set, National Geographic, 1999.

Hurricanes & Tornadoes, Schlessinger Media, 1998.

Flood!!: Nature's Fury. Goldhil Home Media, 1997.

The Most Incredible Disasters, A & E Home Video, 2000.

Natural Disasters, Brentwood Communications, 1998.

Natural Disasters Gift Set, WGBH Boston Video, 1997.

Nova: Earthquake, Vestron Video, 1990.

Nova: Flood!, WGBH Boston Video, 1996.

Nova: Tornado!, WGBH Boston Video, 1985

Raging Planet: Flood, Discovery Communication, 1998.

Storm Force: Floods, TLC Video, 1999.

Storm Force: Tornado, TLC Video, 1999.

Survival in the Sky Boxed Set, Unapix, 2000.

Tornado! Hurricane! Flood!: Wonders of the Weather, Discovery Communication, 1998.

Tornado Video Classics, Goldhil Home Media, 1996 [three volumes, available separately].

20th Century with Mike Wallace - Disasters at Sea, A & E Home Video, 2000.

20th Century with Mike Wallace - Earthquakes: Living on the Edge, A & E Entertainment, 1999.

20th Century with Mike Wallace - Hurricanes: Natural Born Killers, A & E Entertainment, 1999.

20th Century with Mike Wallace - The Terror of Tornadoes, A & E Entertainment, 1998.

Ultimate Fires, Brentwood Communications, 1998.

WEB SITES

About Earthquakes, http://www.crystalinks.com/earthquakes1.html

Aircraft Crash Sites, http://www.geocities.com/CapitolHill/5260/othercrash.html

Airline Disasters, http://dnausers.d-n-a.net/dnetGOjg/Disasters.htm

The Disaster Center, http://www.disastercenter.com/

Great American Disasters, http://www.ezl.com/˜fireball/Disaster.htm

Infamous Hurricanes, http://www.weatherconsultant.com/Feature0.html

Miami Museum of Science - Hurricane Main Menu, http://www.miamisci.org/hurricane/hurricane0.html

National Hurricane Center, http://www.nhc.noaa.gov/

Natural Disaster Reference Database, http://ltpwww.gsfc.nasa.gov/ndrd/

Nova Online - Flood!, http://www.pbs.org/wgbh/nova/flood/

Nuclear Power Plant Accidents, http://www.infoplease.com/ipa/A0001457.html

Researching Shipwrecks, http://www.uscg.mil/hq/g-cp/history/WEBSHIPWRECKS/SHIPWRECKGUIDE.html

Significant Floods in the United States During the 20th Century, http://ks.water.usgs.gov/Kansas/pubs/fact-sheets/fs.024-00.html

Shipwrecks, http://treasurehunt.about.com/hobbies/treasurehunt/cs/shipwrecks/

Tornadoes in the Past, http://www.tornadoproject.com/past/pastts.htm#top

U.S. Geological Survey: Recent and Historical Earthquakes, http://earthquake.usgs.gov/activity/past.html

U.S. News: Hurricanes in History, http://www.usnews.com/usnews/issue/990927/floyd.b.htm

Volcano World, http://volcano.und.nodak.edu/vw.html

Volcanoes.com, http://www.volcanoes.com/

Websites Dedicated to Specific Tornado Events, http://www.spc.noaa.gov/faq/tornado/torpages.html

World Book - Great Fires, http://www.worldbook.com/fun/fire/html/great_fires.htm

World Disasters, http://www.disasterrelief.org/Library/WorldDis/

INDIVIDUAL DISASTERS

GREAT HURRICANE OF 1780

The Deadliest Atlantic Tropical Cyclones, 1492 - Present, http://www.nhc.noaa.gov/pastdeadlytx4_text.html

Millás, José Carlos. *Hurricanes of the Caribbean and Adjacent Regions, 1492-1800*. Academy of the Arts and Sciences of the Americas, 1968.

GALVESTON HURRICANE OF 1900

Bixel, Patricia Bellis, and Elizabeth Hayes Turner. *Galveston and the 1900 Storm*. University of Texas Press, 2000.

Greene, Casey Edward, and Shelly Henley Kelly, eds. *Through a Night of Horrors: Voices from the 1900 Galveston Storm*. Texas A& M University Press, 2000.

Green, Nathan C., ed. *Story of the 1900 Galveston Hurricane*. Pulican Publishing Co., 2000.

Larson, Eric, and Isaac Monroe Cline. *Isaac's Storm: A Man, a Time, and the Deadliest Hurricane in History*. Vintage Books, 1999.

Lester, Paul. *The Great Galveston Disaster: Containing a Full and Thrilling Account of the Most Appalling Calamity of Modern Times*. Pelican Publishing Co., 2000.

The Storm That Changed America: The Galveston Hurricane of 1900, http://www.disasterrelief.org/Disasters/980813Galveston/

LAKE OKEECHOBEE HURRICANE OF 1928

American National Red Cross. *The West Indies Hurricane Disaster, September, 1928: Official Report of Relief Work in Porto Rico, the Virgin Islands and Florida*. American National Red Cross, 1929.

Bean, Rebecca. *The Great Hurricane in Florida and Remarks on Christian Science*. Bee-Hue Publishing Company, 1933.

Hurricane of 1928 by Roger Buckwalter, http://history.jupiter.fl.us/hurricane28.htm

Will, Lawrence Lee. *Okeechobee Hurricane and the Hoover Dike*. Great Outdoors Publishing Company, 1961.

HURRICANE AUDREY, 1957

Ross, Nola Mae Wittler, and Susan McFillen Goodson. *Hurricane Audrey*. Wise, 1997.

Tisdale, John R. "Observational Reporting as Oral History: How Journalists Interpreted the Death and Destruction of Hurricane Audrey." *Oral History Review*, Summer-Fall 2000.

HURRICANE FLORA, 1963

Hurricane Flora - Trinidad & Tobago, http://travel.roughguides.com/content/12774/30710.htm

HURRICANE CAMILLE, 1969

Hurricane Camille, August 20, 1969: A Review. Buena Vista News, 1970.

Prescott, Lyle. "Hurricane!" *Ranger Rick*, Aug. 1996.

Thirty Years After Hurricane Camille: Lessons Learned, Lessons Lost, http://www.esig.ucar.edu/camille/index.html

EAST PAKISTAN TYPHOON OF 1970

Moraes, Dom F. *The Tempest Within: An Account of East Pakistan.* Vikas Publications [Delhi], 1971.

Samad, M. A. *Cyclone of 1970 and Agricultural Rehabilitation.* Agriculture Information Service [Dacca], 1971.

HURRICANE FIFI, 1974

Catholic Institute for International Relations. *Honduras: Anatomy of a Disaster.* Catholic Institute for International Relations [London], 1975.

Sullivan, John H. *United States Post-Disaster Assistance to Honduras: Report of a Staff Survey Mission to Honduras.* U.S. Government Printing Office, 1975.

BANGLADESH TYPHOON OF 1985

Ahmad, Mohiuddin. *The Coastal Tragedy.* Community Development Library [Dhaka], 1985.

DeAngelis, Dick. "The Bangladesh Cyclone." *Weatherwise*, Feb. 1986.

Silver, Eric. "Allah's curse: a deadly wall of water." *Maclean's*, June 10, 1985.

HURRICANE GILBERT, 1988

Berke, Philip R., and Timothy Beatley. *After the Hurricane: Linking Recovery to Sustainable Development in the Caribbean.* Johns Hopkins University Press, 1998.

Clement, David B. *An Analysis of Disaster: Life after Gilbert.* Institute of Social and Economic Research, University of the West Indies, 1989.

Fischer, Henry W. *Hurricane Gilbert: The Media's Creation of the Storm of the Century.* Natural Hazards Research and Applications Information Center, Institute of Behavioral Science, University of Colorado, 1989.

HURRICANE MITCH, 1998

Carrier, Jim. *The Ship and the Storm: Hurricane Mitch and the Loss of the Fantome.* McGraw-Hill Professional Publishing, 2000.

Hurricane Mitch Story Index, http://www.usatoday.com/weather/hurricane/1998/wmitch.htm

Molina, Bruce. *Open Skies Aerial Photography of Selected Areas in Central America Affected by Hurricane Mitch.* U.S. Geological Survey, 1999.

Padgett, Tim. "The Catastrophe Of Hurricane Mitch." *Time International*, Nov. 16, 1998.

Williams, A.R. "After the deluge: Central America's storm of the century." *National Geographic*, Nov. 1999.

NATCHEZ TORNADO OF 1840

Descriptions of the Top Ten US Killer Tornadoes—#2: The Natchez Tornado, http://www.tornadoproject.com/toptens/toptens.htm#2

ST. LOUIS TORNADO OF 1896

Curzon, Julian, comp. *The Great Cyclone at St. Louis and East St. Louis, May 27, 1896: Being a Full History of the Most Terrifying and Destructive Tornado in the History of the World.* Southern Illinois University Press, 1997 [reprint of 1896 ed.].

The East St. Louis, Illinois 1896 Tornado, http://www.iltrails.org/stclair/tornado.htm

TRI-STATE TORNADO OF 1925

Brodt, Jan. "The tri-state tornado, March 18, 1925." *Weatherwise*, Apr. 1986.

Felknor, Peter S. *The Tri-State Tornado: The Story of America's Greatest Tornado Disaster.* Iowa State University Press, 1992.

Tri-State Tornado 75th Anniversary Web Page, http://www.crh.noaa.gov/pah/1925/

TUPELO TORNADO OF 1936

Killer storm leveled 48 blocks in Tupelo, http://www.djournal.com/djournal/site/pages/specialsections/125/wcillers.htm

Moore, Gary. "Trapped in the Great Tupelo Tornado." *Weatherwise*, May-June 1998.

Morse, William Clifford. *The Tupelo Tornado.* University of Mississippi, 1936.

The Tupelo Tornado of 1936, http://rankin.tupeloschools.com/proproj/tupelo/Tornado.html

GAINESVILLE TORNADO OF 1936

Gainesville, GA, Tornado, April 6, 1936, http://ngeorgia.com/feature/gainesvilletornado.html

Gainseville Tornado of 1936, http://www.cviog.uga.edu/Projects/gainfo/1936tornado/gainesvilletornado.htm

PALM SUNDAY TORNADO OUTBREAK OF 1965

Fujita, Tetsuya Theodore. *Palm Sunday Tornadoes of April 11, 1965.* University of Chicago, 1970.

Palm Sunday 1965 Outbreak Article, http://members.nbci.com/d5vbcs/willbanks.html

TORNADO OUTBREAK OF 1974

1974 Tornado Super Outbreak, http://www.weather.com/multimedia/video/specialreports/sotc/superout.html [requres RealAudio player]

NOAA and the 1974 Tornado Outbreak, http://www.publicaffairs.noaa.gov/storms/

Tornado Outbreak of 1974: A Case Study, http://snrs.unl.edu/amet451/kozisek/

United States National Oceanic and Atmospheric Administration, Natural Disaster Survey Team. *The Widespread Tornado Outbreak of April 3-4, 1974: A Report to the Administrator.* U.S. Dept. of Commerce, NOAA, 1974.

EAST FLORIDA TORNADO OUTBREAK OF 1998

Farley, Christopher John. "Twisters, tragedies and miracles." *Time*, March 9, 1998.

Navarro, Mireya. "At least 38 die as tornadoes rip Central Florida; more than 260 injured; hundreds are left homeless after the twisters surprise people near midnight." *New York Times*, Feb. 24, 1998, p. A1.

U.S. Department of Commerce Service Assessment: Central Florida Tornado Outbreak, February 22-23, 1998, http://www.nws.noaa.gov/om/cntrlfl.pdf

OKLAHOMA TORNADO OUTBREAK OF 1999

The Central Oklahoma Tornado Outbreak of May 3, 1999, http://www.srh.noaa.gov/oun/storms/19990503/intro.html

May 3,6, 1999 Tornadoes, http://www.usatoday.com/weather/tornado/storms/1999/w503tor0.htm

Newman, Andy. "30 deaths reported in plains tornadoes; storms rake Oklahoma and Kansas." *New York Times*, May 4, 1999.

YELLOW RIVER FLOOD OF 1887

Deforestation and Floods, http://www.mekongforum.org/qgdeflde.html

Highest Death Toll From a Flood, http://www.guinnessworldrecords.com/record_catagories/recordhome.asp?RecordID=49215

JOHNSTOWN FLOOD OF 1889

Degen, Paula. *Johnstown Flood of 1889: The Tragedy of the Conemaugh.* America's National Parks, 1984.

Dolson, Hildegarde. *Disaster at Johnstown: The Great Flood.* Random House, 1965.

Johnstown Flood Museum, www.jaha.org/flood/main.htm

Johnstown Flood of 1889, http://www.johnstownpa.com/History/hist19.html

McCullough, David. *The Johnstown Flood.* Peter Smith, 1987.

"Museum preserves Johnstown flood artifacts." *Travel Weekly,*

HEPPNER FLOOD OF 1903

Heppner Flood, http://www.rootsweb.com/˜ormorrow/HeppnerFlood.htm

The Heppner Flood - June, 1903,
http://www.ocs.orst.edu/reports/wm/wm_990607.html

OHIO FLOOD OF 1913

Account of 1913 Flood, http://www.fsadayton.org/1913%20Flood.htm

Clatworthy, Linda May. "Ohio Libraries In The Flood." *Library Journal*, Nov. 1913.

1913 Flood, http://wheeling.weirton.lib.wv.us/events/floods/1913/index.htm

1913: The Great Dayton Flood. Victoria Theater [Dayton], 1997.

NETHERLANDS FLOOD OF 1953

Amsterdam Instituut voor Sociaal Onderzoek van het Nederlandse Volk. *Studies in Holland Flood Disaster 1953.* Committee on Disaster Studies of the National Academy of Sciences-National Research Council, 1955.

The Battle of the floods; Holland in February 1953. Netherlands Booksellers and Publishers Association [Amsterdam], 1953.

Norel, K. *Stand By, Boys!: A True Story About Holland's Fight Against the Sea.* William B. Eerdmans, 1955.

BUFFALO CREEK FLOOD OF 1972

Buffalo Creek Disaster, http://www.wvculture.org/history/buffcreek/bctitle.html

The Buffalo Creek Flood Disaster, February 26, 1972,
http://www.rootsweb.com/~wvlogan/buffalo.htm

Erikson, Kai T. *Everything In Its Path: Destruction of Community in the Buffalo Creek Flood.* Simon & Schuster, 1978.

RAPID CITY FLOOD OF 1972

The Rapid City Flood of 1972, http://www.crh.noaa.gov/unr/iwe/1972_Flood/

Schwarz, Francis K. *The Black Hills-Rapid City Flood of June 9-10, 1972: A Description of the Storm and Flood.* U.S. Government Printing Office, 1975.

United States Congress, House Committee on Banking and Currency. *To Provide Additional Relief to the Victims of Hurricane and Tropical Storm Agnes, and to the Victims of the South Dakota Flood Disaster: Hearing, Ninety-Second Congress, Second Session.* U.S. Government Printing Office, 1972.

BIG THOMPSON RIVER FLOOD OF 1976

Heroes of the Big Thompson Flood, http://www.info2000.net/~t-birds/loveland /history/bigtflood/ssflood/scottsch.html

McComb, David G. *Big Thompson Flood: Profile of a Natural Disaster.* Vestige Press, 1996.

Proceedings of the International Seminar on Bangladesh Floods: Regional and Global Environmental Perspectives, Dhaka, 4-7 March, 1989. Bangladesh Research Bureau, 1989 - [series].

BANGLADESH FLOOD OF 1988

Browne, Malcom W. "Once more, the earth visits disaster on the plains of Bangladesh." *New York Times*, Sept. 11, 1988.

Mir, M. Ali, et. al, eds. *Bangladesh Floods: Views From Home and Abroad.* University Press [Dhaka], 1998.

Tefft, Sheila. "South Asian tempers rise as flood waters fall." *Christian Science Monitor*, Sept. 25, 1988.

YANGTZE RIVER FLOOD 1998

Catastrophic Flood Disaster in 1998 and the post factum Ecological and Environmental Reconstruction in China, by Zhang Shougong, http://www.fas.harvard.edu/~asiactr/fs_zhang2.htm

On '98 Extraordinary Floods in Yangtze River Valley of China, by Zhiyong Dong, http://www.iahr.org/membersonly/grazproceedings99/doc/000/000/431.htm

VENEZUELA FLOODS OF 1999

Efectos de las lluvias caídas en Venezuela en diciembre de 1999. CDB Publications, 2000.

Venezuela Floods December 1999, http://www.internetgeographer.co.uk/pages/physgeog/vnzflood.html

MOZAMBIQUE FLOODS OF 2000

Christie, Frances, and Joseph Hanlon. *Mozambique & the Great Flood of 2000.* Indiana University Press, 2001.

Guardian Unlimited - Special Reports - Mozambique Floods, http://www.guardian.co.uk/Mozambique/

Swarns, Rachel L. "Mozambique confronts huge flood losses but sees ray of hope." *New York Times*, Apr. 30, 2000.

EGYPT EARTHQUAKE OF 1201 AD

The 25 Largest Earthquake Disasters in Human History, http://www.geohaz.org/member/news/signif.htm#ref

SICILY EARTHQUAKE OF 1693

History and Legends - The Earthquake of 1693, http://www.ibla.net/eng_stor_terremoto.htm

Nicolosi, Salvatore. *Apocalisse in Sicilia: il terremoto del 1693.* C. Tringale, 1982.

SAN FRANCISCO EARTHQUAKE OF 1906

Barker, Malcom E,, comp. *Three Fearful Days: San Francisco Memoirs of the 1906 Earthquake & Fire.* Londonborn Publications, 1998.

Bronson, William. *The Earth Shook, the Sky Burned: A Photographic Record of the 1906 San Francisco Earthquake and Fire.* Chronicle Books, 1997.

Duey, Kathleen. *San Francisco Earthquake, 1906.* Pocket Books, 1999 [young adult].

Great San Francisco Earthquake, Time-Life Video, 1988.

Hansen, Gladys, et al. *Denial of Disaster: The Untold Story and Photographs of the San Francisco Earthquake and Fire or 1906.* Cameron & Co., 1989.

Kurzman, Dan. *Disaster! The Great San Francisco Earthquake and Fire of 1906.* William Morrow & Co., 2001.

Museum of the City of San Francisco - The Great 1906 Earthquake And Fire, http://www.sfmuseum.org/1906/06.html

TOKYO-YOKOHAMA EARTHQUAKE OF 1923

Great Kanto Earthquake 1923, http://www.japan-guide.com/a/earthquake/

Poole, Otis Manchester. *The Death of Old Yokohama in the Great Japanese Earthquake of September 1, 1923.* Allen & Unwin, 1968.

Seidensticker, Edward. *Tokyo Rising: The City Since the Great Earthquake.* Harvard University Press, 1991.

INDIA EARTHQUAKE OF 1935

1935 India Earthquake, http://www.worldbook.com/fun/bth/earthquake/html/1935india.htm

31st May 1935 - Quetta, Pakistan, Mw8.1, http://www.geocities.com/stasertin/quetta.htm

CHILE EARTHQUAKE OF 1939

Argentine republic. Comisión nacional pro damnificados por el terremoto de Chile. *La Comisión nacional pro ayuda damnificados terremoto Chile.* Compañía impresora argentina, 1939.

Beck, S., et al. "The 1928 and 1939 Subduction Zone Earthquakes Along the Coast of Southern Chile." *Seismological Research Letters* [Mexico], 1993.

Campos, J., and E. Kausel. "The Large 1939 Intraplate Earthquake of Southern Chile." *Seismological Research Letters* [Mexico], 1990.

ALASKA'S GOOD FRIDAY EARTHQUAKE OF 1964

Cohen, Stan. *8.6: The Great Alaska Earthquake March 27, 1964.* Pictorial Histories, 1995.

Dalby, Ron. "A bad Good Friday." *Alaska,* March 1989.

Dynes, Russell. *Reconstruction in the Context of Recovery: Thoughts on the Alaskan Earthquake.* Disaster Reserach Center, 1989.

Garney, Patricia M. Story House Corp., 1973.

Griffin, Joy, comp. *Alaska Earthquake '64.* Wizard Works, 1996.

1964 Alaska Earthquake, http://www.aeic.alaska.edu/Seis/64quake/Alaska_1964_earthquake.html

Shaken To The Core: Alaskan Earthquake—Wrath Of God. A & E Home Video, 2000.

PERU EARTHQUAKE OF 1970

Cromer, Harry C., and Marian A. Czarnecki. *Review of U.S. Assistance Activities Related to the Earthquake Disaster in Peru*. U.S. Government Printing Office, 1970.

Ericksen, George Edward, et al. *Preliminary Report on the Geologic Events Associated with the May 31, 1970, Peru Earthquake*. U.S. Geological Survey, 1970.

1970 Peru Earthquake,
http://www.worldbook.com/fun/bth/earthquake/html/1970peru.htm

Plafker, G., et al. "Geological aspects of the May 31, 1970 Peru earthquake." *Bulletin of the Seismic Association of America*, 1971.

7.8 Earthquake in Peru,
http://www.super70s.com/Super70s/News/1970/May/31-Peru_Earthquake.asp

NORTHEASTERN CHINA EARTHQUAKE OF 1976

Munro, Ross H. "China Experiences A Powerful Quake." *New York Times*, July 28, 1976.

The Tangsham Earthquake, http://www.geo.arizona.edu/K-12/azpepp/education/history/china/

Yong, Chen, Tsoi Kam-ling, et al. *The Great Tangshan Earthquake of 1976: An Anatomy of Disaster*. Pergamon Press [Beijing], 1988.

Zongjin, Ma. *Earthquake Prediction: Nine Major Earthquakes in China (1966-1976)*. Springer Verlag, 1991.

GUATEMALA EARTHQUAKE OF 1976

Espinosa, A. F., ed. *The Guatemalan Earthquake of February 4, 1976: A Preliminary Report*. U.S. Government Printing Office, 1976.

Office of the United Nations Disaster Relief Co-ordinator. *Report of the United Nations Disaster Relief Co-ordinator on the Earthquake in Guatemala, February 1976*. The Co-ordinator [Geneva], 1976.

1976 Guatemala Earthquake,
http://www.worldbook.com/fun/bth/earthquake/html/guatemala.htm

Scanlon, A. Clark. *Hope in the Ruins*. Broadman Press, 1978.

CENTRAL MEXICO EARTHQUAKE OF 1985

Anderson, Harry. "Disaster in Mexico." *Newsweek*, Sept. 30, 1985.

Dynes, Russell. *Individual and Organizational Response to the 1985 Earthquake in Mexico City*. Disaster Research Center, 1989.

The Great Mexico Earthquake and Tsunamis of 19 and 21 September 1985,
http://www.geocities.com/CapeCanaveral/Lab/1029/Tsunami1985Mexico.html

Impressions of the Guerrero-Michoacan, Mexico Earthquake September 19, 1985. Earthquake Engineering Research, 1985.

Romero, Enrique Martinez, ed., and Michael A. Cassaro. *The Mexico Earthquakes-1985: Factors Involved and Lessons Learned.* American Society of Civil Engineers, 1987.

Treaster, Joseph B. "With houses in rubble, thousands are refugees in their hometown." *New York Times,* Sept. 23, 1985.

ARMENIA EARTHQUAKE OF 1988

Armenia: Eyewitnesses Recall Earthquake Of 1988, http://www.rferl.org/nca
l/features/1998/03/F.RU.980317131055.html

Brand, David. "Vision of horror." *Time,* Dec. 26, 1988.

Engholm, Chris. *The Armenian Earthquake.* Lucent Books, 1989.

Filson, John R., ed., and Loring A. Wyllie. *Armenia Earthquake Reconnaissance Report.* Earthquake Engineering Research, 1989.

Urdang, Billiott B. *The Armenian Earthquake Disaster.* Sphinx Press, 1989.

Verluise, Pierre, and Levon Chorbajian, trans. *Armenia in Crisis: The 1988 Earthquake.* Wayne State University Press, 1995.

NORTHERN IRAN EARTHQUAKE OF 1990

Fullwood, Sam. "U.S. puts rancor aside, aids quake relief effort." *Los Angeles Times,* June 23, 1990.

1990 Iran Earthquake,
http://www.worldbook.com/fun/bth/earthquake/html/iran.htm

Northwestern Iran Earthquake 1990,
http://wwwijh.lkwash.wednet.edu/teacher/tarynne.html

Watson, Russell. "Enduring a 'test of God.'" *Newsweek,* July 2, 1990.

KOBE EARTHQUAKE OF 1995

Brebbia, C. A. *The Kobe Earthquake: Geodynamical Aspects.* Computational Mechanics, 1996.

Dickenson, Stephen, E., ed. *Hyogo-Ken Nanbu Earthquake of January 17, 1995: A Post-Earthquake Reconnaissance of Port Facilities.* American Society of Civil Engineers, 1996.

Elliott, Lawrence. "Earthquake at Dawn." *Reader's Digest,* Nov. 1995.

The January 17, 1995 Kobe Earthquake,
http://www.eqe.com/publications/kobe/kobe.htm

Kobe: NFPA Fire Investigation Report,
http://www.nfpa.org/Research/Dormitory_Earthquake/kobe_summary.pdf

Schiff, Ansel J., ed. *Hyogoken-Nanbu (Kobe) Earthquake of January 17, 1995: Lifeline Performance.* American Society of Civil Engineers, 1998.

NORTHERN TURKEY EARTHQUAKE OF 1999

"The Big One: A 3:01 a.m. last Tuesday one of the half-dozen deadliest earthquakes of the century hit Turkey…" *Newsweek*, Aug. 30, 1999.

"Buried Alive: In quake-ravaged Turkey, tales of death, destruction and survival bring home a tragedy beyond comprehension." *Time*, Aug 30, 1999.

IRIS Special Event File - Turkey Earthquake, http://www.iris.washington.edu/DOCS/turkey.htm

United States. Congress. House. Committee on Science. Subcommittee on Basic Research. *The Turkey, Taiwan, and Mexico Earthquakes: Lessons Learned: Hearing Before the Subcommittee on Basic Research of the Committee on Science, House of Representatives, One Hundred Sixth Congress, First Session, October 20, 1999.* U.S. Governmnet Printing Office, 2000.

TAIWAN EARTHQUAKE OF 1999

Fang, Bay. "Mammoth earthquake takes a toll on Taiwan." *U.S. News & World Report*, Oct. 4, 1999.

IRIS Special Event File - Taiwan Earthquake, http://www.iris.washington.edu/DOCS/taiwan.htm

Larmer, Brook. "The Night Heaven Fell: The world's third major earthquake in a month rocks Taiwan, creating a gigantic humanitarian crisis." *Newsweek*, Oct. 4, 1999.

Schiff, Ansel J, and Alex Tang, eds. *Chi-Chi, Taiwan, Earthquake of September 21, 1999: Lifeline Performance.* American Society of Civil Engineers, 2000.

United States. Congress. House. Committee on Science. Subcommittee on Basic Research. *The Turkey, Taiwan, and Mexico Earthquakes: Lessons Learned: Hearing Before the Subcommittee on Basic Research of the Committee on Science, House of Representatives, One Hundred Sixth Congress, First Session, October 20, 1999.* U.S. Governmnet Printing Office, 2000.

INDIA EARTHQUAKE, 2001

"Digging Out." *Current Events*, Feb. 23, 2001.

Gupta, Harsh K, et al. "The Deadliest Intraplate Earthquake." *Science*, March 16, 2001.

Omestead, Thomas, and Soni Sangwan. "Aftershocks in India." *U.S. News & World Report*, Feb. 12, 2001.

THIRA (THERA) ERUPTION OF 1500 B.C.

Bower, B. "Minoan culture survived volcanic eruption." *Science News*, Jan. 13, 1990.

The Eruption of Thera, http://www.fireplug.net/~rshand/restricted/streams/thera/thera.html

Forsyth, Phyllis Young. *Thera in the Bronze Age.* P. Lang, 1997.

McCoy, Floyd W., and Grant Heiken. "Anatomy of an eruption." *Archaeology*, May-June 1990.

McCoy, Floyd W., and G.A. Papadopoulos. "Tsunami generated during the late Bronze Age eruption of Thera: evidence from tsunami deposits on Thera, Crete, Western Turkey, and the Deep Sea." *American Journal of Archaeology*, April 2001

VESUVIUS ERUPTION 79 C.E.

Burgan, Michael. "The day of disaster." *National Geographic World*, Dec. 1999.

The Eruption of Vesuvius - A.D. 79, http://www.humanities-interactive.org/ancient/pompeii/2_LTRS-Eruption_of_Vesuvius.htm

Etienne, Robert. *Pompeii: The Day a City Died.* Harry N. Abrams, 1992.

The 79 A.D. Eruption of Vesuvius, http://search.britannica.com/frm_redir.jsp?query=herculaneum&redir=http://vulcan.fis.uniroma3.it/vesuvio/79_eruption.html

Jashemski, Wilhemina F., and Stanley Jashemski. *The Gardens of Pompeii, Herculaneum & the Villas Destroyed by Vesuvius.*Melissa Media, 1979 [Vol. 2: Appendices, 1993].

Nova:Deadly Shadow of Vesuvius, WGBH Boston Video, 1998.

MOUNT ETNA ERUPTION OF 1669

Chester, D. K., et al. *Mount Etna - Anatomy of a Volcano.* Kluwer Academic, 1985.

1669 Eruption of Etna, http://www.geo.mtu.edu/~boris/ETNA_1669.html

MOUNT TAMBORA ERUPTION OF 1815

CVO Menu - Tambora Volcano, Indonesia, http://vulcan.wr.usgs.gov/Volcanoes /Indonesia/Tambora/framework.html

Harrington, C.R., ed. *The Year Without a Summer?: World Climate in 1816.* Canadian Museum of Nature, 1992.

Stommel, Henry M. *Volcano Weather: The Story of 1816, The Year Without a Summer.* Seven Seas Press, 1983.

Stothers, Richard B. "The great Tambora eruption in 1815 and its aftermath." *Science*, June 15, 1984.

COTOPAXI ERUPTION OF 1877

Geology and Eruptive History of Cotopaxi, http://acasun.eckerd.edu/~wetzellr/ryan-cotopaxi.html

Paulo, Andrzej, et al. *Geology, geochemistry, and petrogenesis of volcanics of Cotopaxi (Ecuador).* Zaklad Narodowy im. Ossolínskich [Poland], 1979.

Pérez de Tudela, César Augusto. *Cotopaxi.* Everest [Madrid], 1981.

KRAKATOA ERUPTION OF 1883

Krakatoa Volcano, http://www.allsands.com/Science/krakatoavolcan_bbo_gn.htm

Simkin, Tom, and Richard S. Fisk, eds. *Krakatau, 1883—The Volcanic Eruption and Its Effects.*Smithsonian Institution Press, 1983.

Thornton, Ian W. B. *Krakatau: The Destruction and Reassembly of an Island Ecosystem*. Harvard University Press, 1996.

Willumsen, Peter. *Krakatau, Events and Geology: A Practical Guide to Krakatau and Surroundings*. P. Willumsen [Jakarta], 1997.

MOUNT PELEE ERUPTION OF 1902

CVO Menu - Mont Pelée, Martinique, West Indies, http://vulcan.wr.usgs.gov/Volcanoes/WestIndies/Pelee/framework.html

Heilprin, Angelo. *The Tower of Pelée: New Studies of the Great Volcano of Martinique*. J.B. Lippincott, 1904.

Kennan, George. *The Tragedy of Pelée*. Greenwood Publishing Group, 2002 [first published 1902].

Peterson, Douglas J. "The glowing avalanche." *Natural History*, Jan. 1985.

Thomas, Gordon, and Max Morgan Witts. *The Day the World Ended*. Scarborough House, 1991 [first published 1969].

Zebrowski, Ernest. *The Last Days of St. Pierre: The Volcanic Disaster That Claimed Thirty Thousand Lives*. Rutgers University Press, 2002.

MOUNT ST. HELENS ERUPTION OF 1980

Carson, Rob, and Geff Hinds. *Mount St Helens: The Eruption and Recovery of a Volcano*. Sasquatch Books, 2000.

Colasurdo, Christine. *Return to Spirit Lake: Journey Through a Lost Landscape*. Sasquatch Books, 1997.

Lipman, Peter W., and Donal R. Mullineaux, eds. *The 1980 Eruptions of Mount St. Helens, Washington*. U.S. Government Printing Office, 1982.

Perry, Ronald W., and Michael K. Lindell. *Living With Mount St. Helens: Human Adjustment to Volcano Hazards*. Washington State University Press, 1990.

Rosenfeld, Charles, and Robert Cooke. *Earthfire: The Eruption of Mount St. Helens*. MIT Press, 1982.

EL CHICHON ERUPTION OF 1982

Aldana, E. Guillermo, and Kenneth Garrett. "The disaster of El Chichon." *National Geographic*, Nov. 1982.

El Chichon Pages, http://www.eps.mcgill.ca/~glyn/latvolc/mexico/elchichon.html

Hoffer, Jerry M., et al. "Eruption of El Chichon volcano, Chiapas, Mexico, 28 March to 7 April 1982." *Science*, Dec. 24, 1982.

Hurtado Martínez, Raúl. *La verdad sobre el volcán "Chichonal" : narración verídica sobre la erupción de 1982*. Impr. La Merced [Mexico], 1982.

NEVADO DEL RUIZ ERUPTION OF 1985

Bruce, Victoria. *No Apparent Danger: The True Story of Volcanic Disaster at Galera and Nevado del Ruiz*. Hapercollins, 2001.

Contreras, Joseph. "'Buried alive'; a volcanic cascade of mud and lava devastates a town in Colombia and kills thousands." *Newsweek*, Nov. 25, 1985.

McDowell, Bart, and Steve Raymer. "Eruption in Columbia; 23,000 villagers perish in volcanic mudflows." *National Geographic*, May 1986.

Mileti, Dennis S. *The Eruption of Nevado del Ruiz volcano, Colombia, South America, November 13, 1985*. National Academy Press, 1991.

Nevado del Ruiz Volcano Pages, http://www.eps.mcgill.ca/~glyn/latvolc/colombia/ruiz.html

Serrill, Michael S. "Aftermath of a disaster; amid tragedy and exhaustion, the cleanup continues." *Time*, Dec. 2, 1985.

FIRE OF ROME, 64 C.E.

Ancient History Sourcebook: Dio Cassius: Nero and the Great Fire 64 CE., http://www.fordham.edu/halsall/ancient/diocassius-nero1.html

The Burning of Rome, 64 A.D., http://www.ibiscom.com/rome.htm

Griffin, Miriam T. *Nero: The End of a Dynasty*. Yale University Press, 1985.

Holland, Richard. *Nero: The Man Behind the Myth*. Sutton, 2000.

Weigall, Arthur Edward Pearse Brome. *Nero, the Singing Emperor of Rome*. Putnam, 1930.

GREAT FIRE OF LONDON, 1666

Bell, Walter G. *The Great Fire of London in 1666*. Greenwood Publishing Company, 1971.

Cowie, Leonard W. *Plague and Fire: London 1665-6*. Wayland Publishers Ltd [London], 1970.

London Gazette Report of Fire of London, Sept 10, 1666, http://www1.britishliterature.com/london/londonfire-gazette.html

London Fire: The Great Fire of London - 1666, http://www.angliacampus.com/education/fire/london/history/greatfir.htm

Porter, Stephen. *The Great Fire of London*. Sutton Publishing, 1998.

Roubaud, Jacques, and Dominic Di Bernardi. *The Great Fire of London : A Story With Interpolations and Bifurcations*. Dalkey Archive Press, 1991.

Vincent, Thomas. *God's Terrible Voice in the City: Wherein You Have 1. The Sound of the Voice in the History of the Two Late Dreadful Judgments of Plague and Fire in London. 2. The Interpretation of the Voice in a Discovery of the Cause and Design of These Judgments*. Soli Deo Gloria Publications, 1997 [first published 1667].

GREAT CHICAGO FIRE, 1871

Colbert, Elias. *Chicago and the Great Conflagration*. Viking Press, 1971 [first published 1871].

The Great Chicago Fire and the Web of Memory, a virtual exhibition, http://www.chicagohs.org/fire/

Cowan, David. *Great Chicago Fires*. Lake Claremont Press, 2001.

Cromie, Robert. *The Great Chicago Fire*. Rutledge Hill Press, 1994.

McIlvaine, Mabel, comp. *Reminiscences of Chicago During the Great Fire*. R. R. Donnelly & Sons Company, 1915.

Miller, Ross. *The Great Chicago Fire*. University of Illinois Press, 2000.

Sawislak, Karen. *Smoldering City: Chicagoans and the Great Fire, 1871-1874*. University of Chicago Press, 1995.

THE GREAT PESHTIGO FIRE, 1871

Fire and Ice: Two Deadly Wisconsin Disasters. Northwood, 1983.

Martin, Michael. "Peshtigo: the fire a nation forgot." *American Forests*, Sept. 1983.

Pernin, Peter. *The Great Peshtigo Fire: An Eyewitness Account*. University of Wisconsin Press, 1999.

Scorched Earth: The Great Peshtigo Fire Remembered,
http://www.iswonline.com/archives/eclectic/peshtigo.shtml

Wells, Robert W. *Fire at Peshtigo*. Prentice-Hall, 1968.

IROQUOIS THEATER FIRE, 1903

CPL Chicago: 1903, December 30: Iroquois Theater Fire,
http://www.chipublib.org/004chicago/disasters/iroquois_fire.html

Guenzel, Louis. *Retrospects: "The Iroqouis Theater Fire."* Champlin-Sealey Company, 1945.

Marshall, Evert. *The Great Chicago Theater Disaster: The Complete Story Told by the Survivors: Presenting a Vivid Picture, Both by Pen and Camera, of One of the Greatest Fire Horrors of Modern Times*. Publishers Union of America, 1904.

Northrop, Henry Davenport. *World's Greatest Calamities, the Baltimore fire and Chicago Theatre Horror*. National Publishing Co., 1904.

TRIANGLE SHIRTWAIST FACTORY FIRE, 1911

McClymer, John F. *The Triangle Strike and Fire*. Harcourt Brace College Publishers, 1998.

McEvoy, Arthur F. "The Triangle Shirtwaist Factory fire of 1911: social change, industrial accidents, and the evolution of common-sense causality." *Law and Social Inquiry*, Spring 1995.

Stein, Leon. *The Triangle Fire*. Cornell University Press, 2001 [first published 1962].

Triangle Shirtwaist Fire - The Encyclopedia of New York City,
http://www.yale.edu/yup/ENYC/triangle_shirtwaist.html

COCOANUT GROVE NIGHTCLUB FIRE, 1942

Anderson, Dave. "The biggest upset, the party, the fire." *New York Times*, Nov. 22, 1942.

Cocoanut Grove Fire, http://www.ezl.com/~fireball/Disaster21.htm

Interview with Thomas Gavin,
http://www.cs.umb.edu/~serl/oralhistory/Calapiz.html

Keyes, Edward. *Cocoanut Grove*. Atheneum, 1984.

Whipple, A. C. "Holiday Inferno." *Reader's Digest*, Nov. 1992.

BEVERLY HILLS SUPPER CLUB FIRE, 1977

The Beverly Hills Tragedy, http://www.cincypost.com/bhfire/

Elliott, Ron. *Inside the Beverly Hills Supper Club Fire*. Turner Publishing, 1996.

"Nightclub fire caused by wiring, jury finds." *New York Times*, July 16, 1985.

Wolfson, Andrew. "After 8 years, a complex case comes to an end; $49 million paid in 1977 blaze." *National Law Journal*, Aug. 19, 1985.

INDONESIAN FOREST FIRES OF 1997 AND 1998

Asia Times: Indonesia's forest fires: a searing indictment,
http://www.atimes.com/se-asia/BG20Ae01.html

Barber, Charles Victor, and James Schweithelm. *Trial by Fire: Forest Fires and Forestry Policy in Indonesia's Era of Crisis and Reform*. World Resources Institute, 2000.

Schweithelm, James. *The Fire This Time: An Overview of Indonesia's Forest Fires in 1997/98*. WWF Indonesia, 1999.

Simons, Lewis M. "Indonesia's plague of fire." *National Geographic*, Aug. 1998.

CHINA NIGHTCLUB FIRE, DECEMBER 2000

"Outrage over a dance-hall fire." *Maclean's*, Jan. 8, 2001.

Poor fire safety kills thousands in China annually,
http://www.timesofindia.com/281200/28nbrs13.htm

Smith, Noah J. "Hundreds of revellers die as fire engulfs dance hall." *The Independent*, Dec. 27, 2000.

"Suspects arrested in deadly fire in central China." *New York Times*, Dec. 27, 2000.

SULTANA, 1865

Berry, Chester D. *Loss of the Sultana and Reminiscences of Survivors*. D. D. Thorpe, 1892.

Elliott, James Walter. *Transport to Disaster*. Holt, Rinehart and Winston, 1962.

Potter, Jerry O. *The Sultana Tragedy: America's Greatest Maritime Disaster*. Pelican Publishing Company, 1992.

The Sultana: Death on the Dark River, http://www.rootsweb.com/~genepool/sultana.htm

Sultana—Mississippi's Titanic. A & E Entertainment, 1998.

GENERAL SLOCUM, 1904

The General Slocum Disaster, http://www.lihistory.com/7/hs743a.htm

Martin, Douglas. "Survivor's life in shadow of 1904 steamboat disaster." *New York Times*, May 24, 1989.

Pace, Eric. "80 years later, New York steamboat disaster is still debated." *New York Times*, June 11, 1984.

"Remains of the General Slocum Located by Clive Cussler and NUMA." *PR Newswire*, Nov. 27, 2000.

Rust, Claude. *The Burning of the General Slocum*. E.P. Dutton, 1981.

Werstein, Irving. *The General Slocum Incident: Story of an Ill-Fated Ship*. John Day Company, 1965.

TITANIC, 1912

Beesley, Lawrence. *The Loss of the S.S. Titanic: Its Story and Its Lessons*. Houghton Mifflin, 2000.

Beesley, Lawrence, and Jack Winocour, eds. *The Story of the Titanic As Told by Its Survivors*. Peter Smith, 1960.

Brown, David D. *The Last Log of the Titanic*. McGraw-Hill, 2000.

Clary, James G. *The Last True Story of the Titanic*. Domhan Books, 1999.

The Lost Film of the Titanic, Kingfisher Productions, 1999.

RMS Titanic Website Index, http://www.titanicindex.com/rms.shtml

Secrets of the Titanic, National Geographic, 1986.

EMPRESS OF IRELAND, 1914

Croall, James. *Fourteen Minutes: The Last Voyage of the Empress of Ireland*. Stein and Day, 1979.

RMS Empress of Ireland, http://www.rmsempressofireland.com/

Wickens, Barbara, and Brenda Branswell. "Lost in the river depths: Canada's worst maritime disaster claimed more than 1,000 lives." *Maclean's*, May 29, 2000.

Wood, Herbert. *Till We Meet Again: The Sinking Of The Empress Of Ireland*. Image Publishing 1982.

Zeni, David. *Forgotten Empress: The Empress of Ireland Story*. Goose Lane, 1998.

EASTLAND, 1915

Eastland Disaster Historical Society, http://www.eastlanddisaster.org/

Hilton, George W. *Eastland: Legacy of the Titanic*. Stanford University Press, 1995.

United States. Congress. House. Committee on merchant marine and fisheries. *Investigation of Accident to the Steamer "Eastland," Chicago, Ill., July 24 to August 5, 1915…* Government Printing Office, 1916.

United States District Court. *Decision of Justice Sessions in Case of Steamship "Eastland."* Government Printing Office, 1915.

LUSITANIA, 1915

Ballard, Robert D., and Spencer Dunmore. *Exploring the Lusitania: Probing the Mysteries of the Sinking That Changed History.* Warner Books, 1995.

Butler, Daniel Allen. *The Lusitania: The Life, Loss, and Legacy of an Ocean Legend.* Stackpole Books, 2001.

Last Voyage of the Lusitania, National Geographic, 1994.

O'Sullivan, Patrick. *The Lusitania: Unravelling the Mysteries.* Sheridan House, 2000.

Simpson, Colin. *The Lusitania.* Little, Brown and Company, 1972.

The Sinking of the Lusitania: 1915, http://campus.northpark.edu/history/WebChron/USA/Lusitania.html

Sinking the Lusitania, PBS Home Video, 2001.

MONT BLANC, 1917

Bird, Michael J. *The Town That Died: The True Story of the Greatest Manmade Explosion Before Hiroshima.* Putnam, 1963.

Boning, Richard. *Seventeen Minutes to Live.* Barnetll Loft Ltd., 1973.

Halifax Explosion, http://www.region.halifax.ns.ca/community/explode.html

KIANGYA, 1948

Great Shipwrecks - Kiangya, http://www.greatshipwrecks.com/kiangya.html

TOYA MARU, 1954

Disaster of the Steamship "Toya Maru,"
http://lib1.nippon-foundation.or.jp/1999/0813/contents/002.htm

ANDREA DORIA, 1956

The Andrea Doria / Stockholm Collision,
http://www.geocities.com/Baja/Dunes/7880/

Collision of the Andrea Doria, Tapeworm Video, 1999.

Goldstein, Richard. Desperate *Hours: The Epic Story of the Sinking and Rescue of the Andrea Doria.* John Wiley & Sons, 2001.

Hoffer, William. *Saved!: The Story of the Andrea Doria, the Greatest Sea Rescue in History.* Summit Books, 1979.

McMurray, Kevin F. Deep *Descent: Adventure and Death Diving the Andrea Doria.* Pocket Books, 2001.

Moscow, Alvin. Collision *Course: The Andrea Doria and the Stockholm.* Easton Press, 1998.

Sinking of the Andrea Doria, A & E Entertainment, 1998.

TAMPOMAS II, 1981

Bya, Arens. *Tragedi kapal Tampomas II.* Padi [Jakarta], 1981.

KdP: GJA - Adili Suharto! (5/10), http://www.gwdg.de/~amutiar/10.html

DONA PAZ, 1987

Chrichton, Tom. "That sinking feeling; tales of a dangerous voyage on an inter-island passenger ship." *Far Eastern Economic Review,* Apr. 27, 1989.

Great Shipwrecks - Dona Paz, http://www.greatshipwrecks.com/dona.html

"Inferno at sea: a holiday disaster; a Philippine ferry sinks." *Newsweek,* Jan. 4, 1988.

Williams, Nick B. "Bodies washing ashore in Philippine disaster; many aboard were believed trapped as ships sank; child reported found clinging to log." *Los Angeles Times,* Dec. 23, 1987.

EXXON VALDEZ, 1989

Exxon Valdez, http://www.epa.gov/oilspill/exxon.htm

Exxon Valdez Oil Spill Trustee Council, http://www.oilspill.state.ak.us/

Kaiser, Jocelyn. "The Exxon Valdez's Scientific Gold Rush." *Science,* Apr. 9, 1999.

Keeble, John. *Out of the Channel: The Exxon Valdez Oil Spill in Prince William Sound.* Eastern Washington University Press, 1999.

Picou, Stephen J., and Duane A. Gill, eds. The *Exxon Valdez Disaster: Readings on a Modern Social Problem.*

"Ten years after the spill." *Newsweek,* March 29, 1999.

Wells, Peter G., et al, eds. *Exxon Valdez Oil Spill: Fate and Effects in Alaskan Waters.* American Society for Testing and Materials, 1996.

SALEM EXPRESS, 1991

"Divers recover bodies of captain and others from Egyptian ferry." *New York Times,* Dec. 18, 1991.

Egypt Red Sea Shipwrecks - The Salem Express, http://www.touregypt.net/vdc/Salemexp.htm

Murphy, Kim. "Up to 470 missing as Egyptian ferry hits Red Sea reef, sinks." *Los Angeles Times,* Dec. 16, 1991.

NEPTUNE, 1993

Freed, Kenneth. "Hundreds dead in sinking of overloaded Haiti ferry." *Los Angeles Times,* Feb. 19, 1993.

Nearly 2,000 Die as Ferry Sinks off Coast of Haiti, http://www-tech.mit.edu/V113/N7/haiti.07w.html

"Of 800 to 1,200 aboard Haitian ferry, 285 lived." *New York Times,* Feb. 20, 1993.

ESTONIA, 1994

Estonia - the ferry disaster '94 (What really happened??), http://www.multi.fi/~stigb/Estonia/

Kielmas, Maria. "New lawsuit in Estonia disaster." *Business Insurance,* Sept. 30, 1996.

Stevenson, Richard W. "Ferry owners say flooding of hold caused sinking." *New York Times,* Sept. 30, 1994.

Tarn, Michael. "One year later, Estonia marks ferry tragedy." *Los Angeles Times*, Sept. 29, 1995.

CAHAYA BAHARI, 2000

"Lost at sea." *Maclean's*, July 10, 2000.

"Search for 'Cahaya Bahari' ends." *Jakarta Post*, July 21, 2000.

World News - The News-Times - Indonesian search ship finds 10 survivors from sunken refuge ferry, http://www.newstimes.com/archive2000/jul02/woa.htm

KURSK, 2000

"A Cry From the Deep: A letter retrieved from the sunken Russian submarine Kursk shows that a few crewmen lived for hours, at least, after the disaster. Could they have been saved?" *Newsweek*, Nov. 6, 2000.

Newman, Richard J., et al. "Desperate hours at sea." *U.S. News & World Report*, Aug. 28, 2000.

Smimov, Aleksei, et al. "Sub rescue effort fails: blame assignment begins." *Current Digest of the Post-Soviet Press*, Sept. 20, 2000.

SSGN Kursk Tragedy, http://www.museum.navy.ru/kursk-e.htm

HINDENBURG, 1937

DiChristina, Mariette. "What really downed the Hindenburg." *Popular Science*, Nov. 1997.

FBI - Freedom of Information Act - The Hindenberg Disaster, http://foia.fbi.gov/hindburg.htm

Hindenburg, A & E Entertainment, 1996.

Hindenburg's Fiery Secret, National Geographic, 2000.

The Hindenburg Historical Society, http://www.hindenburg.net/

Hoeling, Adolph A. *Who Destroyed the Hindenburg!* Little, Brown, 1962.

Mooney, Michael Macdonald. *The Hindenburg.* Dood, Mead, 1972.

PAN AM FLIGHT 1736 AND KLM FLIGHT 4805

Aviation Safety Network: CVR transcript KLM Flight 4805 and Pan Am Flight 1736 collision - 27 MAR 1977, http://aviation-safety.net/cvr/cvr_kl4805.shtml

Pan Am 1736 & KLM 4805, http://pw1.netcom.com/~asapilot/1736.html

JAPAN AIRLINES FLIGHT 123

AirDisaster.com Special Report: Japan Airlines Flight 123, http://www.airdisaster.com/special/special-jal123.shtml

Allen, Glen. "The fatal end of JAL Flight 123." *Maclean's*, Aug. 26, 1985.

The Crew of the Challenger Mission in 1986, http://www.hq.nasa.gov/office/pao/History/Biographies/challenger.html

"Pilot to tower: Immediate, ah, trouble." *New York Times*, Aug. 15, 1985.

CHALLENGER SPACE SHUTTLE EXPLOSION, 1986

Covalt, Craig. "Shuttle crew survived breakup, began emergency procedures." *Aviation Week & Space Technology*, Aug. 4, 1986.

From Disaster to Recovery: The Challenger Explosion and the Rebirth of America's Space Shuttle, MPI Home Video, 1989.

Lydon, Thomas P., et al. *After Challenger*. Defense Marketing Services, 1986.

McConnel, Malcolm. *Challenger: A Major Malfunction / A True Story of Politics, Greed, and the Wrong Stuff*. Doubleday, 1987.

Presidential Commission Report on Space Shuttle Challenger Accident, http://science.ksc.nasa.gov/shuttle/missions/51-l/docs/rogers-commission /table-of-contents.html

Trento, Joseph John. *Prescription for Disaster*. Crown, 1987.

World Spaceflight News. *Challenger Accident: The Tragedy of Space Shuttle Flight 51-L and its Aftermath*. Progressive Management, 2000 [CD-ROM].

IRAN AIR FLIGHT 655

Aviation Safety Network Aircraft accident descritpion, http://aviation-safety.net/database/1988/880703-0.htm

Barry, John, and Roger Charles. "Sea of Lies." *Newsweek*, July 13, 1992.

Rogers, Will, Sharon Rogers, and Gene Gregston, *Storm Center: The USS Vincennes and Iran Air Flight 655: A Personal Account of Tragedy and Terrorism*. United States Naval Institute, 1992.

Van Voorst, Bruce. "Neither 'negligent' nor 'culpable'; the Pentagon rules out punishment for the Iran Airbus shootdown." *Time*, Aug. 29, 1988.

PAN AM FLIGHT 103

"Case Closed?" *Time International*, Feb. 12, 2001.

Cohen, Susan, and Daniel Cohen. *Pan Am 103: The Bombings, the Betrayals, and a Bereaved Family's Search for Justice*. New American Library, 2000.

Deppa, Joan, et al. *The Media and Disasters: Pan Am 103*. New York University Press, 1995.

Emerson, Stephen, and Brian Duffy. *The Fall of Pan Am 103 : Inside the Lockerbie Investigation*. Putnam, 1990.

"The Last Victims." *Newsweek*, Feb. 12, 2001.

WashingtonPost.Com: Pan Am Flight 103 Report, http://cgi.washingtonpost.com/wp-srv/inatl/longterm/panam103/timeline.htm

XIAMEN AIRLINES FLIGHT 8301

AirDisaster.Com: Special Report: Xiamen Airlines Flight 8301, http://www .airdisaster.com/special/special-xi8301.shtml

Aviation Safety Network Accident Description, http://aviation-safety.net/database/1990/901002-3.htm

"Deadly bouquet." *Time*, Oct. 15, 1990.

Kristoff, Nicholas D. "Hijacking sets off shake-up in China." *New York Times*, Oct. 10, 1990.

"Official ays 120 dead in Canton bomb plane crash." *Reuters*, Oct. 2, 1990.

CHINA AIRLINES FLIGHT 140

Aircraft Accident Investigation Report, http://dnausers.d-n-a.net/dnet-GOjg/260494.htm

Sekigawa, Eiichiro, and Michael Mecham. "Pilots, A300 systems cited in Nagoya crash." *Aviation Week & Space Technology*, July 29, 1996.

AMERICAN AIRLINES FLIGHT 965

Accident study by Aeronautica Civil of The Republic of Colombia, http://flightdeck.ie.orst.edu/scripts/dbsqldev/study.idc?study=38

Black box data released from Colombian crash; U.S. lawyers pursue claims, http://archive.nandotimes.com/newsroom/ntn/world/122895/world309_14.html

Peyser, Marc, and Mark Hosenball, "Death in the mountains; did inattentive pilots cause a massive jet crash?" *Newsweek*, Jan. 8, 1996.

Wald, Matthew L. "American Airlines ruled guilty in '95 Cali crash." *New York Times*, Sept. 12, 1997.

VALUJET FLIGHT 592

Fishman, Donald A. "ValuJet Flight 592: Crisis Communication Theory Blended and Extended." *Communication Quarterly*, Fall 1999.

National Transportation Safety Board Abstract of Final Report, http://www.ntsb.gov/Pressrel/970819.htm

Pressley, Sue Anne, and Catherine Skipp. "Jury convicts company for mistakes in ValuJet crash." *International Herald Tribune*, Dec. 8, 1999.

Stern, Willy. "ValuJet: now a criminal probe." *Business Week*, June 24, 1996.

Transcript of final moments of ValuJet Flight 592 released, http://www.cnn.com/US/9611/18/valujet.recordings/

TWA FLIGHT 800

Biema, David Van. "The tiniest terrors: a spark probably doomed TWA 800—and other 747s may not be immune." *Time*, Dec. 22, 1997.

Milton, Pat. *In the Blink of an Eye: The FBI Investigation of Twa Flight 800*. Random House, 1999.

Negroni, Christine. *Deadly Departure: Why the Experts Failed to Prevent the TWA Flight 800 Disaster and How It Could Happen Again*. Cliff Street Books, 2000.

Nightline: Crash of TWA Flight 800, MPI Media Group, 1996.

Sanders, James. *The Downing of TWA Flight 800: The Shocking Truth Behind the Worst Airplane Disaster in U.S. History*. Zebra Books, 1997.

20th Century With Mike Wallace: Crash of TWA Flight 800, A & E Home Video, 1999.

TWA Flight 800 Investigation, http://www.twa800.com/index.htm

SAUDIA FLIGHT 763 AND KAZAKSTAN AIRLINES FLIGHT 1907

Aviation Safety Network Aircraft Accident Description, http://aviation-safety.net/database/1996/961112-0.htm

Burns, John F. "Investigators say one jet in crash that killed 349 over India was off assigned course." *New York Times*, May 5, 1997.

Hundreds killed in jet crash over India, http://www.pub.umich.edu/daily/1996/nov/11-13-96/news/newsf3cr.html

Kataria, Sunil. "Indian panel: midair crash was caused by Kazakh Air." *Journal of Commerce and Commercial*, May 14, 1997.

KOREAN AIR FLIGHT 801

Aviation Safety Network: ATC transcript Korean Air Flight 801, http://aviation-safety.net/cvr/atc_ke801.shtml

Hosenball, Mark, and Russell Watson. "Fly the risky skies: the Guam crash looks like another blot on Korean Air's record." *Newsweek*, Aug. 18, 1997.

Korean Air Flight 801 - Official Guam Crash Site, http://ns.gov.gu/guam/

Malnic, Eric. "Cockpit confusion preceded airliner crash in Guam." *Los Angeles Times*, March 25, 1988.

National Transportation Safety Board Abstract on Korean Air Flight 801: Conclusions, Probable Cause, And Safety Recommendations, http://avstop.com/news/801.html

GARUDA AIRLINES FLIGHT 152

Indonesian plane crashes; all 234 on board feared dead, http://www.s-t.com/daily/09-97/09-27-97/a03wn016.htm

Proctor, Paul. "CFIT eyed in Garuda crash." *Aviation Week & Space Technology*, Oct. 6, 1997.

Tower Tape Transcript of Garuda Flight 152, http://www.avweb.com/other/garuda.html

CHINA AIRLINES FLIGHT 676

"A deadly Taiwan crash." *Maclean's*, March 2, 1998.

AirDisaster.Com: China Airlines 676 CVA Transcript, http://www.airdisaster.com/cvr/ca676tr.shtml

AsiaWeek.com - Hell, Again, http://www.asiaweek.com/asiaweek/98/0227/nat7.html

Thomas, Jeffrey. "Extreme pitch-up noted in Taipei crash." *Aviation Week & Space Technology*, March 16, 1988.

SWISSAIR FLIGHT 111

Kimber, Stephen. "Pity and Providence: A Nova Scotia fisherman who rushed to the horror- filled site of last year's Swissair crash came face-to-face with the big questions of life and death." *Maclean's*, Aug. 23, 1999.

Labi, Nadya. "No safe harbor: a plane crash off Canada rekindles several air-safety controversies." *Time*, Sept. 14, 1998.

Swissair Flight 111 Accident Information and Support, http://www.bhagd.com /swissair/swissair.html

Thomas, Evan, and Mark Hosenball. "Smoke was the first sign of trouble." *Newsweek*, Sept. 14, 1998.

"A Time to Mourn: Relatives of the victims of Flight 111 coped with their loss as the investigation continued." *Maclean's*, Sept. 21, 1998.

EGYPTAIR FLIGHT 990

Jerome, Richard. "Defending His Name: Family and friends of pilot Gameel El Batouty insist he didn't crash Flight 990." *People Weekly*, Dec. 6, 1999.

"'I put my trust in God.'" *Newsweek*, Nov. 29, 1999.

National Transportation Safety Board - EygptAir Flight 990, http://www.ntsb.gov/events/EA990/default.htm

"Only one plausible explanation…" *Newsweek*, Aug. 21, 2000.

GRANDCAMP EXPLOSION, 1947

THREE MILE ISLAND NUCLEAR POWER PLANT ACCIDENT, 1979

The American Experience: Meltdown at Three Mile Island. PBS Home Video, 1999.

Hampton, Wilborn. *Meltdown: Three Mile Island and the Power of Nuclear Energy: A Reporter's Story.* Candlewick Press, 2001.

Houts, Peters S., et al. *The Three Mile Island Crisis: Psychological, Social, and Economic Impacts on the Surrounding Population.* Pennsylvania State University Press, 1988.

Leppzer, Robert. *Voices from Three Mile Island: The People Speak Out.* Crossing Press, 1980.

Moss, Thomas, and David Sills. *The Three Mile Island Nuclear Accident.* New York Academy of Sciences, 1981.

BHOPAL POISONOUS GAS LEAK, 1984

Bhopal - 15th Anniversary Index, http://www.corpwatch.org/bhopal/

Cassels, Jamie. *The Uncertain Promise of Law: Lessons from Bhopal.* University of Toronto Press, 1993.

Chisti, Anees. *Dateline Bhopal: A Newsman's Diary of the Gas Disaster.* South Asia Books, 1986.

Everest, Larry. Behind the Poison Cloud: *Union Carbide's Bhopal Massacre*. Banner Press, 1985.

Mukerjee, Madhusree. "Persistently toxic: the Union Carbide accident in Bhopal continues to harm." *Scientific American*, June 1995.

Shrivastava, Paul. *Bhopal: Anatomy of a Crisis*. Paul Chapman, 1992

Union Carbide Bhopal Disaster, http://www.uoguelph.ca/~rjenning/disaster.html

CHERNOBYL NUCLEAR POWER PLANT EXPLOSION, 1986

Chernobyl Nuclear Disaster, MPI Home Video, 1986.

Chernobyl Plant - Aftermath, MPI Home Video, 1987

McQuerry, Maureen, and Tetiana Havrysh. *Nuclear Legacy: Students of Two Atomic Cities*. Battelle Press, 2000.

Mould, Richard F. *Chernobyl Record: The Definitive History of the Chernobyl Catastrophe*. Institute of Physics Publishing, 2000.

Nuclear Energy Agency: Chernobyl, Ten Years On - Radiological and Health Impact, http://www.nea.fr/html/rp/chernobyl/allchernobyl.html

The Uranium Institute—Nuclear Energy Issues—Chernobyl, http://www.world-nuclear.org/industry/chernobyl/inf07.htm

Vargo, George J., ed., et al. *The Chernobyl Accident: A Comprehensive Risk Assessment*. Battelle Press, 1999.

 ──────────────────────── Glossary

abate to put an end to; nullify.

absolution forgiveness; a pass.

adjacent immediately next to.

adobe a brick or building material consisting of sun-dried earth and straw used in making adobe bricks.

affected country term used to define a country stricken by disaster.

aftershock a minor tremor following the main shock of a larger earthquake.

agrarian rural; farm-based.

aggregation a body, group, or mass of units or parts loosely associated with each other.

alacrity promptness.

altimeter an instrument which measures altitude in an aircraft and registers atmospheric pressure occurring with changes in altitude.

ambivalent indecisive or uncaring.

American Red Cross organization that funnels financial aid, material, and technical personnel to victims of natural disasters all over the world through its main organization and sister organizations.

ammonium nitrate a colorless crystalline salt used in fertilizers and explosives.

antibiotics a substance produced to dilute, inhibit, or kill a microrganism.

appointed decorated and equipped.

apprentice an individual who is learning a skill or trade by practical experience under professional supervision.

arable ability to cultivate crops.

archaeologist an individual who studies the science of material remains.

at-risk populations groups that may suffer the effects of drought, war, food shortages, or other phenomena resulting in humanitarian difficulty and hardship.

ayatollah a religious leader among Shiite Muslims used as a title of respect.

ballast a weighty substance or object used to control the draft and improve the stability of a ship or the ascent of a balloon.

barometric pressure measure of the atmospheric pressure usually expressed by the height of a column of mercury.

benzol a mixture of benzene and other aromatic hydrocarbons.

black box the in-flight voice recorders of the pilots and crew of airline flights.

blockade economic and/or social isolation of an enemy nation by another nation in response to particular policies or actions by means of obstructing movements of ships, supplies, etc.

byproduct something produced in an industrial setting in addition to the principle product.

caldera a crater with a diameter much larger than that of the volcanic vent formed by the collapse of the central part of the volcano.

capacious capable of carrying a great deal of material; having an abundance of space.

capricious characterized by unpredicatable or rapidly changing behavior or patterns.

cataclysmic description of a violent and momentous event marked by extreme devastation and damage.

cesium a silver-white element of the alkali metal group that is the most electropositive element known.

cholera any number of several diseases in humans and domesticated animals usually characterized by severe gastrointestinal problems.

Cold War period of history lasting from the end of World War II to approximately 1991 that the United States and Soviet Union were engaged in mutual suspicion and ideological differences that fell just short of military action and was without strong diplomatic relations.

conflagration a large, diasastrous fire.

congregants churchgoers.

contraband goods being shipped illegally.

countenance mood or expression.

craven fainthearted and lacking in courage or bravery.

culpability fault; responsibility for a wrong or injury.

curie a unit quantity of any radioactive nuclide; named after Marie and Pierre Curie.

cyclone a severe tropical storm in the Indian Ocean and South Pacific Ocean with wind speeds exceeding 120 kilometers per hour.

deluge an overflowing of natural liquids or material on land.

dengue fever an infectious disease caused by a virus and marked by severe joint pain, rashes, and headaches.

Denton Amendment United States law permitting U.S. military operations to airlift or sealift donated humanitarian relief to nations affected by disasters.

depredations plunderings and waste of resources.

dike an artificial course for water; a bank of usually natural material to confine or control water.

dissipate to break apart or spread out before vanishing.

donor country country that provides aid to a developing nation.

Doppler Radar a radar system using the Doppler effect for measuring the velocity of a storm.

dormant temporarily without action but with the capability to resume or begin activity.

dysentery a disease characterized by severe diarrhea and the passage of mucus and blood caused by infection.

earthquakes movements of the earth's crust that generate intense deformations in the earth's interior, accumulating energy that is suddenly released in the form of waves that move to the land surface.

efficacy the power to produce an effect.

emaciated dangerously thin; wasting away.

epicenter the part of the earth's surface directly above an earthquake.

fast onset disasters disasters such as earthquakes, hurricanes, volcanic eruptions, floods, and tsunamis.

festooned decorated.

flagship a ship carrying the commander of a fleet; the most important ship in a network or chain of ships.

FEMA the Federal Emergency Management Agency; United States government agency responsible for coordinating federally declared disasters in the United States and its territories.

forensic belonging to or suitable to courts of law or to public disuccsion and debate.

fuselage the central body portion of an aircraft designed to accommodate the passengers, crew, or cargo.

gale a wind measuring from 32-63 miles per hour.

gargantuan overly large and outsized.

geologist an individual who studies rocks and rock formations.

germinal the earliest stage of development.

G.I. a member of the United States armed forces, from the term "general issue, describing the stock uniform and necessities given to soldiers by the government.

glideslope landing instrument on an aircraft that indicates the angle of a plane's descent.

Gross Domestic Product statistical measure of the goods and services produced by a nation's economy.

guerrillas individuals who engage in irregular warfare tactics, especially as members of an independent unit.

gust a sudden, brief rush of wind.

hazard an external risk factor represented by the potential for a natural or man-made disaster to occur in a particular location.

haphazard without thought or sufficient planning.

hectare a metric measurement of an area equalling 2.47 acres.

helmsman ship's crewmember responsible for steering.

herculean extraordinary strength, power, and stamina; a reference to the mythical Greek hero Hercules.

holocaust thorough destruction.

hubris exaggerated self-confidence or pride that usually results in retribution or tragedy.

hull the frame or body of a ship exclusive of sails, yards, and masts.

hurricane a tropical storm usually occuring in the eastern Pacific and western Atlantic oceans with wind speeds over 120 kilometers per hour.

hypothermia subnormal body temperature.

imminent fast-approaching.

indicted formally accused in writing of an offense by a prosecuting authority and found by a grand jury.

inoculate to introduce an active material such as an antibiotic or other medicine into the bloodstream to prevent disease.

inquest official investigation.

International Red Cross private international relief organization headquartered in Geneva, Switzerland, working as an independent humanitarian organization during emergency situations and disasters.

inundate to cover or overflow.

iodine a nonmetallic halogen element usually obtained as weighty, shiny blackish gray crystals and used in photography, medicine, and analysis.

isotope any of two or more species atoms of a chemical element with the same position on the periodic table and atomic number and virtually the same chemical behavior, though with differing atomic mass and physical properties.

jujitsu an art of weaponless fighting emphasizing the use of throws, holds, and paralyzing strikes to disable an opponent.

kithara an ancient Greek stringed instrument simliar to a lyre, though larger.

knot nautical mile.

kowtowing the act of deferential bowing before a person to show respect or remorse.

lahar a flowing mass of water and volcanic debris.

levee a river landing place or embankment for flood prevention.

litigation action in a court of law; a case before a court.

maelstrom a powerful and sometimes violent whirlpool of activity which draws in objects within a given radius.

magma molten rock material within the earth that eventually results in a rock formation when it cools.

malaria a human disease caused by the bite of anopheline mosquitoes causing periodic episodes of chills and fever.

mantra a mystical formula of incantation; a repeated phrase or set of words.

martial law law applied by military forces invoked by a government in an emergency situation to restore order when civilian law enforcement is unable to maintain safety.

metalurgical description of the science and technology of metals.

meterologist an individual who studies weather patterns and makes forecasts and predictions based on those patterns.

meterology the scientific study of weather patterns.

millierem one-thousandth or a rem; a rem is the dosage of an ionizing radiation that will cause the same effect biologically as one roentgen of an X-ray.

modus vivendi Latin phrase for compromise.

monsoon a wind system characterized by heavy rainfall and shifting wind patterns; most common in Asia.

moratorium a legally authorized period of delay in the performance of a legal obligation or payment of debt.

morgue a place where bodies of persons found dead are kept until claimed or identified by relatives.

munitions ammunition; armaments.

nautical mile unit of distance used for air and sea navigation based on the length of a small arc of a large circle of the earth; a unit equal to 6076.115 feet.

oblong a shape deviating from a square, circular, or spherical form by elongnation in one dimension.

oscillation continued movement from side to side.

parishioners members of a church.

periscope a tubular instrument on a submarine containing lenses and mirrors by which an observer sees a field of view otherwise blocked.

picric acid a toxic explosive yellow crystalline acid used in high explosives, as a dye, or in medications.

plates large sections of the earth's crust on which land rests and moves slightly.

port left side of a ship or plane looking forward; the right side is starboard.

portent a foreshadowing or omen of an event yet to occur.

proprietary relating to the rights of an individually owned entity.

prospectors individuals who explore area for mining deposits in particular.

province an administrative district or division of a country.

provisions material such as food, water, clothing, and other necessities needed during or after a hardship or disaster.

punitive damages monetary reward for damages over and above the normal compensation a plaintiff would receive to further punish a defendant for a serious wrong.

Quaker a member of the religious group known as the Society of Friends; Quakers were thought to actually shudder at the thought of God's power.

queue line.

radar a radio device or system used to locate objects or storms by way of extremely high frequency radio waves.

rations food allowances.

recalcitrant difficult to control or manage.

reconstruction medium and long-term repair of social, economic, and physical damage to a condition or stage of development equal to or better than a disaster.

referendum the practice of submitting to a popular vote on the question of an act passed or proposed in a legislature.

reparations payments by one entity to another for past transgressions or offenses.

response actions carried out in the face of an adverse event aimed at saving lives, healing suffering, and preventing further economic loss.

rivulets a small stream or brook.

saboteurs those engaging in the sabotage of an operation or entity in a criminal fashion.

sandbar a ridge of sand built up by the currents of water, especially in coastal waters and rivers.

savannah a tropical grassland marked by scattered trees and drought-resistant undergrowth.

sectarian limited in character or scope; partisan.

seismology the study of energy produced by activity beneath the surface of the earth.

shoddy clumsily or hastily put together.

silt loose materials of sediment, usually small rock particles deposited by a river.

smorgasbord a lunch or dinner buffet with a variety of foods and dishes; a heterogenous mixture.

sonar an apparatus that detects the location and presence of submerged objects.

starboard right side of a ship or plane looking forward; the left side is port.

steerage passengers passengers on a ship paying the lowest fares and given subpar accommodations.

stevedores individuals who load and unload cargo on ships.

stygian extremely foreboding, dark, or gloomy.

supplicant helpless person or thing in the face of awesome power.

susceptible unresistant and open to a particular agency, stimulus, of influence.

sweatshop a factory or shop in which workers are employed for low wages and must work long hours in unsatisfactory conditions.

tenement an apartment building or house meeting the bare minimum standards of safety, comfort, and sanitation, usually occupied by poorer citizens of larger cities.

tetanus an infectious disease characterized by spasm of voluntary muscles caused by the toxin bacillus.

tornado warning an alert issued by the National Weather Service to an area where a tornado has been spotted on the ground.

tornado watch an alert issued by the National Weather Service to an area where the potential exists for a tornado during a storm.

torrential a violent or sustained flow of liquid, commonly used in association with heavy rainstorms.

tropical depression wind speeds exceeding 25 miles per hour.

tropical storms cyclonic systems with wind speeds betwen 64 and 119 kilometers per hour.

tsumani large sea waves capable of moving thousands of kilometers and caused by the sudden and violent displacement of water; generally generated by earthquakes, volcanic eruptions, and underwater landslides.

typhoid a disease of domestic animals resembling human typhus or typhoid; typhus is marked by high fever, intense headache, and delirium.

typhoon severe tropical storm in the western Pacific Ocean with wind speeds over 120 kilometers per hour.

tyrant a ruler whose power is absolute and unrestrained by law or constitution.

USAID United States Agency for International Development; the official U.S. agency responsible for international assistance and development.

vaudevillian individual actor who participated in vaudeville, a stage performance consisting of acting, singing, and dancing.

viaduct a bridge resting on a series of narrow reinforced concrete usually carrying a road or railroad tracks over a particular obstruction.

vigilante a member of a group or committee organized to suppress and punish crime in the absence or perceived inadequacy of law enforcement.